PLAZA

the times
were a
changin'

ALSO BY IRWIN UNGER

THE BEST OF INTENTIONS
The Great Society Programs of Kennedy, Johnson and Nixon

1968: THE TURNING POINT
(WITH DEBI UNGER)

THE MOVEMENT
A History of the American New Left

the times were a changin'

The Sixties Reader

Edited by IRWIN UNGER
and DEBI UNGER

Three Rivers Press • New York

Published by Three Rivers Press, a division of Crown Publishers, Inc., 201 East 50th Street, New York, New York 10022. Member of the Crown Publishing Group.

Random House, Inc. New York, Toronto, London, Sydney, Auckland
www.randomhouse.com

THREE RIVERS PRESS and colophon are trademarks of Crown Publishers, Inc.

Printed in the United States of America

Library of Congress Cataloging-in-Publication Data

The times were a changin': the sixties reader/edited by Irwin
Unger and Debi Unger. — 1st ed.
1. United States—History—1961–1969—Sources. I. Unger, Irwin.
E839.T58   1998
973.923—dc21   97-39844

ISBN 0-609-80337-9

10 9 8 7 6 5 4 3 2 1

First Edition

To Layla, Emily, Rachel,
Rebecca, Gabriel—our grandchildren

Contents

Acknowledgments

Like all authors and editors we have incurred debts to a number of people, and we would like to express our appreciation for their help.

First, we would like to thank our agent, Alex Hoyt, who made the entire project possible.

We wish to express our appreciation also for Shaye Areheart, Dina Siciliano, and Liana Parry. Their "tough love" immeasurably improved the manuscript.

the times were a changin'

Introduction

The Sixties resound in our historical memory as do few other eras. It was a time when events went into overdrive, and the postwar social trajectory was deflected off line. Life blueprints were rejected; people struck out on new courses. The air resounded with harsh voices demanding, raging, denouncing, promising, accusing, cajoling.

Few who reached adulthood between 1961 and 1971 remained unmarked by the events of those years. For the first time, a generation of American college students contended with real-world politics, where significant gains and losses were at stake. Young men and women just reaching sexual maturity faced novelty, uncertainty, and opportunity as had no previous generation. Nor were the young the only ones whose lives were recast. The attack on authority and hierarchy and the exaltation of the self freed some adults to reconnoiter their options as never before. New careers, new loves, new connections, and new interests and attitudes could now be sampled and indulged.

And beyond the personal, there was the whole society. The Sixties delegitimized all sources of authority—governments, universities, parents, critics, experts, employers, the police, families, the military. In this decade's wake, all hierarchical structures became more pliant, all judgments and critical evaluations and "canons" less definitive and acceptable. The decade also witnessed the "liberation" of whole categories of people who had previously been penalized for their race, age, physical fitness, gender, or sexual preference.

The experiences of the period cut deep crevices into the nation's social and psychic terrain. Even in the blandest "eras of good feelings," consensus had never truly ruled the national mood. But Americans seldom disagreed so angrily about society's course as during the Sixties, especially after 1965. The powerful insurgent wave produced an almost equally strong reaction.

If on one side there were anarchic hippies, riotous inner cities, and angry antiwar protesters, on the other there were vengeful hard hats, foul-tongued racists, and resentful backlash voters. For every Tom Hayden or Malcolm X, there was a George Wallace or Sheriff "Bull" Connor.

As Dickens said of an earlier but similar era: "It was the best of times, it was the worst of times, it was the age of wisdom, it was the age of foolishness, it was the epoch of belief, it was the epoch of incredulity, it was the season of Light, it was the season of Darkness, it was the spring of hope, it was the winter of despair, we had everything before us, we had nothing before us, we were all going direct to Heaven, we were all going direct the other way."

•   •   •

The Sixties began with the inauguration of a president who had been "born in this century" and who promised to get "the country moving again." Youth was replacing age in the White House, and that alone promised change. But few could guess that the ten years following the inauguration of John F. Kennedy would witness a world turned upside down.

America, on that blustery inauguration day in January 1961, was still deep in the throes of postwar conformity. Skirts were worn below the knee, dresses were tailored, and women's shoes had high heels and pointy toes. On prime-time TV, the favorite programs were *The Flintstones, Ozzie and Harriet, One Happy Family,* and *The Bob Hope Show.* In film, the 1961 Academy Award for best picture went to a musical fable about feuding New York gangs, but *West Side Story* was monumentally innocent despite its subject matter. On Broadway, *My Fair Lady* was still drawing crowds after 2,300 performances. Elvis had already stirred the rage of parents and moralists with his swiveling hips and suggestive phrasing, but the most popular recording artist in 1961 was Eddie Fisher, the quintessential boy next door. Sexual mores were strict. Illegitimacy was rare in the middle class, and most Americans considered homosexuality a sin, and drove its practitioners deep into the closet. The suburbs defined the lives of millions, and no one had yet noticed the quiet desperation of women living in houses with lawns and picture windows. On college campuses, except for a sprinkling of the most "progressive" and cosmopolitan ones, fraternities and sororities, pledge week, pep rallies, dances, and "sandbox" politics were the dominant extracurricular activities.

In general, political discourse was timid and self-congratulatory. In 1959, the New York intelligentsia had announced "the end of ideology"—a rejec-

tion of utopianism and the radical visions of the gene
America, they said, was a success, prosperous and orde
little fine-tuning. In the future, the task of governing
experts, who would apply social science skills to prob
the awkward impediment of all-encompassing social formulas.

There was, in fact, one destablizing domestic issue on that January d.,
Ever since the 1954 Supreme Court decision *Brown v. Board of Education,*
the clamor for racial justice had been growing louder. On February 1,
1960, a small group of black college students in Greensboro, North
Carolina, had given new life to the civil rights movement by sitting down
at the "whites only" local Woolworth's lunch counter and waiting to be
served. The Second Reconstruction was well under way, yet all through
Dixie in January 1961 Jim Crow still reigned in schools, theaters, playgrounds, restaurants, hotels, and other facilities. In most of the Deep
South, few blacks were yet registered to vote, and there were almost no
black public officials. And if blacks were finally raising their voices to
demand their place in the sun, other outsiders—Hispanics, Asians, Native
Americans, women, gays—still had not begun to stir. *2ⁿᵈ paragraph*

The time was not without foreign anxieties. By 1961, Joseph McCarthy
was dead and the "ism" he spawned had abated, but the fear of
Communism and the cold war were very much alive. The new president's
inaugural address that January day emphasized foreign policy and the
resolve of the United States to fend off international Communism. "Let
every nation know, whether it wishes us well or ill, that we shall pay any
price, bear any burden, meet any hardship, support any friend, oppose any
foe, to assure the survival and the success of liberty." The Soviet Union, Red
China, and Fidel Castro's Cuba loomed as threats to the American way of
life. In January 1961, no one was shooting at anyone, but both "the West"
and "the Communist bloc" were piling up arms against the day of reckon-
ing and releasing lethal clouds of strontium 90 into the atmosphere as they
tested ever bigger H-bombs in the South Pacific, Siberia, and the American
Southwest. The cold war made many Americans uneasy, but only a few took
action. A handful of pacifists and humanists sought to stop the war
machine. Yet in the winter of 1961, few Americans disputed the policy of
containment and the need for continued vigilance and sacrifice to prevent
Communist conquest.

Just beneath the surface, however, forces stirred that would soon transform the lives of almost everyone. First, the political pendulum was about
to shift leftward. John F. Kennedy was a Democrat, elected after a two-
term Republican, but he was never an extreme liberal. Until he visited the

ws" of West Virginia in 1960 on his campaign tour, poverty for him only a rumor. But with a party tradition to confirm and a party constituency to satisfy, he found himself father of a program—the New Frontier—that aimed to complete the promises of Roosevelt and Truman. Once in office, Kennedy extracted relatively little in the way of liberal social legislation from a still-conservative Congress unimpressed by his razor-thin victory. Yet Jack and his first lady, Jacqueline Bouvier Kennedy, created a glittering facade of glamour and success. Camelot hid ugly currents of narcissism, callowness, recklessness, and deception, but by the time he flew off to Texas with Jackie in November 1963 to mend political fences, John Kennedy was widely admired, and most pundits assumed he would be easily reelected in 1964.

Ineffectual on Capitol Hill, JFK grew increasingly adept at foreign policy. He stumbled at first by approving a badly planned, badly conceived, undermanned invasion of Castro's Cuba by CIA-trained Cuban exiles, then abandoning the invaders when they faced defeat. But Kennedy redeemed himself by staring down Nikita Khrushchev's reckless emplacement of Soviet missiles in Cuba. Kennedy also forced the Soviets to back down from their threat to strangle Allied-occupied Berlin. In the fall of 1963, responding to public fears of atmospheric radioactive pollution, he negotiated a partial nuclear test ban treaty with the USSR.

Kennedy's tragic death in Dallas was a defining event of the decade. The assassination and the police blunders that followed it shook the public's basic trust in the political system and set in motion a process that would erode values and delegitimize institutions in the years ahead. Yet for a time, the nation seemed to recover. Lyndon Johnson reassured the public by his tact and sensitivity during the first days of national grief and shock. Vowing to continue his predecessor's policies, he exploited the public's guilts and sorrows to push through stalled social legislation, securing a major tax cut and the Civil Rights Act of 1964. In May 1964, before eighty thousand University of Michigan graduates and their guests, he described his vision of a Great Society that would not only round out the New Deal–Fair Deal but also augment the quality of life of a society that had already achieved material abundance.

In the remaining months of his predecessor's unfinished term, Johnson launched a War on Poverty. In his view, a rich society would provide the means for people who had been left behind to pull themselves out of ignorance and indigence. In November 1964, running against Barry Goldwater, a far-right Republican who spoke for the chronic nay-sayers and the newly rich, LBJ won the most resounding presidential victory on record and carried into office a raft of liberal Democratic representatives and senators. Buoyed up by an ever widening and deepening prosperity that promised painless revenue growth, what followed was the greatest outpouring of social legislation in a generation. The Eighty-ninth Congress enacted Medicare and Medicaid, the first general federal-aid-to-education bill, immigration reform, highway beautification, air and water pollution acts, federal scholarships to college students, the Voting Rights Act, and laws creating the National Endowments for the Arts and Humanities. Tom Wicker of *The New York Times* would note of the first session of that Congress, "they are rolling the bills out . . . these days the way Detroit turns supersleek, souped-up autos off the assembly line. . . . The list of achievements is so long that it reads better than the legislative achievements of most two-term presidents."

Liberalism thrived in all three branches of government. In the Supreme Court, under Chief Justice Earl Warren, "the Brethren" churned out decisions that turned into laws of the land, principles that the country's liberal thinkers had long supported. The Court outlawed prayer in public schools. It mandated the principle of "one man, one vote." It struck down laws forbidding the sale of contraceptives. It mandated that suspects in criminal cases be informed of their legal rights. It liberalized the laws against obscenity.

In 1965, at the peak of the liberal surge, the nation would also begin a process of uncontrolled social and cultural fission. By mid-decade, the Second Reconstruction had dismantled Jim Crow and restored black Americans to full civil rights citizenship. But there it had stalled. The Reverend Martin Luther King, Jr., the eloquent black Baptist minister who, since the late 1950s, had led the movement for racial justice, had arrived at an impasse. Achieving social and economic parity was a more intractable goal than attaining equality before the law, and as a result, the black ghettos were growing restless and angry. In August 1965, the Los Angeles neighborhood of Watts erupted in a spasm of looting, burning, and smashing. This was the first of four "long, hot summers" of violence that lasted until King himself became an assassin's victim.

But as the decade reached midpoint, blacks were not alone in their disenchantment. By now, younger civil rights activists were questioning the whole principle of "black and white together" and the tactics of peaceful civil disobedience. In 1966, youthful new leaders took over the Student Non-Violent Coordinating Committee and the Congress of Racial Equality and proclaimed "Black Power," a form of black separatism that rejected nonviolence and posed an angry challenge to the system. That same year, two Oakland students founded the Black Panthers, a paramilitary band of black youths who marched through the streets in black berets and leather jackets, carrying rifles and taunting the police.

By mid-decade, Vietnam had changed from a trouble spot into a war. Kennedy instigated American military intervention, but Johnson continued and expanded it. A master of domestic policy but a novice in foreign affairs, LBJ saw the North Vietnamese drive to reunite the country under their control as an act of totalitarian aggression like Nazi expansion during the 1930s. During the 1964 presidential campaign, he had fudged the Vietnam issue. "American boys," he told the voters, should not "do the fighting for Asian boys." But in early 1965, he concluded that the Vietnamese Communists could be stopped only by direct American military action. In February, he launched a bombing campaign against Hanoi; on March 8, the first U.S. combat troops splashed ashore at Da Nang. By the end of the year, the number of American combat troops in Vietnam had reached 200,000.

Vietnam loosened the nation at all its joints. A limited war, one without clear goals and of uncertain utility, it dismayed left and right alike. Conservatives saw America fighting a war with one hand tied behind its back. The young and the liberal saw a superpower brutally exercising aggression against a weak people fighting for their freedom. "Out now!" "America the ugly!" "Bring the boys home!" became their slogans.

The antiwar proponents were the more passionate and effective protesters. Pacifists who had long been active in the antinuclear ban-the-bomb campaign mounted the first protests against the Vietnam involvement. They were soon joined by Students for a Democratic Society, a New Left campus group that sought a juster, kinder nation through "participatory democracy." In the spring of 1965, campus anti-Vietnam teach-ins and marches on Washington foretold a surge of protest against the war that would broaden to challenge all American establishment institutions.

Meanwhile, society as a whole began to register the growing insurgent mood. By mid-decade, mind-altering drugs—magic buttons, hash, LSD— were capturing the hearts and minds of students and with-it adults. Embracing the ethic of a Harvard psychology professor, Timothy Leary, to "turn on, tune in, drop out," the psychedelic drug culture generated a dissenting critique of mainstream society as repressed, coercive, and materialistic. By 1966, in the low-rent bohemias of big American cities, "flower children," young refugees from white suburbia, were gathering to live in "tribes" and "free associations" based, they said, on "making love, not war." In mid-1967, San Francisco's Haight-Ashbury district became the locale of a spontaneous "hippie" experiment in living informed by LSD. The new movement proclaimed itself a "counterculture," a liberated alternative to the life and institutions of "square" America.

Rock 'n' roll was the theme music of psychedelia. A merger of black rhythm and blues with jazz and country, it was the sound of youth revolt that began with Chuck Berry and Elvis Presley. In the form of "acid rock," along with strobe lights, LSD, and marijuana, it accompanied unbuttoned counterculture celebrations in San Francisco's Fillmore auditorium and its imitators east and west. In 1964, Bob Dylan, a nasal former "folkie," composed the anthem for the era: "The Times They Are A-Changin'."

The Pill, announced with little fanfare in 1960, had ended fear of pregnancy; penicillin had diminished fear of disease. Sex, in any position, in any form, was considered good; denial was bad. The new sexual liberation movement soon spread beyond youthful flower-child dropouts. All through middle-class and working-class America ran a new current of permissiveness. The magazine and TV commentators began to report "wife-swapping" as the latest suburban diversion. Divorce rates soared as both men and women, hitherto resigned to sexual disappointment, sought erotic adventure and fulfillment outside marriage. The federal courts, in the name of the First Amendment right to free speech, began to provide protection to erotic and even pornographic publications. The movie industry moved with the tide to allow "mature" audiences to be exposed to bad language and nudity. In 1968, Hollywood adopted a new rating system, including "R" (restricted) for obscenity and bare breasts and "X" for outright explicit sex acts.

Women were also at the forefront of the new sexual revolution. Good sex and free sex were feminine rights that had not been acceptable during the repressive 1950s. But women now wanted to reclaim them. In 1963, a suburban housewife, Betty Friedan, wrote a book, *The Feminine Mystique,* that identified a hidden emotional malaise that afflicted women. In 1966, Friedan and like-minded women organized the National Organization for Women (NOW), to fight for equality for women "in truly equal partnership with men."

To some militant women, however, this equal-rights feminism seemed pallid. Western society, they proclaimed, exploited, degraded, and neglected women in more fundamental ways than NOW recognized. It was a patriarchy, dominated by males, whose values, attitudes, aesthetics, and morals pervaded every aspect of the culture and created norms that diminished the lives of girls and women. Men were the enemies, and they and their values had to be resisted. Led by strong-willed women, radical feminist groups were created to raise feminine consciousness to the disparity in

America's traditionally patriarchal society. In September 1968, radical feminists picketed the Miss America Pageant in Atlantic City. To most Americans, this rejection of a long-held and adored tradition provided the first glimpse of a new mood of feminist militancy, and many, inevitably, were dismayed.

The restless, angry mood infected college students too. By the later Sixties, the postwar baby boom had created a youth population larger in proportion to the population as a whole than any since the previous century. Activated by the new prosperity, by new federal aid, and by the growing sense that a college degree was indispensable for success in the modern "knowledge society," young people poured into the colleges. In 1960, there were fewer than 3 million college undergraduates; by 1970, there were more than 6.3 million. Many campuses became bloated, impersonal places where required courses overflowed lecture halls and students were identified by IBM-card digits. Along with an unpopular war and a job market that permitted generous career detours, this anomie was a perfect formula for campus revolt.

The opening gun in the decade-long campus wars was the Berkeley Free Speech Movement of 1964–65, which shut down the flagship University of California campus over restrictions on political advocacy and recruitment. Later campus upheavals were generally fueled by resentment of university "complicity" with the "war machine" or of campus recruitment by war-implicated firms like napalm manufacturer Dow Chemical. But some of the rebellions were aimed more broadly against the repressive institutions of society, of which the universities themselves were prime instances. Led by SDS, the rebellions followed a standard configuration of picketing, classroom boycotts, laboratory trashings, and administration building takeovers. The endgame was the police "bust," in which broken bones and bloodied heads radicalized student bodies and faculties.

By 1966, Lyndon Johnson and his Great Society were under siege. The War on Poverty often incited, rather than inhibited, anger and social unrest. Militant activists, rip-off artists, and freeloaders—as the establishment media told it—benefited more from the Office of Economic Opportunity's programs than did the "deserving poor." In turn, more and more white Americans came to resent costly social programs as wasteful and one-sided. White "backlash," which identified with Governor George Wallace of Alabama, was first described in that year. During the 1966 off-year elections, many of the liberals elected to Congress in 1964 went down to defeat. Johnson would find the Ninetieth Congress far less willing to give him what he wanted than the Eighty-ninth.

Inflation also reared its nasty head in 1966. The economy had raced along, since the tax cut in 1964, swelling output by well over four percent a year and bringing unemployment down to three and a half percent of the labor force by 1969. The Great Society floated on a sea of federal revenues. But Vietnam and the Great Society programs busted the budget and lifted prices. In 1967, Johnson asked Congress for an income tax surcharge to siphon off excess purchasing power and reduce inflationary pressures. He got it in 1968, but he had to promise cutbacks in domestic social programs. The programs in place would survive and even grow, but there would be no more Great Society experiments.

By early 1968, Johnson felt besieged and had already decided not to run for a second full term. Accused by the media and the intellectuals of lying to Americans, he had estranged the students over Vietnam. Wherever he went he could hear them chanting, "Hey, hey, LBJ / How many kids did you kill today?" Intellectuals, writers, and academics had also deserted him. Cruelest of all, important leaders of the civil rights movement now rejected Johnson. Despite the Civil Rights Act of 1964 and the landmark Voting Rights Act of 1965, black leaders, even Martin Luther King, turned against the president over Vietnam, a war being fought disproportionately by minorities. In 1968, the counterculture rock musical *Hair* announced that "war is white people sending black people to make war on yellow people to save the land they stole from red people."

In late 1967, Eugene McCarthy, the metaphysical senator from Minnesota, for the sake of peace and his own conscience, challenged Johnson for the 1968 Democratic presidential nomination. In early March of the election year, a "Clean for Gene" band of young anti-Vietnam activists helped McCarthy get 42 percent of the Democratic vote in the New Hampshire primary, an astounding moral victory over the president. Days later, Robert Kennedy, now senator from New York, announced that he too would seek the Democratic nomination on a peace platform. Facing humiliating defeat in the primaries, weakened by bad health, and worn down by the cares of long public service, Johnson announced on March 31, in a speech also proposing peace talks in Paris, that he would not run for reelection.

During the next three months, McCarthy and Kennedy fought it out on the primary trail for the vacated spot, going head to head in a dozen state contests. But the nation underwent a convulsion of racial anger and despair when, on April 4, 1968, Martin Luther King was shot and killed in Memphis, where he had gone to rally support for a sanitation workers' strike. More than a hundred cities exploded in riots, and the ghastly record of political violence quickly resumed. On June 3, after winning the

California primary in a squeaker, Bobby Kennedy was shot and killed in his campaign hotel in Los Angeles by an irate Arab-American.

In late January 1968, at the time of Tet, the Vietnamese lunar New Year, the Vietnamese Communists launched a major countrywide uprising. The Vietcong were repulsed with frightful losses, but the magnitude and initial successes of their offensive jolted the media and the American public. An enemy that the administration had said was on the ropes and about to collapse clearly had plenty of fight left. Tet raised to a new level public distrust of the Johnson administration and the military experts. The delegitimization process rose another notch.

Publicly, Johnson proclaimed Tet a Communist defeat and vowed to fight on, but even the hawks' will had been weakened. When General Westmoreland asked for another 206,000 troops, the administration said no and began to reassess the American role in Vietnam. After 1968, there would be no further increases in American troop levels. What did not expand inevitably began to contract.

With both LBJ and Kennedy out of the race, McCarthy contested Vice President Hubert Humphrey for the Democratic nomination. Humphrey was loyal to his chief and saddled with the Vietnam incubus. But he came to the Chicago convention in August well ahead of his remaining opponent in delegates, all from the nonprimary states. The convention was a party disaster. Several thousand peace advocates descended on the Windy City to support McCarthy and denounce the Democrats' "politics of death." Some of the protesters were Yippies, counterculture activists led by Jerry Rubin and Abbie Hoffman, determined to make a shambles of the convention process. As the TV cameras rolled, Yippies clashed with brutal Chicago police, and the appalled American public saw contorted faces, shattered glass, tear gas, and blood. Humphrey won the nomination, but the Battle of Chicago may have cost him the election.

Meanwhile, in Miami, the Republicans nominated Richard Nixon on a platform that emphasized law and order. The former vice president had made a spectacular comeback since 1962 when, running for governor of California, he lost to Pat Brown and ruefully promised never to run for office again. But GOP leaders, grateful for his loyalty to the party in 1964, when so many mainstream Republicans had deserted Goldwater, gave him their votes in Miami. Nixon also won the support of southerners by promising to slow the process of integration and give the white South a larger say in Washington.

The Republicans' worst fear was conservative voters' defection to George Wallace. The Alabama governor had decided to run on a separate third-party ticket that promised backlash voters a true alternative to both major parties: the Vietnam War would be concluded by victory, and the "pointy-headed professors" who had concocted the Great Society social programs would be exiled from Washington. In an early poll, Wallace scored only eight percentage points behind Humphrey.

In the end, the race between the major party candidates was close. After early dithering, Humphrey adopted an independent Vietnam line that brought dovish Democrats back to the fold. At the same time, organized labor rallied blue-collar trade unionists behind the party that had advanced their interests for so many years. On Election Day, Nixon won, but less than a percentage point in the popular vote separated him from Humphrey. Wallace got only 13 percent of the total.

The counterculture peaked in 1969. On the weekend of August 15–17, near Woodstock, New York, 400,000 youths gathered for a rock festival that promised the Jefferson Airplane, the Family Stone, Jimi Hendrix, Janis Joplin, and Joan Baez. The weather was rainy and the grounds became a quagmire. The scene included nudity, public sex, and open use of drugs. But there was no violence and little crime, and the event became a peak experience for thousands, giving a name to a whole generation of young men and women—the Woodstock Nation.

Nineteen sixty-nine would mark the death of one dissenting movement and the birth of another. In June, at its ninth annual convention, SDS split into two factions: Progressive Labor, loyal to Mao Tse-Tung's People's Republic of China, and the Black Panther–allied Weathermen, fantasists possessed by apocalyptic visions of white "Amerika" destroyed by urban guerrillas. Following a rash of violent tryout "actions," the Weathermen—and Weatherwomen—went underground, into the "belly of the beast," to fight for revolution. Many would not emerge for years.

Meanwhile, another underground broke through to the full light of day. Homosexuals were the last minority to confront their oppressors during the decade. Victims of ridicule, violence, and brutal legal repression, they had disguised their sexual preferences or accepted their oppression while groups defined by race or gender were demanding respect and equality. Then spontaneously, on June 27, gay, lesbian, and transvestite patrons at the Stonewall Inn on Christopher Street in Greenwich Village decided to fight back when police raided the establishment. Two nights of rioting followed. Stonewall was gay America's Concord and Lexington, the shot heard 'round the world. In July, a group of homosexual and lesbian activists organized the Gay Liberation Front, setting in motion forces that would alter collective American sensibilities and our perception of fundamental social institutions.

Some would say the Sixties did not end on December 31, 1969. The United States would not fully detach from the Vietnam War until January 1973, when the combatants signed a peace treaty in Paris. And the war itself was not over until the conquest of the South by the Communists in 1975. The New Left and the counterculture deflated only gradually, and even the Great Society—or at least its major programs—survived and, for a time under Nixon, even expanded. It is not possible, then, to squeeze the Sixties precisely into the chronological decade. And yet an uncommon cultural, social, and political coherence to the period 1960–69 justifies its distinctive treatment.

1

The Economic Miracle

Affluence made possible the Sixties as we know it. Only the wealth generated by a surging economy could have sustained the politics, the lifestyles, the tastes, and the opinions of Sixties Americans.

The whole era following World War II had been prosperous compared with the 1930s. In 1945, the United States emerged from victory over the Axis powers as the only unscathed nation with its technology enhanced, its economy renewed, and its leaders and people supremely confident in their industrial prowess. Rather than collapse to Great Depression levels, as many experts had predicted during the war, the country reached full employment soon after 1945 and, despite several recessions, never returned to the bad old days of the prewar era. But in the twenty-five years following V-J Day, no period was as thriving as the middle segment of the Sixties. In the miraculous year of 1965–66, unemployment was under four percent, GNP grew at about six percent, and inflation advanced at less than three percent. By 1968, economic analysts were proclaiming the "longest uptrend in history."

The economic boom and the general sense of confidence it fostered made possible the expanded social programs of the Great Society. Each year during the Sixties, government revenues rose without any increase in tax rates and, in fact, even when rates were cut. Social generosity seemed a free ride; a little redistribution from rich to poor seemed painless. As Walter Heller wrote in 1966, "when the cost of fulfilling people's aspirations can be met out of a growing horn of plenty—instead of robbing Peter to pay Paul—ideological roadblocks melt away." The boom also underwrote the decade's radical insurgency. Prosperous times made possible wide detours from careers into dissenting politics and alternative lifestyles that college students took with abandon. If you dropped out, you could later painlessly drop in. Minimal risk was involved.

The Sixties, however, had its economic worries and concerns. Good times are never good enough. Under Eisenhower, the economy had suffered several recessions, some of them moderately severe. The last began in 1958 and, after a brief recovery, resumed in early 1960. During the presidential campaign, the Democrats had capitalized on voters' continued worries by promising to "get the country moving again." The economic picture had improved by the time the new Kennedy administration was ensconced in Washington, but the president had promised action and his economic policy advisers, led by Walter Heller of the Council of Economic Advisers, were determined to further reduce the unemployment rate and accelerate the growth of GNP beyond the modest showing of the Eisenhower years.

Heller was a disciple of John Maynard Keynes, the British economist who, during the dismal 1930s, had propounded a new theory of business cycles and proposed a new way to deal with them. Keynes believed that depressions are caused by a weak propensity to invest and insufficient aggregate demand for goods and services. In the face of the persistent unemployed resources of capital and labor that resulted, the government must step in and by expansive fiscal policies—an excess of expenditures over revenues—compensate for the shortfall of the private economy. In effect, when private spending is unable to sustain full employment, the government must take over. The Keynesians rejected the balanced budget orthodoxies of the day. Saving the economy and sparing the public were far more important than making the Treasury's balance come out in the black. The president himself was not a Keynesian, but his economic advisers undertook a campaign to make the young leader see the error of his old-fashioned ways.

Heller's remedy for the sluggish economy was a federal tax cut. This was a conservative version of Keynesianism. The added spending needed would come by increasing the personal income of taxpayers. With more money in their pockets, they would, presumably, buy more cars, houses, restaurant meals, books, and movie tickets, and the economy would rebound. Another version of Keynesianism defended by John K. Galbraith, a Harvard professor who was close to the president, and Leon Keyserling, a former adviser to Truman, proposed to increase government spending without increasing government revenues. In this case, the added demand would take the form of new highways, better schools and hospitals, upgraded national parks, larger libraries, and improved welfare services. In his 1958 book *The Affluent Society,* Galbraith had talked about private wealth and public squalor. His sort of Keynesian economic stimulation promised to redress the imbalance between the two.

Fearing the wrath of fiscal conservatives and the widespread public view that deficits were somehow wicked, Kennedy delayed acting on his advisers' concerns. Not until June 1962 did the president formally propose a tax cut, and not until early the following year did a bill begin to find its way through Congress. It had not yet passed when Kennedy met his tragic fate in Dallas, and it did not become law until February 26, 1964. Thereafter, revival and rapid growth, already under way, truly surged, bringing to the nation some of the most prosperous years of the century.

Other economic issues besides unemployment and sluggish growth rates required attention. There was "structural" unemployment: the poor fit of people to jobs. Many workers lacked the knowledge and skills needed for a new age. The situation promised to become worse down the road as the new computers, linked to robotized machinery, began to make their impact. Structural unemployment was also related to regional obsolescence. Substantial parts of the nation had been left out of the growth surge, and their inhabitants remained sunk in poverty. Given these persistent difficulties, it was no wonder that pockets of private poverty remained. Literate Americans read and acclaimed two books of this decade that revealed the rust spots under the shiny surface of prosperity: Galbraith's *The Affluent Society* and Michael Harrington's *The Other America*.

Finally, prosperity was not enough. In fact, it produced its own class of existential discontents. When society had solved its problems of material scarcity, it found itself beset with urgent new questions of meaning, purpose, fulfillment, choice, love, and life and death.

Yet without question, in the first half of the decade, optimism about the future and satisfaction about the present reached levels seldom before attained, and much of what we consider characteristic of the Sixties floated on a bounding sea of prosperity.

Council of Economic Advisers Report, 1965

In 1946, just after World War II, Congress created the Council of Economic Advisers (CEA) to help the president formulate economic policy. The bill establishing the CEA was intended by its sponsors to commit the government to a full-employment policy using elements of Keynesian fiscal policy. These elements, seemingly, had proven themselves during the war, when massive federal deficits had finally ended the chronic underemployment of labor and capital of the 1930s. In the course of the bill's passage through a conservative Congress, however, the legal commitment had been eliminated, and the bill that finally became law did little more than create an advisory body to serve the president as a board of experts and to issue annual reports.

This did not mean that the CEA was powerless. Under Kennedy and Johnson, the council was led by articulate and forceful men—Walter Heller and Gardner Ackley—who had the ear of their chiefs and were able to powerfully influence national economic policy. It was these men who sold the famous 1964 tax cut to Kennedy and who elevated Keynesianism to the position of orthodox policy for a modern capitalist economy.

The CEA's 1965 report, as excerpted here, describes triumphantly the successes of the American economy. It conveys the economic optimism that undergirded much of the Great Society and helped create the sense of new possibilities in which dissent could flourish. It also reveals the triumph of Keynesian ideas. Ackley and his colleagues were certain that Keynesian fiscal policy, as embedded in the Revenue Act of 1964, had given the economy a big boost. Admittedly, the extraordinary economic expansion had begun before the 1964 tax cut officially passed, but the recent surge, the council claimed, stemmed from consumer anticipation of its advent.

Reading the document today, we are struck by its hubris. The council members clearly believed that they knew how to tame the business cycle. But before many months had passed, inflation would rear its unlovely head, and the council would recommend a surtax on personal income. Down the road, even the basic principles of the Keynesians would come into question.

[*From* **Annual Report of the Council of Economic Advisers, 1965** *(Washington, DC: U.S. Government Printing Office, 1966), pp. 35–38.*]

The Sustained Expansion of 1961–64

As 1965 begins, most Americans are enjoying a degree of prosperity unmatched in their experience, or indeed in the history of their nation. In 1964, some 70 million of them were at work, producing $622 billion worth of goods and services.

The gains of four years of uninterrupted economic expansion had brought fuller pay envelopes, greater sales, larger dividend checks, a higher standard of living, more savings, and a stronger sense of security than ever before. Over that period industrial production grew at an annual rate of 7 percent, and the total output of all goods and services . . . increased at an average rate of 5 percent. . . . These gains brought jobs to 4 million more persons and raised total consumer income after taxes by 6 percent a year. All this was accomplished with essentially stable prices.

That the extent and duration of these gains exceeded the two preceding postwar expansions can be seen from Chart I [not included.] Indeed, in a few months, the duration of this expansion will have surpassed any other on record—except only the prolonged advance before and during World War II.

An Overall View of the Expansion

This gratifying record reflects the strength and elasticity of the private economy and its favorable response to a series of policy measures deliberately designed to invigorate it. The upturn of 1961 was quick and strong, in part through an early recovery of private demand and in part through forceful policy actions. Prompt steps to boost consumers' purchasing power taken by President Kennedy's administration were later reinforced by increases in Government expenditures necessary to strengthen America's basic defenses and to achieve the precautionary buildup required by the Berlin crisis.*

Following the rapid recovery, the outlook appeared favorable in 1962. Many observers, recognizing that there were special explanations for the weakness and brevity of the recovery of 1958–60, expected a return of the vigorous expansionary strength of 1954–57. In fact, conditions had changed. The backlogs of demand for housing, consumer durable goods, and additions to manufacturing plant and equipment, which had existed in 1954–55, were gone. Even after the expansionary fiscal measures of 1961, the federal budget remained more restrictive than it had been in the 1954–57 period. . . .

In the course of 1962, the pace of expansion slowed. By mid-1962 it had become apparent that, given the level and structure of federal tax rates, the strength of private demand would be insufficient to carry the economy up to full employment of its resources. Consequently, President Kennedy announced in August that he would propose a major tax bill in 1963, reducing the rates of personal income and corporate profits taxes from levels which had been determined in large part by the need to fight the postwar and Korean [War] inflations. The year 1963 saw prolonged debate over this measure and enactment came only in February 1964. But by mid-1963, increasing confidence that prosperity would be maintained with the aid of the expected tax cut, the continuing support of an expansionary monetary policy, the fuller response of business investment to the 1962 tax measures, and the strong demand for automobiles once again began to accelerate the pace of expansion. Thus, as the Revenue Act of 1964 became effective, the economy was already moving ahead strongly.

The Economy in 1964

In its Report a year ago, the Council of Economic Advisers found that ". . . the outlook this year calls for a significant acceleration in the growth of

---

*This refers to the tensions during 1961 between the United States and the Soviet Union over the status of Berlin that resulted in the calling up of military reserves by the Kennedy administration and the request to Congress for additional defense funds—ed.

output. At the midpoint of the forecast range, current dollar GNP for 1964 is estimated to increase 6.5 percent above the level of 1963, and the real GNP about 5 percent . . . the more rapid expansion of production in 1964 should lower the unemployment rate. By the end of the year, it is expected to fall to approximately 5 percent." These expectations were realized. Gross National Product (GNP) for the year as a whole exceeded that of 1963 by 6.5 percent and the unemployment rate in December was 5.0 percent.

The optimistic forecast for 1964 depended on the tax cut, and its fulfillment is a measure of the tax cut's accomplishments. . . .

These four years of expansion have demonstrated that the American economy is capable of sustained balanced growth in peacetime. No law of nature compels a free market economy to suffer from recessions or periodic inflations. As the postwar experience of Western Europe and Japan already indicates, future progress need not be interrupted even though its pace may vary from year to year. We need not judge the life expectancy of the current expansion by measuring the time it has already run. The economy is in good health, and its prospects for continued expansion are in no wise dimmed by the fact that the upswing began four years ago rather than one or two years ago. . . .

The Other America: Poverty in the United States *by Michael Harrington*

A majority of Americans felt flush in the Sixties, but many did not feel happy. Too many of their fellow citizens had been left behind—or so Michael Harrington informed them in 1962.

Harrington was a young man of thirty-four when he wrote The Other America, *a small book about a then-largely-unnoticed social phenomenon. A democratic socialist who had worked for Dorothy Day's Catholic Worker movement, a precursor to the radical Liberation Theology of recent Latin America, Harrington did not share in the self-congratulatory mood of mainstream social observers. As a socialist, he was naturally skeptical of capitalism, and when he looked into the hidden corners of American life, he found poverty and inequality in abundance.*

Relatively few books, in the annual publishers' deluge, have made much difference except to their authors. But some have. Harriet Beecher Stowe's Uncle Tom's Cabin *forced antebellum Americans to confront the evil of slavery and contributed to growing strife between North and South. Upton Sinclair's* The Jungle *made the literate public fear for its health and led to the 1906 Pure Food and Drug Act. The Other America pricked the conscience of the middle class and forced them to confront the continued presence of the poor in a society that basked in affluence.*

The book's most significant reader was the president. John Kennedy may actually have only read Dwight Macdonald's review of Harrington in The New Yorker, *but it was enough to alert him to poverty as a potential political issue. In December 1962, he called in Walter Heller, his economic adviser, and told him: "Now look! I want to go beyond the things that have already been accomplished. Give me the facts on the things we will have to do. For example, what about the poverty problem in the United States." Heller, who himself had been thinking about the country's pockets of poor people, gathered up experts from the Social Security Administration, the Department of Labor, and the Department of Health, Education, and Welfare to put together a federal program to reduce the poverty rate in America. After Kennedy's death, Heller brought the antipoverty issue to Lyndon Johnson's attention and so planted the seed that became the Great Society's War on Poverty.*

The selection below is an excerpt from Harrington's book, a book that actually made a difference.

There is a familiar America. It is celebrated in speeches and advertised on television and in the magazines. It has the highest mass standard of living the world has ever known.

In the 1950s this America worried about itself, yet even its anxieties were products of abundance. The title of a brilliant book was widely misinterpreted, and the familiar America began to call itself "the affluent society." There was introspection about Madison Avenue and tail fins; there was discussion of the emotional suffering taking place in the suburbs. In all this, there was an implicit assumption that the basic grinding economic problems had been solved in the United States. In this theory the nation's problems were no longer a matter of basic human needs, of food, shelter, and clothing. Now they were seen as qualitative, a question of learning to live decently amid luxury.

While this discussion was carried on, there existed another America. In it dwelt somewhere between 40 million and 50 million citizens of this land. They were poor. They still are.

To be sure, the other America is not impoverished in the same sense as those poor nations where millions cling to hunger as a defense against starvation. This country has escaped such extremes. That does not change the fact that tens of millions of Americans are, at this very moment, maimed in body and spirit, existing at levels beneath those necessary for human decency. If these people are not starving, they are hungry, and sometimes fat with hunger, for that is what cheap foods do. They are without adequate housing and education and medical care.

The government has documented what this means to the bodies of the poor, and the figures will be cited throughout this book. But even more basic, this poverty twists and deforms the spirit. The American poor are pessimistic and defeated, and they are victimized by mental suffering to a degree unknown in suburbia.

This book is a description of the world in which these people live; it is about the other America. Here are the unskilled workers, the migrant farm workers, the aged, the minorities, and all the others who live in the economic underworld of American life. In all this, there will be statistics, and that offers the opportunity for disagreement among honest and sincere men. I would ask the reader to respond critically to every assertion, but not to allow statistical quibbling to obscure the huge, enormous, and intolerable fact of poverty in America. For, when all is said and done, the reality of poverty is unmistakable, whatever its exact dimensions, and the truly human reaction can only be outrage. As W. H. Auden wrote:

Hunger allows no choice
To the citizen or the police;
We must love one another or die.

I

The millions who are poor in the United States tend to become increasingly invisible. Here is a great mass of people, yet it takes an effort of the intellect and will even to see them.

I discovered this personally in a curious way. After I wrote my first article on poverty in America, I had all the statistics down on paper. I had proved to my satisfaction that there were around 50 million poor in this country. Yet, I realized I did not believe my own figures. The poor existed in the government reports; they were percentages and numbers in long, close columns, but they were not part of my experience. I could prove that the other America existed, but I had never been there.

My response was not accidental. It was typical of what is happening to an entire society, and it reflects profound social changes in this nation. The other America, the America of poverty, is hidden today in a way that it never was before. Its millions are socially invisible to the rest of us. No wonder that so many misinterpreted Galbraith's title and assumed that "the affluent society" meant that everyone had a decent standard of life. The misinterpretation was true as far as the actual day-to-day lives of two-thirds of the nation were concerned. Thus, one must begin a description of the other America by understanding why we do not see it.

There are perennial reasons that make the other America an invisible land.

Poverty is often off the beaten track. It always has been. The ordinary tourist never left the main highway, and today he rides interstate turnpikes. He does not go into the valleys of Pennsylvania where the towns look like movie sets of Wales in the thirties. He does not see the company houses in rows, the rutted roads (the poor always have bad roads whether they live in the city, in towns, or on farms), and everything is black and dirty. And even if he were to pass through such a place by accident, the tourist would not meet the unemployed men in the bar or the women coming home from a runaway sweatshop.

Then, too, beauty and myths are perennial masks of poverty. The traveler comes to the Appalachians in the lovely season. He sees the hills, the streams, the foliage—but not the poor. Or perhaps he looks at a run-down mountain house and, remembering Rousseau rather than seeing with his eyes, decides that "those people" are truly fortunate to be living the way they are and that they are lucky to be exempt from the strains and tensions of the middle class. The only problem is that "those people," the quaint inhabitants of those hills, are undereducated, underprivileged, lack medical care, and are in the process of being forced from the land into a life in the cities, where they are misfits.

These are normal and obvious causes of the invisibility of the poor. They operated a generation ago; they will be functioning a generation hence. It is more important to understand that the very development of American society is creating a new kind of blindness about poverty. The poor are increasingly slipping out of the very experience and consciousness of the nation.

If the middle class never did like ugliness and poverty, it was at least aware of them. "Across the tracks" was not a very long way to go. There were forays into the slums at Christmas time; there were charitable organizations that brought contact with the poor. Occasionally, almost everyone passed through the Negro ghetto or the blocks of tenements, if only to get downtown to work or to entertainment.

Now the American city has been transformed. The poor still inhabit the miserable housing in the central area, but they are increasingly isolated from contact with, or sight of, anybody else. Middle-class women coming in from suburbia on a rare trip may catch the merest glimpse of the other America on the way to an evening at the theater, but their children are segregated in suburban schools. The business or professional man may drive along the fringes of slums in a car or bus, but it is not an important experience to him. The failures, the unskilled, the disabled, the aged, and the minorities are right there, across the tracks, where they have always been. But hardly anyone else is.

In short, the very development of the American city has removed poverty from the living, emotional experience of millions upon millions of middle-class Americans. Living out in the suburbs, it is easy to assume that ours is, indeed, an affluent society.

This new segregation of poverty is compounded by a well-meaning ignorance. A good many concerned and sympathetic Americans are aware that there is much discussion of urban renewal. Suddenly, driving through the city, they notice that a familiar slum has been torn down and that there are towering, modern buildings where once there had been tenements or hovels. There is a warm feeling of satisfaction, of pride in the way things are working out: the poor, it is obvious, are being taken care of.

The irony in this (as the chapter on housing will document) is that the truth is nearly the exact opposite to the impression. The total impact of the various housing programs in postwar America has been to squeeze more and more people into existing slums. More often than not, the modern apartment in a towering building rents at $40 a room or more. For, during the past decade and a half, there has been more subsidization of middle- and upper-income housing than there has been of housing for the poor.

Clothes make the poor invisible too: America has the best-dressed poverty the world has ever known. For a variety of reasons, the benefits of mass production have been spread much more evenly in this area than in many others. It is much easier in the United States to be decently dressed than it is to be decently housed, fed, or doctored. Even people with terribly depressed incomes can look prosperous.

This is an extremely important factor in defining our emotional and existential ignorance of poverty. In Detroit the existence of social classes became much more difficult to discern the day the companies put lockers in the plants. From that moment on, one did not see men in work clothes on the way to the factory, but citizens in slacks and white shirts. This process has been magnified with the poor throughout the country. There are tens of thousands of Americans in the big cities who are wearing shoes, perhaps even a stylishly cut suit or dress, and yet are hungry. It is not a matter of planning, though it almost seems as if the affluent society had given out costumes to the poor so that they would not offend the rest of society with the sight of rags.

Then, many of the poor are the wrong age to be seen. A good number of them (over 8 million) are sixty-five years of age or better; an even larger number are under eighteen. The aged members of the other America are often sick, and they cannot move. Another group of them live out their lives in loneliness and frustration: they sit in rented rooms, or else they stay close to a house in a neighborhood that has completely changed from the old days. Indeed, one of the worst aspects of poverty among the aged is that these people are out of sight and out of mind, and alone.

The young are somewhat more visible, yet they too stay close to their neighborhoods. Sometimes they advertise their poverty through a lurid tabloid story about a gang killing. But generally they do not disturb the quiet streets of the middle class.

And finally, the poor are politically invisible. It is one of the cruelest ironies of social life in advanced countries that the dispossessed at the bottom of society are unable to speak for themselves. The people of the other America do not, by and large, belong to unions, to fraternal organizations, or to political parties. They are without lobbies of their own; they put forward no legislative program. As a group, they are atomized. They have no face; they have no voice.

Thus, there is not even a cynical political motive for caring about the poor, as in the old days. Because the slums are no longer centers of powerful political organizations, the politicians need not really care about their inhabitants. The slums are no longer visible to the middle class, so much of the idealistic urge to fight for those who need help is gone. Only the social agencies have a really direct involvement with the other America, and they are without any great political power.

To the extent that the poor have a spokesman in American life, that role is played by the labor movement. The unions have their own particular idealism, an ideology of concern. More than that, they realize that the existence of a reservoir of cheap, unorganized labor is a menace to wages and working conditions throughout the entire economy. Thus, many union legislative proposals—to extend the coverage of minimum wage and social security, to organize migrant farm laborers—articulate the needs of the poor.

That the poor are invisible is one of the most important things about them. They are not simply neglected and forgotten as in the old rhetoric of reform; what is much worse, they are not seen. . . .

● ● ●

Forty to 50 million people are becoming increasingly invisible. That is a shocking fact. But there is a second basic irony of poverty that is equally important: if one is to make the mistake of being born poor, he should choose a time when the majority of the people are miserable too.

J. K. Galbraith develops this idea in *The Affluent Society*, and in doing so defines the "newness" of the kind of poverty in contemporary America. The old poverty, Galbraith notes, was general. It was the condition of life of an entire society, or at least of that huge majority who were without special skills or the luck of birth. When the entire economy advanced, a good many of these people gained higher standards of living. Unlike the poor today, the majority poor of a generation ago were an immediate (if cynical) concern of political leaders. The old slums of the immigrants had the votes; they provided the basis for labor organizations; their very numbers could be a powerful force in political conflict. At the same time the new technology required higher skills, more education, and stimulated an upward movement for millions.

Perhaps the most dramatic case of the power of the majority poor took place in the 1930s. The Congress of Industrial Organizations literally organized millions in a matter of years. A labor movement that had been declining and confined to a thin stratum of the highly skilled suddenly embraced masses of men and women in basic industry. At the same time this acted as a pressure upon the Government, and the New Deal codified some of the social gains in laws like the Wagner Act. The result was not a basic transformation of the American system, but it did transform the lives of an entire section of the population.

In the thirties one of the reasons for these advances was that misery was general. There was no need then to write books about unemployment and poverty. That was the decisive social experience of the entire society, and the apple sellers even invaded Wall Street. There was political sympathy from middle-class reformers; there were an élan and spirit that grew out of a deep crisis.

Some of those who advanced in the thirties did so because they had unique and individual personal talents. But for the great mass, it was a question of being at the right point in the economy at the right time in history, and utilizing that position for common struggle. Some of those who failed did so because they did not have the will to take advantage of new opportunities. But for the most part the poor who were left behind had been at the wrong place in the economy at the wrong moment in history.

These were the people in the unorganizable jobs, in the South, in the minority groups, in the fly-by-night factories that were low on capital and high on labor. When some of them did break into the economic mainstream—when, for instance, the CIO opened up the way for some Negroes to find good industrial jobs—they proved to be as resourceful as anyone else. As a group, the other Americans who stayed behind were not originally composed primarily of individual failures. Rather, they were victims of an impersonal process that selected some for progress and discriminated against others.

Out of the thirties came the welfare state. Its creation had been stimulated by mass impoverishment and misery, yet it helped the poor least of all. Laws like unemployment compensation, the Wagner Act, the various farm programs, all these were designed for the middle third in the cities, for the organized workers, and for the upper third in the country, for the big market farmers. If a man works in an extremely low-paying job, he may not even be covered by social security or other welfare programs. If he receives unemployment compensation, the payment is scaled down according to his low earnings.

One of the major laws that was designed to cover everyone, rich and poor, was social security. But even here the other Americans suffered discrimination. Over the years social security payments have not even provided a subsistence level of life. The middle third have been able to supplement the federal pension through private plans negotiated by unions, through joining medical insurance schemes like Blue Cross, and so on. The poor have not been able to do so. They lead a bitter life, and then have to pay for that fact in old age.

Indeed, the paradox that the welfare state benefits those least who need help most is but a single instance of a persistent irony in the other America. Even when the money finally trickles down, even when a school is built in a poor neighborhood, for instance, the poor are still deprived. Their entire environment, their life, their values, do not prepare them to take advantage of the new opportunity. The parents are anxious for the children to go to work; the pupils are pent up, waiting for the moment when their education has complied with the law.

Today's poor, in short, missed the political and social gains of the thirties. They are, as Galbraith rightly points out, the first minority poor in history, the first poor not to be seen, the first poor whom the politicians could leave alone. . . .

2

The New Frontier–Great Society

he victory of John F. Kennedy over Richard Nixon in the 1960 presidential race marked in many ways the beginning of the Sixties. Though both men were "born in this century," to use Kennedy's inaugural phrase, and both were veterans of World War II, JFK was a better icon of the new era than his opponent. Even if only four years older, Nixon—awkward physically, personally insecure, and closely identified with the Eisenhower administration—*seemed* to belong to the previous generation. After eight drowsy years of the GOP, Kennedy's Democratic affiliations, and his image of youthful irreverence and boldness, promised a new start in the nation's public life and perhaps a new beginning in its culture and values as well.

In fact, Kennedy was scarcely a political innovator. His politics were inspired more by the practical give-and-take of Irish-American Boston than by the reformist zeal of the party's thinkers. In the fight for the nomination in 1960, the Democratic liberals had rejected the son of Joseph Kennedy, a man tainted by sharp dealings in business and appeasement of Hitler, in favor of two-time loser Adlai Stevenson. Yet Kennedy could not ignore his party's traditions. For a generation, the Democrats had been the party of innovation. The New Deal, the offspring of crisis and opportunity, had made the federal government into the driving force for social and political change. It had not ended the Great Depression, but it had created a modified social welfare system that sought reduced inequality and greater protection against the uncertainties of life in capitalist society.

Kennedy's New Frontier aimed at rounding out Roosevelt's New Deal and Harry Truman's Fair Deal. It proposed a higher minimum wage, subsidized housing, federal assistance for public schools, and hospital insurance for retirees.

The young president got little of what he wanted. The public mood was timid, and Kennedy's wafer-thin 1960 victory deprived him of the psychological mandate needed to overcome it. The Democrats had majorities in both houses, but a conservative coalition of southerners and northern Republicans prevented passage of most liberal social legislation. There were also Kennedy's own limitations. Lawmaking seemed to bore him. He much preferred the excitement of foreign policy and crisis management. Now, as president, he lacked the will, or the skill, to cajole and bully Congress to achieve his goals. A third of the way through JFK's "thousand days," a leader of the liberal Americans for Democratic Action declared that the president had been "a bitter disappointment."

But Kennedy's flaws as a reformer must not be exaggerated. His personal experience in West Virginia during the presidential primary campaign, reinforced by the press exposés of Appalachian poverty, led him to sponsor the Area Redevelopment Act to encourage revival in the nation's impoverished rural regions. The measure passed in May 1961. It was Kennedy, moreover, who proposed a federal program targeting the nation's remaining poor. He had absorbed the message of Harrington's *The Other America* and concluded that the administration should submit a general antipoverty bill to Congress. His antipoverty task force was at work on the measure when Kennedy visited Dallas in late 1963 to smooth over the rifts in the Texas Democratic Party and was gunned down by Lee Harvey Oswald.

Lyndon Baines Johnson, Kennedy's successor, was a very different sort of man. The former Senate majority leader lived for the give-and-take of Congress, the wheeling and dealing of the legislative process. Not since James K. Polk, over a century before, did a president have so intimate an acquaintance with the workings of the national legislature and the details of how to make laws. During the remaining months of his predecessor's term, moreover, LBJ could count on the public's desire to honor the memory of the fallen hero by endorsing his programs posthumously. The second session of the Eighty-eighth Congress would give LBJ a number of significant measures still pending when Kennedy died, including a Wilderness Preservation Act, a food stamp plan for the poor, and an economy-stimulating federal tax cut.

But meanwhile Johnson was defining his own reform program, one that differed from the New Frontier in its greater reach. More than his predecessor's, LBJ's program looked ahead to new issues relevant to the affluence of the Sixties.

In November 1964, running in his own right for president, Johnson won the most lopsided victory over an opponent in American political history. His defeat of Barry Goldwater gave Johnson the mandate Kennedy never had. Besides the psychological advantage, Congress was now so solidly Democratic that the president could ignore the conservative North-South

coalition. What followed in the Eighty-ninth Congress was the most spectacular flood of social and cultural legislation since the New Deal, going
far to create what Lyndon Johnson, the Franklin Roosevelt protégé from
the Texas hill country, called the Great Society.

The golden age was short-lived. The Vietnam War, the creep of inflation,
the ghetto riots, campus strikes, political assassinations, congressional battle fatigue—all exacted their toll. In November 1966, many of the new liberals who had been elected to Congress in the Goldwater sweep went down
to defeat. The Ninetieth Congress failed to reverse the liberal tide but did
little to keep it going. After 1968, under Nixon, many of the Great Society
programs expanded fiscally as automatic entitlements grew, but few new
ones were created. Reform and change resumed their slow crawl. Whether
it was the calamities and defeats of the years after 1965 that ended reform
and checked the liberal surge or whether America merely reverted to the
norm of political life, we will never know.

Camelot

*The thousand days of John F. Kennedy's presidency were destined for mythological
transfiguration. The youth and good looks of the president and first lady, their circle of brilliant and glamorous friends, Kennedy's family wealth, and his martyrdom
and early death—these guaranteed that the public would remember the Kennedy
administration as a moment of magic.*

*Kennedy, along with his wife and the vice president, had gone to Texas in
November 1963 to bring peace to the Texas Democrats, whose feuding threatened to
deliver the state to the Republicans. In Dallas, while traveling in an open convert-
ible through cheering crowds, the president was shot and killed by a sniper. A shocked
and sorrowful nation experienced a wrenching week of obsequies and several days of
further dismay when the putative assassin, Lee Harvey Oswald, was himself shot
and killed by a local nightclub owner, Jack Ruby, while in police custody.*

*The sense of a lost paradise was strongest soon after the tragic events in Dallas of
November 22, 1963. In the days following, the public was immersed in a succession
of wrenching ceremonies to mark its grief.*

*But nothing contributed as much to the Edenic sense as a brief piece written by
Theodore White, the journalist whose book on the 1960 presidential campaign would
launch a series of brilliant narratives of later presidential races. A friend of the
Kennedys, White had been summoned to the Kennedy home in Hyannisport by the
young widow just a week after the assassination to help neutralize what she considered critical evaluations of the Kennedy administration and the Kennedy era. White,
she hoped, would compose a piece for Life magazine that would rescue her husband's
reputation and the Kennedy White House from the gloom that had collected around*

it. Unable to fly because of a fierce northeaster, White drove up to Cape Cod from New York by hired limousine.

For two hours at the family compound, he listened to the angry and unfocused widow talk about the "bitter old men" who wrote history and would inevitably blacken her husband's name. White must, as a preemptive strike, convey her own vision of the meaning of the previous three years.

Jackie's view was utterly romantic and mostly fictitious. She wanted Americans to think of the Kennedy White House as Camelot, where King Arthur and his knights of the Round Table performed their acts of gallantry and derring-do with laughter, wit, and matchless style. White himself, though a strong Kennedy partisan, found this formula cloying and false, but he dutifully phoned the story in to Life, *which printed it. Few who knew the administration well found the picture faithful to the flawed workaday original. It assuredly clashes with our knowledge of Kennedy's obsessive and covert womanizing. But it fed the public's sentimental need to mourn the lost glamour of 1961–63, and it remains an icon of the decade.*

[*Theodore H. White, "For President Kennedy: An Epilogue,"* Life *magazine, December 6, 1963. Copyright © 1963 Time Inc. Reprinted with permission.*]

FOR PRESIDENT KENNEDY

She remembers how hot the sun was in Dallas, and the crowds—greater and wilder than the crowds in Mexico or in Vienna. The sun was blinding, streaming down: yet she could not put on sunglasses for she had to wave to the crowd.

And up ahead she remembers seeing a tunnel around a turn and thinking that there would be a moment of coolness under the tunnel. There was the sound of the motorcycles, as always in a parade, and the occasional backfire of a motorcycle. The sound of the shot came, at that moment, like the sound of a backfire and she remembers Connally saying, "No, no, no, no, no. . . ."

She remembers the roses. Three times that day in Texas they had been greeted with the bouquets of yellow roses of Texas. Only, in Dallas they had given her *red* roses. She remembers thinking, how funny—red roses for me; and then the car was full of blood and red roses.

Much later, accompanying the body from the Dallas hospital to the airport, she was alone with Clint Hill—the first Secret Service man to come to their rescue—and with Dr. Burkley, the White House physician. Burkley gave her two roses that had slipped under the President's shirt when he fell, his head in her lap.

All through the night they tried to separate him from her, to sedate her and take care of her—and she would not let them. She wanted to be with him. She remembered that Jack had said of his father, when his father suffered the stroke, that he could not live like that. Don't let that happen to me, he had said, when I have to go.

• • •

Now, in her hand she was holding a gold St. Christopher's medal.

She had given him a St. Christopher's medal when they were married, but when Patrick* died this summer, they had wanted to put something in the coffin with Patrick that was from them both, and so he had put in the St. Christopher's medal.

Then he had asked her to give him a new one to mark their tenth wedding anniversary, a month after Patrick's death.

He was carrying it when he died, and she had found it. But it belonged to him—so she could not put *that* in the coffin with him. She wanted to give him something that was hers, something that she loved. So she had slipped off her wedding ring and put it on his finger. When she came out of the room in the hospital in Dallas, she asked: "Do you think it was right? Now I have nothing left." And Kenny O'Donnell said, "You leave it where it is."

That was at 1:30 P.M. in Texas.

But then, at Bethesda Hospital in Maryland, at 3 A.M. the next morning, Kenny slipped into the chamber where the body lay and brought her back the ring, which, as she talked now, she twisted.

On her little finger was the other ring: a slim, gold circlet with green emerald chips—the one he had given her in memory of Patrick.

• • •

There was a thought, too, that was always with her. "When Jack quoted something, it was usually classical," she said, "but I'm so ashamed of myself—all I keep thinking of is this line from a musical comedy.

"At night, before we'd go to sleep, Jack liked to play some records; and the song he loved most came at the very end of this record. The lines he loved to hear were: *Don't let it be forgot, that once there was a spot, for one brief shining moment that was known as Camelot.*"

She wanted to make sure that the point came clear and went on: "There'll be great Presidents again—and the Johnsons are wonderful, they've been wonderful to me—but there'll never be another Camelot again.

"Once, the more I read of history, the more bitter I got. For a while I thought history was something that bitter old men wrote. But then I real-

*Patrick is the son they lost two days after his birth—ed.

ized history made Jack what he was. You must think of him as this little boy, sick so much of the time, reading in bed, reading history, reading the Knights of the Round Table, reading Marlborough. For Jack, history was full of heroes. And if it made him this way—if it made him see the heroes—maybe other little boys will see. Men are such a combination of good and bad. Jack had this hero idea of history, the idealistic view."

But she came back to the idea that transfixed her: *"Don't let it be forgot, that once there was a spot, for one brief shining moment that was known as Camelot*—and it will never be that way again."

• • •

As for herself? She was horrified by the stories that she might live abroad. "I'm *never* going to live in Europe. I'm not going to 'travel extensively abroad.' That's a desecration. I'm going to live in the places I lived with Jack. In Georgetown, and with the Kennedys at the Cape. They're my family. I'm going to bring up my children. I want John to grow up to be a good boy."

As for the President's memorial, at first she remembered that, in every speech in their last days in Texas, he had spoken of how in December this nation would loft the largest rocket booster yet into the sky, making us first in space. So she had wanted something of his there when it went up—perhaps only his initials painted on a tiny corner of the great Saturn, where no one need even notice it. But now Americans will seek the moon from Cape Kennedy. The new name, born of her frail hope, came as a surprise.

The only thing she knew she must have for him was the eternal flame over his grave at Arlington.

"Whenever you drive across the bridge from Washington into Virginia," she said, "you see the Lee Mansion on the side of the hill in the distance. When Caroline was very little, the mansion was one of the first things she learned to recognize. Now, at night you can see his flame beneath the mansion for miles away."

She said it is time people paid attention to the new President and the new First Lady. But she does not want them to forget John F. Kennedy or read of him only in dusty or bitter histories:

For one brief shining moment there was Camelot.

The Warren Commission Report

The assassination of President Kennedy on November 22, 1963, bruised the nation's soul as no other event of the Sixties. Whatever his failings as a legislator and a man, he represented outwardly all that was most attractive about the republic's political life. He had not been universally popular. The far right and upholders of the racial status quo despised him, but to the broad middle, three years into his administration, he seemed an admirable representative of American political culture. The polls, however premature, showed that he would be reelected handily in 1964.

On November 29, a week after the tragic events in Dallas, President Johnson established a seven-man commission headed by Chief Justice Earl Warren to get to the truth of the assassination, which was already being encrusted with rumors and speculation amplified by Oswald's murder before he could be tried in court. The Warren Commission held extensive hearings and drew on the investigations of the FBI, the Secret Service, the attorney general of Texas, and the State Department. It submitted its report on September 24, 1964, in a single volume of conclusions and twenty-six additional ones of testimony and exhibits. The commission's summary conclusions, as indicated below, were that a single assassin, Lee Harvey Oswald, fired all three of the shots that killed Kennedy and wounded Texas governor John Connally. Further, the commission concluded that neither Oswald nor his killer, Jack Ruby, was engaged in a wider conspiracy.

The commission report, as we know, did not settle the issues in the minds of many Americans. To the public at the time, the disproportion between the means and the end, between the confused motives of the feckless misfit and the magnitude of his deed, made the conclusions unsatisfactory and unbelievable. In the years since 1963, literally thousands of books have been written about the assassination, and virtually all have pushed some conspiracy theory in which the murderers are identified variously with Castro's Cuba, the mafia, the Soviet Union, the far right, the CIA, the FBI, or even Lyndon Johnson. By now, the mythologies of the assassination have become as interesting a phenomenon as the events in Dallas themselves. Psychologists and cultural historians have had a field day uncovering the roots of these mythologies deep in the individual and collective psyche of the American people and in the experience of cold war intrigues and actual attempts, from the 1970s on, by the highest American officials to conceal embarrassing truths.

The brief excerpt below is from the report's conclusions.

[*From* **The Warren Commission Report: Report of the President's Commission on the Assassination of President John F. Kennedy** (*New York: St. Martin's Press*), *pp. 18–23.*]

CONCLUSIONS

This Commission was created to ascertain the facts relating to the preceding summary of events and to consider the important questions which they raised. The Commission has addressed itself to this task and has reached certain conclusions based on all the available evidence. No limitations have been placed on the Commission's inquiry; it has conducted its own investigation, and all Government agencies have fully discharged their responsibility to cooperate with the Commission in its investigation. These conclusions represent the reasoned judgment of all members of the Commission and are presented after an investigation which has satisfied the Commission that it has ascertained the truth concerning the assassination of President Kennedy to the extent that a prolonged and thorough search makes this possible.

1. The shots which killed President Kennedy and wounded Governor Connally were fired from the sixth floor window at the southeast corner of the Texas School Book Depository. This determination is based upon the following:

   a. Witnesses at the scene of the assassination saw a rifle being fired from the sixth floor window of the Depository Building, and some witnesses saw a rifle in the window immediately after the shots were fired.

   b. The nearly whole bullet found on Governor Connally's stretcher at Parkland Memorial Hospital and the two bullet fragments found in the front seat of the Presidential limousine were fired from the 6.5-millimeter Mannlicher-Carcano rifle found on the sixth floor of the Depository Building to the exclusion of all other weapons.

   c. The three used cartridge cases found near the window on the sixth floor at the southeast corner of the building were fired from the same rifle which fired the above-described bullet and fragments, to the exclusion of all other weapons.

   d. The windshield in the Presidential limousine was struck by a bullet fragment on the inside surface of the glass, but was not penetrated.

   e. The nature of the bullet wounds suffered by President Kennedy and Governor Connally and the location of the car at the time of the shots establish that the bullets were fired from above and behind the Presidential limousine, striking the President and the Governor as follows:

      (1) President Kennedy was first struck by a bullet which entered at the back of his neck and exited through the lower front portion of his neck, causing a wound which would not necessarily have been lethal. The President was struck a second time by a bullet which entered the right-rear portion of his head, causing a massive and fatal wound.

      (2) Governor Connally was struck by a bullet which entered on the right side of his back and traveled downward through the right side of his chest, exiting below his right nipple. This bullet then passed through his right wrist and entered his left thigh where it caused a superficial wound.

    f. There is no credible evidence that the shots were fired from the Triple Underpass, ahead of the motorcade, or from any other location.

2. The weight of the evidence indicates that there were three shots fired.

3. Although it is not necessary to any essential findings of the Commission to determine just which shot hit Governor Connally, there is very persuasive evidence from the experts to indicate that the same bullet which pierced the President's throat also caused Governor Connally's wounds. However, Governor Connally's testimony and certain other factors have given rise to some difference of opinion as to this probability but there is no question in the mind of any member of the Commission that all the shots which caused the President's and Governor Connally's wounds were fired from the sixth floor window of the Texas School Book Depository.

4. The shots which killed President Kennedy and wounded Governor Connally were fired by Lee Harvey Oswald. This conclusion is based upon the following:

    a. The Mannlicher-Carcano 6.5-millimeter Italian rifle from which the shots were fired was owned by and in the possession of Oswald.

    b. Oswald carried this rifle into the Depository Building on the morning of November 22, 1963.

    c. Oswald, at the time of the assassination, was present at the window from which the shots were fired.

    d. Shortly after the assassination, the Mannlicher-Carcano rifle belonging to Oswald was found partially hidden between some cartons on the sixth floor and the improvised paper bag in which Oswald brought the rifle to the Depository was found close by the window from which the shots were fired.

    e. Based on testimony of the experts and their analysis of films of the assassination, the Commission has concluded that a rifleman of Lee Harvey Oswald's capabilities could have fired the shots from the rifle used in the assassination within the elapsed time of the shooting. The Commission has concluded further that Oswald possessed the capability with a rifle which enabled him to commit the assassination.

f. Oswald lied to the police after his arrest concerning important substantive matters.

  g. Oswald had attempted to kill Maj. Gen. Edwin A. Walker (Resigned, U.S. Army) on April 10, 1963, thereby demonstrating his disposition to take human life.

5. Oswald killed Dallas Police Patrolman J. D. Tippit approximately 45 minutes after the assassination. This conclusion upholds the finding that Oswald fired the shots which killed President Kennedy and wounded Governor Connally and is supported by the following:

  a. Two eyewitnesses saw the Tippit shooting and seven eyewitnesses heard the shots and saw the gunman leave the scene with revolver in hand. These nine eyewitnesses positively identified Lee Harvey Oswald as the man they saw.

  b. The cartridge cases found at the scene of the shooting were fired from the revolver in the possession of Oswald at the time of his arrest to the exclusion of all other weapons.

  c. The revolver in Oswald's possession at the time of his arrest was purchased by and belonged to Oswald.

  d. Oswald's jacket was found along the path of flight taken by the gunman as he fled from the scene of the killing.

6. Within 80 minutes of the assassination and 35 minutes of the Tippit killing Oswald resisted arrest at the theatre by attempting to shoot another Dallas police officer.

7. The Commission has reached the following conclusions concerning Oswald's interrogation and detention by the Dallas police:

  a. Except for the force required to effect his arrest, Oswald was not subjected to any physical coercion by any law enforcement officials. He was advised that he could not be compelled to give any information and that any statements made by him might be used against him in court. He was advised of his right to counsel. He was given the opportunity to obtain counsel of his own choice and was offered legal assistance by the Dallas Bar Association, which he rejected at that time.

  b. Newspaper, radio, and television reporters were allowed uninhibited access to the area through which Oswald had to pass when he was moved from his cell to the interrogation room and other sections of the building, thereby subjecting Oswald to harassment and creating chaotic conditions which were not conducive to orderly interrogation or the protection of the rights of the prisoner.

c. The numerous statements, sometimes erroneous, made to the press by various local law enforcement officials, during this period of confusion and disorder in the police station, would have presented serious obstacles to the obtaining of a fair trial for Oswald. To the extent that the information was erroneous or misleading, it helped to create doubts, speculations, and fears in the mind of the public which might otherwise not have arisen.

8. The Commission has reached the following conclusions concerning the killing of Oswald by Jack Ruby on November 24, 1963:

a. Ruby entered the basement of the Dallas Police Department shortly after 11:17 A.M. and killed Lee Harvey Oswald at 11:21 A.M.

b. Although the evidence on Ruby's means of entry is not conclusive, the weight of the evidence indicates that he walked down the ramp leading from Main Street to the basement of the police department.

c. There is no evidence to support the rumor that Ruby may have been assisted by any members of the Dallas Police Department in the killing of Oswald.

d. The Dallas Police Department's decision to transfer Oswald to the county jail in full public view was unsound. The arrangements made by the police department on Sunday morning, only a few hours before the attempted transfer, were inadequate. Of critical importance was the fact that news media representatives and others were not excluded from the basement even after the police were notified of threats to Oswald's life. These deficiencies contributed to the death of Lee Harvey Oswald.

9. The Commission has found no evidence that either Lee Harvey Oswald or Jack Ruby was part of any conspiracy, domestic or foreign, to assassinate President Kennedy. The reasons for this conclusion are:

a. The Commission has found no evidence that anyone assisted Oswald in planning or carrying out the assassination. In this connection it has thoroughly investigated, among other factors, the circumstances surrounding the planning of the motorcade route through Dallas, the hiring of Oswald by the Texas School Book Depository Co. on October 15, 1963, the method by which the rifle was brought into the building, the placing of cartons of books at the window, Oswald's escape from the building, and the testimony of eyewitnesses to the shooting.

b. The Commission has found no evidence that Oswald was involved with any person or group in a conspiracy to assassinate the

President, although it has thoroughly investigated, in addition to other possible leads, all facets of Oswald's associations, finances, and personal habits, particularly during the period following his return from the Soviet Union in June 1962.

c. The Commission has found no evidence to show that Oswald was employed, persuaded, or encouraged by any foreign government to assassinate President Kennedy or that he was an agent of any foreign government, although the Commission has reviewed the circumstances surrounding Oswald's defection to the Soviet Union, his life there from October of 1959 to June of 1962 so far as it can be reconstructed, his known contacts with the Fair Play for Cuba Committee, and his visits to the Cuban and Soviet Embassies in Mexico City during his trip to Mexico from September 26 to October 3, 1963, and his known contacts with the Soviet Embassy in the United States.

d. The Commission has explored all attempts of Oswald to identify himself with various political groups, including the Communist Party, U.S.A., the Fair Play for Cuba Committee, and the Socialist Workers Party, and has been unable to find any evidence that the contacts which he initiated were related to Oswald's subsequent assassination of the President.

e. All of the evidence before the Commission established that there was nothing to support the speculation that Oswald was an agent, employee, or informant of the FBI, the CIA, or any other governmental agency. It has thoroughly investigated Oswald's relationships prior to the assassination with all agencies of the U.S. Government. All contacts with Oswald by any of these agencies were made in the regular exercise of their different responsibilities.

f. No direct or indirect relationship between Lee Harvey Oswald and Jack Ruby has been discovered by the Commission, nor has it been able to find any credible evidence that either knew the other, although a thorough investigation was made of the many rumors and speculations of such a relationship.

g. The Commission has found no evidence that Jack Ruby acted with any other person in the killing of Lee Harvey Oswald.

h. After careful investigation the Commission has found no credible evidence either that Ruby and Officer Tippit, who was killed by Oswald, knew each other or that Oswald and Tippit knew each other.

Because of the difficulty of proving negatives to a certainty the possibility of others being involved with either Oswald or Ruby cannot be established categorically, but if there is any such evidence it has been beyond the reach of all the investigative agencies and resources of the United States and has not come to the attention of this Commission.

10. In its entire investigation the Commission has found no evidence of conspiracy, subversion, or disloyalty to the U.S. Government by any Federal, State, or local official.

11. On the basis of the evidence before the Commission it concludes that Oswald acted alone. Therefore, to determine the motives for the assassination of President Kennedy, one must look to the assassin himself. Clues to Oswald's motives can be found in his family history, his education or lack of it, his acts, his writings, and the recollections of those who had close contacts with him throughout his life. The Commission has presented with this report all of the background information bearing on motivation which it could discover. Thus, others may study Lee Oswald's life and arrive at their own conclusions as to his possible motives.

The Commission could not make any definitive determination of Oswald's motives. It has endeavored to isolate factors which contributed to his character and which might have influenced his decision to assassinate President Kennedy. These factors were:

a. His deep-rooted resentment of all authority which was expressed in a hostility toward every society in which he lived;

b. His inability to enter into meaningful relationships with people, and a continuous pattern of rejecting his environment in favor of new surroundings;

c. His urge to try to find a place in history and despair at times over failures in his various undertakings;

d. His capacity for violence as evidenced by his attempt to kill General Walker;

e. His avowed commitment to Marxism and communism, as he understood the terms and developed his own interpretation of them; this was expressed by his antagonism toward the United States, by his defection to the Soviet Union, by his failure to be reconciled with life in the United States even after his disenchantment with the Soviet Union, and by his efforts, though frustrated, to go to Cuba.

Each of these contributed to his capacity to risk all in cruel and irresponsible actions.

The Great Society Speech

Meeting with Congress a week after John F. Kennedy's assassination, Lyndon Johnson intoned, "Let us continue." He intended to take up the unfinished business of the New Frontier, he told the assembled legislators and the American public, and carry it through to completion. Six months later, he stood before eighty thousand parents, dignitaries, faculty, and students at the University of Michigan spring graduation. His address would convey to the nation his vision of the future, his plan for remaking America.

In the tradition of most liberal presidents in the twentieth century, Johnson had a name for his program: the Great Society. It was a label that he borrowed from Richard Goodwin, a brilliant young aide and speechwriter he had inherited from Kennedy. A bellwether of his times, Goodwin shared the view of liberal mid-Sixties intellectuals that the postwar economic surge called for a refocusing of long-term social goals and perspectives. Want and scarcity were no longer serious specters. America was now an affluent society and the domestic problems ahead were qualitative, not quantitative. These views Goodwin made the core of the commencement address he wrote for his new chief.

As he delivered his blessedly short speech that sunny graduation day at Ann Arbor, Lyndon Johnson was transmitting the blueprint for a new sort of reform, one suited to the new postscarcity age. This new agenda would add beauty, intellect, spiritual values, and justice to material benefits as the goals of government. A later generation would not be kind to the Great Society, but on that warm May day the future seemed astonishingly bright.

[*Lyndon B. Johnson, "The Great Society,"* in **Public Papers of the Presidents of the United States: Lyndon B. Johnson, 1963–64,** *vol. 1 (Washington, DC: U.S. Government Printing Office, 1965), pp. 704–707.*]

THE GREAT SOCIETY

I have come today from the turmoil of your capital to the tranquility of your campus to speak about the future of your country.

The purpose of protecting the life of our nation and preserving the liberty of our citizens is to pursue the happiness of our people. Our success in that pursuit is the test of our success as a nation.

For a century we labored to settle and to subdue a continent. For half a century we called upon unbounded invention and untiring industry to create an order of plenty for all of our people.

The challenge of the next half century is whether we have the wisdom to use that wealth to enrich and elevate our national life, and to advance the quality of our American civilization.

Your imagination, your initiative, and your indignation will determine whether we build a society where progress is the servant of our needs, or a society where old values and new visions are buried under unbridled growth. For in your time we have the opportunity to move not only toward the rich society and the powerful society, but upward to the Great Society.

The Great Society rests on abundance and liberty for all. It demands an end to poverty and racial injustice, to which we are totally committed in our time. But that is just the beginning.

The Great Society is a place where every child can find knowledge to enrich his mind and to enlarge his talents. It is a place where leisure is a welcome chance to build and reflect, not a feared cause of boredom and restlessness. It is a place where the city of man serves not only the needs of the body and the demands of commerce but the desire for beauty and the hunger for community.

It is a place where man can renew contact with nature. It is a place which honors creation for its own sake and for what it adds to the understanding of the race. It is a place where men are more concerned with the quality of their goals than the quantity of their goods.

But most of all, the Great Society is not a safe harbor, a resting place, a final objective, a finished work. It is a challenge constantly renewed, beckoning us toward a destiny where the meaning of our lives matches the marvelous products of our labor.

So I want to talk to you today about three places where we begin to build the Great Society—in our cities, in our countryside, and in our classrooms.

Many of you will live to see the day, perhaps fifty years from now, when there will be 400 million Americans—four-fifths of them in urban areas. In the remainder of this century urban population will double, city land will double, and we will have to build homes, highways, and facilities equal to all those built since this country was first settled. So in the next forty years we must rebuild the entire urban United States.

Aristotle said: "Men come together in cities in order to live, but they remain together in order to live the good life." It is harder and harder to live the good life in American cities today.

The catalogue of ills is long: there is the decay of the centers and the despoiling of the suburbs. There is not enough housing for our people or transportation for our traffic. Open land is vanishing and old landmarks are violated.

Worst of all expansion is eroding the precious and time-honored values of community with neighbors and communion with nature. The loss of these values breeds loneliness and boredom and indifference.

Our society will never be great until our cities are great. Today the frontier of imagination and innovation is inside those cities and not beyond their borders. . . .

A second place where we begin to build the Great Society is in our countryside. We have always prided ourselves on being not only America the strong and America the free, but America the beautiful. Today that beauty is in danger. The water we drink, the food we eat, the very air that we breathe, are threatened with pollution. Our parks are overcrowded, our seashores overburdened. Green fields and dense forests are disappearing.

A few years ago we were greatly concerned about the "Ugly American." Today we must act to prevent an ugly America.

For once the battle is lost, once our natural splendor is destroyed, it can never be recaptured. And once man can no longer walk with beauty or wonder at nature, his spirit will wither and his sustenance be wasted.

A third place to build the Great Society is in the classrooms of America. There your children's lives will be shaped. Our society will not be great until every young mind is set free to scan the farthest reaches of thought and imagination. We are still far from that goal. . . .

Each year more than 100,000 high school graduates, with proved ability, do not enter college because they cannot afford it. And if we cannot educate today's youth, what will we do in 1970 when elementary school enrollment will be 5 million greater than 1960? And high school enrollment will rise by 5 million. College enrollment will increase by more than 3 million.

In many places, classrooms are overcrowded and curricula are outdated. Most of our qualified teachers are underpaid, and many of our paid teachers are unqualified. So we must give every child a place to sit and a teacher to learn from. Poverty must not be a bar to learning, and learning must offer an escape from poverty.

But more classrooms and more teachers are not enough. We must seek an educational system which grows in excellence as it grows in size. This means better training for our teachers. It means preparing youth to enjoy their hours of leisure as well as their hours of labor. It means exploring new techniques of teaching, to find new ways to stimulate the love of learning and the capacity for creation.

These are three of the central issues of the Great Society. While our government has many programs directed at those issues, I do not pretend that we have the full answer to those problems. . . .

But I do promise this: We are going to assemble the best thought and the broadest knowledge from all over the world to find those answers for America. I intend to establish working groups to prepare a series of White

House conferences and meetings—on the cities, on natural beauty, on the quality of education, and on other emerging challenges. And from these meetings and from this inspiration and from these studies we will begin to set our course toward the Great Society.

The solution to these problems does not rest on a massive program in Washington, nor can it rely solely on the strained resources of local authority. They require us to create new concepts of cooperation, a creative federalism, between the national capital and the leaders of local communities.

Within your lifetime powerful forces, already loosed, will take us toward a way of life beyond the realm of our experience, almost beyond the bounds of our imagination.

For better or for worse, your generation has been appointed by history to deal with those problems and to lead America toward a new age. You have the chance never before afforded to any people in any age. You can help build a society where the demands of morality, and the needs of the spirit, can be realized in the life of the nation.

So, will you join in the battle to give every citizen the full equality which God enjoins and the law requires, whatever his belief, or race, or the color of his skin?

Will you join in the battle to give every citizen an escape from the crushing weight of poverty?

Will you join in the battle to make it possible for all nations to live in enduring peace—as neighbors and not as mortal enemies?

Will you join in the battle to build the Great Society, to prove that our material progress is only the foundation on which we will build a richer life of mind and spirit?

There are those timid souls who say this battle cannot be won, that we are condemned to a soulless wealth. I do not agree. We have the power to shape the civilization that we want. But we need your will, your labor, your hearts if we are to build that kind of society.

Those who came to this land sought to build more than just a new country. They sought a new world. So I have come here today to your campus to say that you can make their vision our reality. So let us from this moment begin our work so that in the future men will look back and say, It was then, after a long and weary way, that man turned the exploits of his genius to the full enrichment of his life.

The War on Poverty

The War on Poverty has often overshadowed the remainder of Lyndon Johnson's Great Society, but this is a misplaced emphasis. Conceived by a band of aides and experts surrounding John Kennedy, it was inherited by LBJ after Kennedy's death and pushed by him in the months following the tragedy in Dallas, well before the May 1964 Ann Arbor Great Society speech. Though it stirred the imagination of the media and the public, it was never more than a piece of the Great Society.

This conclusion does not deny the innovative quality of the Economic Opportunity Act of 1964, the chief War on Poverty measure. Even in the United States, the world's bastion of individualistic capitalism, the federal government had intervened in the past to keep people from starving and freezing and had imposed progressive income taxes to reduce the extremes of wealth and poverty. The new program, however, went far beyond these measures. Now, the American president announced, in a time of overall prosperity, the government would seek to end once and for all an age-old evil of humanity. Poverty would cease to exist in America.

The War on Poverty was innovative in its bureaucratic approach as well. It would be administered from the White House by a separate agency, not part of any executive department, and headed by a czar, directly responsible to the president. And yet the Office of Economic Opportunity would not be a traditional top-down body. Reflecting the thinking of a new breed of social workers who wished to encourage community competence, the bill provided for "community action" agencies, representing the local poor, to design antipoverty programs and help administer them.

The War on Poverty, in the end, was a disappointment. The Community Action Programs (CAPs) usually proposed by local groups shifted control of a healthy amount of federal money away from powerful elected city officials to beneficiaries of the programs themselves. The complaints of the mayors could not be ignored on Capitol Hill and the White House. The CAPs, moreover, sometimes fell under the control of black militants and white radicals who used them to further a revolutionary social agenda. Inevitably, much money was wasted. The Job Corps, another program under the Economic Opportunity Act, also achieved marginal results. Few of the poor youths who attended Job Corps camps learned the skills needed to make it on their own in the private economy, though the economy was booming in these years.

The "war" was by no means an unrelieved failure. Special programs like free legal services, local health clinics, and Head Start probably made the lives of poor Americans better than they would otherwise have been. Yet in the end, what had started with such soaring hope deflated to a modest set of programs that undoubtedly helped poor people cope but scarcely achieved the "total victory" over poverty that Johnson promised.

This selection is from Johnson's March 16, 1964, message transmitting his War on Poverty bill to Congress. It summarizes the measure and conveys some of the decade's optimistic spirit that America was capable of solving fundamental problems.

[The War on Poverty: The Economic Opportunity Act of 1964, *U.S. Senate, 88th Cong., 2nd sess.,* **Document No. 86.]**

We are citizens of the richest and most fortunate nation in the history of the world. One hundred and eighty years ago we were a small country struggling for survival on the margin of a hostile land. Today we have established a civilization of free men which spans an entire continent. . . .

The path forward has not been an easy one. But we have never lost sight of our goal—an America in which every citizen shares all the opportunities of his society, in which every man has a chance to advance his welfare to the limit of his capacities.

We have come a long way toward this goal. We still have a long way to go. The distance which remains is the measure of the great unfinished work of our society. To finish that work I have called for a national war on poverty. Our objective: total victory. There are millions of Americans—one-fifth of our people—who have not shared in the abundance which has been granted to most of us, and on whom the gates of opportunity have been closed.

What does this poverty mean to those who endure it? It means a daily struggle to secure the necessities for even a meager existence. It means that the abundance, the comforts, the opportunities they see all around them are beyond their grasp. Worst of all, it means hopelessness for the young. The young man or woman who grows up without a decent education, in a broken home, in a hostile and squalid environment, in ill health or in the face of racial injustice—that young man or woman is often trapped in a life of poverty. He does not have the skills demanded by a complex society. He does not know how to acquire those skills. He faces a mounting sense of despair which drains initiative and ambition and energy.

Our tax cut will create millions of new jobs—new exits from poverty. But we must also strike down all the barriers which keep many from using those exits. The war on poverty is not a struggle simply to support people, to make them dependent on the generosity of others. It is a struggle to give people a chance. It is an effort to allow them to develop and use their capacities, as we have been allowed to develop and use ours, so that they can share, as others share, in the promise of this nation. . . .

Because it is right, because it is wise, and because, for the first time in our history, it is possible to conquer poverty, I submit, for the consideration of the Congress and the country, the Economic Opportunity Act of 1964. The act does not merely expand old programs or improve what is already being done. It charts a new course. It strikes at the causes, not just the consequences of poverty. It can be a milestone in our 180-year search for a better life for our people.

This act provides five basic opportunities:

It will give almost half a million underprivileged young Americans the opportunity to develop skills, continue education, and find useful work.

It will give every American community the opportunity to develop a comprehensive plan to fight its own poverty—and help them to carry out their plans.

It will give dedicated Americans the opportunity to enlist as volunteers in the war against poverty.

It will give many workers and farmers the opportunity to break through particular barriers which bar their escape from poverty.

It will give the entire nation the opportunity for a concerted attack on poverty through the establishment, under my direction, of the Office of Economic Opportunity, a national headquarters for the war against poverty.

This is how we propose to create these opportunities. *First,* we will give high priority to helping young Americans who lack skills, who have not completed their education or who cannot complete it because they are too poor. The years of high school and college age are the most critical stage of a young person's life. If they are not helped then, many will be condemned to a life of poverty which they, in turn, will pass on to their children.

I therefore recommend the creation of a Job Corps, a work-training program, and a work-study program. A new national Job Corps will build toward an enlistment of 100,000 young men. They will be drawn from those whose background, health, and education make them least fit for useful work. Those who volunteer will enter more than one hundred camps and centers around the country. Half of these young men will work, in the first year, on special conservation projects to give them education, useful work experience, and to enrich the natural resources of the country. Half of these young men will receive, in the first year, a blend of training, basic education, and work experience in job training centers. These are not simply camps for the underprivileged. They are new educational institutions, comparable in innovation to the land-grant colleges. Those who enter them will emerge better qualified to play a productive role in American society.

A new national work-training program operated by the Department of Labor will provide work and training for 200,000 American men and women between the ages of sixteen and twenty-one. This will be developed through state and local governments and nonprofit agencies. Hundreds of thousands of young Americans badly need the experience, the income, and the sense of purpose which useful full- or part-time work can bring. For them such work may mean the difference between finishing school or dropping out. Vital community activities from hospitals and playgrounds to libraries and settlement houses are suffering because there are not enough people to staff them. We are simply bringing these needs together.

A new national work-study program operated by the Department of Health, Education, and Welfare will provide federal funds for part-time jobs for 140,000 young Americans who do not go to college because they cannot afford it. There is no more senseless waste than the waste of the brainpower and skill of those who are kept from college by economic circumstance. Under this program they will, in a great American tradition, be able to work their way through school. They and the country will be richer for it.

Second, through a new community action program we intend to strike at poverty at its source—in the streets of our cities and on the farms of our countryside among the very young and the impoverished old. This program asks men and women throughout the country to prepare long-range plans for the attack on poverty in their own local communities. These are not plans prepared in Washington and imposed upon hundreds of different situations. They are based on the fact that local citizens best understand their own problems, and know best how to deal with those problems. These plans will be local plans striking at the many unfilled needs which underlie poverty in each community, not just one or two. Their components and emphasis will differ as needs differ. These plans will be local plans calling upon all the resources available to the community—federal and state, local and private, human and material. And when these plans are approved by the Office of Economic Opportunity, the federal government will finance up to 90 percent of the additional cost for the first two years. . . .

Third, I ask for the authority to recruit and train skilled volunteers for the war against poverty. . . . If the state requests them, if the community needs and will use them, we will recruit and train them and give them the chance to serve.

Fourth, we intend to create new opportunities for certain hard-hit groups to break out of the pattern of poverty. Through a new program of loans and guarantees we can provide incentives to those who will employ the unemployed. Through programs of work and retraining for unemployed fathers and mothers we can help them support their families in dignity while preparing themselves for new work. Through funds to purchase needed land, organize cooperatives, and create new and adequate family farms we can help those whose life on the land has been a struggle without hope.

Fifth, I do not intend that the war against poverty become a series of uncoordinated and unrelated efforts—that it perish for lack of leadership and direction. Therefore this bill creates, in the Executive Office of the President, a new Office of Economic Opportunity. Its director will be my personal chief of staff for the war against poverty. I intend to appoint Sargent Shriver to this post. He will be directly responsible for these new programs. He will work with and through existing agencies of the government. This program—the Economic Opportunity Act—is the foundation of our war against poverty. . . .

And this program is much more than a beginning. Rather it is a commitment. It is a total commitment by this President, and this Congress, and this nation, to pursue victory over the most ancient of mankind's enemies. On many historic occasions the President has requested from Congress the authority to move against forces which were endangering the well-being of our country. This is such an occasion.

On similar occasions in the past we have often been called upon to wage war against foreign enemies which threatened our freedom. Today we are asked to declare war on a domestic enemy which threatens the strength of our nation and the welfare of our people. If we now move forward against this enemy—if we can bring to the challenges of peace the same determination and strength which has brought us victory in war—then this day and this Congress will have won a secure and honorable place in the history of the nation, and the enduring gratitude of generations of Americans yet to come.

Medicare

Today, the health care innovations of the Great Society seem its most significant legacy. At the heart of the Johnson program to improve the nation's health was Medicare, a medical and hospital insurance plan for retirees financed through the Social Security system.

Government-run medical insurance schemes had been part of the welfare state agenda that emerged at the end of the nineteenth century in a number of the most advanced industrial countries. They had been debated in the United States during the Progressive era, and a few of the more experimental states had actually adopted modest health insurance programs. In 1935, Roosevelt toyed with the idea of including a health insurance provision in the Social Security bill but dropped it when the medical profession's opposition threatened to kill the whole measure. Harry Truman, inspired by Britain's postwar adoption of its National Health scheme, had proposed an ambitious all-inclusive federal health insurance plan in the late 1940s.

Truman's bold proposal got nowhere. But over the next decade, the liberal bureau-crats and politicians and the active portion of the liberal electorate worked for some form of federal health insurance. With more and more working people covered by employer-funded private health payment programs, these schemes came to focus pri-marily on hospital insurance for retirees linked to the popular system of federal old-age pensions created in the 1930s. A federal hospital insurance scheme for pensioners was part of Kennedy's New Frontier submitted in 1962. The bill failed to pass. Under remorseless pressure from the American Medical Association, and dominated by the conservative coalition of southern Democrats and Republicans that had run Congress since 1938, the legislators refused to move. In his first year, while filling out Kennedy's uncompleted term, Johnson revived the Kennedy bill, but also could not get it enacted.

The logjam broke after LBJ's astonishing victory over Barry Goldwater in 1964. The Johnson mandate convinced even the AMA that some form of Medicare was inevitable and that the doctors would be well advised to support a bill that would pro-tect their incomes and their interests. With opposition muted and with the liberals now in tight control of Congress, Johnson succeeded. He got not only hospital insurance but a plan to pay doctors' fees and, in addition, Medicaid—a joint federal-state pro-gram to pay the medical bills of the indigent. But the new programs not only insured the aged and the poor; they guaranteed that the interests of the private practitioners of medicine were not ignored.

But Johnson was concerned with more than health insurance. In the message to Congress accompanying the Medicare bill, he proposed a broad program to improve the nation's health.

Besides health insurance for retirees, Johnson wanted to get rid of the "asylums" that warehoused the mentally ill and release patients into local community facilities; he wanted to improve the medical care of children and youth; he sought to encour-age medical research; he hoped to increase the number of doctors, dentists, and nurses through scholarship programs. Much of his health program was enacted but not all of it worked. The "deinstitutionalization" of mental patients added to the homeless problems of the 1980s and 1990s. The leap in the number of physicians helped send health costs in later years through the roof. (Many of those doctors became "special-ists," and charged accordingly.)

This proposal, submitted in the heady days of January 1965, conveys the presi-dent's unbounded optimism about the possibilities of medical science if made avail-able to all. In the new age of affluence, the nation could not only conquer poverty; it could also conquer disease. (One wonders if LBJ did not ultimately believe that the right legislation could defeat death itself!)

[**Lyndon B. Johnson, Special Message to the Congress, "Advancing the Nation's Health,"** January 7, 1965, in **Public Papers of the Presidents: Lyndon Johnson, 1965,** vol. 2 (Washington, DC: U.S. Government Printing Office, 1966), pp. 12–21.]

SPECIAL MESSAGE TO THE CONGRESS:
ADVANCING THE NATION'S HEALTH

To the Congress of the United States:

In 1787, Thomas Jefferson wrote that, "Without health there is no happiness. An attention to health, then, should take the place of every other object."

That priority has remained fixed in both the private and public values of our society through generations of Americans since. . . .

Today . . . we are privileged to contemplate new horizons of national advance and achievement in many sectors. But it is imperative that we give first attention to our opportunities—and our obligations—for advancing the nation's health. For the health of our people is, inescapably, the foundation for fulfillment of all our aspirations.

In these years of the 1960s, we live as beneficiaries of this century's great . . . revolution of medical knowledge and capabilities. Smallpox, malaria, yellow fever, and typhus are conquered in this country. Infant deaths have been reduced by half every two decades. Poliomyelitis which took 3,154 lives so recently as 1952 cost only five lives in 1964. Over the brief span of the past two decades, death rates have been reduced for influenza by 88 percent, tuberculosis by 87 percent, rheumatic fever by 90 percent.

A baby born in America today has a life expectancy half again as long as those born in the year the twentieth century began.

The successes of the century are many.

The pace of medical progress is rapid.

The potential for the future is unlimited.

But we must not allow the modern miracles of medicine to mesmerize us. The work most needed to advance the nation's health will not be done for us by miracles. We must undertake that work ourselves through practical, prudent, and patient programs—to put more firmly in place the foundation for the healthiest, happiest, and most hopeful society in the history of man.

Our first concern must be to assure that the advance of medical knowledge leaves none behind. We can—and we must—strive now to assure the availability of and accessibility to the best health care for all Americans, regardless of age or geography or economic status.

With this as our goal, we must strengthen our nation's health facilities and services, assure the adequacy and quality of our health manpower, continue to assist our States and communities in meeting their health responsibilities, and respond alertly to the new hazards of our new and complex environment.

We must, certainly, continue and intensify our health research and research facilities. . . . In our struggle against disease, great advances have been made, but the battle is far from won. While that battle will not end in our lifetime . . . we have the high privilege and high promise of making longer strides forward now than any other generation of Americans.

The measures I am outlining today will carry us forward in the oldest tradition of our society—to give "an attention to health" for all our people. Our advances, thus far, have been most dramatic in the field of health knowledge. We are challenged now to give attention to advances in the field of health care—and this is the emphasis of the recommendations I am placing before you at this time.

I. Removing Barriers to Health Care

In this century, medical scientists have done much to improve human health and prolong human life. Yet as these advances come, vital segments of our populace are being left behind—behind barriers of age, economics, geography, or community resources. . . .

A. Hospital Insurance for the Aged

Thirty years ago, the American people made a basic decision that the later years of life should not be years of despondency and drift. The result was enactment of our Social Security program, a program now fixed as a valued part of our national life. Since World War II, there has been increasing awareness of the fact that the full value of Social Security would not be realized unless provision were made to deal with the problem of costs of illnesses among our older citizens.

I believe this year is the year when, with the sure knowledge of public support, the Congress should enact a hospital insurance program for the aged.

The facts of the need are well and widely known:

- Four out of five persons 65 or older have a disability or chronic disease.
- People over 65 go to the hospital more frequently and stay twice as long as younger people.
- Health costs for them are twice as high as for the young.

Where health insurance is available it is usually associated with an employer-employee plan. However, since most of our older people are not employed, they are usually not eligible under these plans.

- Almost half of the elderly have no health insurance at all.
- The average retired couple cannot afford the cost of adequate health protection under private health insurance.

I ask that our Social Security system—proved and tested by three decades of successful operation—be extended to finance the cost of basic health services. In this way, the specter of catastrophic hospital bills can be lifted from the lives of our older citizens. *I again strongly urge the Congress to enact a hospital insurance program for the aged.* Such a program should:

- Be financed under social security by regular, modest contributions during working years;
- Provide protection against the costs of hospital and post-hospital extended care, home nursing services, and outpatient diagnostic services;
- Provide similar protection to those who are not now covered by social security, with the costs being paid from the administrative budget;
- Clearly indicate that the plan in no way interferes with the patient's complete freedom to select his doctor or hospital.

Like our existing social security cash retirement benefits, this hospital insurance plan will be a basic protection plan. It should cover the heaviest cost elements in serious illnesses. In addition, we should encourage private insurance to provide supplementary protection.

I consider this measure to be of utmost urgency. Compassion and reason dictate that this logical extension of our proven social security system will supply the prudent, feasible, and dignified way to free the aged from the fear of financial hardship in the event of illness.

Also, I urge all states to provide adequate medical assistance under the existing Kerr-Mills program* for the aged who cannot afford to meet the noninsured costs.

B. Better Health Services for Children and Youth

America's tradition of compassion for the aged is matched by our traditional devotion to our most priceless resource of all—our young. Today, far

*The Kerr-Mills act, passed in 1960, following defeat of a broader health insurance measure, provided that under a joint state-federal plan those with *very low incomes* could receive aid for hospitalization and other medical services. The "means test" provision cut out all but a minority from benefits; the states often refused to make the fifty percent contribution mandated—ed.

more than many realize, there are great and growing needs among our children for better health services.

• • •

[Here follows a description of the existing inadequacies of health care for children and youths.]

• • •

The states and localities bear the major responsibility for providing modern medical care to our children and youth. But the federal government can help. *I recommend legislation to:*

- *Increase the authorizations for maternal and child health and crippled children's services,* earmarking funds for project grants to provide health screening and diagnosis for children of preschool and school age, as well as treatment and follow-up care services for disabled children and youth. . . .

C. Improved Community Mental Health Services

Mental illness afflicts one out of ten Americans, fills nearly one-half of all the hospital beds in the nation, and costs $3 billion annually. Fortunately, we are entering a new era in the prevention, treatment, and care of mental illness. Mere custodial care of patients in large, isolated asylums is clearly no longer appropriate. Most patients can be cared for and cured in their own communities.

An important beginning toward community preparation has been made through the legislation enacted by the 88th Congress authorizing aid for constructing community mental health centers. But facilities alone cannot assure services.

• • •

[Here follows a description of how the programs fall short in terms of facilities and trained psychiatrists.]

• • •

I therefore recommend legislation to authorize a five-year program of grants for the initial costs of personnel to man community mental health centers which offer comprehensive services.

II. Strengthening the Nation's Health Facilities and Services

In our urbanized society today, the availability of health care depends uniquely upon the availability and accessibility of modern facilities, located in convenient and efficient places, and on well organized and adequately supported services. . . .

A. Multipurpose Regional Medical Complexes

• • •

[Here follows a description of the challenges of cancer, heart disease, and stroke.]

• • •

I recommend legislation to authorize a five-year program of project grants to develop multipurpose regional medical complexes for an all-out attack on heart disease, cancer, stroke, and other major diseases.

III. Manpower for the Health Services

The advance of our nation's health in this century has . . . been possible because of the unique quality and fortunate quantity of men and women serving in our health professions. Americans respect and are grateful for our doctors, dentists, nurses, and others who serve our nation's health. But it is clear that the future requires our support now to increase the quantity and assure the continuing high quality of such vital personnel.

In all sectors of health care, the need for trained personnel continues to outstrip the supply.

• • •

[Here follows a description of the shortage of doctors and dentists.]

• • •

I therefore recommend legislation to authorize scholarships for medical and dental students who would otherwise not be able to enter or complete such training.

IV. Health Research and Research Facilities

•   •   •

[Here follows a recommendation for increased federal funding of medical research.]

•   •   •

Conclusion

I believe we have come to a rare moment of opportunity and challenge in the evolution of our society. In the message I have presented to you—and in other messages I shall be sending—my purpose is to outline the attainable horizons of a greater society which a confident and prudent people can begin to build for the future.

Whatever we aspire to do together, our success in those enterprises—and our enjoyment of the fruits that result—will rest finally upon the health of our people. We cannot and we will not overcome all the barriers—or surmount all the obstacles—in one effort, no matter how intensive. But in all the sectors I have mentioned we are already behind our capability and our potential. Further delay will only compound our problems and deny our people the health and happiness that could be theirs. . . .

3

The New Left

An important component of the Sixties insurgency was a restored political left. Usually called the "New Left," in fact it mixed old and new. It was composed of several overlapping layers but had a common denominator that justifies treating it as an entity with a distinct name.

The New Left was predominantly a youth movement. During the Great Depression, World War II, and the immediate postwar era, radicals had generally been adults with jobs and families. There were "reds" on campuses, but they belonged to student auxiliaries; they did not control the major organizations. By the Sixties, however, McCarthyite intimidation along with the aging process had decimated a generation of American radicals. Though the students were often inspired and occasionally guided by middle-aged gurus, they themselves led the cutting-edge organizations of the political left. This youthful quality was undoubtedly one source of the New Left's impetuosity and militancy; it was also a source of conflict with the surviving Old Left.

The New Left, at least initially, confronted the existing system with a new analysis and new critique. The Old Left had been predominantly Marxist, whether Socialist, Communist, or Trotskyist. It had glorified the proletariat and marked it as the primary agent for socialist revolution. In the version of Marx elaborated by Lenin, the oppressed workers would be led by a small cadre of dedicated revolutionaries with the practical and theoretical skills to serve as a vanguard and, in the name of the proletariat, establish a successful revolutionary regime.

This picture of capitalism's fate and the role of the wage earners beguiled millions during the generation preceding World War I. It was strengthened by the victory of the Russian Bolsheviks in 1917 and the formation of the Soviet Union. During the catastrophic Great Depression, Marxism attracted industrial workers and blocs of artists, journalists, academics, literati, and

of the country's most talented men and women, disillu-
...lism, joined the Communist Party, USA, a group that
...e to the Moscow-based world Communist movement, or
...ravelers who invariably supported its policies. There
...able exceptions to the slavish Old Left acceptance of pro-
Soviet p... both before and after 1945, but these independents were
outside the mainstream of radicalism in the United States.

Meanwhile, after World War II, the emerging cold war called into question all radicalism in America. Growing antagonism between the Soviet
Union and the United States stirred wide fears of the Communist menace.
Ferreting out spies, subversives, and dissenters became a major domestic
industry, with Senator Joseph McCarthy of Wisconsin as chief executive
officer. McCarthyism created a fog of fear that discouraged almost all radicalism. Thousands left the Communist Party and other radical groups to
slip back into private life. Others, while remaining skeptical of capitalism,
joined in the cold war campaign against Soviet expansionism. A feeble dissenting voice continued to exist in politics, but half a generation of new
recruits failed to enlist in the left; the remaining Old Left became truly old
and enfeebled.

In 1954, the "establishment" finally lost patience with McCarthy's reckless charges and helped destroy his credibility. He would die disgraced. An
exaggerated anti-Communism continued in some circles, but overall fears
of dissent receded. It was now possible to criticize capitalism, American foreign policy, and racial practices without stiff penalties, and in the new
atmosphere, bold souls began to attack mainstream values and opinions.
Many of these were the children of Old Leftists, "red diaper babies" who,
in the less coercive environment of the late 1950s, took up the banners that
their parents had dropped.

To explain the New Left, prosperity must be added to youthful zeal and
the rebound from McCarthyism. Whatever its faults, the nation's economy
was flourishing as the 1950s ended, and affluence provided a margin of
error that made personal experimentation with causes relatively risk free.
Indeed, the very prosperity revealed a whole new class of faults, related to
"quality of life," that needed to be redressed. To young men and women,
born during the war or just after, America, though it had largely solved the
problems of scarcity that bedeviled their parents, seemed a deeply flawed
society in its racial practices, its bureaucratic rigidities, and its headlong
pursuit of material things.

A final ingredient of the New Left brew was the extravagant number of
Sixties youth and their strategic placement. In 1945, 13 million GIs

returned from war and began to procreate exuberantly. Between 1946 and 1964, some 70 million babies first saw the world, creating the largest contingent of young Americans in our history. Their sheer numbers gave the Sixties baby boomers cohort significance. It was difficult to ignore the views and desires of such a large part of the nation's active population. During the decade the youth culture came to fascinate even older Americans.

Just as relevant as the youth cohort's numbers was their location. More than ever before, the young were now packed into college dorms, student unions, and lecture halls. In 1960, there were 3 million college students in the United States. In the fall of 1964, the first baby boomers hit the campuses. By the following year, there were 5 million, and by 1973, 10 million. Never before had so many bright young people been collected together in one spot to question and vex their elders.

Given the New Left's timing and youth, most of its differences with its predecessors were predictable. Born too late to remember the old battles, the New Left was not pro-Communist, but neither was it especially anti-Communist. The Soviet Union was undoubtedly a repressive dictatorship, but its threat to world peace was exaggerated and probably no worse than America's. As for domestic anti-Communism, all too often it had been a cover for right-wing repression of dissent.

The New Left, unlike the Old, was also skeptical of the working class and its leaders. To the children of the suburban bourgeoisie, wage earners seemed fat and complacent, without revolutionary potential. The new agents of social change quite possibly were the engineers, the teachers, the technicians, and above all, the students—parts of the educated middle class—who, though they shared in much of the new material prosperity, suffered from alienation from work, from their society, and from one another.

The young radicals' indictment of modern industrial society disparaged their elders' emphasis on material gain. Capitalism had proved its capacity to create wealth and even to spread its benefits, but it had failed to provide meaningful, useful, and fulfilling lives for those who existed within its embrace. Here the young radicals borrowed from the ideas of Herbert Marcuse, Norman O. Brown, and Paul Goodman, whose versions of "liberation" merged Marx with Freud. Utopia would enjoy not only economic equality and boundless wealth but satisfying work, loving relationships, and bountiful instinctual gratification as well.

Such attitudes and ideas proved compelling to thousands of young people who considered themselves members of the New Left. Many would join, or loosely affiliate with, Students for a Democratic Society (SDS), created in the early Sixties by red diaper babies from a youth auxiliary of the moderate social-democratic League for Industrial Democracy. Whatever their affiliation, many New Leftists were inspired by the civil rights struggle or, after 1964, by the antiwar movement. As time passed and the world did not turn, they became increasingly impatient with liberal society and increasingly apocalyptic in their expectations. By 1968, they had abandoned their faith in democratic participation and been drawn to totalitarian antiliberalism, including the most militant forms of revolutionary millennialism. In 1969, SDS broke up, and some of its veteran members would join the violent Weather Underground to attack "Amerika" from the "belly of the beast."

The New Left did not abruptly disappear. It continued into the 1970s, only fading with American withdrawal from Vietnam and the economic deterioration following the OPEC oil crisis. In a sense, it never vanished completely, for many who passed through its ranks brought with them—into professional life, journalism, and academe—the lessons they had learned on the firing line of Sixties dissent.

Letter to the New Left

Many prophetic movements have their John the Baptist, a precursor who foreshadows the mature movement to come. For the New Left, this figure was C. Wright Mills, a Columbia University professor of sociology who had resisted the tide of self-congratulation and acquiescence that marked American intellectual life in the 1950s.

Mills was a maverick all his life. Born in Texas, he took his graduate training at the University of Wisconsin, when it still retained the progressive shading of the La Follettes, the political dynasty that made early twentieth-century Wisconsin the pioneer Progressive state. At decorous Columbia, which he joined as professor of sociology in 1946, he raised eyebrows by wearing working-class clothes and riding a motorcycle. He was an intellectual maverick as well. At a time when his colleagues in sociology were proclaiming the "end of ideology" and the triumph of consensus, he remained a leftist.

Mills was aware of the continued vitality of the left in Britain. There, following the 1956 Soviet invasion of Hungary and the shocking Khrushchev revelations of Stalin's brutal excesses, a group of younger radicals had broken with the Communist Party. In 1959, they began to publish a journal called New Left Review *as a forum for fresh ideas on the left.*

Mills's article, reprinted here, was an attempt to deal with a worrisome circumstance of the contemporary world left. There no longer existed a reliable "agency" of revolution. Marx and his successors had counted on the progressive worsening material conditions of the working class to undermine capitalism, but everywhere wage earners seemed fat and content, willing to accept the status quo without question.

Who, then, would make the revolution? Mills concluded that the educated young would be the agency of social transformation. In his "Letter to the New Left," he transmitted a message that would powerfully influence the young intellectuals who made up the first generation of Sixties American radicals.

[C. Wright Mills, *"Letter to the New Left,"* New Left Review, September–October 1960, *pp. 18–23.*]

LETTER TO THE NEW LEFT

We have frequently been told by an assorted variety of dead-end people that the meanings of left and of right are now liquidated, by history and by reason. I think we should answer them in some such way as this:

The *Right,* among other things, means what you are doing: celebrating society as it is, a going concern. *Left* means, or ought to mean, just the opposite. It means structural criticism and reportage and theories of society, which at some point or another are focused politically as demands and programs. These criticisms, demands, theories, programs are guided morally by the humanist and secular ideals of Western civilization—above all, the ideals of reason, freedom and justice. To be "left" means to connect up cultural with political criticism, and both with demands and programs. And it means all this inside *every* country of the world.

Only one more point of definition: absence of public issues there may well be, but this is not due to any absence of problems or of contradictions, antagonistic and otherwise. Impersonal and structural changes have not eliminated problems or issues. Their absence from many discussions is an ideological condition, regulated in the first place by whether or not intellectuals detect and state problems as potential *issues* for probable publics, and as *troubles* for a variety of individuals. One indispensable means of such work on these central tasks is what can only be described as ideological analysis. To be actively left, among other things, is to carry on just such analysis.

To take seriously the problem of the need for a political orientation is not, of course, to seek for A Fanatical and Apocalyptic Vision, for An Infallible and Monolithic Lever of Change, for Dogmatic Ideology, for A Startling New Rhetoric, for Treacherous Abstractions, and all the other bogeymen of the dead-enders. These are, of course, "the extremes," the straw men, the red herrings used by our political enemies to characterize the polar opposite of where they think they stand.

They tell us, for example, that ordinary men cannot always be political "heroes." Who said they could? But keep looking around you; and why not search out the conditions of such heroism as men do and might display?

They tell us that we are too "impatient," that our "pretentious" theories are not well enough grounded. That is true, but neither are our theories trivial. Why don't they get to work to refute or ground them? They tell us we "do not really understand" Russia and China today. That is true; we don't; neither do they. We at least are studying the question. They tell us we are "ominous" in our formulations. That is true: we do have enough imagination to be frightened, and we don't have to hide it. We are not afraid we'll panic. They tell us we are "grinding axes." Of course we are: we do have, among other points of view, morally grounded ones, and we are aware of them. They tell us, in their wisdom, that we do not understand that The Struggle is Without End. True: we want to change its form, its focus, its object.

We are frequently accused of being "utopian" in our criticisms and in our proposals and, along with this, of basing our hopes for a new left *politics* "merely on reason," or more concretely, upon the intelligentsia in its broadest sense.

There is truth in these charges. But must we not ask: What now is really meant by *utopian*? And is not our utopianism a major source of our strength? *Utopian* nowadays, I think, refers to any criticism or proposal that transcends the up-close milieux of a scatter of individuals, the milieux which men and women can understand directly and which they can reasonably hope directly to change. In this exact sense, our theoretical work is indeed utopian—in my own case, at least, deliberately so. What needs to be understood, and what needs to be changed, is not merely first this and then that detail of some institution or policy. If there is to be a politics of a new left, what needs to be analyzed is the *structure* of institutions, the *foundation* of policies. In this sense, both in its criticisms and in its proposals, our work is necessarily structural, and so—*for us,* just now—utopian.

This brings us face to face with the most important issue of political reflection and of political action in our time: the problem of the historical agency of change, of the social and institutional means of structural change. There are several points about this problem I would like to put to you.

•   •   •

First, the historic agencies of change for liberals of the capitalist societies have been an array of voluntary associations, coming to a political climax in a parliamentary or congressional system. For socialists of almost all varieties, the historic agency has been the working class—and later the peasantry, or parties and unions composed of members of the working class, or (to blur, for now, a great problem) of political parties acting in its name, "representing its interests."

I cannot avoid the view that both these forms of historic agency have either collapsed or become most ambiguous. So far as structural change is concerned, neither seems to be at once available and effective as *our* agency anymore. I know this is a debatable point among us, and among many others as well; I am by no means certain about it. But surely, if it is true, it ought not to be taken as an excuse for moaning and withdrawal (as it is by some of those who have become involved with the end-of-ideology); and it ought not to be bypassed (as it is by many Soviet scholars and publicists, who in their reflections upon the course of advanced capitalist societies simply refuse to admit the political condition and attitudes of the working class).

Is anything more certain than that in 1970—indeed, at this time next year—our situation will be quite different, and—the chances are high—decisively so? But of course, that isn't saying much. The seeming collapse of our historic agencies of change ought to be taken as a problem, an issue, a trouble—in fact, as *the* political problem which *we* must turn into issue and trouble.

Second, it is obvious that when we talk about the collapse of agencies of change, we cannot seriously mean that such agencies do not exist. On the contrary, the means of history-making—of decision and of the enforcement of decision—have never in world history been so enlarged and so available to such small circles of men on both sides of The Curtains as they now are. My own conception of the shape of power, the theory of the power elite, I feel no need to argue here. This theory has been fortunate in its critics, from the most diverse political viewpoints, and I have learned from several of these critics. But I have not seen, as of this date, an analysis of the idea that causes me to modify any of its essential features.

The point that is immediately relevant does seem obvious: what is utopian for us, is not at all utopian for the presidium of the Central Committee in Moscow, or the higher circles of the Presidency in Washington, or, recent events make evident, for the men of SAC and CIA. The historic agencies of change that have collapsed are those which were at least thought to be open to *the left* inside the advanced Western nations, to those who have wished for structural changes of these societies. Many things follow from this obvious fact; of many of them, I am sure, we are not yet adequately aware.

Third, what I do not quite understand about some new-left writers is why they cling so mightily to "the working class" of the advanced capitalist societies as *the* historic agency, or even as the most important agency, in the face of the really impressive historical evidence that now stands against this expectation.

Such a labor metaphysic, I think, is a legacy from Victorian Marxism that is now quite unrealistic.

It is an historically specific idea that has been turned into an ahistorical and unspecific hope.

The social and historical conditions under which industrial workers tend to become a class-for-themselves, and a decisive political force, must be fully and precisely elaborated. There have been, there are, there will be such conditions. These conditions vary according to national social structure and the exact phase of their economic and political development. Of course we cannot "write off the working class." But we must *study* all that, and freshly. Where labor exists as an agency, of course we must work with it, but we must not treat it as The Necessary Lever, as nice old Labour Gentlemen in Britain and elsewhere tend to do.

Although I have not yet completed my own comparative studies of working classes, generally it would seem that only at certain (earlier) stages of industrialization, and in a political context of autocracy, *etc.*, do wage workers tend to become a class-for-themselves, *etc.* The *etceteras* mean that I can here merely raise the question.

•   •   •

It is with this problem of agency in mind that I have been studying, for several years now, the cultural apparatus, the intellectuals, as a possible, immediate, radical agency of change. For a long time, I was not much happier with this idea than were many of you; but it turns out now, at the beginning of the 1960s, that it may be a very relevant idea indeed.

In the first place, is it not clear that if we try to be realistic in our utopianism—and that is no fruitless contradiction—a writer in our countries on the left today *must* begin with the intellectuals? For that is what we are, that is where we stand.

In the second place, the problem of the intelligentsia is an extremely complicated set of problems on which rather little factual work has been done. In doing this work, we must, above all, not confuse the problems of the intellectuals of West Europe and North America with those of the Soviet bloc or with those of the underdeveloped worlds. In each of the three major components of the world's social structure today, the character and the role of the intelligentsia is distinct and historically specific. Only by detailed comparative studies of them in all their human variety can we hope to understand any one of them.

In the third place, who is it that is getting fed up? Who is it that is getting disgusted with what Marx called "all the old crap"? Who is it that is thinking and acting in radical ways? All over the world—in the bloc, and in between—the answer is the same: it is the young intelligentsia.

I cannot resist copying out for you, with a few changes, some materials I recently prepared for a 1960 paperback edition of a book of mine on war:

"In the spring and early summer of 1960, more of the returns from the American decision and default are coming in. In Turkey, after student riots, a military junta takes over the state, of late run by Communist Container Menderes. In South Korea, too, students and others knock over the corrupt American-puppet regime of Syngman Rhee. In Cuba, a genuinely left-wing revolution begins full-scale economic reorganization, without the domination of U.S. corporations. Average age of its leaders: about 30—and certainly a revolution without Labor As Agency. On Taiwan, the eight million Taiwanese under the American-imposed dictatorship of Chiang Kai-shek, with his two million Chinese, grow increasingly restive. On Okinawa, a U.S. military base, the people get their first chance since World War II ended to demonstrate against U.S. seizure of their island; and some students take that chance, snake-dancing and chanting angrily to the visiting President: 'Go home, go home—take away your missiles.' (Don't worry, 12,000 U.S. troops easily handle the generally grateful crowds; also the President is 'spirited out' the rear end of the United States compound—and so by helicopter to the airport.) In Japan, weeks of student rioting succeed in rejecting the President's visit, jeopardizing a new treaty with the U.S.A., and displacing the big-business, pro-American Prime Minister, Kishi. And even in our own pleasant Southland, Negro and white students are—but let us keep that quiet: it really *is* disgraceful.

"That is by no means the complete list; that was yesterday; see today's newspaper. Tomorrow, in varying degree, the returns will be more evident. Will they be evident enough? They will have to be very obvious to attract real American attention: sweet complaints and the voice of reason—these are not enough. In the slum countries of the world today, what are they saying? The rich Americans, they pay attention only to violence—and to money. You don't care what they say, American? Good for you. Still, they may insist; things are no longer under the old control; you're not getting it straight, American: your country—it would seem—may well become the target of a world hatred the like of which the easy-going Americans have never dreamed. Neutralists and Pacifists and Unilateralists and that confusing variety of Leftists around the world—all those tens of millions of people, of course they are misguided, absolutely controlled by small conspiratorial groups of trouble-makers, under direct orders from Moscow and Peking. Diabolically omnipotent, it is *they* who create all this messy unrest. It is *they* who have given the tens of millions the absurd idea that they shouldn't want to remain, or to become, the seat of American nuclear bases—those gay little outposts of American civilization. So now they don't want U-2's on their territory; so now they want to contract out of the American military machine; they want to be neutral among the crazy big antagonists. And they don't want their own societies to be militarized.

"But take heart, American: you won't have time to get really bored with your friends abroad: they won't be your friends much longer. You don't need *them;* it will all go away; don't let them confuse you."

Add to that: In the Soviet bloc, who is it that has been breaking out of apathy? It has been students and young professors and writers; it has been the young intelligentsia of Poland and Hungary, and of Russia, too. Never mind that they have not won; never mind that there are other social and moral types among them. First of all, it has been these types. But the point is clear, isn't it?

That is why we have got to study these new generations of intellectuals around the world as real live agencies of historic change. Forget Victorian Marxism, except when you need it; and read Lenin again (be careful)—Rosa Luxemburg, too.

"But it is just some kind of moral upsurge, isn't it?" Correct. But under it: no apathy. Much of it is direct nonviolent action, and it seems to be working, here and there. Now we must learn from the practice of these young intellectuals and with them work out new forms of action.

"But it's all so ambiguous—Cuba, for instance." Of course it is; history-making is always ambiguous. Wait a bit; in the meantime, help them to focus their moral upsurge in less ambiguous political ways. Work out with them the ideologies, the strategies, the theories that will help them con-solidate their efforts: new theories of structural changes of and by human societies in our epoch.

"But it is utopian, after all, isn't it?" No, not in the sense you mean. Whatever else it may be, it's not that. Tell it to the students of Japan. Tell it to the Negro sit-ins. Tell it to the Cuban Revolutionaries. Tell it to the people of the Hungry-nation bloc.

Studies on the Left

The American New Left started in the late 1950s as a student movement on a few liberal, cosmopolitan campuses. The first fruits of the revived left were a cluster of student political parties and publications that sought to bring to the serene halls-of-ivy a dissenting, adversarial voice.

The University of Wisconsin at Madison was one early nursery of the New Left. The university had a long progressive history dating to early in the twentieth century, when the campus was the source of liberal ideas and personnel for Governor Robert M. La Follette and his successors. Even during the timid, repressive 1950s, it provided a haven on its faculty for left dissenters. In addition, the university enrolled many liberal-to-left out-of-state students from the big cities, especially Chicago and New York, who were attracted by its low cost, fine academic reputation, and adversarial intellectual traditions.

It was a group of graduate students, many of them disciples of historian William Appleman Williams, who organized Studies on the Left *in 1959 to serve as a dissenting intellectual voice in the emerging post-McCarthy era. The founders, including Lloyd Gardner, Lee Baxandall, and Saul Landau, hoped to make* Studies *a fount of dissenting views and theories to counter the prevailing conservatism in academic history and the social sciences. Best exemplified by the "consensus" historians and the "value-free" social science of Daniel Bell and others, this conservatism fit the conformist mood of the day by celebrating the American past and defending the American present. To counter this school, as the editorial below notes, the* Studies *founders would practice a "radicalism of disclosure." In the end, the New Left intellectuals would be eclipsed by the radical activists, but in 1959,* Studies *seemed an exciting challenge to the blandness and self-congratulation of the times.*

[*From* **Studies on the Left, Fall 1959, pp. 2–4.**]

In academic circles, the term "objectivity" is generally used to indicate the dispassion, the nonpartisanship with which the "true scholar" approaches his work. It is also frequently used to indicate the prevalent, or "majority" view. For example, there are not very many students who will stand up for their "subjective" evaluation of another scholar's work in opposition to the supposedly objective judgment inherent in the fact that the man has been given a professorship at a prominent Ivy League university, and a great deal of praise by established scholars. Many, perhaps most, students will distrust their own subjective opinion in the face of all this objective data, and they may even state that there is no other standard of evaluation. In other words, they have made the subtle and all-important equation between quality on the one hand, and acceptability or market value on the other, and are well on their way to a bright academic future. The objectivity here assumed is reducible to the weight of authority, the viewpoint of those who are in position to enforce standards, the value judgments of the not so metaphorical marketplace of ideas.

Similarly, the use of the term to indicate scholarly dispassion is, at bottom, a way of justifying acceptance (either active or passive) of the status quo. When a man is digging up facts to support traditional and accepted interpretations, or when he has no interest in the significance of these facts for larger theoretical questions, he may, without too much difficulty, prevent himself from becoming impassioned. When he is turning out an obviously marketable piece showing that the American Constitution is the best guarantee of freedom that man will ever come up with, that the causes of some historical event are so complex that they are beyond discovery, or that some poet had an aversion to dogs, he may understandably remain unimpassioned. But this does not necessarily mean that he is any less biased than his neighbor, although it might very well mean that he cares less. On the other hand, when a scholar arrives at a radical or unconventional interpretation, he may very well become excited by what he is doing. For the act of contradiction involves emotions more tumultuous than those aroused by the state of acceptance. Scholarly dispassion is the true medium of the scholar satisfied with (or browbeaten by) things as they are.

As graduate students anticipating academic careers, we feel a very personal stake in academic life, and we feel that, as radicals, we are hampered in our work by the intrusion of prevailing standards of scholarship, which set up a screen between ourselves and our product, an automatic censoring device which trims and deflates and confines our work, under the pretext of what is supposed to be "objective scholarship," until we no longer know it as our own. Like little boys writing poems in the style of Terence, we learn the traditional, acceptable genres in our fields, and then develop the skills necessary to produce similar work, until slowly, subtly, but surely, we come to look upon our work, not as the expression of our union with man and society, but merely as our means of livelihood and security—a product for sale, neither our possession nor our creation. And the closer we come to taking our places as working people in the profession, the harder it is to remember who we are, what we have to say, and why we got into the intellectual racket in the first place.

But when we think back, we recall that at some point in our education we thought that life was interesting and challenging, and that we wanted to know more about it. We wanted to understand the phenomena which excited us: the functioning of the galaxy; the role of men in history; the creative process. And we wanted to know how we could participate creatively in life. We wanted to learn the origins of racism so that we could help to stamp it out; we wanted to know why people suffer, so that we could help to make suffering less in our time. We were not very dispassionate about our work then, because it is not easy to be dispassionate about racism, or the creative process, or the galaxy, about war and peace, and the fate of man. We did not think, at that time, that history is dull, and the search for knowledge, drudgery.

Nor do we think so yet. There is work for the radical scholar, the thinker who is committed to the investigation of the origins, purposes and limitations of institutions and concepts, as well as for the conservative or liberal scholar who is committed to their efficient maintenance and improvement. There is room in scholarship for the application of reason to the *reconstruction* of society, as well as to legalistic interpretation and reform. There is a place for the scholar who looks upon traditional formulations, theories, structures, even "facts" with a habitually critical attitude stemming from his distaste for things as they are, and from his distrust of the analyses of those who are committed to the maintenance of the status quo.

There is a place for him because, if he is a scholar as well as a malcontent, an honest researcher as well as a radical, his very partisanship, bias—call it what you will—gives him a kind of objectivity. Because he stands opposed to established institutions and conventional conceptions, the radical scholar possesses an unconcern for their safety or preservation which enables him to carry inquiry along paths where the so-called "objective" conservative or liberal scholar would not care to tread. Arnold Hauser has observed that the French bourgeoisie of the nineteenth century rejected naturalism in art from its "perfectly correct feeling that every art that describes life without bias and without restraint is in itself a revolutionary art." In 1912, Woodrow Wilson shrewdly expressed a similar feeling current within the American bourgeoisie. "The radicalism of our time," he observed, ". . . does not consist in the things that are proposed, but in the things that are disclosed." The relentless disclosure of the nature and causes of social institutions and developments is, in our own time, also radical. The Hon. Henry Cabot Lodge, Jr., unlike his more candid forebear, would even like to shroud in secrecy the now radical fact that the United States economy is capitalistic (he calls it *economic humanism*). And he has his counterparts among the scholars.

There are men and women in this country, both in and out of the academic profession, who still pursue their intellectual labor with a combination of scholarly integrity and commitment to the humanization of society. There are many more who retain a desire to do so, but who are prevented from fulfilling themselves and contributing significantly to knowledge by the paralyzing effect of forcefully maintained academic standards. The waste perhaps is tragic. It is our conviction that academic acceptance of the radical scholar's work as a contribution worthy of respect and consideration would increase both the quality and quantity of such work, and revitalize all of American intellectual life in an important way. But this respect must be earned and fought for, and it is not easy to fight alone. It is difficult for the isolated individual to maintain belief in the legitimacy of radical scholarship, even though history attests to it, and individuals in our own time demonstrate it. Even for those who believe in it, as many do, it is difficult to exercise their radicalism in individual opposition to the weight of the authorities who control our professional future. *Studies on the Left* wishes to participate in the struggles of radical scholars by existing as a meeting place where, in spite of philosophical and political differences, they can join in their common dissatisfaction with present academic standards and myths, and work harmoniously and creatively toward the future; and by helping such scholars demonstrate to the academic world the unique contribution which the radically committed thinker, by the very nature of his emotional and intellectual partisanship, is able to make. We hope that the radicalism of what is disclosed, as it increases and matures, may provide knowledge and theory for the future growth of a radicalism of what is proposed.

An Essay on Liberation

No thinker came closer to supplying a philosophical rationale to the student left than Herbert Marcuse. A Jewish refugee from Nazi Germany, Marcuse was one of the key figures of the Frankfurt School of "critical theory," a kind of think tank dating from the 1920s that sought to apply neo-Marxist analyses to modern capitalism. With most of his associates, Marcuse fled to America when Hitler came to power, and set up shop at Columbia University. In 1954, he became a professor of philosophy at Brandeis University.

Marcuse never felt at home in American society. America was the frame of reference for his critical evaluations of late capitalism, but it always seemed alien to him. His understanding of the affluent society around him in the Sixties seems drawn from popular sociology rather than from firsthand experience. To the end of his stay in America, he remained a Germanic Herr Doktor Professor.

Like his Frankfurt School colleagues, Marcuse took as a given the idea that capitalist society was undemocratic and exploitative by its nature. Like all societies of the past, it was one where "dominance" of the masses by an elite was the ultimate reality. A disciple of Freud as well as Marx, Marcuse saw capitalism as evil not only because it denied the masses material benefits but because it denied them instinctual satisfactions as well. The capitalists not only limited the income and wealth of the proletariat; they also restricted their sexual pleasure. A certain amount of instinctual self-denial was undoubtedly necessary for society to function, he acknowledged, but capitalism imposed a regime of puritanism on the masses that was excessive.

Marcuse's dislike of capitalism was not blunted by the new age of affluence and relative permissiveness that the post–World War II era brought. Both apparent advances were deceptive, he asserted; the masses remained deprived and repressed. Neither had ushered in democracy, equality, and joy, and the need for revolution remained.

Marcuse cheered the arrival of Sixties insurgency and tried to nurture and guide it. To some extent he succeeded. The more literate and bookish of New Left student leaders treated Eros and Civilization *(1955) and* One-Dimensional Man *(1964), theoretical works about the nature of modern capitalist societies, as intellectual bibles. But Marcuse also spoke directly to the "Movement" itself. In this excerpt from the brief book,* An Essay on Liberation, *written in 1967–68,* he praises the student left, especially the counterculture. Suspending his residual Marxist focus on the working class and its material exploitation, he acknowledges the cultural grievances of the young rebels and sees them as the potential agents of revolutionary change. But he also refuses to abandon his old Marxist faith in rationality, and he warns the young radicals that while mind-altering drugs might provide temporary relief from the cultural tyranny of Western capitalism, they could not be an end in themselves.*

Ultimately, the young radicals wanted validation, not criticism, and they found the transplanted German professor a disappointment as a guide and guru.

[*Herbert Marcuse,* An Essay on Liberation. *Copyright © 1969 by Herbert Marcuse. Reprinted by permission of Beacon Press.*]

AN ESSAY ON LIBERATION

The new sensibility has become a political factor. This event, which may well indicate a turning point in the evolution of contemporary societies, demands that critical theory incorporate the new dimension into its concepts, project its implications for the possible construction of a free society. Such a society presupposes throughout the achievements of the existing societies, especially their scientific and technical achievements. Released from their service in the cause of exploitation, they could be mobilized for the global elimination of poverty and toil. . . .

The new sensibility, which expresses the ascent of the life instincts over aggressiveness and guilt, would foster, on a social scale, the vital need for

*Though this essay was written in the late Sixties, it expressed views that Marcuse had already broadcast widely through his earlier works and which form part of the intellectual background of the decade's radicalism.

the abolition of injustice and misery and would shape the further evolution of the "standard of living." The life instincts would find rational expression (sublimation) in planning the distribution of the socially necessary labor time within and among the various branches of production. . . . The liberated consciousness would promote the development of a science and technology free to discover and realize the possibilities of things and men in the protection and gratification of life, playing with the potentialities of form and matter for the attainment of this goal. Technique would then tend to become art, and art would tend to form reality: the opposition between imagination and reason, higher and lower faculties, poetic and scientific thought, would be invalidated. Emergence of a new Reality Principle: under which a new sensibility and a desublimated scientific intelligence would combine in the creation of an *aesthetic ethos.*

The term "aesthetic," in its dual connotation of "pertaining to the senses" and "pertaining to art," may serve to designate the quality of the productive-creative process in an environment of freedom. . . . This would be the sensibility of men and women who do not have to be ashamed of themselves anymore because they have overcome their sense of guilt: they have learned not to identify themselves with the false fathers who have built and tolerated and forgotten the Auschwitzs and Vietnams of history, the torture chambers of all the secular and ecclesiastical inquisitions and interrogations, the ghettos and the monumental temples of the corporations, and who have worshiped the higher culture of this reality. If and when men and women act and think free from this identification, they will have broken the chain which linked the fathers and the sons from generation to generation. They will not have redeemed the crimes against humanity, but they will have become free to stop them and prevent their recommencement. . . .

The new sensibility . . . emerges in the struggle against violence and exploitation where this struggle is waged for essentially new ways and forms of life: negation of the entire Establishment, its morality, culture; affirmation of the right to build a society in which the abolition of poverty and toil terminates in a universe where the sensuous, the playful, the calm, and the beautiful become forms of existence and thereby the *Form* of the society itself.

The aesthetic as the possible Form of a free society appears at that stage of development where the intellectual and material resources for the conquest of scarcity are available, where previously progressive repression turns into regressive repression, where the higher culture in which the aesthetic . . . had been monopolized and segregated from the reality collapses and dissolves in desublimated "lower," and destructive forms, where the hatred of the young bursts into laughter and song, mixing the barricade and the dance floor, love play and heroism. And the young also attack the *esprit de sérieux* in the socialist camp: miniskirts against the apparatchiks, rock 'n' roll against Soviet Realism. The insistence that a socialist society can and ought to be light, pretty, playful, that these qualities are essential elements of freedom, the faith in the rationality of the imagination, the demand for a new morality and culture—does this great anti-authoritarian rebellion indicate a new dimension and direction of radical change, the appearance of new agents of radical change, and a new vision of socialism in its qualitative difference from the established societies? Is there anything in the aesthetic dimension which has an essential affinity with freedom not only in its sublimated cultural (artistic) but also in its desublimated political, existential form, so that the aesthetic can become a . . . factor in the technique of production . . . ?

[T]he aesthetic dimension can serve as a sort of gauge for a free society. A universe of human relationships no longer mediated by the market, no longer based on competitive exploitation or terror, demands a sensitivity freed from the repressive satisfactions of the unfree societies; a sensitivity receptive to forms and modes of reality which thus far have been projected only by the aesthetic imagination. For the aesthetic needs have their own social content: they are the claims of the human organism, mind and body, for a dimension of fulfillment which can be created only in the struggle against the institutions which, by their very functioning, deny and violate these claims. The radical social content of the aesthetic needs becomes evident as the demand for their most elementary satisfaction is translated into group action on an enlarged scale. From the harmless drive for better zoning regulations and a modicum of protection from noise and dirt to the pressure for closing whole city areas to automobiles, prohibition of transistor radios in all public places, decommercialization of nature, total urban reconstruction, control of the birth rate—such action would become increasingly subversive of the institutions of capitalism and of their morality. The quantity of such reforms would turn into the quality of radical change to the degree to which they would critically weaken the economic, political, and cultural pressure and power groups which have a vested interest in preserving the environment and ecology of profitable merchandising.

The aesthetic morality is the opposite of puritanism. It does not insist on a daily bath or shower for people whose cleaning practices involve systematic torture, slaughtering, poisoning; nor does it insist on clean clothes for men who are professionally engaged in dirty deals. But it does insist on cleaning the earth from the very material garbage produced by the spirit of capitalism, and from this spirit itself. And it insists on freedom as a biological necessity: being physically incapable of tolerating any repression other than that required for the protection and amelioration of life. . . .

The order and organization of class society, which have shaped the sensibility and the reason of man, have also shaped the freedom of the imagination. . . . In the great historical revolutions, the imagination was, for a short period, released and free to enter into projects of a new social morality and of new institutions of freedom; then it was sacrificed to the requirements of effective reason.

If now, in the rebellion of the young intelligentsia, the right and truth of the imagination become the demands of political action, if surrealistic forms of protest and refusal spread throughout the movement, this apparently insignificant development may indicate a fundamental change in the situation. . . .

Today, the rupture with the linguistic universe of the Establishment is more radical [than during revolutions in the past]: in the most militant areas of protest, it amounts to a methodical reversal of meaning. It is a familiar phenomenon that subcultural groups develop their own language, taking the harmless words of everyday communication out of their context and using them for designating objects or activities tabooed by the Establishment. This is the Hippie subculture: "trip," "grass," "pot," "acid," and so on. But a far more subversive universe of discourse announces itself in the language of black militants. Here is a systematic linguistic rebellion, which smashes the ideological context in which the words are employed and defined, and places them into the opposite context. . . . Thus, the blacks "take over" some of the most sublime and sublimated concepts of Western civilization, desublimate them, and redefine them. For example, the "soul" (in its essence lily-white ever since Plato) . . . has been desublimated and . . . migrated to the Negro culture: they are soul brothers, the soul is black, violent, orgiastic; it is no longer in Beethoven, Schubert, but in the blues, in jazz, in rock 'n' roll, in "soul food." Similarly, the militant slogan "black is beautiful" redefines another central concept of the traditional culture by reversing its symbolic value and associating it with the anti-color of darkness, tabooed magic, the uncanny. The ingression of the aesthetic into the political also appears at the other pole of the rebellion against the society of affluent capitalism, among the nonconformist youth. Here, too, the reversal of meaning, driven to the point of open contradiction: giving flowers to the police, "flower power"—

the redefinition and very negation of the sense of "power"; the erotic belligerency in the songs of protest; the sensuousness of long hair, of the body unsoiled by plastic cleanliness.

These political manifestations of a new sensibility indicate the depth of the rebellion, of the rupture with the continuum of repression. They bear witness to the power of the society in shaping the whole of experience, the whole metabolism between the organism and its environment. . . . Today's rebels want to see, hear, feel new things in a new way: they link liberation with the dissolution of ordinary and orderly perception. The "trip" involves the dissolution of the ego shaped by the established society—an artificial and short-lived dissolution. But the artificial and "private" liberation anticipates, in a distorted manner, an exigency of social liberation: the revolution must be at the same time a revolution in perception which will accompany the material and intellectual reconstruction of society, creating the new aesthetic environment.

Awareness of the need for such a revolution in perception, . . . is perhaps the kernel of truth in the psychedelic search. But it is vitiated when its narcotic character brings temporary release not only from the reason and rationality of the established system but also from that other rationality which is to change the established system, when sensibility is freed not only from the exigencies of the existing order but also from those of liberation. Intentionally noncommitted, the withdrawal creates its artificial paradises within the society from which it withdrew. . . . In contrast, the radical transformation of society implies the union of the new sensibility with a new rationality. The imagination becomes productive if it becomes the mediator between sensibility on the one hand, and theoretical as well as practical reason on the other, and in this harmony of faculties . . . guides the reconstruction of society. . . .

The Free Speech Movement

Student dissent began with campus political parties and a handful of new critical journals in the waning years of the 1950s. Student rebellions began with the uprising at the University of California at Berkeley during the 1964–65 academic year.

The Bay Area was long a catch-basin for every brand of nonconformist and radical. Pacifists and refugees from McCarthyism flocked to the region during the 1940s and 1950s. Beat poets and writers, during these same decades, found a comfortable home in San Francisco's North Beach bohemia. In the early Sixties, Berkeley harbored the first of the student activists and a large contingent of young white civil rights militants. On the campus of the flagship branch of the University of California, the politicized students were only a minority, but they were passionate and articulate and soon found the university administration a suitable target for their wrath.

The head of the vast University of California system was Clark Kerr, a former professor of industrial relations. A Quaker and a liberal, Kerr had eased the McCarthyite state loyalty-oath rules for faculty members and ended the policy of excluding leftist campus speakers. But he had also proclaimed the university's role as the sparkplug of economic growth and the ally of the state's primary economic interests. The University of California, then, by its president's own assertion, was no ivory tower but a part of the establishment and a bastion of the "system."

Activists were alerted to the university's conservative role in the fall of 1964, when classes resumed after the summer break. Until now, they had been allowed to man recruiting tables and conduct rallies favoring a wide range of political positions and causes outside the university. Now, suddenly, the dean of students declared that on-campus political advocacy for off-campus issues would be forbidden. Many students suspected that recent student picketing of the Oakland Tribune, *owned by a powerful conservative U.S. senator, William Knowland, was behind the rules change.*

The administration's ukase offended student moderates as well as activists. It seemed a throwback to the militant anti-Communism of just a few years before and a blatant denial of fundamental civil liberties. Free speech on campus became the core issue of the student revolt and would give its name to the movement that soon emerged.

The administration's actions awakened other student discontents. Berkeley enrollments had exploded in the early Sixties as the first of the postwar baby boomers graduated from high school. By the fall of 1965, there were some 25,000 students attending UCB full or part time. Many classes were very large and divided into sections supervised by graduate student teaching assistants. Senior faculty were difficult to see; many were too busy with their scholarship or consulting work to talk to students. To keep track of the mass of bodies, the administration employed computers using IBM punch cards that bore the legend "neither fold, spindle, or mutilate." The anomic nature of campus life would create grievances that Free Speech Movement (FSM) leaders would both share and use.

The response to the dean's directive followed what would become the standard trajectory of campus confrontations during the decade. Militants ignored the rulings and were suspended, drawing sympathy from moderates. Further attempts at disciplinary action by the administration soon led to greater militancy and ultimately to the use of civil disobedience tactics learned from the civil rights movement, in this case the occupation of Sproul Hall, the administration building. Unable to negotiate a peaceful evacuation, university officials felt compelled to call in the police, and the "bust" that followed further radicalized the campus, including the younger faculty, especially those in the humanities and social sciences. In Berkeley, the student activists ultimately won. The dean's rules were liberalized, and in the wake of the upheaval, the campus was radicalized. For the next dozen years the Berkeley community would be the staging ground of every sort of political and cultural insurgency, from Maoism to Filthy Speech.

This selection is a speech by Mario Savio, a twenty-year-old undergraduate in philosophy, delivered from the steps of Sproul Hall during the height of the anti-administration excitement. A member of the FSM steering committee, Savio had spent the summer of 1964 in Mississippi, and his words, echoing the tones and rhythms of the civil rights movement, seek to equate the university with the racist establishment of the South. Savio also expresses the sense of the university as an immense, heartless machine, indifferent to the needs and feelings of its students.

[Mario Savio, "An End to History," from the Bancroft Library, University of California at Berkeley.]

Last summer I went to Mississippi to join the struggle there for civil rights. This fall I am engaged in another phase of the same struggle, this time in Berkeley. The two battlefields may seem quite different to some observers, but this is not the case. The same rights are at stake in both places—the right to participate as citizens in democratic society and the right to due process of law. Further, it is a struggle against the same enemy. In Mississippi an autocratic and powerful minority rules, through organized violence, to suppress the vast, virtually powerless, majority. In California, the privileged minority manipulates the University bureaucracy to suppress the students' political expression. That "respectable" bureaucracy masks the financial plutocrats; that impersonal bureaucracy is the efficient enemy in a "Brave New World."

In our free speech fight at the University of California, we have come up against what may emerge as the greatest problem of our nation—depersonalized, unresponsive bureaucracy. We have encountered the organized status quo in Mississippi, but it is the same in Berkeley. Here we find it impossible usually to meet with anyone but secretaries. Beyond that, we find functionaries who cannot make policy but can only hide behind the rules. We have discovered total lack of response on the part of the policy makers. To grasp a situation which is truly Kafkaesque, it is necessary to understand the bureaucratic mentality. And we have learned quite a bit about it this fall, more outside the classroom than in.

As bureaucrat, an administrator believes that nothing new happens. He occupies an ahistorical point of view. In September, to get the attention of this bureaucracy which had issued arbitrary edicts suppressing student political expression and refused to discuss its action, we held a sit-in on the campus. We sat around a police car and kept it immobilized for over thirty-two hours. At last, the administrative bureaucracy agreed to negotiate. But instead, on the following Monday, we discovered that a committee had been appointed, in accordance with usual regulations, to resolve the dispute. Our attempt to convince any of the administrators that an event had occurred, that something new had happened, failed. They saw this simply as something to be handled by normal university procedures.

The same is true of all bureaucracies. They begin as tools, means to certain legitimate goals, and they end up feeding their own existence. The conception that bureaucrats have is that history has in fact come to an end. No events can occur now that the Second World War is over which can change American society substantially. We proceed by standard procedures as we are.

The most crucial problems facing the United States today are the problem of automation and the problem of racial injustice. Most people who will be put out of jobs by machines will not accept an end to events, this historical plateau, as the point beyond which no change occurs. Negroes will not accept an end to history here. All of us must refuse to accept history's final judgment that in America there is no place in society for people whose skins are dark. On campus, students are not about to accept it as fact that the university has ceased evolving and is in its final state of perfection, that students and faculty are respectively raw material and employees, or that the University is to be autocratically run by unresponsive bureaucrats.

Here is the real contradiction: the bureaucrats hold history as ended. As a result significant parts of the population both on campus and off are dispossessed, and these dispossessed are not about to accept this ahistorical point of view. It is out of this that the conflict has occurred with the university bureaucracy and will continue to occur until that bureaucracy becomes responsive or until it is clear the university cannot function.

The things we are asking for in our civil rights protests have a deceptively quaint ring. We are asking for the due process of law. We are asking for our actions to be judged by committees of our peers. We are asking that regulations ought to be considered as arrived at legitimately only from the consensus of the governed. These phrases are all pretty old, but they are not being taken seriously in America today, nor are they being taken seriously on the Berkeley campus.

I have just come from a meeting with the Dean of Students. She notified us that she was aware of certain violations of university regulations by certain organizations. University friends of SNCC [Student Non-Violent Coordinating Committee], which I represent, was one of these. We tried to draw from her some statement on these great principles: consent of the governed, jury of one's peers, due process. The best she could do was to evade or to present the administration party line. It is very hard to make any contact with the human being who is behind these organizations.

The university is the place where people begin seriously to question the conditions of their existence and raise the issue of whether they can be committed to the society they have been born into. After a long period of apathy during the fifties, students have begun not only to question but, having arrived at answers, to act on those answers. This is part of a growing understanding among many people in America that history has not ended, that a better society is possible, and that it is worth dying for.

This free speech fight points up a fascinating aspect of contemporary campus life. Students are permitted to talk all they want so long as their speech has no consequences.

One conception of the university, suggested by a classical Christian formulation, is that it be in the world but not of the world. The conception of Clark Kerr, by contrast, is that the university is part and parcel of this particular stage in the history of American society; it stands to serve the need of American industry; it is a factory that turns out a certain product needed by industry or government. Because speech does often have consequences which might alter this perversion of higher education, the university must put itself in a position of censorship. It can permit two kinds of speech: speech which encourages continuation of the status quo, and speech which advocates changes in it so radical as to be irrelevant in the foreseeable future. Someone may advocate radical change in all aspects of American society, and this I am sure he can do with impunity. But if someone advocates sit-ins to bring about changes in discriminatory hiring practices, this can not be permitted because it goes against the status quo of which the university is a part. And that is how the fight began here.

The administration of the Berkeley campus has admitted that external, extra-legal groups have pressured the university not to permit students on campus to organize picket lines, not to permit on campus any speech with consequences. And the bureaucracy went along. Speech with consequences, speech in the area of civil rights, speech which some might regard as illegal, must stop.

Many students here at the university, many people in society, are wandering aimlessly about. Strangers in their own lives, there is no place for them. They are people who have not learned to compromise, who for example have come to the university to learn to question, to grow, to learn—all the standard things that sound like clichés because no one takes them seriously. And they find at one point or other that for them to become part of society, to become lawyers, ministers, businessmen, people in government, that very often they must compromise those principles which were most dear to them. They must suppress the most creative impulses that they have; this is a prior condition for being part of the system. The university is well structured, well tooled, to turn out people with all the sharp edges worn off, the well-rounded person. The university is well equipped to produce that sort of person, and this means that the best among the people who enter must for four years wander aimlessly much of the time questioning why they are on campus at all, doubting whether there is any point in what they are doing, and looking toward a very bleak existence afterward in a game in which all of the rules have been made up, which one cannot really amend.

It is a bleak scene, but it is all a lot of us have to look forward to. Society provides no challenge. American society in the standard conception it has of itself is simply no longer exciting. The most exciting things going on in America today are movements to change America. America is becoming ever more the utopia of sterilized, automated contentment. The "futures" and "careers" for which American students now prepare are for the most part intellectual and moral wastelands. This chrome-plated consumers' paradise would have us grow up to be well-behaved children. But an important minority of men and women coming to the front today have shown that they will die rather than be standardized, replaceable, and irrelevant.

The Columbia Uprising

By 1968, the student New Left had become militant. The persistent agony of Vietnam, the explosive "long, hot summers" in the cities, the murders of the people's tribunes—Martin Luther King, Jr., and Robert Kennedy—the apparent failure of the War on Poverty, the rise of Black Power ideology—all fused to create an apocalyptic mood among white student radicals. SDS, which had fathered the new student left, was swept along with the overheated rhetoric and imperatives. The Port Huron Statement of 1962 had positioned SDS only a little to the left of Americans for Democratic Action, the repository of New Deal liberalism. Now, in the nadir year of the decade, SDS leaders considered themselves "revolutionary communists," whose goals were the destruction of American liberal capitalism and its replacement by an ill-defined Marxist utopia.

The ties between higher education and the apparatus of the cold war, as revealed in spurts during the decade, confirmed the place of the university as a prop of bourgeois society and validated student activists' focus on their own home base. A blow struck against the university would be a blow struck against the "beast" of America. And there was another reason to consider the campus battles important: it was in the blazing furnace of campus confrontation that otherwise apolitical or even conservative students could be transformed into radical enthusiasts ready to attack the world headquarters of the counterrevolution.

The SDS chapter at Columbia University on Morningside Heights was prepared to act on this concept. Formed in early 1965, Columbia SDS had at first been a moderate and rather languid organization. By 1968, moving with the times, it had become more radical and more active as the "action faction," led by Mark Rudd, took control. A swaggering sophomore from New Jersey, Rudd believed that campus confrontation could radicalize the "new ruling class" and determine the future of the entire society. As he would say, the university's only valid function was "the creation and expansion of revolution."

Fortunately for the SDS militants, Columbia was enmeshed in a cluster of issues that could be used to radicalize the campus. First, it was a member of the Institute for Defense Analysis (IDA), a consortium of research universities under contract to test weapons and perform other services for the Pentagon. The university's complicity in the Vietnam War and the "warfare state" was also expressed in authorized campus recruiting by the military services and by private companies that were major defense contractors.

More immediate to most students was the gymnasium problem. Columbia needed a new gym and had begun to construct one, with the permission of the city, on city-owned property along the edge of Morningside Park, a steep stretch of trees, undergrowth, and boulders that separated the university from black Harlem directly to the east. Even when provisions were made for access to the sports facilities and pool by Harlem residents, it appeared, in the militant mood of 1968, that "whitey," in the shape of the university, was ignoring the wishes of black people and stealing their property. The gym was an imperialist intrusion into Harlem.

On April 23, SDS held a noon rally to protest IDA at the Sundial, between the administration building and Butler Library. The protesters intended to briefly invade the administration building in defiance of the rule against indoor demonstrations. Little was said of the gym or Harlem. But what ensued was a week of confrontation exceeded in passion only by Berkeley's Free Speech Movement and in media coverage by no other action of SDS or the Sixties student movement.

The selection here is an account by Jeff Shero, a participant in the "siege of Morningside Heights." A former University of Texas student and one of the founders of SDS, Shero at this point was editor of Rat, *a New York–based underground publication, part of a nationwide explosion of dissenting "alternative" media. The piece is of course biased; Shero never doubted that the university was coercive and that its cause was wrong. He would have been even more biased if he had written later in the week, when the Columbia administration called in the police to evict students*

who had taken over university buildings, an action the cops performed with great
zeal and little concern for the safety of the demonstrators or even innocent bystanders.

Shero anticipated many Columbians. And he was right. Over the next two years,
dozens of campuses detonated, though none of the explosions were as resonant as the
one atop Morningside Heights. And yet the revolution never came. The campuses,
in the end, were not the triggers of society's final overthrow.

[*Jeff Shero, "Blockade and Siege,"* Rat: Subterranean News, *May 13–18, 1968.*]

BLOCKADE AND SIEGE

With the aid of the ill-laid plans of Grayson Kirk and the Board of Trustees, Columbia University made history last week. The news has focused on the startling events, the beating, the barricades, and taken issue on the opposing forces' positions, but no one has attempted to explain how just another protest demonstration grew into a militant movement qualitatively different from any yet in an American university.

A week ago Tuesday, SDS called a noon rally. A petition was to be carried into Low Library in defiance of an order banning indoor demonstrations. A line of jocks blocked the marchers, and they returned to the center of campus. What looked like another failure of the left was saved by the impromptu idea of marching to the gym construction site in Morningside Park. With a frustrated energy, the demonstrators began tearing down the chain link fence surrounding the property, and when the friendly local police were called in to protect the property and apprehend the culprits, fighting ensued. Arrested demonstrators were freed from the clutches of the police, and several police were knocked into the mud puddles. It was the first hint that the mood was beginning to change.

Back on campus, Mark Rudd, the blond-haired, impulsive, and aggressive SDS leader, called to the throng to take their grievances to Dean Coleman in Hamilton Hall. It was a matter of practicality; it was impossible to gain entrance into Low Library, the seat of administrative power. The crowd trailed behind the leaders; there was no surge, no great anger. Inside, Dean Coleman was surrounded, imprisoned by the mass of bodies around him. Mark Rudd demanded that he deal with us. When the crew-cut, tight-lipped dean refused, citing our rudeness and retreating into his office, the logic of the situation made him our hostage—we were going to hold him there until he reached someone with enough power to discuss our grievances.

We had a hostage! High spirits and community swept through the crowd. Black student leaders and white student leaders began speaking, explaining the issues and making demands in militant tones. As the time passed, the mood became more militant. People were preparing to sit into the night. The speakers began engaging the curious crowd which surrounded the perimeter of the demonstration. One black speaker who had earlier fought with the police at the gym site captured the idea which was to move people in the following days. He looked into the eyes of the spectators and hecklers and movingly explained, "I love peace and order . . . But I love justice more."

Early that evening the administration attempted their first peacekeeping ploy. Dean Coleman emerged from his office and announced that he had contacted Vice President [David] Truman, and that he would deign to discuss the issues with us if we left Hamilton Hall and proceeded to Wollman Auditorium. It was clear we had no bargaining power if we released the Dean. Our response was direct—have Truman come to us. An impasse, and we were headed into the first long night.

That night students and community people from Harlem poured in. Separate meetings were held to debate strategy and plan for the next day. The white students divided on the issue of whether to barricade the hall or merely keep the Dean hostage while still letting students attend classes. Much the same tactical debate occurred in the black meeting. One point clearly arose, though; the black students had a higher degree of commitment than did the bulk of whites. Rumors abounded about the number of guns brought in by blacks, and the whites knew the black leadership proposed barricading the building. Many were edgy. As the night wore on, it became obvious that while we shared common demands, tensions threatened our solidarity. At five in the morning, when blacks declared that they were going to blockade the building and that whites who shared their determination should seize another, a clear and positive resolution to the internal political turmoil was reached.

Just before six o'clock the whites streamed out of the building and headed for Low Library. A window was smashed, and students hurried by the startled security guards who sat at their desks and made only feeble protests. Quickly, and with a sense of awe at being in the inner sanctum, students took over Grayson Kirk's executive office and tightly barricaded the doors. Everyone expected the police to arrive in force at any moment. Between the frantic periods of scurrying irrationally, when people dashed about accomplishing nothing, frozen moments, like in WWII movies of submarine crews holding tight while depth charges slowly descended and exploded, gripped the suite. People lived in ten-second spurts.

Later in the day when the police hadn't come, the mood changed to liberated jubilation. The President's sherry and cigars were broken out, the mood was festive—the peasants had taken over the palace. Two prophy-lactics and a skin magazine were found in Kirk's drawer—ah! the emperor also stands naked.

The hours hustled by. While *The New York Times* editorialized about the hooliganism, the demonstrators were finding a new empowered sense of themselves, and support was spreading. New halls were taken. Faculty members for the first time attempted forcibly to keep cops away and were injured in the process. That night at one o'clock, two thirty-man teams fanned out in a coordinated move and seized the Mathematics Building. It was secured, barricaded throughout, in thirty minutes.

Segmented time lost its normal meaning, sleepless hours blurred into sleepless days. While events crashed, racing through the minds of the participants, changing them more swiftly than months of arguments ever would, certain moments, sometimes inconsequential, stand out like rays of clarity in the jumbled joy and strain of the time. . . . A Negro sergeant, supposedly guarding the ledge outside the Presidential suite, made friends with the window-watchers and, when he got too cold, gladly took a glass of the President's imported sherry. . . . Sir Stephen Spender, the elderly British poet, climbed through the second story window to greet the students. Some, unaware of their guest's fame, demanded forcefully to know if he was a reporter. Reporters aren't allowed. . . . Chalked on a blackboard by someone unknown: "Fellow classmates: Although I am spending the night here I want to tell you that I love the idea of a classroom as any student can, and that I'm not taking part in, but rather doing my best to prevent any damage to it or the ideas it represents." On another blackboard, "Create two, three, many Columbias." . . . More moments. . . . After many long hours of debate it was decided to attempt to hold the barricades. A police attack was imminent; people prepared themselves, a great sense of pride glowed through those who were to protect the barricades. Pride in themselves; pride in their work. . . . After a tense period in Fayerweather Hall, a couple announced to the crowd that they were going to get married. They didn't have a license, but they wanted to be married now. Jubilation and unity. The priest married them and pronounced them children of the new age. A totally happy wedding.

The vignettes are pleasing, they give a certain reassurance that everything is the same, that the status quo oscillates and then returns to normalcy. But during the first few days new political precedents slowly formed and solidified. Participants by the hundreds realized new concrete possibilities in their lives and were forever changed. Alliances between black and white, between the campus and the community, the exaltation of people over property and the unchallenged participation of outsiders in the struggle—ideas found only in the radicals' fondest pot dreams slowly merged into reality.

During the siege, whites and blacks held separate halls, with little communication, yet the blacks refused deals for amnesty just for themselves; instead they told the mediators and the public—amnesty for all, and not only an end to gym construction, but get rid of IDA as well. The distrust woven into the minds of whites and blacks for hundreds of years unraveled just a little.

The press screamed about the disrespect for property and the destruction brought about by the demonstrators. The administration called in the police which spread more destruction in hours than the demonstrators did for days. The demonstrators began to work on a new principle. If the cause is just, if we are right that Columbia's role in the counterinsurgency of the IDA means more efficient death for Vietnamese and [that] its seizure of property in East Harlem perpetuates crippling racism, then we should hold our position as effectively as possible. Tear off a door of Grayson Kirk's cabinet to build a stronger barricade or smash a window to get desks to block up a basement; it's judged much better than smashing another person's skull.

A third precedent was set, a problem which is still a matter of great debate at Berkeley. During the blockade nonstudents from both the black community and the white radical community joined in, and no students bothered to raise the issue of outsiders. It became as legitimate for a radical to go to Columbia as to the Pentagon. The university was no longer seen as a protected island, freed from outside involvement and participation. Just as the administration worked with the corporate leaders and fronts projects for the CIA and the military, so the students work with all forces outside their narrow community.

The development which held the most [pathos?] was the tortured self-searching role of the faculty; except for the handful of radical professors who backed the political demand [i.e., Columbia's withdrawal from IDA], most of the faculty attempted to save their position by being mediators protective of order. But the conflict was polarized. Some who wanted to maintain harmony in a discordant atmosphere had no real power or position. The faculty . . . [was] more faint-hearted after the initial leftward surge; as employees of the university, they identified with the institution they had learned to live with. Maintenance of the institution was repeatedly stated as more important than the issues at stake. Most barricaders felt the university was an integral part of an oppressive system, an idea which the professors who built their lives on academia would not accept.

The conflict still unfolds. It seems the administration made the fatal mistake of overplaying its hand, and has done great damage to itself. But then another possibility exists. Steve Weissman during the Berkeley Free Speech Movement observed that the administration saved the movement time and again from extinction through its blunders. Good luck? No, he would respond, the bureaucracy is so rigid, unresponsive to the needs of the community, and subject to a system of outside control, that it couldn't help but blunder into mistakes which outraged the academic community. He argued it was the nature of the system.

And so may it be now. Leaders like Mark Rudd are singled out as instigators, but the crises are more thoroughgoing. The struggle at Columbia has sparked new dreams in students throughout the country. It's now only time before "Columbia" is imitated with new intensity throughout the country.

Weatherman

From the moderate Port Huron Statement in 1962 to the Weathermen in 1969 was a brief period of time. But in the world of SDS, it was a lifetime. During those seven years the New Left moved from earnest and often thoughtful criticism of formalized democratic institutions and support of grassroots participation, to revolutionary terrorism against a totally depraved and irredeemable "Amerika."

The change in SDS was the result of forces both without and within. As the Vietnam War escalated, as efforts at social reform stalled, as racial violence flared, as legitimacy of authority declined, as assassination became endemic, dissent and protest grew angrier and more despairing. By decade's end, many educated Americans feared the nation was tottering at the edge of revolution. For committed radicals, the last days now seemed imminent.

But SDS was also suffering from painful internal strains. In 1968, its "national office" leaders were facing challenges from Trotskyists, Communists, and Maoists—Marxist-Leninists of several kinds who had infiltrated the organization when, against the advice of older democratic leftists, SDS leaders had lowered their guard. Meanwhile, black militants and activist women had declared their independence of white male radicals, cutting sharply into the SDS leadership's confidence and moral authority. A final challenge came from the hippie culture, which mocked the "square" attitudes of SDS and the political radicals generally.

The leaders at the Chicago headquarters sought to fend off the die-hard orthodox Marxists by accommodating the newest activists. This meant allying SDS with black militants, rebellious youth, and radical feminists. At the same time, given the growing sense of world capitalist crisis, a Leninist depiction of capitalism in its death throes—the stage of "imperialism"—had to be incorporated into the SDS message.

The end result, in ideological terms, was the Weatherman statement presented at the June 1969 annual convention in Chicago. This turgid sixteen-thousand-word document targeted positions that the powerful Maoist faction, Progressive Labor, was seeking to impose on SDS. It denied the revolutionary primacy of the proletariat and the claim that other oppressed groups—blacks, women, youths—had interests distinctive from the working class. It depicted black militants and Third World radicals generally, whether abroad or in America itself, as the preeminent instruments of revolution. In so doing, it abandoned the Port Huron focus on students as the agents of social change in advanced capitalist societies.

SDS broke up at this ninth annual convention. The national office leaders, now calling themselves Weathermen, expelled Progressive Labor* and set off on a course of revolutionary extremism that included street riots, bank robberies, bomb making, and classroom disruptions. What remained of the national office faction split into small "collectives," many of whose members went underground, there to spout apocalyptic rhetoric and practice sexual excesses to confirm how far they had moved from their bourgeois roots.

This document is an immediate precursor of the Weatherman statement. Written by Bill Ayers and Jim Mellen, two young men who soon became "Weatherleaders" and were indicted in April 1970 by authorities for inciting to riot, it is far briefer than the Weatherman statement. Nevertheless, it captures the essential ideas and mood of that overblown manifesto.

[*Bill Ayers and Jim Mellen, "Hot Town: Summer in the City Or I Ain't Gonna Work on Maggie's Farm No More,"* **New Left Notes,** *April 4, 1969; reprinted in Harold Jacobs, ed.,* **Weatherman** *(Berkeley: Ramparts Press, 1970), pp. 29–38.*]

HOT TOWN: SUMMER IN THE CITY OR I AIN'T GONNA WORK ON MAGGIE'S FARM NO MORE

I. Toward a Revolutionary Movement

Over the past few months, SDS has developed a correct transitional strategy for itself. That strategy is based on an understanding of the class nature of this society; on an understanding that the sharpest struggles against the ruling class are being waged by the oppressed nations against U.S. imperialism, and that all our actions must flow from our identity as part of an

---

*Denying the legitimacy of their expulsion, the Progressive Laborites sought to take over SDS's shell. For a time a PL-dominated organization calling itself SDS operated out of Boston. But no one was fooled, and it soon disbanded.

international struggle against U.S. imperialism. It is a strategy that understands the need for SDS to tie itself to these struggles, and to make itself something more than it is: to transform itself into a student movement into a working-class youth movement.

It is clear that, although a successful revolution in this country is in no way inevitable, any revolution—to have even a small chance of success—would have to be a revolution of the working class. This is not to say that SDS as an organization should move immediately to organizing workers, or that we have, at this point, a precise enough understanding of the various segments and characteristics of the working class. It is only to assert an understanding of the fact that the struggle for freedom that we are involved in can never succeed without the total, fundamental economic and social transformation in which the working class overthrows and liquidates the ruling class.

Up until recently, SDS has been exclusively a student movement. Furthermore, it has been a student movement concentrated primarily on the elite campuses of Harvard, Chicago, Berkeley, Michigan. This is beginning to change. San Francisco State replaces Berkeley, Michigan State replaces Michigan, as the important centers of struggle. And SDS begins to spring up in the high schools and off the campus altogether.

But more importantly, the movement begins to happen in these places. In most cities, high schools are blowing up so fast that SDS organizers can't keep up with them. Community and junior colleges are increasingly the scenes of struggle and confrontation. And the army has become the time bomb of the ruling class.

We're faced with two realities: that, in the past, SDS has been primarily an elite student group, and that, at this point in history, young people in the schools generally, and in the army, are actively resisting the special oppression they face. Given what SDS is, what is happening in this society, and what the movement must become in order to have even a chance of success, it is clear that SDS must begin to consciously transform itself from a student movement into a working-class youth movement. That is, SDS must become more than itself, must move, in the only organic way open to it, to become a self-conscious working-class movement. And it must do this by emphasizing the commonality of the oppression and struggles of youth, and by making these struggles class conscious.

This is possible because of the material basis of the oppression of youth. The majority of young people in America today are either in school, in the army, or unemployed. Specifically in the schools and in the army, young people perform tasks that have no relevance to their own needs but are key to the functioning of capitalism: training young people to fit into a more highly skilled work force, forcing them to defend imperialism and the Empire in struggles against national liberation movements, and, in all cases, deferring young people for longer and longer periods of time from the productive work force. Thus, there is significant class content to the oppression of the vast majority of young people. This is not to say that youth is a class—or that young people's struggles are always in the interest of the working class as a whole. While it's true that youth aren't hardened into class positions and generally reflect all the different class interests, it is clear that the oppression of youth by imperialism hits hardest on working-class youth, especially black and brown youth. We must attack this oppression in a class way, that is, raise the interests of the most oppressed sectors first. That is the only basis that exists for revolutionary class unity. Our task must be to understand the class content of youth's oppression, to specify it in practice, and to build class consciousness through struggle.

Discipline Needed

In order for SDS to succeed at this task, it will take tremendous self-consciousness and discipline from the membership. It will involve high school organizers consciously organizing among the lowest tracked kids. It will involve organizers consciously developing bases in community colleges. And it will involve disciplined cadre entering the armed forces and work places as organizers.

There are two important developments that would help this process. These should be seen as urgent tasks. First is the development of cadre. Seriousness and self-consciousness inside the organization are essential as SDS begins to transform itself into a revolutionary movement. Through collective political experience and study, cadre can be developed who can bring these things to SDS. The function of cadre—through exemplary action and through political education—is to broaden the movement and build class consciousness in a self-conscious way, as well as help consolidate growth and fight uneven development.

A second important task is the concretization of our politics through practice. The development of our politics in the past few months leaves us with an understanding of the oppression of youth, only in a general way. We see that working-class youth are oppressed in specific ways and that the existing base of SDS in colleges and universities has much in common with youth in all sectors of the working class. We must now learn more about the issues which face city youth especially, the kind of consciousness which is developing there, and the organizational forms which can make struggle around those issues and that consciousness coherent. In order to make SDS, now basically a student movement, something more than it is, a revolutionary youth movement, we must learn more about city youth and the class content of their struggle. We must bring organizers from our existing constituency more directly into organizing situations of our potential constituency, thereby creating a material force for the further development of our politics.

The task of developing cadres, as well as the task of broadening our constituency to other sections of white working-class youth, both have a special urgency at this time. This is due to the advanced level of political struggle of the black liberation movement. To recognize the vanguard character of the black liberation struggle means to recognize its importance to the "white" movement. The black liberation struggle has been instrumental in winning much of the white movement to a clearer understanding of imperialism, class oppression within the U.S., the reactionary nature of pacifism, the need for armed struggle as the only road to revolution, and other essential truths which were not predominant within our movement in the past. It must be clear that setbacks to the vanguard are tremendous setbacks to the people's movement as a whole.

White Fighting Force

Yet repression at this time is very serious against the political vanguard of the black liberation struggle, the Black Panther Party. And this repression is facilitated by the absence of substantial material support—power—by the white movement. Unless we recognize the urgency of fighting white supremacy by building the material strength of the white movement to be a conscious, organized, mobilized fighting force capable of giving real support to the black liberation struggle, we will be deserting the most advanced leadership of that struggle to the free hand of ruling-class repression.

Thus the urgency of broadening the movement to more proletarian sections of white industrial workers and youth is not because in some way concern with the white working class is an alternative political direction from the support for the black struggle. Rather, it is a necessary extension of the support. Nor is "white working-class organizing" an alternative to the struggle within the "student movement" against pacifism and social democratic and revisionist ideas, which feed on the isolation of the student movement from the masses of working people. In both cases, we seek to expand our base not in conflict with the black liberation struggle or "student organizing" but because of it.

In terms of cadre development, an investigation of and intimacy with the real life situation and struggles of the oppressed sections of working-class youth will give formerly "student" cadres a clearer identification with and understanding of the interests of the class as a whole. Thus, on return to a campus situation, they will be better equipped to fight the go-slowism of student provincialism.

II. Program

A large number of SDS people should come to Detroit to participate in a summer of work and study. A program that calls for SDS people to work as a group in the cities should first understand the history and failures of past SDS programs. While it is beyond the scope of this paper to develop a detailed critical history of SDS programs relating to the cities, we will make a couple of general comments that are particularly relevant.

In our past organizing we incorrectly thought that SDS people should totally follow the direction of the people with whom they were working. This on two levels: first, we assumed that SDS people were foreign elements who had to transform their identities, emulate others; and second, we thought that SDS people should totally take political direction from the people with whom they were organizing. Both of these are incorrect. The task should be to retain one's sense of identity, retain a sense of struggle from the campus, and at the same time build a movement which includes a broader constituency. This process may lead to SDS people undergoing fundamental changes, but consciousness must develop dialectically, not mechanically (like by getting a haircut).

Selection and Training

Participation in the summer program will be based primarily on self-selection, but we will emphasize that those who do become involved should see themselves as full-time SDS cadre, willing to work intensively for the development of the summer collective.

In preparation for the summer, we will continue our program of movement schools which we've developed over the past few months in Michigan. This is a program which involves chapters in intensive weekends of study around questions such as racism, imperialism, and corporate power. This program will intensify as we come closer to this summer.

Furthermore, we will set up special training sessions in Detroit for those who plan to participate in the summer program. These special sessions will include resource people leading discussions on such topics as the history of labor struggles in Detroit, the role of law in society and legal rights, and the political economy of the city. These special sessions will concentrate on preparing people for the summer experience and will be attended by people from all over the state who are coming to Detroit.

Jobs

People involved in the program will try to get jobs in the city. They will be made aware of the job situation in Detroit and urged to seek employment where it will provide the best experiences. Participants will get jobs in bars, restaurants, taxicabs, and shops, as well as a few working out of day-labor slave markets. Women will be urged to work in jobs where the employment of women is high: specific factories, as secretaries, waitresses, maids. The selection of the job place should be done on the basis that it is preferential for our people to work where there are either a great number of young workers, or a great number of unskilled workers; a company union or no union, or where there is rank and file dissent or black caucuses, etc. This is to be done so that the people involved are involved in the most relevant political experiences and for the greatest possible time. The jobs will be necessary to maintain the summer program financially, as well as to provide practical experience necessary toward the concretization of our politics.

Study

Workable study groups will be organized which will help people develop political perspective and intellectual background. Study will include revolutionary theory and organization, the political economy of monopoly capitalism, the history and development of racism, the history of the labor movement, as well as more specific areas of study, like Vietnam, the Middle East, and Cuba. A major area of study, which will involve some original research, will be the translation of economic power into political power in the city of Detroit. Toward the end of the summer study groups will be tying together their intellectual and practical work and attempting to make specific plans for fall strategy. This will include some campus work as well as GI organizing, high schools, and some on-the-job work.

Skill-Building

The summer should provide an opportunity to develop much-needed skills that SDS people have had neither the time nor the organization to develop in the past. We will organize groups to learn self-defense skills, printing, propaganda, auto mechanics, and how to do research. More groups will develop depending on the needs and interests of those involved.

Life in the City

People will be living in small groups throughout the city. There should be involvement by SDS people in the neighborhood issues as they come up: a fight in the park, a protest against the pigs. Further, the group as a whole can anticipate certain issues it will become involved in. For instance, we're sure that we'll have to deal with racism in a number of concrete situations. Detroit, with its giant auto corporations and sprawling universities, has created one of the largest ghettos in the country. Detroit is also the home of a large Panther organization and other militant black groups. Working out a relationship with these groups and becoming involved in issues to fight racism will be of primary importance.

The labor situation in Detroit will, almost certainly, be in intensive turmoil this summer. The existence of militant black caucuses in auto [unions] (DRUM, FRUM, ELRUM, etc.) has created a tense situation for the corporations and union bureaucracies, and has provided an alternative for workers. Some people from the SDS project will be in shops as will organizers from Detroit's National Organizing Committee and will be relating to these struggles on a day-to-day basis. The project as a whole must work out ways to support the struggles of revolutionaries in the shops.

Some people, especially those who've been drafted or plan to enter the armed forces soon, will be working around Fort Wayne handing out *Vietnam GI* and *The Bond*. They will try to develop an understanding of GI problems that will be valuable in the future.

Others are planning to work with high school kids around the Grande ballroom, hippie capitalist center of Detroit. They hope to develop in these kids an understanding of the ways in which revolutionary rhetoric and hippie culture can be made into commodities by the capitalists.

There will of course be other types of involvement in community issues which we can't foresee. But with this amount of activity going on, it's clear that logistics and coordination are going to be a problem. We will try to have a large meeting weekly to keep people in touch with what overall things are going on, and to maintain a sense of the strength and dynamic of the group.

An important tension should develop in a program between the collective life and training among the SDS people and the political outreach into the community. It will be important to maintain this tension and each person should adjust to the duality. Merely living together and studying would promote isolation and elitism (the value of study undirected by practical political activity is also questionable). Merely working in the community without a self-conscious development of cadre skills and organizational training would promote an undirected activism and lack of concrete political development.

Clearly, an important part of the white movement's fight against white chauvinism is the propaganda effect of the very existence of whites who are on the side of the blacks against the system. This begins to show the masses of white working people that the struggle is a class and political struggle, not a racial struggle. Thus, open, overt, visible political activity of our movement in support of the black struggle must be prominent in our priorities for the summer. Yet we must also understand that this "action propaganda" is not a substitute for going among the working masses, learning directly what their experiences and ideas are about, and doing direct propaganda among them. To correctly balance these two needs will be a central task of our summer effort.

The whole program should be seen as a step towards a strong revolutionary youth movement in Michigan. It should not be seen as an attempt to organize all of Detroit. After the summer, many people will probably return to their campuses to continue on-going SDS work. Many will stay in Detroit to help build a strong movement there, and some will be going into the armed forces and other constituencies to begin work. That this program develop is of crucial importance for the advancement of all this work, and the development of these organizers.

4

The New Right

adicalism was not the only extreme ideology that flourished in the Sixties. The leftward surge of the decade found conservatism well entrenched among the public, the politicians, and the intellectual community. In fact, the revived left was in part a reaction against that conservative mood. Yet despite the shift, during the course of these turbulent Sixties years, the political and cultural left never ceased to be challenged by the defenders of conservative values.

From Plato on, there have, of course, been thinkers who despised both change and equality and concocted arguments to refute them. In America, there were Alexander Hamilton among the Founding Fathers, John C. Calhoun among antebellum politicians, James Fenimore Cooper among the writers, William Graham Sumner among the sociologists, and Irving Babbitt among the literary critics; they had all defended hierarchy and the status quo against democrats and apostles of progress. Yet all told, conservatism has been weakly represented in the American intellectual tradition. Before 1945, much of what passed for conservatism had been little more than a crude defense of wealth inequalities or a temperamental distrust of change.

The postwar era was different. The United States emerged from the flames of World War II with revived faith in its institutions. But if Americans felt renewed confidence, they also felt renewed challenges. With one enemy—fascism—defeated, another—Communism—seemed equally menacing.

Two groups on the right sought to inoculate America against dangers external and internal with a conservative ideology. The libertarian antitoxin glorified the autonomous individual. The great enemy was the state, and the highest good was personal freedom, even freedom to do dangerous, perverse things so long as they did not harm others. In their economic views, libertarians took as gospel Adam Smith's "invisible hand" of competing self-interest as maximizer of productivity and material well-being. In their view of society as a whole, they followed Charles Darwin's principle that progress comes only from the ruthless struggle for existence, and they concluded that social intervention to save individuals from their own mistakes and inadequacies was certain to produce more misery than good. In the short run, libertarians assumed constant flux, marked by much "creative destruction" with many winners and even more frequent losers.

Overlapping with but also disputing the libertarians were the traditionalists. These thinkers and activists prized human attachments over competition. In their view, the good society was organic, based on mutual respect and mutual obligations derived from generations of shared experience. People were not isolated individuals but members of communities with defined relationships, many of which predated capitalism and were based on values other than the mere pursuit of wealth. Traditionalists respected religion as the best guide to timeless principles and as a source of order and discipline in a potentially chaotic world, and they were not averse to imposing its values on the community. They invariably supported a traditional code of social and sexual behavior.

Both kinds of conservatives—the libertarian and the traditionalist— were elitists, skeptical of equality. Libertarians believed in equality of opportunity but acknowledged the inevitability of unequal outcomes since humans did not have equal capacities. Traditionalists were also certain that some humans were inherently inferior to others, and they often despised majoritarian democracy as rule of the incompetent mob. Their ideal society was hierarchical too, but they admired privilege based on tradition or moral authority more than privilege based on superior marketplace ruthlessness or sheer competitive skills.

Libertarianism made its major intellectual breakthrough with economist Friedrich Hayek's *The Road to Serfdom* (1944) attacking the "collectivism" of both right and left as the enemy of freedom and the source of totalitarianism. The book awakened and invigorated a class of thinkers and theorists who admired American capitalism and deplored the big-government trends of the previous generation. In later years, the outstanding spokesman of this group would be the University of Chicago economist Milton Friedman.

The postwar traditionalist revival was led by Russell Kirk, a sometime historian and academic strongly influenced by the romantic nostalgia of the 1920s Southern Agrarians and of Edmund Burke, the Anglo-Irish critic of the French Revolution. In 1953, Kirk published a compendious volume, *The Conservative Mind,* that sought to rescue the Western conservative tradition from claims that it was merely a vulgar defense of self-interest and unworthy of intellectual respect.

During the 1950s a surprisingly large public welcomed Hayek, Kirk, and a clutch of new conservative intellectuals. But it was William Buckley, a rich young man from Texas, who gave conservatism a national forum and a popular vernacular twist.

Buckley began his conservative career in 1951 with a powerful blast at his alma mater, Yale, as a fount of antireligious and collectivist thinking and teaching. *God and Man at Yale* scandalized the left and made the handsome, articulate young elitist a conservative celebrity. In 1955, he became editor of *The National Review,* which became the voice of conservatism of all varieties: libertarian, traditionalist, and anti-Communist.

As the Sixties drew to a close, a fresh conservative current emerged. Neoconservatism was the invention of former liberal-to-radical intellectuals who had applauded the exciting new left dissent when it first appeared. Its leaders—Irving Kristol, Nathan Glazer, Daniel Bell, Norman Podheretz, William Bennett, even Daniel Moynihan—had observed the growing anarchy of the inner cities and the campuses, feared for America's core institutions, and deplored the headlong drive to anarchy. In 1966, they established *The Public Interest,* which warned against lowering America's cold war guard, buying off ghetto radicals, and coddling student disrupters.

It would be a mistake to reduce the conservatism of the postwar era to a handful of intellectual positions. Conservatism, like its left counterparts, also drew on interests, prejudices, fears, and frustrations. In the country's South and West, the newly rich oil barons, ranchers, and lumber magnates embraced conservatism, especially of the libertarian variety, as a defense of their profits against a high-taxing, interventionist federal government. Pious Catholics and disillusioned former Marxists allied themselves with conservative positions as a way of opposing godless international Communism. Fundamentalist Protestants embraced conservatism because it repudiated the social permissiveness and immorality that seemed to be sweeping the country. Bigots South and North turned to the right as a way to defeat the drive to integration and racial equality.

During the Sixties, the intellectual dimensions of the movement having already been established, conservatives found much new fuel for outrage. The Great Society, the civil rights movement, and the Supreme Court's defenses of free speech, defendants' rights, personal privacy, and secularism helped to reinvigorate the political right. On the national stage, Governor George Wallace became the catch-basin for all the conservative fears, doubts, regrets, and yearnings of the decade. As governor of Alabama in 1963, Wallace had become a hero of the right when he defied the Kennedy administration's effort to desegregate the state university. Thereafter he was the beneficiary of a "backlash," an angry reaction to the supposed excessive leniency toward blacks, student militants, antiwar protesters, hippies, feminists, and criminals.

In 1964, Wallace decided to challenge President Johnson in the Democratic primaries. His surprising level of support in Maryland and Indiana made him a political presence in the Democratic Party and encouraged him to run on a separate ticket four years later, after Johnson renounced a second full term. The Wallace ticket faded badly in the stretch, but for a time, the former Alabama governor, capitalizing on resentments of the Sixties felt by millions, ran neck and neck with the unapologetic liberal, Johnson's vice president, Hubert Humphrey.

The defeat of Goldwater in 1964 and of Wallace four years later—and the narrow victory of Nixon in that 1968 presidential race—show that the conservative impulse still lagged. But clearly, as the Sixties wound down, the drive to turn back the political, social, and cultural clock was surging. By the end of the following decade, it would come into its own with the Moral Majority and Ronald Reagan. It is still with us today as the century staggers to a close.

Fundamentalist Conservatism

We think of the 1980s as the triumphant era of religious conservatism. It was in that decade that the Moral Majority burst on the scene with an agenda merging Christian fundamentalism and politics and in the process, one might say, put the fear of God into the liberals.

Of course, biblical fundamentalism predates the 1980s. In its modern version, it reaches back to the early part of the century, when a group of orthodox Protestant churches adopted as "fundamental" to Christian belief five dogmas: the Virgin birth, Christ's atonement for mankind, his Resurrection, the Second Coming, and the inerrancy of the Bible. During the 1920s, the fundamentalists sought to prevent the teaching of Darwinian evolution and suffered a serious setback when, at the famous "monkey trial" in Dayton, Tennessee, they were made to seem like ignorant rubes.

But fundamentalism never disappeared, and in the Sixties fire-and-brimstone preachers flourished throughout the rural Midwest and the South. Much of the time, they dwelt on salvation and personal sin, leaving so **98** *"social gospel" churches, which were especially active in th* *and the War on Poverty. At times, in fact, the fundame* *liberal colleagues for their social activism. Not all of them* *the public forum to the Protestant left. Especially on t* *Communism" and the all-powerful state, fundamentalists* *among God-fearing believers with passion and good effect, preparing the way for the breakthrough of the 1980s.*

This selection is from a 1966 talk by the popular preacher Billy James Hargis at the Anti-Communist Leadership School in Tulsa. During the 1950s, Hargis had been an ardent supporter of Senator Joseph McCarthy, the anti-Communist crusader. His Christian Crusade continued to fight the good fight into the next decade.

[*Billy James Hargis, "Political Planning for Victory over Communism," excerpted from George* Thayer, **The Farther Shores of Politics: The American Political Fringe Today** *(New York: Simon and Schuster, 1967), pp. 232–34.*]

POLITICAL PLANNING FOR VICTORY OVER COMMUNISM

I am a Christian conservative today because only conservatism in the United States espouses the philosophy of Christ. . . . The liberal churches today preach a social gospel. This is misnamed; it's really a socialist gospel. Or, in the common vernacular, they preach the gospel according to Martin Luther King instead of the gospel according to Matthew, Mark, Luke and John. . . .

I believe the Bible is inspired, I believe it's God's word, I believe in heaven and hell, I believe in God and Satan, I believe in right and wrong, I believe God *gave* us America, I believe America was God's greatest nation under the living Sun and the ideal of governments, and I believe the only hope to maintain freedom is this orthodox Christian traditionalist viewpoint. . . .

Then you have the anti-communists who say "I would rather be dead than Red" and I'm one of those that say that . . . I would rather see my children destroyed and *my* life destroyed, and my wife's life destroyed in a nuclear bombing, than the thought of them having to live under a communist slave state. This wouldn't be living, this would be hell on earth and death would be merciful! [shouts of *"Right!"* from the audience] . . .

Now my friends, if you don't think that . . . world government is the goal then you had better become convinced on that *one* point or you will not be an effective conservative because it all hinges on that. This is their goal: world government, as fantastic as it sounds. . . .

lived through liberalism since the days of Franklin Delano
velt and I have seen my country go bankrupt economically; and I've
n our churches become apostate; and I've seen our schools emphasize
internationalism instead of nationalism and even turn against the faith of
our fathers. I've seen this country in the name of progress become a bankrupt—morally and economically—republic and it's not even a republic any
longer. I'm afraid that we have the seeds of a dictatorship in Washington,
D.C., today, and I'm concerned and I have a *right* to be concerned and as
long as I live I will *express* that concern. . . .

As I have already told you in Ezekiel and Revelations both, the Anti-Christ
builds a world government and a world church. It's built on compromise
and appeasement; it's built on surrender of convictions, not on orthodoxy,
not on principles. . . . You don't achieve ecumenical unity without compromise and compromise is evil! . . . Internationalism, liberalism, welfare sta-
tism, Marxism, fascism, communism, Nazism are nothing but an attack
upon man's correct relationship with God. It is concealed atheism. . . .

Don't talk to me of liberalism! It is a double standard, Satanic hypocrisy! . . . The
only people that I ever met in my life that I think are worth knowing are
those little ol' Bible-believing Christian people who love the Lord and who
love America and they're willing even in their feeble way to the best of their
ability to give their lives to the defense of both. They're the only people I
want to know, and they're the ones I want to hold my hand as I walk
through the Valley of the Shadow of Death.

The Catholic Right

The National Review, *published by William Buckley, was a mainstay of the political right during the Sixties. It was a forum for many varieties of conservatism,
though Buckley drew the line at John Birchism, which he considered outrageous and
paranoid on the issue of Communist infiltration of the American government. But
if the journal emphasized one kind of conservatism over the others, it was Catholic
conservatism.*

Buckley himself was a devout Catholic, and many around him on the Review
*were as well. Though the journal sought a broad readership and avoided too close
an identification with sectarian Catholicism, its vision had a distinctive Catholic
cast. This focus could be detected in its reverence for Christian tradition and its rig-
orous anti-Communism.*

In the selection below, Frank S. Meyer, one of The National Review's *editors,
attacks* Commonweal, *a liberal Catholic journal, for failing to see that anti-
Communism was a "holy war" in which civilization itself was at stake. Meyer was a*

former Communist who repudiated his radical views and formulated for the Review
a conservative philosophy that combined a libertarian respect for freedom in the eco-
nomic and political realms with a Christian focus on virtue as the goal of society.

PRINCIPLES AND HERESIES

One thing the Liberal mind cannot stomach is the concept that some
things have greater values than others, that there can be among human
beings, nations, and civilizations a higher and a lower. So it was predictable
that when Brent Bozell, in "The Strange Drift of Liberal Catholicism"
(*National Review,* August 12), dared to say that Western civilization has a
unique and transcendent value, and that our war against Communism is a
holy war, Liberalism would rise in its wrath.

It is somewhat disconcerting, however, that the attack has been spear-
headed by a Liberal journal which is also a Catholic journal, *Commonweal,*
and that the attack has the content that it has. Were it not for that content, and for the further fact that the editors of *Commonweal* attack not
only the article but the "professional competence" of the editors of
National Review, the non-Catholics as well as the Catholic editors, "in dealing with the relation between Catholicism and socio-political matters," I
should leave the matter to Mr. Bozell, who is perfectly capable of defending himself and his article, and to my Catholic colleagues on the editorial board.

But the issue is wider. *Commonweal* not only challenged the several and
individual competencies of the editors of *National Review,* who strongly
approved of the article, whatever their faith; it drove a knife into the heart
of any man who, recognizing the fearful potentialities of modern warfare,
is nonetheless willing to stand up and fight for his country and his civilization. Obviously, the horrendous potentialities of nuclear warfare would give
pause to any sane man if all that were at stake between surrender and resistance were moderate preferences between one civilization and another,
varying shades of gray that held nothing approximating black and white.

But Communism, in actual and objective fact, does represent an
absolute black, and the West as a civilization is *in its essence* as close to an
absolute white as is possible in the subdued light which illuminates this
imperfect world. Sharp and vivid extremes do exist in reality, no matter
how much the Liberal and relativist mind strives to cloak the real presence
of glorious and desperate alternatives. As Brent Bozell wrote: "God is

involved in the Cold War; but more to the point: God's civilization is involved. The West makes this claim over against the rest of the world: that it has been vouchsafed the truth about the nature of man and his relationship to the universe, and has been commissioned to construct and preserve an earthly city based on this truth."

This statement it is which so scandalizes *Commonweal*. Blinding in its simple directness, it blazes upon the gimcrack structure of "if, and, and but," of "maybe and perhaps," of "everything is relative," behind which the Liberals take refuge from reality. So sharp a confrontation of good and evil is too painful for them. The West is nice, they concede, "of high merit and great value," and Communism is nasty; we are right to conduct "a continuing and unremitting opposition to Communism." But Heaven forbid that the issue be placed too sharply or too clearly: "To speak of the West as God's civilization is almost blasphemous. . . ." To assert that the West's war against Communism is a holy war is "to enlist God as the Supreme Commander of our natural forces [and] hopelessly to confuse the sacral and the secular order."

Of course, "to enlist God" for a human end would be immeasurably blasphemous; but what if God has enlisted us, through the heritage of our long history and His revelation of good and truth, to resist to the utmost, to bend our every energy to destroy, an incarnate evil? It is sad to have to remind Catholics, even Liberal Catholics, that this is a sacramental, not a Manichean world, that our secular actions as ordinary men partake of the sacred when we act with good faith and motive and grace towards truth and good.

With all the human imperfections that attended their wars, were the Crusaders who defended the West against the tide of Islam "hopelessly misguided," "almost blasphemous," as they fought for the Honor of God and for the West which carried that Honor and that Truth? We may be more historically sophisticated than they, but if we are not blinded by historical relativism, the essence of their understanding of the role of the West remains true of us—that, in Cardinal Newman's words, "this commonwealth [is] pre-eminently and emphatically human society, and its intellect the human mind, and its decisions the sense of mankind, and its disciplined and cultivated state civilization in the abstract. . . . [It is] the state also of that supernatural society and system which our Maker has given us directly from Himself, Christian Polity. . . ."

If to fight for this civilization with the belief that we do God's will is blasphemous, then not the Western but the Buddhist view of things of this world is true; they are but shadows to which no man should give a moment's allegiance. But this the West has always denied. Its Christian vision has seen this sentient world as reflecting and embodying, however imperfectly, issues of transcendent significance.

It is only this understanding that can strengthen and justify us against the hazards of these fearful times. *Commonweal* may raise its hands in horror if we see a divine sanction for our mission; the patriots of the early Republic had a more profound view of the relations between things divine and human:

"Then conquer we must,
For our cause it is just,—
And this be our motto,—
In God is our trust!"

Barry Goldwater

If William Buckley and the National Review *circle were the brains of the Sixties conservative movement, Senator Barry Goldwater of Arizona was its sinews. Goldwater was an uncomplicated man, with few new ideas of his own. He was also an honest and principled man, less willing than most politicians to trim his sails to the winds of popularity. Viewed with horror by many moderates during the Sixties, he would eventually win the respect and even affection of the broad American public after he retired from active politics.*

Goldwater came from an interesting background. His grandfather was a Jewish immigrant from Poland whose son, Baron Goldwater, established a successful department store in Phoenix in 1896. Baron married a Protestant woman and their first son, named Barry, was born in 1909. Barry was raised as an Episcopalian but could not be thought of as a traditional Wasp with roots running back to the colonial era.

Goldwater's conservatism derived from a combination of experiences. Rugged individualism came naturally to a young man born in the Great Basin West with its freewheeling cowboy-rancher traditions and mythology. As an air corps officer during the Second World War, moreover, he learned patriotism and respect for hierarchy and authority. Both influences were reflected in his dress. Goldwater was as likely to wear cowboy boots and a Stetson, or his air force reserve general's uniform, as an ordinary business suit.

Elected to the Senate in 1952, he offended most liberals. But he quickly became the favorite of the emerging new right, especially its western and southern wing. To the ranchers, miner owners, and timber and oil barons of the mountain states and West Coast, his stands against intrusive government resource regulation were appealing. Southern conservatives liked his skeptical views of federal civil rights initiatives. Both groups found him preferable to traditional conservative Robert Taft, the dour patrician senator from Ohio, whose father had been both president and chief justice of the Supreme Court. Goldwater was quickly embraced by the new conservative intellectuals, who were thrilled to have a disciple among potential presidential candidates.

In 1960, Goldwater published his testament, The Conscience of a Conservative, *which was actually written by L. Brent Bozell, brother-in-law of William Buckley. It became a guidebook for the faithful and helped keep Goldwater's name before the public. In 1964, the Goldwater wing of the Republican Party, using hardball tactics that outraged the more sedate party moderates and liberals, captured the Republican presidential nomination for their favorite. The Goldwater candidacy was probably doomed in any case. Lyndon Johnson, still reflecting the glow of his martyred predecessor, was unbeatable. Yet the Republican candidate seemed seized by a death wish. In his acceptance speech at the convention, he defended "extremism"—if in "defense of liberty"— and confirmed his opponents' demonic image of him as a trigger-happy warmonger and an intransigent reactionary who would turn back the clock to William McKinley's day. Millions of Republican centrists deserted him to vote for LBJ. In the end, the Arizona senator got the smallest proportion of the popular vote of any major candidate in history and carried only six states—five in the deep South, plus his native Arizona.*

Obviously, the mid-Sixties were not prime time for the political right in America. Yet Goldwater and his followers had blazed a trail that others would follow more successfully in later years.

THE CONSCIENCE OF A CONSERVATIVE

I have been much concerned that so many people today with Conservative instincts feel compelled to apologize for them. Or if not to apologize directly, to qualify their commitment in a way that amounts to breast-beating. "Republican candidates," Vice President Nixon has said, "should be economic conservatives, but conservatives with a heart." President Eisenhower announced during his first term, "I am conservative when it comes to economic problems but liberal when it comes to human problems." Still other Republican leaders have insisted on calling themselves "progressive" Conservatives. These formulations are tantamount to an admission that Conservatism is a narrow, mechanistic *economic* theory that may work very well as a bookkeeper's guide, but cannot be relied upon as a comprehensive political philosophy.

The same judgment, though in the form of an attack rather than an admission, is advanced by the radical camp. "We liberals," they say, "are interested in *people.* Our concern is with human beings, while you Conservatives are preoccupied with the preservation of economic privilege and status." Take them a step further, and the Liberals will turn the accusations into a class argument: it is the little people that concern us, not the "malefactors of great wealth."

Such statements, from friend and foe alike, do great injustice to the Conservative point of view. Conservatism is *not* an economic theory, though it has economic implications. The shoe is precisely on the other foot: it is Socialism that subordinates all other considerations to man's material well-being. It is Conservatism that puts material things in their proper place— that has a structured view of the human being and of human society, in which economics plays only a subsidiary role.

The root difference between the Conservatives and the Liberals of today is that Conservatives take account of the *whole* man, while the Liberals tend to look only at the material side of man's nature. The Conservative believes that man is, in part, an economic, an animal creature; but that he is also a spiritual creature with spiritual needs and spiritual desires. What is more, these needs and desires reflect the *superior* side of man's nature, and thus take precedence over his economic wants. Conservatism therefore looks upon the enhancement of man's spiritual nature as the primary concern of political philosophy. Liberals, on the other hand—in the name of a concern for "human beings"—regard the satisfaction of economic wants as the dominant mission of society. They are, moreover, in a hurry. So that their characteristic approach is to harness the society's political and economic forces into a collective effort to *compel* "progress." In this approach, I believe they fight against Nature.

Surely the first obligation of a political thinker is to understand the nature of man. The Conservative does not claim special powers of perception on this point, but he does claim a familiarity with the accumulated wisdom and experience of history, and he is not too proud to learn from the great minds of the past.

The first thing he has learned about man is that each member of the species is a unique creature. Man's most sacred possession is his individual soul—which has an immortal side, but also a mortal one. The mortal side establishes his absolute differentness from every other human being. *Only a philosophy that takes into account the essential differences between men, and, accordingly, makes provision for developing the different potentialities of each man can claim to be in accord with Nature.* We have heard much in our time about "the common man." It is a concept that pays little attention to the history of a nation that grew great through the initiative and ambition of uncommon men. The Conservative knows that to regard man as part of an undifferentiated mass is to consign him to ultimate slavery.

Secondly, the Conservative has learned that the economic and spiritual aspects of man's nature are inextricably intertwined. He cannot be economically free, or even economically efficient, if he is enslaved politically; conversely, man's political freedom is illusory if he is dependent for his economic needs on the State.

The Conservative realizes, thirdly, that man's development, in both its spiritual and material aspects, is not something that can be directed by outside forces. Every man, for his individual good and for the good of his society, is responsible for his *own* development. The choices that govern his life are choices that *he* must make: they cannot be made by any other human being, or by a collectivity of human beings. If the Conservative is less anxious than his Liberal brethren to increase Social Security "benefits," it is because he is more anxious than his Liberal brethren that people be free throughout their lives to spend their earnings when and as they see fit.

So it is that Conservatism, throughout history, has regarded man neither as a potential pawn of other men, nor as a part of a general collectivity in which the sacredness and the separate identity of individual human beings are ignored. Throughout history, true Conservatism has been at war equally with autocrats and with "democratic" Jacobins. The true Conservative was sympathetic with the plight of the hapless peasant under the tyranny of the French monarchy. And he was equally revolted at the attempt to solve that problem by a mob tyranny that paraded under the banner of egalitarianism. The conscience of the Conservative is pricked by *anyone* who would debase the dignity of the individual human being. Today, therefore, he is at odds with dictators who rule by terror, and equally with those gentler collectivists who ask our permission to play God with the human race.

With this view of the nature of man, it is understandable that the Conservative looks upon politics as the art of achieving the maximum amount of freedom for individuals that is consistent with the maintenance of social order. The Conservative is the first to understand that the practice of freedom requires the establishment of order: it is impossible for one man to be free if another is able to deny him the exercise of his freedom. But the Conservative also recognizes that the political power on which order is based is a self-aggrandizing force; that its appetite grows with eating. He knows that the utmost vigilance and care are required to keep political power within its proper bounds.

In our day, order is pretty well taken care of. The delicate balance that ideally exists between freedom and order has long since tipped against freedom practically everywhere on earth. In some countries, freedom is altogether down and order holds absolute sway. In our country the trend is less far advanced, but it is well along and gathering momentum every day. Thus, for the American Conservative, there is no difficulty in identifying the day's overriding political challenge: it is *to preserve and extend freedom*. As he surveys the various attitudes and institutions and laws that currently prevail in America, many questions will occur to him, but the Conservative's first concern will always be: *Are we maximizing freedom?* I suggest we examine some of the critical issues facing us today with this question in mind.

Young Americans for Freedom

Formed in the fall of 1960 at a meeting held on the Connecticut estate of William Buckley, editor of The National Review, *Young Americans for Freedom (YAF) reflected the growing élan and intellectual respectability of American conservative thought.*

The Sharon Statement, YAF's founding manifesto, expressed a particular kind of conservatism. Its targets were big government and restrictions on freedom, especially in the economic realm. It also reaffirmed the aggressive anti-Communism of the Buckley circle. It says nothing about "family values," or obscenity, or "right to life." Clearly, it took the unsettling experience of the decade just beginning, plus its extensions through the 1970s, to change the focus of the conservative agenda.

THE SHARON STATEMENT

*Adopted by the Young Americans for Freedom
in conference at Sharon, Conn., September 9–11, 1960*

In this time of moral and political crisis, it is the responsibility of the youth of America to affirm certain eternal truths.

We, as young conservatives, believe:

That foremost among the transcendent values is the individual's use of his God-given free will, whence derives his right to be free from the restrictions of arbitrary force;

That liberty is indivisible, and that political freedom cannot long exist without economic freedom;

That the purposes of government are to protect these freedoms through the preservation of internal order, the provision of national defense, and the administration of justice;

That when government ventures beyond these rightful functions, it accumulates power which tends to diminish order and liberty;

That the Constitution of the United States is the best arrangement yet devised for empowering government to fulfill its proper role, while restraining it from the concentration and abuse of power;

That the genius of the Constitution—the division of powers—is summed up in the clause which reserves primacy to the several states, or to the people, in those spheres not specifically delegated to the Federal Government;

That the market economy, allocating resources by the free play of supply and demand, is the single economic system compatible with the requirements of personal freedom and constitutional government, and that it is at the same time the most productive supplier of human needs;

That when government interferes with the work of the market economy, it tends to reduce the moral and physical strength of the nation; that when it takes from one man to bestow on another, it diminishes the incentive of the first, the integrity of the second, and the moral autonomy of both;

That we will be free only so long as the national sovereignty of the United States is secure; that history shows periods of freedom are rare, and can exist only when free citizens concertedly defend their rights against all enemies;

That the forces of international Communism are, at present, the greatest single threat to these liberties;

That the United States should stress victory over, rather than coexistence with, this menace; and

That American foreign policy must be judged by this criterion: does it serve the just interests of the United States?

THE IVORY TOWER

A new organization was born last week, and just possibly it will influence the political future of this country, as why should it not, considering that its membership is young, intelligent, articulate, and determined, its principles enduring, its aim to translate these principles into political action in a world which has lost its moorings and is looking about for them desperately?

One wonders why an organized conservative political youth movement was not begun before, so naturally does it fit, now that it is on the scene, and so plain is the need for it. It could be that the nonexistence of such an organization ten years ago is fortunate, for it might have piled on the rocks. It is only in the last decade that American conservatism has been freed from the exclusive hold which the narrow dogmas of vested business interests had upon it. The National Association of Manufacturers is a splendid organization that has accomplished a great deal of good; but it is wrong to suppose that it was ever equipped to generate a *Weltanschauung* which could galvanize the intellectual, creative, and moral energies of students who had been indoctrinated over thirty years by their teachers to believe that conservatism was merely a highbrow word for the profit system—that there was nothing in conservatism beyond the vaults of the Chase National Bank.

The Young Americans for Freedom have the benefit of perspectives which ten years ago could only have been intuited. In ten years much has happened. History proved the irrelevance of liberal doctrine. The critique of liberalism has been made, if not definitively, at least sufficiently; and it is a total critique. The word *conservatism* is accepted both by Russell Kirk and Frank Meyer as designating their distinct but complementary, even symbiotic positions. In the last ten years more important books have been written than there is time here to catalogue, books of journalistic, philosophical, economic, historical, and cultural import—all of them concentrically pointing an accusing finger at the tottering idols of liberalism. The great renewal of the last decade is reflected in the nuances in the Young Americans' statement of first principles. . . . Here is mention of the moral aspect of freedom; of transcendent values; of the nature of man. All this together with a tough-as-nails statement of political and economic convictions which Richard Nixon couldn't read aloud without fainting.

• • •

The students were called to the founding conference in Sharon, Connecticut, by Douglas Caddy, until recently a student at Georgetown University, now with the McGraw-Edison Committee for Public Affairs in New York. Ninety students turned up from 24 states, representing 44 colleges. The age limits for members were set in the original draft of the bylaws at between 16 and 28; but the conference overruled the committee and with a low bow to the achievements of geriatrics, moved the old age limit up to 35 and made at least this bystander feel young again. Caddy was elected National Director, and all inquiries should be addressed to him at 343 Lexington Avenue, New York 16, N. Y. Enclose a dollar bill, if you want to help with the cost of setting the organization up. Robert

Schuchman of the Yale Law School is chairman. There are six regional directors. In the Northeast it is Walter McLaughlin, Jr., of the Harvard Law School. For the Central Atlantic states, Robert Harley of Georgetown University. For the South, George Gaines of Tulane University. For the West, Dick Noble of Stanford University. For the Southwest, Jim Kolbe of Northwestern University, and for the Midwest, Robert Croll, also of Northwestern University. The twelve members of the Board of Directors are David Franke (New School for Social Research), Richard Cowan (Yale), Tom Colvin (Davidson), Carol Dawson (Washington, D.C.), Carl McIntire (Shelton), Bill Madden (Holy Cross), William Schulz (Antioch), James Abstine (Indiana), Howard Phillips (Harvard), Scott Stanley, Jr. (University of Kansas Law School), Lee Edwards (press assistant to Senator John Marshall Butler), and Herbert Kohler (Knox).

•　　•　　•

What will the Young Americans for Freedom do? What did the Young Socialists do? What do the Students for Industrial Democracy do? The American Youth for Democracy? The Students for Democratic Action? The left never lacked for things to do; neither does the right. Every chapter of YAF in every college will shape a program rooted in the principal concerns of its own campus; except that no one will be accepted as a member who does not endorse the Sharon Statement. There will be annual meetings. Perhaps they will find the funds to publish a newsletter. They will have the help of the Intercollegiate Society of Individualists, a nonpolitical organization whose aim it is to advance an understanding of freedom at the college level.

But what is so striking in the students who met at Sharon is their appetite for power. Ten years ago the struggle seemed so long, so endless, even, that we did not even dream of victory. Even now the world continues to go left, but all over the land dumbfounded professors are remarking the extraordinary revival of hard conservative sentiment in the student bodies. It was Goldwater, not Nixon or Eisenhower, who was the hero of the bright and dominant youth forces at the Chicago Convention. It is quixotic to say that they or their elders have seized the reins of history. But the difference in psychological attitude is tremendous. They talk about *affecting* history; we have talked about *educating* people to want to affect history. It may be that, as Russell Kirk keeps reminding us, the Struggle Availeth. No one would doubt it who talked to the founding fathers of the Young Americans for Freedom.

Ayn Rand's "Objectivism"

Ayn Rand was an extraordinary figure in American intellectual life. Born in Russia in 1905, she stayed long enough in her native country to experience the triumph of Bolshevism. In 1926, she escaped from the Soviet Union and emigrated to the United States, where she lived the rest of her life.

For a number of years she worked in Hollywood as script reader, wardrobe girl, and screenwriter. In 1943, she published The Fountainhead, *a novel that became a colossal best-seller and brought her fame and a forum for her ideas.*

Rand was a radical individualist who believed egoism to be a supreme good. She was not afraid to glorify selfishness, for she believed it a virtue, not a vice. Her chief enemy was "collectivism" of all sorts. This included the collectivism of the socialists and of those near-socialists, the big-government liberals. But it also included the traditional conservatives, those who glorified an "organic" society, what the Germans referred to as Gemeinschaft, *a social system closely knit by common origins and shared values. These conservatives she viewed as worshipers of irrationality epitomized by mysticism and traditional Christian piety. She herself was a daughter of the rationalist Enlightenment of the eighteenth century and denied the existence of God. She also thought the traditionalist conservatives were all too often "soft on altruism," a quality she considered as dubious as collectivism. In 1957, she perfected her views in* Atlas Shrugged, *a 1,168-page brief in the form of a novel.*

In this selection, Rand describes Objectivism, as she calls her uncompromising version of political and economic laissez-faire. In the Sixties these views seemed totally obscurantist and reactionary. They would remain poised beneath the surface, however, waiting to come to the top in the great 1980s conservative surge.

[*"Collectivized Ethics, pp. 93–99,"* from **The Virtue of Selfishness** *by Ayn Rand. Copyright ©* *1961, 1964 by Ayn Rand. Used by permission of Dutton Signet, a division of Penguin Putnam, Inc.*]

COLLECTIVIZED ETHICS

Certain questions which one frequently hears are not philosophical queries, but psychological confessions. This is particularly true in the field of ethics. It is especially in the discussions of ethics that one must check one's premises (or remember them) and more: one must learn to check the premises of one's adversaries.

For instance. Objectivists will often hear a question such as: "What will be done about the poor or the handicapped in a free society?"

The altruist-collectivist premise, implicit in that question, is that men are "their brothers' keepers" and that the misfortune of some is a mortgage on others. The questioner is ignoring or evading the basic premises of Objectivist ethics and is attempting to switch the discussion on to his own collectivist base. Observe that he does not ask: "*Should* anything be done?" but: "*What* will be done?"—as if the collectivist premise had been tacitly accepted and all that remains is a discussion of the means to implement it.

Once, when Barbara Branden* was asked by a student: "What will happen to the poor in an Objectivist society?—she answered: "If *you* want to help them, you will not be stopped."

This is the essence of the whole issue and a perfect example of how one refuses to accept an adversary's premises as the basis of discussion.

Only individual men have the right to decide when or whether they wish to help others; society—as an organized political system—has no rights in the matter at all.

On the question of when and under what conditions is it morally proper for an individual to help others, I refer you to Galt's speech in *Atlas Shrugged.*† What concerns us here is the collectivist premise of regarding this issue as political, as the problem or the duty of "society as a whole."

Since nature does not guarantee automatic security, success, and survival to any human being, it is only the dictatorial presumptuousness and the moral cannibalism of the altruistic-collectivist code that permits man to suppose . . . that *he* can somehow guarantee such security to some men at the expense of others.

If a man speculates on what "society" should do for the poor, he accepts thereby the collectivist premise that men's lives belong to society and that *he,* as a member of society, has the right to dispose of them, to set their goals or to plan the "distribution" of their efforts.

This is the psychological confession implied in such questions and in many issues of the same kind.

At best, it reveals a man's psycho-epistemological chaos. . . . More often, however, that psychological confession reveals a deeper evil: it reveals the enormity of the extent to which altruism erodes men's capacity to grasp the concept of *rights* or the value of an individual life; it reveals a mind from which the reality of a human being has been wiped out.

---

*Barbara Branden was the wife of a prominent disciple and lieutenant of Rand's, Nathaniel Branden—ed.

†John Galt is the hero of Rand's 1957 novel *Atlas Shrugged,* which describes a global strike of the world's creative people against the existing order when they become fed up with the burdens imposed on them by their inferiors in the name of altruism. His credo insists that helping sufferers is only legitimate if the beneficiaries have been unjustly victimized and if they are worthy of help—ed.

Humility and presumptuousness are always two sides of the same premise and always share the task of filling the space vacated by self-esteem in a collectivized mentality. The man who is willing to serve as a means to the ends of others will necessarily regard others as the means to *his* ends. The more neurotic he is or the more conscientious in the practice of altruism . . . , the more he will tend to devise schemes "for the good of mankind" or of "society" or of "the public" or of "future generations"—or of anything except actual human beings.

Hence the appalling recklessness with which men propose, discuss, and accept "humanitarian" projects which are to be imposed by political means, that is, *by force,* on an unlimited number of human beings. If, according to collectivist caricatures, the greedy rich indulged in profligate material luxury, on the premise of "price no object"—then the social progress brought by today's collectivized mentalities consists of indulging in altruistic political planning, on the premise of "human lives no object."

The hallmark of such mentalities is the advocacy of some grand scale *public* goal, without regard to context, costs, or means. *Out of context,* such a goal can usually be shown to be desirable; it has to be public, because the *costs* are not to be earned but to be expropriated; and a dense patch of venomous fog has to shroud the issue of *means*—because the means are to be *human lives.*

"Medicare" is an example of such a project. "Isn't it desirable that the aged should have medical care in times of illness?" its advocates clamor. Considered out of context, the answer would be: yes, it is desirable. Who would have a reason to say no? And it is at this point that the mental processes of a collectivized brain are cut off; the rest is fog. Only the *desire* remains in his sight—it's the good, isn't it?—it's not for myself, it's for others, it's for the public, for the helpless, ailing public. . . . The fog hides such facts as the enslavement and, therefore, the destruction of medical science and disintegration of all medical practice, and the sacrifice of the professional integrity, the freedom, the careers, the ambitions, the achievements, the happiness, the *lives* of the very men who are to provide that "desirable" goal—the doctors. . . .

It is men's views of the public or *political* existence that the collectivized ethics of altruism has protected from the march of civilization and has preserved as a reservoir, a wildlife sanctuary, ruled by the mores of prehistoric savages. If men have grasped some faint glimmer of respect for individual rights in their private dealings with one another, that glimmer vanishes when they turn to public issues—and what leaps into the political arena is a cave man who can't conceive of any reason why the tribe may not bash in the skull of any individual if it so desires.

The distinguishing characteristic of such tribal mentality is: the axiomatic, the almost "instinctive" view of human life as the fodder, fuel, or means for every public project.

The examples of such projects are innumerable: "Isn't it desirable to clean up the slums?" (Dropping the context of what happens to those in the next income bracket)—"Isn't it desirable to have beautiful, planned cities, all of one harmonious style?" (Dropping the context of *whose* choice of style is to be forced on the home builders)—"Isn't it desirable to have an educated public?" (Dropping the context of *who* will do the educating, *what* will be taught, and *what* will happen to dissenters)—"Isn't it desirable to liberate the artists, the writers, and the composers from the burden of financial problems and leave them free to create?"—(Dropping the context of *which* artists, writers, and composers?—chosen by whom?—at whose expense?—at the expense of the artists, writers, and composers who have no political pull and whose miserably precarious incomes will be taxed to "liberate" that privileged elite?)—"Isn't *science* desirable? Isn't it desirable for man to conquer space?"

And here we come to the essence of the unreality—the savage, blind, ghastly unreality—that motivates a collectivized soul.

The unanswered and unanswerable in all of their "desirable" goals is: To *whom?* Desires and goals presuppose *beneficiaries*. Is science desirable? To *whom?* Not to the Soviet serfs who die of epidemics, filth, starvation, terror, and firing squads—while some bright young men wave to them from space capsules circling over their human pigsties. And not to the American father who died of heart failure brought on by overwork, struggling to send his son through college—or to the boy who could not afford college—or to the couple killed in an automobile wreck, because they could not afford a new car—or to the mother who lost her child because she could not afford to send him to the best hospital—not to any of these people whose taxes pay for the support of our subsidized science and *public* research projects.

Science is a value only because it expands, enriches, and protects man's life. It is not a value outside that context. Nothing is a value outside that context. And "man's life" means the single, specific, irreplaceable lives of individual men.

The discovery of new knowledge is a value to men only when and if they are free to use and enjoy the benefits of the previously known. New discoveries are a *potential* value to all men, but *not* at the price of sacrificing all of their *actual* values. A "progress" extended into infinity, which brings no benefit to anyone, is a monstrous absurdity. And so is the "conquest of space" by some men, when and if it is accomplished by expropriating the labor of other men who are left without means to acquire a pair of shoes.

Progress can come only out of men's surplus, that is: from the work of those men whose ability produces more than their personal consumption requires, those who are intellectually and financially able to venture out in pursuit of the new. Capitalism is the only system where such men are free to function and where progress is accompanied, not by forced privations, but by a constant rise in the general level of prosperity, of consumption and of enjoyment of life.

It is only to the frozen unreality inside a collectivized mind that human lives are interchangeable—and only such a brain can contemplate as "moral" or "desirable" the sacrifice of generations of living men for the alleged benefits which *public* science or *public* industry or *public* concerts will bring to the unborn.

Soviet Russia is the clearest, but not the only, illustration of the achievements of collectivized mentalities. Two generations of Russians have lived, toiled, and died in misery, waiting for the abundance promised by their rulers, who pleaded for patience and commanded austerity, while building public "industrialization" and killing public hope in five-year installments. At first, the people starved while waiting for electric generators and tractors; they are still starving, while waiting for atomic energy and interplanetary travel.

That waiting has no end—the unborn profiteers of that wholesale sacrificial slaughter will never be born—the sacrificial animals will merely breed new hordes of sacrificial animals—as the history of all tyrannies has demonstrated—while the unfocused eyes of a civilized brain will stare on, undeterred, and speak of a vision of service to mankind, mixing interchangeably the corpses of the present with the ghosts of the future, but seeing no *men*.

All public projects are mausoleums, not always in shape, but always in cost.

The next time you encounter one of those "public-spirited" dreamers who tells you rancorously that "some very desirable goals cannot be achieved without *everybody's* participation," tell him that if he cannot obtain everybody's *voluntary* participation, his goals had jolly well better remain unachieved—and that men's lives are not his to dispose of.

And, if you wish, give him the following example of the ideals he advocates. It is medically possible to take the corneas of a man's eyes immediately after his death and transplant them to the eyes of a living man who is blind, thus restoring his sight (in certain types of blindness). Now, according to collectivized ethics, this poses a social problem. Should we wait until a man's death to cut out his eyes, when other men need them? Should we regard everybody's eyes as public property and devise a "fair method of distribution"? Would you advocate cutting out a living man's eyes and giving them to a blind man, so as to "equalize" them? No? Then don't struggle any further with questions about "public projects" in a free society. You know the answer. The principle is the same.

5

The Civil Rights Movement

The struggle against black oppression and inequality in America goes back to the earliest days of modern Western slavery, when the first African bondsman refused to obey the order of a white master. The abolitionist movement before the Civil War was the ultimately successful effort, by blacks and whites alike, to destroy the "peculiar institution," the very basis of exploitation and servitude. After emancipation in 1863, former slaves, allied with white Radical Republicans, struggled to achieve legal equality in the ex-Confederate states. They failed, and by the 1880s Southern black leaders, personified by Booker T. Washington, accepted a compromise that accepted legal segregation ("Jim Crow") and disfranchisement in the South in exchange for a minimum of economic opportunity.

During the opening years of the twentieth century, the civil rights movement took a more militant turn when W. E. B. Du Bois and a group of northern-born black professionals rejected the accommodationist views of Washington and once more insisted that black Americans be granted full and equal citizenship. In 1909, blacks and white liberals joined to create the National Association for the Advancement of Colored People (NAACP) as a weapon against the oppressive racial regimes of both sections.

Meanwhile, demography was transforming the race issue. To the end of the nineteenth century, the great majority of blacks had been rural southerners, often tied to the sharecrop system of the cotton belt. Beginning in the early years of the new century and accelerating in the 1920s, thousands of black men and women moved to the commercial-industrial cities of the North. There they found legal equality and improved economic and professional opportunity, but nonetheless encountered discrimination in jobs, housing, and social relations. Most middle class blacks during this period were assimilationists who sought racial justice through an integrated society. Many working-class blacks of the northern ghettos, however, were attracted to the black nationalism and separatism purveyed by Marcus Garvey, a Jamaican immigrant.

The 1930s were especially hard years for black Americans. Less securely entrenched in industry, trade, and the professions than whites, they were often the first to be fired as the Great Depression settled over the land. In the South, the collapse of farm prices made the plight of black sharecroppers even worse. Fortunately, African Americans benefited from new federal welfare programs that, for the first time, were often applied without regard for race. Wherever they could vote, they repaid Franklin Roosevelt and his party by shifting from their traditional Republican political allegiance.

World War II was a watershed in American race relations. For some time, academic anthropologists and sociologists had been teaching the primacy of environment over heredity and the mental and moral equality of the races. Hatred of Nazism and its lethal racism, and the need to achieve national unity for the sake of victory reinforced egalitarian ideals. After 1945, thousands of black service men and women returned home determined to tear down the remaining structures of discrimination.

In the late 1940s and early 1950s, the chief engine of racial change was the NAACP's Legal Defense and Education Fund, which successfully challenged in the courts the Jim Crow higher-education systems of the South. In 1954, its attack on segregated public schools produced a unanimous landmark decision by the Warren Supreme Court. *Brown v. Board of Education of Topeka* swept aside *Plessy v. Feguson,* the 1896 decision that declared segregation to be legal under the Constitution if the accommodations for both races were equal.

The *Brown* decision marked the beginning of the modern civil rights movement. The Court had removed the legal foundation of racial separation in the schools, but there was still the difficult task of enforcing compliance with *Brown* against the growing resistance by southern state officials and vigilante groups such as the Ku Klux Klan and the White Citizens' Councils. Segregation remained embedded, moreover, in many other aspects of southern life besides education—in transportation, parks, playgrounds, and public services generally, as well as in jobs and housing. Nor had *Brown* remedied the disfranchisement of black voters. As of the mid-1950s, few if any blacks in large parts of the South could evade the hurdles to voting—poll taxes, literacy tests, and plain intimidation—erected by local and state officials.

In the decade following *Brown,* the civil rights army of white and black activists continued to challenge the Jim Crow system in the courts and constantly increased the pressure on Congress and the Kennedy and Johnson administrations for new, tougher civil rights and voting rights legislation. Increasingly, they employed civil disobedience tactics—sit-ins, traffic disruptions, building occupations, illegal marches—to goad the authorities into action. The approach counted on the overreaction of local authorities to offend public opinion and compel federal intervention.

For most of the period, the leader of the movement was the black Baptist clergyman Dr. Martin Luther King, Jr. A learned man with advanced degrees in theology and philosophy, King possessed eloquence and courage that gave extraordinary impetus to civil rights. He came to the forefront of the movement in 1955–56 when, as the young pastor of Montgomery's Dexter Avenue Baptist Church, he led the black community in a successful boycott of the city's Jim Crow bus system. In 1957, he founded the Southern Christian Leadership Conference (SCLC), which soon took the lead in organizing civil disobedience demonstrations all over the South, targeting police brutality, segregation, and denial of voting rights. King's tactics and goals were reinforced in February 1960, when black students from the North Carolina Agricultural and Technical College at Greensboro sat down at the segregated lunch counter of a local Woolworth's and asked to be served. Abused and berated by white customers and employees and denied service, they persisted, and their brave example inspired sit-ins all through the South and boycotts of five-and-dime chains near scores of liberal northern campuses. The sit-in movement soon evolved into the Student Non-Violent Coordinating Committee (SNCC), which formally affiliated with King's SCLC.

King's goal was a color-blind society where race no longer counted and everyone was judged by merit. Many whites found his message of racial cooperation and his tactics of nonviolent civil disobedience appealing and nonthreatening, and they supplied much of the money for his movement and some of the personnel for his demonstrations. This phase of the civil rights campaign culminated in the dazzling August 1963 March on Washington for Jobs and Freedom, where over 250,000 people, a third of them white, gathered to demand that Congress pass legislation to advance racial equality. At the end of the day the marchers heard King's soaring speech "I Have a Dream," calling for "a beautiful symphony of brotherhood."

In the next two years, Congress enacted two measures that brought full citizenship to southern blacks. The Civil Rights Act of 1964 barred all discrimination in public accommodations and employment. The Voting

Rights Act the next year eliminated many of the devices that southern officials had used to prevent blacks from voting. Much remained to end the
informal racial discrimination that could hide behind personal preferences, but Jim Crow and disfranchisement were soon both dead.

Until mid-decade, the SCLC and its philosophy were the core of the civil
rights movement. But as gains in public access and voting left behind the
more intractable problems of inadequate housing, poor education, and
low incomes, more militant groups challenged King and his disciples.
Going to an integrated school or casting a ballot for mayor or senator often
seemed hollow to those who could not get a decent job or afford to pay a
reasonable rent for a livable apartment.

After 1966, King and the SCLC were challenged by the Congress of
Racial Equality (CORE), by the Nation of Islam (Black Muslims), by the
Black Panthers, and by SCLC's own newly militant auxiliary, SNCC. These
groups differed from one another in points of philosophy and tactics, but
all of them rejected white members, and all but the Panthers refused to
make alliances with white liberals or radicals. All, moreover, appealed to
black pride and at least flirted with reverse racism. They derided King's
nonviolence and replaced his message of forgiveness with militant, even
incendiary rhetoric. This new approach, called Black Power, threatened
many white citizens.

King deplored black separatism and antiwhite attitudes but understood
the anger of the firebrands. He had to harness it or find himself reduced
to an irrelevant has-been. Even more difficult to contain and channel was
the nihilistic violence of the black inner cities. Starting in 1965, in the
Watts district of Los Angeles, each summer for three years, the nation's
black urban neighborhoods exploded in spasms of rage and destruction.
Civil rights leaders and white liberals asked the public to understand the
rioters' frustrations if not their actions. But many white citizens resented
the descent into arson, looting, and violence.

In 1966, King moved his campaign to Chicago, where his new targets
were job discrimination and housing segregation. There he hit a brick wall.
Suburban Chicago homeowners were more ferociously hostile to having
black neighbors than southern white parents had been to admitting black
students to all-white schools. King's march through Marquette Park was
greeted with obscenities and flying rocks and bottles. In the end, he left
Chicago with little besides some empty promises from the mayor, the landlords, and the real estate agents to fight housing discrimination.

Meanwhile, the civil rights left flank was plunging ever deeper into
angry, self-destructive behavior. In 1966, CORE and SNCC replaced their

moderate leaders with Black Power advocates Floyd McKissick and Stokely Carmichael and expelled all their white members. That same year, the Panthers, organized in Oakland originally to monitor police brutality, began to parade on the streets wearing menacing paramilitary uniforms and carrying rifles. In 1967, the Black Power Conference in Newark denounced Zionism as imperialism, thus offending Jewish liberals. The rhetoric of the newer groups became ever more intimidating. That July, H. Rap Brown of SNCC announced that "if America don't come around we're going to burn it down."

King refused to go along with this self-indulgent extremism, but he still had to move beyond the old agenda and in late 1967 proposed an inter-racial "poor people's" march on Washington for mid-1968 to demand an Economic Bill of Rights that would outlaw housing discrimination and cre-ate a massive federal jobs program. He would not live to see the realization of the Poor People's Campaign. On the evening of April 4, 1968, as he stood on a motel balcony in Memphis before dinner, he was shot to death by a paid killer. More than a hundred cities erupted in rage as blacks sought to retaliate against the system that had murdered their noblest champion.

King's death destroyed whatever coherence and unity of purpose the civil rights movement still possessed. The Poor People's Campaign, now led by the Reverend Ralph Abernathy, proved a fiasco. In May, several hun-dred demonstrators of all races arrived in Washington and constructed a tent-and-plywood Resurrection City on the Mall as the staging area for the new economic demands. The campaign soon deteriorated into a round of ethnic squabbles, and Resurrection City became a hellhole of crime and predatory behavior inflicted by a small criminal element. Endless rain, meanwhile, turned the community into a squalid and unhealthy mudhole. Reflecting a growing resentment of black militancy and a new political con-servatism, Congress and the Johnson administration gave the campaign leaders little of what they wanted. On June 24, with many demonstrators already gone, the Washington police dismantled the shacks and the remaining occupants dispersed.

The collapse of the Poor People's Campaign marked the end of the main phase of the postwar civil rights movement. Richard Nixon's elec-tion as president brought to the White House an administration that owed little to black voters and much to the white South. The Republican admin-istration sought to turn down the sound on black militancy. Yet ironically, it was under Nixon that federal agencies began to establish affirmative action procedures, under the Sixties civil rights legislation, to compensate minorities and women for past discrimination in jobs and education by giving them offsetting advantages. Over the next decade, a quiet revolution took place that brought the races and the sexes closer to statistical parity in college and professional school admissions, job enrollment, and incomes. Nixon, moreover, did not block progress toward black voter registration in the South.

But deep discontents remained. Left behind in the inner cities were many thousands of black Americans who were unable to use the new instruments of mobility and whose lives seemed ever more proscribed by crime, drugs, ill-health, illegitimacy, and deeply embedded poverty. Unfortunately, race continued to be a deeply divisive influence in American life. White resentment of "reverse discrimination" and of inner city crime fueled racist angers. On the other side, black frustration at police brutality and white racist violence continued to nurture a sense of grievance.

There are skeptics today who, in light of continuing racial antagonisms, belittle the achievements of the Sixties civil rights movement. But they fail to understand the oppressive racial regime it transformed. The civil rights movement did not create a racial paradise. But then, it is difficult to see how it is possible to achieve a social system where racial differences only have benign consequences. Meanwhile, the only fair conclusion is that the civil rights movement of the Sixties was a giant step along the road to a fairer and more decent America.

Brown v. Board of Education of Topeka

In May 1954, the Supreme Court, with Chief Justice Earl Warren presiding, handed down the landmark decision Brown v. Board of Education of Topeka, *declaring unconstitutional the South's segregated school system. Soon after the* Brown *decision, the Court also struck down publicly mandated segregation in public buildings, in housing, in transportation, and in recreational and eating facilities. By 1963, it could assert that "it is no longer open to question that a State may not constitutionally require segregation of public facilities." Taken together, the Court had begun to demolish the notorious system of legal segregation that the South had erected after emancipation to keep its black population in a position of permanent subordination.*

The basis for the Court's decision in Brown *was a reinterpretation of the clause in the Fourteenth Amendment, passed during Reconstruction, that denied any state the power to refuse "to any person within its jurisdiction the equal protection of the laws." As the* Brown *decision notes, the Court had decided in* Plessy v. Ferguson *(1896) that the equal protection clause did not invalidate separate facilities so long as they were* equal. *This ruling allowed the system of segregation that was then fast evolving in the South and in fact did little to ensure "equal" facilities. Almost everywhere in the South the Jim Crow school, or playground, or bathroom was more decrepit and dirty than its white equivalent.*

After World War II, the NAACP, through its Legal Defense and Education Fund, won a series of court victories in segregation cases that suggested a changing attitude within the federal judiciary. But in 1953, when Earl Warren became chief justice of the Supreme Court, the edifice of Jim Crow was still largely intact and the Plessy *principle still in force. A firm believer in the equality of the races, Warren had little doubt that segregation was both immoral and unconstitutional. Influenced by the liberal sociology and social psychology of the day, he understood the wounds that were inflicted on black children by being separated from their white peers in the public schools.* *

Warren never had to ponder his own decision in the Brown *case, but the chief justice had no illusions about how a decision in favor of the plaintiffs would be greeted in the South. He wished to avoid a massive collision between the southern states and federal authority. This meant that he must seek not just a majority against school segregation; he must try for a unanimous decision. With two justices of the nine justices conservative southerners,*[†] *this promised to be a daunting task.*

Warren was equal to the challenge. A bluff, hearty extrovert, he was no legal scholar. But he was a forceful and skilled manager, and in several preliminary conferences, he succeeded in maneuvering his more skeptical colleagues into supporting the Court's unanimous opinion. In writing the decision, moreover, he avoided a judgmental or disapproving tone that might have offended the South, and rather than laying out detailed procedures for quick implementation of the decision, he postponed the issue of compliance to a later day.

It would take years before the Brown *decision was widely implemented. Massive resistance and even physical violence would accompany its course. In more recent times, of course, resegregation through middle-class flight from the inner-city public schools has become widespread. Still, Justice Felix Frankfurter was right when he called Monday, May 17, 1954, "a day that will live in glory."*

[Brown v. Board of Education of Topeka, 347 Supreme Court Reporter, 483.]

---

*Whether the works of recent social scientists, as cited in the decision's famous footnote 11, strongly influenced the Court's decision has been the subject of much argument. Even if, as has been stated, the note was tacked on as an afterthought, the body of the opinion itself betrays the influence of new views by psychologists of the adverse effects of Jim Crow schools on minority children's personality and morale.

[†]The two conservatives were Tom Clark of Texas and Stanley Reed of Kentucky. There was one other southerner on the Court, Hugo Black of Alabama, but his section notwithstanding, he was one of the most liberal of "the Brethren."

BROWN V. BOARD OF EDUCATION OF TOPEKA

Mr. Chief Justice WARREN delivered the opinion of the Court.

• • •

These cases come to us from the States of Kansas, South Carolina, Virginia, and Delaware. They are premised on different facts and different local conditions, but a common legal question justifies their consideration together in this consolidated opinion.

In each of the cases minors of the Negro race . . . seek the aid of the courts in obtaining admission to the public schools of their community on a nonsegregated basis. In each instance they have been denied admission to schools attended by white children under laws requiring or permitting segregation according to race. This segregation was alleged to deprive the plaintiffs of the equal protection of the laws under the Fourteenth Amendment. In each of the cases other than the Delaware case, a three-judge federal district court denied relief to the plaintiffs on the so-called "separate but equal" doctrine announced by this Court in *Plessy v. Ferguson*. . . . Under that doctrine, equality of treatment is accorded when the races are provided substantially equal facilities, even though these facilities are separate. . . .

The plaintiffs contend that segregated public schools are not "equal" and cannot be made "equal," and that hence they are deprived of the equal protection of the laws. Because of the obvious importance of the question presented, the Court took jurisdiction. . . .

Reargument was largely devoted to the circumstances surrounding the adoption of the Fourteenth Amendment in 1868. . . . This discussion and our own investigation convince us that . . . the most avid proponents of the postwar Amendments undoubtedly intended them to remove all legal distinctions among "all persons born or naturalized in the United States." Their opponents, just as certainly, were antagonistic to both the letter and the spirit of the Amendments and wished them to have the most limited effect. . . .

In the first cases in this Court construing the Fourteenth Amendment, decided shortly after its adoption, the Court interpreted it as proscribing all state-imposed discrimination against the Negro race. The doctrine of "separate but equal" did not make its appearance in this Court until 1896 in the case of *Plessy v. Ferguson*, . . . involving not education but transportation. . . . In more recent cases, all on the graduate school level, inequality was found in that specific benefits enjoyed by white students were denied to Negro students of the same educational qualifications. . . .

In none of these cases was it necessary to re-examine the doctrine to grant relief to the Negro plaintiff. . . .

In the instant cases, that question is directly presented. Here . . . there are findings . . . that the Negro and white schools involved have been equalized, or are being equalized, with respect to buildings, curricula, qualifications and salaries of teachers, and other "tangible" factors. Our decision, therefore, cannot turn on merely a comparison of these tangible factors in the Negro and white schools involved. . . .

[1] In approaching this problem, we cannot turn the clock back to 1868 when the Amendment was adopted, or even to 1896 when *Plessy v. Ferguson* was written. We must consider public education in the light of its full development and its present place in American life throughout the nation. Only in this way can it be determined if segregation in public schools deprives these plaintiffs of the equal protection of the laws.

[2] Today, education is perhaps the most important function of state and local governments. . . . It is required in the performance of our most basic public responsibilities. . . . It is the very foundation of good citizenship. Today it is a principal instrument in awakening the child to cultural values, in preparing him for later professional training, and in helping him to adjust normally to his environment. In these days it is doubtful that any child may reasonably be expected to succeed in life if he is denied the opportunity of an education. Such an opportunity, where the state has undertaken to provide it, is a right which must be made available to all on equal terms.

[3] We come then to the question presented: Does segregation of children in public schools solely on the basis of race, even though the physical facilities and other "tangible" factors may be equal, deprive the children of the minority group of equal educational opportunities? We believe it does.

In *Sweat v. Painter*, . . . in finding that a segregated law school for Negroes could not provide them equal educational opportunities, this Court relied in large part on "those qualities which are incapable of objective measurement which make for greatness in a law school." In *McLaurin v. Oklahoma State Regents* . . . the Court, in requiring that a Negro admitted to a white graduate school be treated like all other students, again resorted to intangible considerations. . . .

Such considerations apply with added force to children in grade and high schools. To separate them from others of similar age and qualifications solely because of their race generates a feeling of inferiority as to their status in the community that may affect their hearts and minds in a way unlikely ever to be undone. . . . Whatever may have been the extent of psychological knowledge at the time of *Plessy v. Ferguson,* this finding is amply supported by modern authority.* Any language in *Plessy v. Ferguson* contrary to this finding is rejected.

[4] We conclude that in the field of public education the doctrine of "separate but equal" has no place. Separate educational facilities are inherently unequal. Therefore, we hold that the plaintiffs and others similarly situated for whom the actions have been brought are, by reason of the segregation complained of, deprived of the equal protection of the laws guaranteed by the Fourteenth Amendment.

White Citizens' Councils

Resistance to school desegregation as ordered by the Supreme Court in the 1954 Brown *decision began almost at once. In several southern states, white supremacists actually proposed nullification in order to avoid compliance with the decision. In early 1956, nineteen U.S. senators and eighty-one representatives signed a "Southern Manifesto" declaring their intention to use "all lawful means" to reverse the school desegregation policy. On the grassroots level, one hostile response was the formation of Conservative White Citizens' Councils in communities all over the South.*

The councils were called "Uptown Ku Klux Klans." The Klan proper recruited primarily from the bottom layers of southern white society: mill workers, truck drivers, marginal farmers, filling station attendants, and store clerks. People with minimal education, Klan members were often rough men who were not afraid of violence. Their tactics relied heavily on psychological intimidation, and often progressed to arson, beatings, and even murder. It was a band of Mississippi Klansmen who, in 1964 during the Freedom Summer voter registration drive, murdered three civil rights workers—James Chaney, Andrew Goodman, and Michael Schwerner—and buried their bodies in an earthen dam.

The local White Citizens' Council was composed of more respectable people: the school principal, a prominent lawyer, the manager of the five-and-dime store, the owner of the Texaco station, a real estate developer, the Ford dealer, a Baptist minister, and the president of the savings and loan. They were often pillars of the white community, but they loathed the school desegregation decision and the racial change it heralded. They also deplored the tactics of the Klan: parading around in white robes, burning crosses, and beating NAACP workers were not for them. The White Citizens' Councils instead turned to the tactic of imposing economic sanctions on black civil rights activists and the few whites who supported desegregation. Their tools were boycotts, job dismissals, denial of credit, and mortgage foreclosures.

*At this point the famous footnote 11 cited a collection of articles by social psychologists and others about the adverse effects on the minds and personalities of children in segregated schools. Their inclusion led to the view that the Court had been deeply influenced by extralegal data—ed.

They also distributed propaganda to counter the desegregation movement. The document here is taken from a 1965 issue of the White Citizens' Councils' publication, The Citizen. *It directly addresses the question of mixed-race schools and expresses the concerns of many whites, in the North as well as the South, who feared that admitting blacks to white schools would lower the quality of education and penalize their sons and daughters.*

[*White Citizens' Councils, "How Can We Educate Our Children?" Citizen, November 1965, pp. 4–7.*]

How Can We Educate Our Children?

Schools are not merely the mark of a civilization. They are the means of maintaining civilization.

Our American school system is at once an inheritance from Europe and an original contribution to the modern world. Ultimately, our system derives from the medieval universities such as Oxford and Cambridge, and from the "grammar" and other schools established to prepare for those universities. . . .

All the universities of the Middle Ages and the earliest universities or colleges in America were established by groups of Christians, whose basic concern was perpetuation of the gospel.

American state universities were frankly imitative of these educational institutions of the Christian church. Early American schools, like their European predecessors, aimed at beginning for children a course of study leading toward college. In this country, however, a new element came to be emphasized—the training of every child, whether he would or would not go to college. This vital feature of our society has now reached the point of undertaking to see that every child goes to college.

It is this widening of the doors of opportunity which has been the special contribution of America to the world, for to some degree the rest of the world is following us in it.

What needs to be remembered is that there is no point in widening the doors if the treasure within be lost in the process. Our schools and colleges became valuable because they led their students to skill in the arts and knowledge in the sciences, very specifically including the Holy Scripture and the Christian life.

Too often in our time the curriculum has been broadened at the expense of becoming shallower, and recently all religious content has been dictatorially excluded from state-operated schools. Of course some positive attitude toward religion is inseparable from an educational enterprise. . . .

In the world revolution now being everywhere attempted, the conscious overthrow of the traditional American school system, with its roots in the Christian culture of Western Europe, is a priority item. Many revolutionary techniques have been employed, many massive assaults have been made on the ramparts of the "three R's" and especially of the fourth "R," religion. . . .

No other blow against our educational structure has been quite so violent or damaging as the hysterical attack of the racial integrationists. The results in the District of Columbia are notorious. The school system of the nation's capital was once among the finest in the country. Today it is an educational desert—with one oasis in the far Northwest thanks to a process of de facto resegregation.

Central High School in Little Rock was found by a survey in the mid-1950s to be one of the twenty-five best secondary schools in the United States. Today, even though integration there is hardly more than a token, it is scarcely thought of in terms of overall excellence.

Dr. Henry Garrett and other experts have shown that a sound program of schooling is intrinsically impossible where significant numbers of white and black children are herded together in one classroom. The essential disparity, mentally and temperamentally, is just too great. The mania for homogenization has not yet reached the point where high school boys and girls are integrated in the same gym classes. Yet it would be hardly more absurd than the forced congregation of Negro with white children above the preschool level.

(In the Old South, white children played with Negro children regularly before reaching school age, and even later—outside the school. This fact sometimes caused painful personal readjustments later, which integrationists attribute to the eventual segregation, but which could just as well be attributed to the early integration. More reasonably, one could simply recognize that a full life involves many readjustments.)

Some object to segregationist arguments based on IQ differences by saying: "Well then, group them in class by IQ, or other ability test, without reference to race!" The rejoinder to this is twofold: (1) it is not at all what the militant integrationists want, since it would leave a racially unbalanced situation; and (2) it would create new psychological problems, possibly much more serious than any we now have, and would result in an ever widening gap between the predominantly white group, with its adopted superior Negroes, and the predominantly Negro group, with its adopted subnormal whites.

Intelligence is not everything—not enough to justify breaking up groups with other sources of internal cohesion. But a group's average intelligence is important enough to justify separate education for groups with significantly different averages, even if there is some "overlap." By way of analogy, the existence of Amazonian women and effeminate men does not justify drafting women for combat military service (though the Russians have used women for such service).

Not to pursue further the speculative reasons for segregation, a recent analysis of practical school problems which gives the strongest kind of objective support to the segregationist position appeared in, of all places, *The New York Times Magazine* (May 2, 1965) by one Martin Mayer—subjectively, it would appear, an integrationist, but an intelligent observer and skillful writer. Following are excerpts from this revealing article:

> *Public confidence in the [New York City] school system is fearfully low and dropping: White children are leaving the city public schools at a rate of 40,000 a year. . . . Of the leaders of the school system itself—the nine-member Board of Education and the 20-odd deputy and associate superintendents— only a handful have children who attend or ever did attend a New York public school. . . . Of the Negro leaders of the integration drive, . . . not one has or has had a child in a New York public school.*

Integration is the main, but not the only threat to the American school system. Indeed, integration itself would not be promoted so fanatically if too many educators had not adopted a philosophy which says that the spirit of man is the result of material processes, and that there is no spirit beyond.

Materialism begins by exalting the schools, for it holds that through them society and the nature of man himself may undergo a revolutionary transformation. Yet materialism ends by destroying the schools, for it reduces them to budgets, buildings, and bureaucracy, where blossom at best the beatniks of Berkeley, and from which finer spirits escape altogether. . . .

Because of the integration-at-any-cost policy of both the federal government and the majority of the nation's educational bureaucrats, the public is daily losing faith in the "serviceability of public education." This is not a condition which the Citizens' Councils have created, but it is one which we recognize. The purpose of the Chattanooga Leadership Conference is to promote the rapidly expanding private school movement as a means of protecting both racial integrity and American education.

Letter from a Birmingham Jail

Much of Martin Luther King's success as a civil rights leader derived from the moral grandeur of his cause. But it also stemmed from his own splendid eloquence. No orator since Daniel Webster in the mid-nineteenth century could so move listeners by the power of his voice as King. But King was also a cogent polemical writer, and nothing that he wrote was as effective as his "Letter from a Birmingham Jail."

In early 1963, King had shifted the resources of his Atlanta-based Southern Christian Leadership Conference to Birmingham, Alabama, a city that had refused to budge from the Jim Crow system that was beginning to collapse in other southern communities. King considered Birmingham so segregated that when there, he felt he was "within a cab ride of being in Johannesburg, South Africa." It was also a violent city. Civil rights advocates called it "Bombingham." Its police chief was the notorious Eugene "Bull" Connor, a throwback to the worst period of brutal racist law enforcement in the South.

King had been invited to bring his staff, with their skills and training in nonviolent civil disobedience, to Birmingham by the Reverend Fred Shuttleworth, a local black leader. King could not refuse Shuttleworth's request, but he also saw Birmingham as an opportunity to knock out a major prop of the Jim Crow system generally. "As Birmingham goes," he noted, "so goes the South."

The campaign started with sit-ins at downtown lunch counters. On April 6, Shuttleworth led a march on City Hall. Connor arrested all the marchers. Soon after, the SCLC announced a boycott by blacks of downtown stores that practiced segregation. On April 10, after securing a court order forbidding racial demonstrations, Connor arrested King and the Reverend Ralph Abernathy, his second in command, as they led another march on City Hall.

King used his stay in the Birmingham jail to reply to a claim by white Birmingham clergymen that the SCLC was composed of "outsiders coming in" and that its campaign was "unwise and untimely." Shrewdly placing himself and his followers at the center of the civil rights movement, he warned that if the approach of the SCLC did not work, then the white community might well have to face the methods of militant black nationalists. Blood might flow on the streets. Taken as a whole, the piece is the best brief statement of the nonviolent civil disobedience strategies that King so successfully used to break down the remnants of Jim Crow.

Forbidden writing materials, King wrote the article on odd pieces of paper, including toilet paper. It was smuggled out to the media by a black jail trustee.

[**Martin Luther King, Jr., "Letter from a Birmingham Jail." With permission of Intellectual Properties Management.**]

LETTER FROM A BIRMINGHAM JAIL

My dear Fellow Clergymen,

While confined here in the Birmingham City Jail, I came across your recent statement calling our present activities "unwise and untimely". . . . Since I feel that you are men of genuine good will and your criticisms are sincerely set forth, I would like to answer your statement in what I hope will be patient and reasonable terms.

I think I should give the reason for my being in Birmingham, since you have been influenced by the argument of "outsiders coming in." I have the honor of serving as president of the Southern Christian Leadership Conference, an organization operating in every Southern state. . . . Several months ago our local affiliate here in Birmingham invited us to be on call to engage in a nonviolent direct action program if such were deemed necessary. We readily consented, and when the hour came we lived up to our promises. . . .

Beyond this, I am in Birmingham because injustice is here. Just as the eighth-century prophets left their little villages and carried their "thus saith the Lord" far beyond the boundaries of the home towns, and just as the Apostle Paul left his little village of Tarsus and carried the gospel of Jesus Christ to practically every hamlet and city of the Graeco-Roman world, I too am compelled to carry the gospel of freedom beyond my particular home town. . . .

You deplore the demonstrations that are presently taking place in Birmingham. But I am sorry that your statement did not express a similar concern for the conditions that brought the demonstrations into being. . . . I would not hesitate to say that it is unfortunate that so-called demonstrations are taking place in Birmingham at this time, but I would say in more emphatic terms that it is even more unfortunate that the white power structure of this city left the Negro community with no other alternative.

In any nonviolent campaign there are four basic steps: (1) Collection of fact to determine whether injustices are alive, (2) Negotiation, (3) Self-purification and (4) Direct action. We have gone through all of these steps in Birmingham. There can be no gainsaying of the fact that racial injustice engulfs this community.

Birmingham is probably the most thoroughly segregated city in the United States. Its ugly record of police brutality is known in every section of this country. Its unjust treatment of Negroes in the courts is a notorious reality. There have been more unsolved bombings of Negro homes and churches in Birmingham than any other city in the nation. These are the hard, brutal, and unbelievable facts. On the basis of these conditions Negro leaders sought to negotiate with the city fathers. But the political leaders consistently refused to engage in good faith negotiation.

Then came the opportunity last September to talk with some of the leaders of the economic community. In these negotiating sessions certain promises were made by the merchants—such as the promise to remove the humiliating racial signs from the stores. On the basis of these promises Rev. [Fred] Shuttlesworth and the leaders of the Alabama Christian Movement for Human Rights agreed to call a moratorium on any type of demonstrations. As the weeks and the months unfolded, we realized that we were the victims of a broken promise. The signs remained. . . . So we had no alternative except that of preparing for direct action, whereby we would present our very bodies as a means of laying our case before the conscience of the local and national community. . . . We decided to set our action program around the Easter season, realizing that with the exception of Christmas, this was the largest shopping period of the year. Knowing that a strong economic withdrawal program would be the by-product of direct action, we felt that this was the best time to bring pressure on the merchants for needed changes. . . .

Creative Tension

You may well ask, "Why direct action? Why sit-ins, marches, etc.? Isn't negotiation a better path?" You are exactly right in your call for negotiation. Indeed, this is the purpose of direct action. Nonviolent direct action seeks to create such a crisis and establish such creative tension that a community that has constantly refused to negotiate is forced to confront the issue. It seeks to so dramatize the issue that it can no longer be ignored. I just referred to the creation of tension as part of the work of the nonviolent resister. This may sound rather shocking. But I must confess that I am not afraid of the word tension. I have earnestly worked and preached against violent tension, but there is a type of constructive nonviolent tension that is necessary for growth. . . . We must see the need of having nonviolent gadflies to create the kind of tension in society that will help men rise from the dark depths of prejudice and racism to the majestic heights of understanding and brotherhood. So the purpose of the direct action is to create a situation so crisis-packed that it will inevitably open the door to negotiation. . . .

We know through painful experience that freedom is never voluntarily given by the oppressor: it must be demanded by the oppressed. Frankly, I have never engaged in a direct action that was "well timed," according to the timetable of those who have not suffered unduly from the disease of segregation. For years now I have heard the word "Wait!" It rings in the ear of every Negro with a piercing familiarity. This "Wait" has almost always meant "Never". . . . We have waited for more than three hundred and forty years for our constitutional and God-given rights. The nations of Asia and Africa are moving with jetlike speed toward the goal of political independence, and we still creep at a horse and buggy pace toward the gaining of a cup of coffee at a lunch counter. I guess it is easy for those who have never felt the stinging darts of segregation to say "Wait." But when you have seen vicious mobs lynch your mothers and fathers at will and drown your sisters and brothers at whim; when you have seen hate-filled policemen curse, kick, brutalize, and even kill your black brothers and sisters with impunity; when you see the vast majority of your twenty million Negro brothers smothering in an air-tight cage of poverty in the midst of an affluent society; when you suddenly find your tongue twisted and your speech stammering as you seek to explain to your six-year-old daughter why she can't go to the public amusement park that has just been advertised on television, and see tears welling up in her little eyes when she is told that Funtown is closed to colored children, and see the depressing clouds of inferiority begin to form in her little mental sky, and see her begin to distort her little personality by unconsciously developing a bitterness toward white people; when you have to concoct an answer for a five-year-old son asking in agonizing pathos: "Daddy, why do white people treat colored people so mean?"; when you take a cross-country drive and find it necessary to sleep night after night in the uncomfortable corners of your automobile because no motel will accept you; when you are humiliated day in and day out by nagging signs reading "white" and "colored"; when your first name becomes "nigger" and your middle name becomes "boy" (however old you are) . . . , and when your wife and mother are never given the respected title "Mrs."; when you are harried by day and haunted by night by the fact that you are a Negro, living constantly at tip-toe stance, never knowing what to expect next, and plagued with inner fears and outer resentments; when you are forever fighting a degenerating sense of "nobodiness"; then you will understand why we find it difficult to wait. There comes a time when the cup of endurance runs over, and men are no longer willing to be plunged into an abyss of injustice where they experience the blackness of corroding despair. I hope, sirs, you can understand our legitimate and unavoidable impatience.

Breaking the Law

You express a great deal of anxiety over our willingness to break laws. This is certainly a legitimate concern. Since we so diligently urge people to obey the Supreme Court's decision of 1954 outlawing segregation in the public schools, it is rather strange and paradoxical to find us consciously breaking laws. One may well ask, "How can you advocate breaking some laws and obeying others?" The answer is found in the fact that there are two types of laws. There are just and there are *unjust* laws. I would agree with Saint Augustine that "an unjust law is no law at all."

Now what is the difference between the two? How does one determine when a law is just or unjust? A just law is a man-made code that squares with the moral law or the law of God. An unjust law is a code that is out of harmony with the moral law. . . . Any law that uplifts human personality is just. Any law that degrades human personality is unjust. All segregation statutes are unjust because segregation distorts the soul and damages the personality. It gives the segregator a false sense of superiority, and the segregated a false sense of inferiority. . . .

Let me give another explanation. An unjust law is a code inflicted upon a minority which that minority had no part in enacting or creating because they did not have an unhampered right to vote. . . . Throughout the state of Alabama all kinds of conniving methods are used to prevent Negroes from becoming registered voters, and there are some counties without a single Negro registered to vote despite the fact that the Negro constitutes a majority of the population. Can any law set up in such a state be considered democratically structured? . . .

I hope you can see the distinction I am trying to point out. In no sense do I advocate defying the law as the rabid segregationist would do. This would lead to anarchy. One who breaks an unjust law must do it *openly, lovingly* (not hatefully, as the white mothers did in New Orleans when they were seen on television screaming "nigger, nigger, nigger") and with a willingness to accept the penalty by staying in jail to arouse the conscience of the community over its injustice. It is in reality expressing the very highest respect for law. . . .

The White Moderate

. . . I must make two honest confessions to you, my Christian and Jewish brothers. First, I must confess that over the last few years I have been gravely disappointed with the white moderate. I have almost reached the regrettable conclusion that the Negro's great stumbling block in the stride toward freedom is not the white Citizen's Council-er or the Ku Klux Klanner, but the white moderate who is more devoted to "order" than to justice; who prefers a negative peace which is the absence of tension to a positive peace which is the presence of justice. . . . Shallow understanding from people of good will is more frustrating than absolute misunderstanding from people of ill will. . . .

In your statement you asserted that our actions, even though peaceful, must be condemned because they precipitate violence. But can this assertion be logically made? Isn't this like condemning the robbed man because his possession of money precipitated the evil act of robbery? . . .

You spoke of our activity in Birmingham as extreme. . . . I started thinking about the fact that I stand in the middle of two opposing forces in the Negro community. One is a force of complacency made up of Negroes who, as a result of long years of oppression, have been so completely drained of self-respect and a sense of "somebodiness" that they have adjusted to segregation, and, of a few Negroes in the middle class who . . . have unconsciously become insensitive to the problems of the masses. The other force is . . . expressed in the various black nationalist groups that are springing up over the nation, the largest and best known being Elijah Muhammad's Muslim movement.* This movement is nourished by the contemporary frustration over the continued existence of racial discrimination. It is made up of people who have lost faith in America, who have absolutely repudiated Christianity and have concluded that the white man is an incurable "devil." I have tried to stand between these two forces, saying that we need not follow the "do-nothingism" of the complacent or the hatred and despair of the black nationalist. There is the more excellent way of love and nonviolent protest. I'm grateful to God that, through the Negro church, the dimension of nonviolence entered our struggle. If this philosophy had not emerged, I am convinced that by now many streets of the South would be flowing with floods of blood. And I am further convinced that if our white brothers dismiss as "rabble rousers" and "outside agitators" those of us who are working through the channels of nonviolent direct action and refuse to support our nonviolent efforts, millions of Negroes, out of frustration and despair, will seek solace and security in black nationalist ideologies, a development that will lead inevitably to a frightening racial nightmare.

Oppressed people cannot remain oppressed forever. The urge for freedom will eventually come. This is what happened to the American Negro. Something within has reminded him of his birthright of freedom; something without has reminded him that he can gain it. Consciously and unconsciously, he has been swept in by what the Germans call the *Zeitgeist*, and with his black brothers of Africa, and his brown and yellow brothers of Asia, South America, and the Caribbean, he is moving with a sense of cosmic urgency toward the promised land of racial justice. . . .

---

*The Black Muslims, or the Nation of Islam, a group founded in the 1930s and led for many years by Elijah Muhammad, preached a separatist, antiwhite doctrine that appealed to many inner-city blacks. Malcolm X was a lieutenant of Muhammad who later broke with him—ed.

Bull Connor's Police

I must close now. But before closing I am impelled to mention one other point in your statement that troubled me profoundly. You warmly commended the Birmingham police force for keeping "order" and "preventing violence." I don't believe you would have so warmly commended the police force if you had seen its angry violent dogs literally biting six unarmed nonviolent Negroes. I don't believe you would so quickly commend the policemen if you would observe their ugly and inhuman treatment of Negroes here in the city jail; if you would watch them push and curse old Negro women and young Negro girls; if you would see them slap and kick old Negro men and young boys; if you would observe them, as they did on two occasions, refuse to give us food because we wanted to sing our grace together. I'm sorry I can't join you in your praise for the police department. . . .

I wish you had commended the Negro sit-inners and demonstrators of Birmingham for their sublime courage, their willingness to suffer, and their amazing discipline in the midst of the most inhuman provocation. One day the South will recognize its real heroes. They will be the James Merediths,* courageously and with a majestic sense of purpose, facing jeering and hostile mobs and the agonizing loneliness that characterizes the life of the pioneer. They will be old, oppressed, battered Negro women, symbolized in a seventy-two-year-old woman of Montgomery, Alabama, who rose up with a sense of dignity and with her people decided not to ride the segregated buses, and responded to one who inquired about her tiredness with ungrammatical profundity; "My feet is tired, but my soul is rested." They will be the young high school and college students, young ministers of the gospel, and a host of their elders courageously and nonviolently sitting in at lunch counters and willing to go to jail for conscience's sake. One day the South will know that when these disinherited children of God sat down at lunch counters, they were in reality standing up for the best in the American dream and the most sacred values in our Judeo-Christian heritage, and thusly, carrying our whole nation back to those great walls of democracy which were dug deep by the founding fathers in the formulation of the Constitution and the Declaration of Independence. . . .

> Yours for the cause of
> Peace and Brotherhood
> Martin Luther King, Jr.

*James Meredith was the young man whose successful suit for admission finally desegregated the University of Mississippi. In 1966, while leading a voter registration march from Memphis to Jackson, he was severely wounded by a white racist—ed.

To Fulfill These Rights

No president did more to further the cause of civil rights than Lyndon Johnson. Representing in Congress a former slave state that fought in the Confederacy and that had adopted legal segregation after the Civil War, Johnson had had to accommodate to the racial mentality of Texas. But he had never been an outright defender of white supremacy. In 1956, he was only one of three senators from the South who had refused to sign the Southern Manifesto, a declaration of regional opposition to the Supreme Court's 1954 school desegregation decision.

As president, Johnson had a new constituency—the entire American people—and by 1964, a clear majority of Americans had lost all patience with legalized racial discrimination. In that year, using his famous tactics of cajolery, intimidation and persistence, he induced Congress to pass the most comprehensive civil rights bill in the republic's history. By mid-1965, Johnson was preparing to add a new measure to the Civil Rights Act to ensure the right of black Americans to vote in the South. By championing the civil rights movement, then, the President was riding a popular wave. But there were also dangers in positioning himself at the van of the movement. The new torrent of legislation put the Democratic Party at risk, threatening as it did to make the Republicans in the South the party of the white voter. It required conviction on Johnson's part as well as political savvy to take the lead on civil rights. A supple political operator, the tall Texan in the White House was at the same time a passionate believer in the Jeffersonian vision of human equality and was willing to risk political capital to achieve it.

By mid-1965, Johnson, like other civil rights proponents, had concluded that the "Negro Revolution" must move beyond securing formal legal equality. It was time to address the issue of inequality in other realms. Blacks were disproportionately poor, unskilled, illiterate, sick, and powerless, and even if the legal barriers to access to jobs, education, health care, and voting came down, other barriers would remain behind for the indefinite future. It was this knotty problem that the president chose to address in his famous speech at Washington's Howard University, the flagship of the nation's black institutions of higher education.

The address was consistent with Johnson's views, of course, but it was written by two young aides, Richard Goodwin and Daniel Moynihan. Many of the ideas were Moynihan's, developed in his 1965 in-house report, The Negro Family: The Case for National Action. *A brilliant expounder of fresh concepts, Moynihan had concluded that black Americans were personally handicapped by their group past, especially slavery, and that its long-term effects on family cohesion and structure still damaged their ability to compete in the race of life. In a version of the then popular "culture of poverty" idea, he sought to explain why lowering the legal barriers was not enough. In retrospect, the Moynihan report was insightful, but it tripped off a firestorm of protest among black leaders and white radicals who perceived it as "blaming the victim"—holding blacks themselves responsible for their plight when in fact it was white racism that was to blame.*

The Howard University address not only advanced a theory of black cultural impairment, it also suggested a novel solution. In some ways, the key phrase of the president's speech was "we seek . . . not just equality as a right and a theory, but equality as a fact and equality as a result." Lyndon Johnson, surely without recognizing its full implications, was announcing a goal whose fulfillment would require active government intervention in the job market and other areas in favor of minorities. It was, in retrospect, the opening gun in the battle for affirmative action that would peak under his successors and stir powerful feelings for and against in the years to come.

[*Lyndon Johnson, "To Fulfill These Rights," Public Papers of the Presidents: Lyndon Johnson, 1965, vol. 2 (Washington, DC: U.S. Government Printing Office, 1966), pp. 635–40.*]

To Fullfill These Rights

I am delighted at the chance to speak at this important and this historic institution. Howard has long been an outstanding center for the education of Negro Americans. Its students are of every race and color, and they come from many countries of the world. It is truly a working example of democratic excellence.

Our earth is the home of revolution. In every corner of every continent men charged with hope contend with ancient ways in the pursuit of justice. They reach for the newest of weapons to realize the oldest of dreams, that each may walk in freedom and pride, stretching his talents, enjoying the fruits of the earth.

Our enemies may occasionally seize the day of change, but it is the banner of our revolution they take. And our own future is linked to this process of swift and turbulent change in many lands in the world. But nothing in any country touches us more profoundly, and nothing is more freighted with meaning for our own destiny, than the revolution of the Negro American.

In far too many ways American Negroes have been another nation; deprived of freedom, crippled by hatred, the doors of opportunity closed to hope.

In our time change has come to this nation, too. The American Negro, acting with impressive restraint, has peacefully protested and marched, entered the courtrooms and the seats of government, demanding a justice that has long been denied. The voice of the Negro was the call to action. But it is a tribute to America that, once aroused, the courts and the

Congress, the President and most of the people, have been the allies of progress.

Thus we have seen the high court of the country declare that discrimination based on race was repugnant to the Constitution, and therefore void. We have seen in 1957, and 1960, and again in 1964, the first civil rights legislation in this nation in almost an entire century.

As majority leader of the United States Senate, I helped to guide two of these bills through the Senate. And, as your President, I was proud to sign the third. And now very soon we will have the fourth—a new law guaranteeing every American the right to vote.

No act of my entire administration will give me greater satisfaction than the day when my signature makes this bill, too, the law of this land.

The voting rights bill will be the latest, and among the most important, in a long series of victories. But this victory—as Winston Churchill said of another triumph for freedom—"is not the end. It is not even the beginning of the end. But it is, perhaps, the end of the beginning."

That beginning is freedom; and the barriers to that freedom are tumbling down. Freedom is the right to share, share fully and equally, in American society—to vote, to hold a job, to enter a public place, to go to school. It is the right to be treated in every part of our national life as a person equal in dignity and promise to all others.

But freedom is not enough. You do not wipe away the scars of centuries by saying: Now you are free to go where you want, and do as you desire, and choose the leaders you please.

You do not take a person who for years has been hobbled by chains and liberate him, bring him up to the starting line of a race, and then say, "you are free to compete with all the others," and still justly believe that you have been completely fair.

Thus it is not enough just to open the gates of opportunity. All our citizens must have the ability to walk through those gates.

This is the next and the more profound stage of the battle for civil rights. We seek not just freedom but opportunity. We seek not just legal equity but human ability, not just equality as a right and a theory but equality as a fact and equality as a result.

For the task is to give 20 million Negroes the same chance as every other American to learn and grow, to work and share in society, to develop their abilities—physical, mental, and spiritual—and to pursue their individual happiness.

To this end equal opportunity is essential, but not enough, not enough. Men and women of all races are born with the same range of abilities. But ability is not just the product of birth. Ability is stretched or stunted by the family that you live with, and the neighborhood you live in—by the school you go to and the poverty or the richness of your surroundings. It is the product of a hundred unseen forces playing upon the little infant, the child, and finally the man.

This graduating class at Howard University is witness to the indomitable determination of the Negro American to win his way in American life.

The number of Negroes in schools of higher learning has almost doubled in fifteen years. The number of nonwhite professional workers has more than doubled in ten years. The median income of Negro college women tonight exceeds that of white college women. And there are also the enormous accomplishments of distinguished individual Negroes, many of them graduates of this institution, and one of them the first lady ambassador in the history of the United States.

These are proud and impressive achievements. But they tell only the story of a growing middle-class minority, steadily narrowing the gap between them and their white counterparts.

But for the great majority of Negro Americans—the poor, the unemployed, the uprooted, and the dispossessed—there is a much grimmer story. They still, as we meet here tonight, are another nation. Despite the court orders and the laws, despite the legislative victories and the speeches, for them the walls are rising and the gulf is widening.

Here are some of the facts of this American failure.

Thirty-five years ago the rate of unemployment for Negroes and whites was about the same. Tonight the Negro rate is twice as high.

In 1948 the 8 percent unemployment rate for Negro teenage boys was actually less than that of whites. By last year that rate had grown to 23 percent, as against 13 per cent for whites unemployed.

Between 1949 and 1959, the income of Negro men relative to white men declined in every section of this country. From 1952 to 1963 the median income of Negro families compared to white actually dropped from 57 percent to 53 percent.

In the years 1955 through 1957, 22 percent of experienced Negro workers were out of work at some time during the year. In 1961 through 1963 that proportion had soared to 29 percent.

Since 1947 the number of white families living in poverty has decreased 27 percent, while the number of poorer nonwhite families decreased only 3 percent.

The infant mortality of nonwhites in 1940 was 70 percent greater than whites. Twenty-two years later it was 90 percent greater.

Moreover, the isolation of Negro from white communities is increasing, rather than decreasing, as Negroes crowd into the central cities and become a city within a city.

Of course Negro Americans as well as white Americans have shared in our rising national abundance. But the harsh fact of the matter is that in the battle for true equality too many—far too many—are losing ground every day.

We are not completely sure why this is. We know the causes are complex and subtle. But we do know the two broad basic reasons. And we do know that we have to act.

First, Negroes are trapped—as many whites are trapped—in inherited, gateless poverty. They lack training and skills. They are shut in, in slums, without decent medical care. Private and public poverty combine to cripple their capacities.

We are trying to attack these evils through our poverty program, through our education program, through our medical care and our other health programs, and a dozen more of the Great Society programs that are aimed at the root causes of this poverty.

We will increase, and we will accelerate, and we will broaden this attack in years to come until this most enduring of foes finally yields to our unyielding will.

But there is a second cause—much more difficult to explain, more deeply grounded, more desperate in its force. It is the devastating heritage of long years of slavery; and a century of oppression, hatred, and injustice.

For Negro poverty is not white poverty. Many of its causes and many of its cures are the same. But there are differences—deep, corrosive, obstinate differences—radiating painful roots into the community, and into the family, and the nature of the individual.

These differences are not racial differences. They are solely and simply the consequence of ancient brutality, past injustice, and present prejudice. They are anguishing to observe. For the Negro they are a constant reminder of oppression. For the white they are a constant reminder of guilt. But they must be faced and they must be dealt with and they must be overcome, if we are ever to reach the time when the only difference between Negroes and whites is the color of their skin.

Nor can we find a complete answer in the experience of other American minorities. They made a valiant and a largely successful effort to emerge from poverty and prejudice.

The Negro, like these others, will have to rely mostly upon his own efforts. But he just cannot do it alone. For they did not have the heritage of centuries to overcome, and they did not have a cultural tradition which had been twisted and battered by endless years of hatred and hopelessness, nor were they excluded—these others—because of race or color—a feeling whose dark intensity is matched by no other prejudice in our society.

Nor can these differences be understood as isolated infirmities. They are a seamless web. They cause each other. They result from each other. They reinforce each other.

Much of the Negro community is buried under a blanket of history and circumstance. It is not a lasting solution to lift just one corner of that blanket. We must stand on all sides, and we must raise the entire cover if we are to liberate our fellow citizens.

One of the differences is the increased concentration of Negroes in our cities. More than 73 percent of all Negroes live in urban areas compared with less than 70 percent of the whites. Most of these Negroes live in slums. Most of these Negroes live together—a separated people.

Men are shaped by their world. When it is a world of decay, ringed by an invisible wall, when escape is arduous and uncertain, and the saving pressures of a more hopeful society are unknown, it can cripple the youth and it can desolate the men.

There is also the burden that a dark skin can add to the search for a productive place in our society. Unemployment strikes most swiftly and broadly at the Negro, and this burden erodes hope. Blighted hope breeds despair. Despair brings indifference to the learning which offers a way out. And despair, coupled with indifference, is often the source of destructive rebellion against the fabric of society.

There is also the lacerating hurt of early collision with white hatred or prejudice, distaste, or condescension. Other groups have felt similar intolerance. But success and achievement could wipe it away. They do not change the color of a man's skin. I have seen this uncomprehending pain in the eyes of the little, young Mexican-American schoolchildren that I taught many years ago. But it can be overcome. But for many, the wounds are always open.

Perhaps most important—its influence radiating to every part of life— is the breakdown of the Negro family structure. For this, most of all, white America must accept responsibility. It flows from centuries of oppression and persecution of the Negro man. It flows from the long years of degradation and discrimination, which have attacked his dignity and assaulted his ability to produce for his family.

This, too, is not pleasant to look upon. But it must be faced by those whose serious intent is to improve the life of all Americans.

Only a minority—less than half—of all Negro children reach the age of 18 having lived all their lives with both of their parents. At this moment, tonight, little less than two-thirds are at home with both of their parents. Probably a majority of all Negro children receive federally aided public assistance sometime during their childhood.

The family is the cornerstone of our society. More than any other force it shapes the attitude, the hopes, the ambitions, and the values of the child. And when the family collapses, it is the children that are usually damaged. When it happens on a massive scale, the community itself is crippled.

So, unless we work to strengthen the family, to create conditions under which most parents will stay together—all the rest: schools, and playgrounds, and public assistance, and private concern—will never be enough to cut completely the circle of despair and deprivation.

There is no single easy answer to all of these problems.

Jobs are part of the answer. They bring the income which permits a man to provide for his family.

Decent homes in decent surroundings and a chance to learn—an equal chance to learn—are part of the answer.

Welfare and social programs better designed to hold families together are part of the answer.

Care for the sick is part of the answer.

An understanding heart by all Americans is another big part of the answer.

And to all of these fronts—and a dozen more—I will dedicate the expanding efforts of the Johnson Administration.

But there are other answers that are still to be found. Nor do we fully understand even all of the problems. Therefore, I want to announce tonight that this fall I intend to call a White House conference of scholars, and experts, and outstanding Negro leaders—men of both races—and officials of government at every level.

This White House conference's theme and title will be "To Fulfill These Rights."

Its object will be to help the American Negro fulfill the rights which, after the long time of injustice, he is finally about to secure.

To move beyond opportunity to achievement.

To shatter forever not only the barriers of law and public practice, but the walls which bound the condition of man by the color of his skin.

To dissolve, as best we can, the antique enmities of the heart which diminish the holder, divide the great democracy, and do wrong—great wrong—to the children of God.

And I pledge you tonight that this will be a chief goal of my administration, and of my program next year, and in the years to come. And I hope, and I pray, and I believe, it will be a part of the program of all America.

For what is justice?

It is to fulfill the fair expectations of man.

Thus, American justice is a very special thing. For, from the first, this has been a land of towering expectations. It was to be a nation where each man could be ruled by the common consent of all—enshrined in law, given life by institutions, guided by men themselves subject to its rule. And all—all of every station and origin—would be touched equally in obligation and in liberty.

Beyond the law lay the land. It was a rich land, glowing with more abundant promise than man had ever seen. Here, unlike any place yet known, all were to share the harvest.

And beyond this was the dignity of man. Each could become whatever his qualities of mind and spirit would permit—to strive, to seek, and if he could, to find his happiness.

This is American justice. We have pursued it faithfully to the edge of our imperfections, and we have failed to find it for the American Negro.

So, it is the glorious opportunity of this generation to end the one huge wrong of the American nation and, in so doing, to find America for ourselves, with the same immense thrill of discovery which gripped those who first began to realize that here, at last, was a home for freedom.

All it will take is for all of us to understand what this country is and what this country must become.

The Scripture promises: "I shall light a candle of understanding in thine heart, which shall not be put out."

Together, and with millions more, we can light that candle of understanding in the heart of all America.

And, once lit, it will never again go out.

Black Power

King's prediction that black nationalism would gain if racial justice were delayed was fulfilled. Nineteen sixty-six saw the advent of the Black Power movement that abandoned nonviolence and repudiated the integrationist, black-and-white-together goal of King and the leaders of the older civil rights organizations.

The Black Power movement of the last half of the Sixties had several precursors. In the 1920s the Marcus Garvey movement preached a black pride and separatist back-to-Africa message. The Black Muslims (the Nation of Islam), founded in the 1930s, rejected Christianity as the white man's religion, called whites "blue-eyed dev-

ils," and favored a separate black nation. Black Power also drew on the pan-Africanism that inspired the anticolonial movements of sub-Saharan Africa beginning in the late 1950s.

Black Power appeared suddenly in 1966 during the course of a "walk against fear" from Memphis to Jackson, organized by James Meredith, to assert the rights of blacks to use the highways of Mississippi freely. When, at the demonstration's start, Meredith was wounded by a gunshot fired by a white racist, civil rights leaders rushed to Memphis to rescue the march. Upon their arrival King and the leaders of the integrationist NAACP and Urban League ran into a militant group of young activists, members of CORE and SNCC, who refused to accept white participants and urged using a militant black defense group, Deacons for Defense, to protect the demonstrators. Unwilling to accept the proposals of the firebrands, the moderate leaders left Memphis in a huff. King and the SCLC went along reluctantly.

It was in Greenwood, Mississippi, halfway through the march, that the young radicals led by Stokely Carmichael of SNCC began to chant "Black Power! Black Power!" King's SCLC contingent tried to drown out the militants' cry with their own: "Freedom now! Freedom now!" But their voices were too few, and more and more the militants' anger and belligerence became the predominant tone of the march. By the time the weary marchers arrived in Jackson, the national media had noticed the menacing new tone of the civil rights movement.

In reality, Black Power had a protean quality. Undoubtedly, for some of the hotblooded young radicals, it awakened emotionally satisfying visions of harsh vengeance against white people. At the other extreme, white conservatives were equally certain that it sanctioned race war and would encourage the sort of blind violence that had erupted in the Los Angeles suburb of Watts the previous year. Within the mainstream civil rights movement, Roy Wilkins of the NAACP condemned it as "the father of hatred and the mother of violence." For his part, King clearly considered it a repudiation of his biracial, Gandhian movement, but for the sake of the cause he sought to find common ground with the young firebrands while holding on to his white liberal backers.

The negative reaction of most whites and the civil rights mainstream forced Carmichael and other Black Power advocates onto the defensive. Not yet ready to proclaim apocalypse, they at first tried to define the new approach in reasonable and positive terms. "It doesn't mean that you take over the country," Carmichael explained. Floyd McKissick of CORE claimed Black Power was an attempt "to grab our bootstraps, consolidate our political power and act in the framework of this democracy to change our lives." Defenders of the new movement insisted that its primary purpose was to counter black self-hatred and raise black esteem. And clearly that was part of its message. One of the famous Black Power slogans was "Black is beautiful."

But however reasonable it may have been at first, in the hothouse of the late Sixties, where new movements sprouted, grew, and died in a matter of months, the anger of

Black Power became increasingly unrestrained. In this 1967 selection, SNCC leaders let down their guard and admitted to their willingness to accept, even initiate, violence and intimidation.

[*Student Non-Violent Coordinating Committee, "We Want Black Power," 1967, pamphlet in Tamiment Library, New York University.*]

WE WANT BLACK POWER

Black Men of America Are a Captive People

The black man in America is in a perpetual state of slavery no matter what the white man's propaganda tells us.

The black man in America is exploited and oppressed the same as his black brothers are all over the face of the earth by the same white man. We will never be free until we are all free and that means all black oppressed people all over the earth.

We are not alone in this fight, we are a part of the struggle for self-determination of all black men everywhere. We here in America must unite ourselves to be ready to help our brothers elsewhere.

We must first gain BLACK POWER here in America. Living inside the camp of the leaders of the enemy forces, it is our duty to our Brothers to revolt against the system and create our own system so that we can live as MEN.

We must take over the political and economic systems where we are in the majority in the heart of every major city in this country as well as in the rural areas. We must create our own black culture to erase the lies the white man has fed our minds from the day we were born.

The Black Man in the Ghetto Will Lead the Black Power Movement

The black Brother in the ghetto will lead the Black Power Movement and make the changes that are necessary for its success.

The black man in the ghetto has one big advantage that the bourgeois Negro does not have despite his "superior" education. He is already living outside the value system white society imposes on all black Americans.

He has to look at things from another direction in order to survive. He is ready. He received his training in the streets, in the jails, from the ADC* check his mother did not receive in time and the head-beatings he got from the cop on the corner.

---

*Aid to Dependent Children, a major feature of the federal welfare system.

Once he makes that first important discovery about the great pride you feel inside as a BLACK MAN and the great heritage of the mother country, Africa, there is no stopping him from dedicating himself to fight the white man's system.

This is why the Black Power Movement is a true revolutionary movement with the power to change men's minds and unmask the tricks the white man has used to keep black men enslaved in modern society.

The Bourgeois Negro Cannot Be a Part of the Black Power Movement

The bourgeois Negro has been force-fed the white man's propaganda and has lived too long in the half-world between white and phony black bourgeois society. He cannot think for himself because he is a shell of a man full of contradictions he cannot resolve. He is not to be trusted under any circumstances until he has proved himself to be "cured." There are a minute handful of these "cured" bourgeois Negroes in the Black Power Movement, and they are most valuable but they must not be allowed to take control. They are aware intellectually but under stress will react emotionally to the pressures of white society in the same way a white "liberal" will expose an unconscious prejudice that he did not even realize he possessed.

What Brother Malcolm X Taught Us about Ourselves

Malcolm X* was the first black man from the ghetto in America to make a real attempt to get the white man's fist off the black man. He recognized the true dignity of man—without the white-society prejudices about status, education, and background that we all must purge from our minds.

Even today, in the Black Power Movement itself we find Brothers who look down on another Brother because of the conditions that life has imposed upon him. The most beautiful thing that Malcolm X taught us is that once a black man discovers for himself a pride of his blackness, he can throw off the shackles of mental slavery and become a MAN in the truest sense of the word. We must move on from the point our Great Black Prince had reached.

We Must Become Leaders for Ourselves

We must not get hung up in the bag of having one great leader who we depend upon to make decisions. This makes the Movement too vulnerable to those forces the white man uses to keep us enslaved, such as the draft, murder, prison, or character assassination.

---

*The former Malcolm Little, a convert to the Nation of Islam, a black separatist group. He was eventually assassinated, apparently by a rival black group.

We have to all learn to become leaders for ourselves and remove all white values from our minds. When we see a Brother using a white value through error, it is our duty to the Movement to point it out to him. We must thank our Brothers who show us our own errors. We must discipline ourselves so that if necessary we can leave family and friends at a moment's notice, maybe forever, and know our Brothers have pledged themselves to protect the family we have left behind.

As a part of our education, we must travel to other cities and make contacts with the Brothers in all the ghettos in America so that when the time is right we can unite as one under the banner of BLACK POWER.

Learning to Think Black and Remove White Things from Our Minds

We have got to begin to say and understand with complete assuredness what black is. Black is an inner pride that the white man's language hampers us from expressing. Black is being a complete fanatic, who white society considers insane.

We have to learn that black is so much better than belonging to the white race with the blood of millions dripping from their hands that it goes far beyond any prejudice or resentment. We must fill ourselves with hate for all white things. This is not vengeance or trying to take the white oppressors' place to become new black oppressors but is a oneness with a worldwide black brotherhood.

We must regain respect for the lost religion of our fathers, the spirits of the black earth of Africa. The white man has so poisoned our minds that if a Brother told you he practiced Voodoo, you would roll around on the floor laughing at how stupid and superstitious he was.

We have to learn to roll around on the floor laughing at the black man who says he worships the white Jesus. He is truly sick.

We must create our own language for these things that the white man will not understand because a Black Culture exists, and it is not the wood-carvings or native dancing—it is the black strength inside of true men.

Ideas on Planning for the Future of Black Power

We must infiltrate all government agencies. This will not be hard because black clerks work in all agencies in poor-paying jobs and have a natural resentment of the white men who run these jobs.

People must be assigned to seek out these dissatisfied black men and women and put pressure on them to give us the information we need. Any man in overalls, carrying a tool box, can enter a building if he looks like he knows what he is doing.

Modern America depends on many complex systems such as electricity, water, gas, sewerage, and transportation, and all are vulnerable. Much of the government is run by computers that must operate in air conditioning. Cut off the air conditioning and they cannot function.

We must begin to investigate and learn all of these things so that we can use them if it becomes necessary. We cannot train an army in the local park, but we can be ready for the final confrontation with the white man's system.

Remember your Brothers in South Africa and do not delude yourselves that it could not happen here. We must copy the white man's biggest trick, diversion (Hitler taught them that), and infiltrate all civil rights groups, keep them in confusion so they will be neutralized and cannot be used as a tool of the white power structure.

The civil rights, integrationist movement says to the white man, "If you please, sir, let us, the 10 percent minority of Americans, have our rights. See how nice and nonviolent we are?"

This is why SNCC calls itself a Human Rights Organization. We believe that we belong to the 90 percent majority of the people on earth that the white man oppresses and that we should not beg the white man for anything. We want what belongs to us as human beings, and we intend to get it through BLACK POWER.

How to Deal with Black Traitors

Uncle Tom is too kind a word. What we have are black traitors, quislings, collaborators, sell-outs, white Negroes.

We have to expose these people once and for all for what they are and place them on the side of the oppressor where they belong. Their black skin is a lie and their guilt the shame of all black men. We must ostracize them and if necessary exterminate them.

We must stop fighting a "fair game." We must do whatever is necessary to win BLACK POWER. We have to hate and disrupt and destroy and blackmail and lie and steal and become blood-brothers like the Mau-Mau.

We must eliminate or render ineffective all traitors. We must make them fear to stand up like puppets for the white men, and we must make the world understand that these so-called men do not represent us or even belong to the same black race because they sold out their birthright for a mess of white society pottage. Let them choke on it.

Pitfalls to Avoid on the Path to Black Power

We must learn how close America and Russia are politically. The biggest lie in the world is the cold war. Money runs the world, and it is controlled completely by the white man.

Russia and America run the two biggest money systems in the world, and they intend to keep it under their control under any circumstances. Thus, we cannot accept any help from Communism or any other "ism."

We must seek out poor people's movements in South America, Africa, and Asia and make our alliances with them. We must not be fooled into thinking that there is a ready-made doctrine that will solve all our problems.

There are only white man's doctrines, and they will never work for us. We have to work out our own systems and doctrines and culture.

Why Propaganda Is Our Most Important Tool

The one thing that the white man's system cannot stand is the TRUTH because his system is all based on lies.

There is no such thing as "justice" for a black man in America. The white man controls everything that is said in every book, newspaper, magazine, TV and radio broadcast.

Even the textbooks used in the schools and the bible that is read in the churches are designed to maintain the system for the white man. Each and every one of us is forced to listen to the white man's progaganda every day of our lives.

The political system, economic system, military system, educational system, religious system, and anything else you name is used to preserve the status quo of white America getting fatter and fatter while the black man gets more and more hungry.

We must spend our time telling our Brothers the truth.

We must tell them that any black woman who wears a diamond on her finger is wearing the blood of her Brothers and Sisters in slavery in South Africa, where one out of every three black babies dies before the age of one, from starvation, to make the white man rich.

We must stop wearing the symbols of slavery on our fingers.

We must stop going to other countries to exterminate our Brothers and Sisters for the white man's greed.

We must ask our Brothers which side they are on.

Once you know the truth for yourself, it is your duty to dedicate your life to recruiting your Brothers and to counteract the white man's propaganda.

We must disrupt the white man's system to create our own. We must publish newspapers and get radio stations. Black Unity is strength—let's use it now to get BLACK POWER.

The Black Panthers

The Black Panthers epitomized the late Sixties political climate. Formed in 1966 by Huey Newton and Bobby Seale, two Oakland, California, community college stu-

dents, they were responding to notorious police brutality in the Oakland ghetto. To monitor and constrain police behavior toward ghetto citizens, Panthers, equipped with cameras, tape recorders, and a copy of the state penal code, shadowed police patrols.

There is little evidence that the Panthers improved police behavior, but there is no doubt that, with their paramilitary dress style and open carrying of rifles, they expressed the defiance and go-for-broke mood of many young black males by mid-decade. The organization grew slowly until May 1967, when thirty rifle-toting Panthers marched into the California capitol building in Sacramento to protest a pending bill outlawing the carrying of loaded weapons within city limits. The invasion of the capitol shocked many whites but established the Panthers' bona-fides as the "baddest dudes" around and brought a flood of young black recruits. Black Panther chapters sprang up in major cities across the country.

From the outset, the police and the Panthers were sworn enemies and were soon engaged in bloody shoot-outs in the Bay Area, in New Haven, in Chicago, and in other cities in which neither side was guiltless. At the time, the left considered the Panthers innocent victims of brutal police repression. And they were. But today we know that Panther leaders also cynically used radical and liberation ideology as a cover for larceny, drug dealing, and even murder.

Despite their violence and military posturing—or perhaps because of them—the Panthers became heroes of the left. Adopting a version of Marxism, the Black Panther Party—unlike SNCC, CORE, and the Black Muslims—favored alliances with white radicals, making it possible for white New Leftists to rejoin the battle for racial equity. It was admiration for Panther "authenticity" that led SDS, late in its career, into the camp of anti-imperialism and defense of Third World causes. That admiration also explains the famous "radical chic" party hosted by conductor Leonard Bernstein in his Park Avenue apartment, in which rich and famous liberals mixed with indicted Panther leaders to express their sympathy and support.

The Panthers sought respectability by developing a program of school breakfasts in the ghettos that seemed benevolent and nurturing, but the social programs paled beside the militant revolutionary rhetoric and posturing.

In this document, the Panther Party for Self Defense, using the Declaration of Independence as its model, lays out its program for public view.

[*Black Panther Party for Self Defense, "What We Want, What We Believe," pamphlet in Tamiment Library, New York University.*]

WHAT WE WANT   WHAT WE BELIEVE

What we want now!:

1. We want freedom. We want power to determine the destiny of our black community.

2. We want full employment for our people.
3. We want an end to the robbery by the white man of our black community.
4. We want decent housing fit for shelter of human beings.
5. We want education for our people that exposes the true nature of this decadent American society. We want education that teaches us our true history and our role in the present day society.
6. We want all black men to be exempt from military service.
7. We want an immediate end to *police brutality* and *murder* of black people.
8. We want freedom for all black men and women held in federal, state, county, and city prisons and jails.
9. We want all black people, when brought to trial, to be tried in court by a jury of their peer group or people from their black communities, as defined by the Constitution of the United States.
10. We want land, bread, housing, education, clothing, justice, and peace.

What we believe:

1. We believe that black people will not be free until we are able to determine our destiny.
2. We believe that the federal government is responsible and obligated to give every man employment or a guaranteed income.

    We believe that if the white American business men will not give full employment, then the means of production should be taken from the business men and placed in the community so that the people of the community can organize and employ all of its people and give [them] a high standard of living.
3. We believe that this racist government has robbed us, and now we are demanding the overdue debt of forty acres and two mules. Forty acres and two mules was promised 100 years ago as retribution for slave labor and mass murder of black people. We will accept the payment in currency which will be distributed to our many communities. The Germans are now aiding the Jews in Israel for the genocide of the Jewish people. The Germans murdered 6 million Jews. The American racist has taken part in the slaughter of over 50 million black people; therefore, we feel that this is a modest demand that we make.
4. We believe that if the white landlords will not give decent housing to our black community, then the housing and the land should be made into cooperatives so that our community, with government aid, can build and make decent housing for its people.

5. We believe in an educational system that will give to our people a knowledge of self. If a man does not have knowledge of himself and his position in society and the world, then he has little chance to relate to anything else.

6. We believe that black people should not be forced to fight in the military service to defend a racist government that does not protect us. We will not fight and kill other people of color in the world who, like black people, are being victimized by the white racist government of America. We will protect ourselves from the force and violence of the racist police and the racist military, by whatever means necessary.

7. We believe we can end police brutality in our black community by organizing black *self defense* groups that are dedicated to defending our black community from racist police oppression and brutality. The Second Amendment of the Constitution of the United States gives us a right to bear arms. We therefore believe that all black people should arm themselves for *self defense.*

8. We believe that all black people should be released from the many jails and prisons because they have not received a fair and impartial trial.

9. We believe that the courts should follow the United States Constitution so that black people will receive fair trials. The 14th Amendment of the U.S. Constitution gives a man a right to be tried by his peer group. A peer is a person from a similar economic, social, religious, geographical, environmental, historical, and racial background. To do this the court will be forced to select a jury from the black community from which the black defendant came. We have been and are being tried by all-white juries that have no understanding of the "average reasoning man" of the black community.

10. When in the course of human events, it becomes necessary for one people to dissolve the political bonds which have connected them with another, and to assume among the powers of the earth, the separate and equal station to which the laws of nature and nature's God entitle them, a decent respect to the opinions of mankind requires that they should declare the causes which impel them to the separation.

    We hold these truths to be self-evident, that all men are created equal, that they are endowed by their Creator with certain unalienable rights, that among these are life, liberty, and the pursuit of happiness. That to secure these rights, governments are instituted among men, deriving their just powers from the consent of the governed—*that whenever any form of government becomes destructive of these ends, it is the right of people to alter or to abolish it, and to institute new government, laying its foundation on such principles and organizing its powers in such form, as to them shall seem most likely to effect their safety and happiness.*

Prudence, indeed, will dictate that governments long established should not be changed for light and transient causes; and accordingly all experience hath shewn, that mankind are more disposed to suffer, while evils are sufferable, than to right themselves by abolishing the forms to which they are accustomed. *But when a long train of abuses and usurpations, pursuing invariably the same object, evinces a design to reduce them under absolute despotism, it is their right, it is their duty, to throw off such government, and to provide new guards for their future security.*

Resurrection City

Wherever you looked in 1968, there was another crisis. The Tet offensive had dashed hopes of an early victory in Vietnam. The economy was faltering under a surge of inflation. In politics the Democratic Party, at its Chicago convention, had revealed its disunity and inflicted on itself a dangerous political wound. For the civil rights movement, it was undoubtedly the worst year of the decade. Martin Luther King, Jr., fell to an assassin's bullet that April and in the early summer, the Poor People's Campaign came to an inglorious end.

The Poor People's Campaign was conceived by King as an answer to the question, Whither the civil rights movement? The brave work of the past decade had restored voting rights to blacks in the South but everywhere they remained poor, sick, and ill-educated. The civil rights movement, in alliance with organizations of other poor people, had to grapple with these tougher problems at a time when the country seemed in headlong retreat from social commitment.

In December 1967, the Southern Christian Leadership Conference drew up proposals for a campaign the following spring that would force the federal government to end poverty in America once and for all. It would demand enactment of an Economic Bill of Rights to guarantee housing integration, provide jobs, and establish a guaranteed annual income for all. King was now being derided by young black activists as an Uncle Tom, and to prove his militancy, he promised to use confrontational tactics if needed. Thousands of poor people—white, black, brown—would descend on the nation's capital and create "major massive dislocations" until their demands were met. For King, this campaign would be, he said, his "last, greatest dream."

After his murder in Memphis, the Reverend Ralph Abernathy took over the campaign. According to the plan, it would open in early spring with several caravans of "poor people" moving in mule trains to Washington. Its centerpiece would be a large encampment in West Potomac Park. During the weeks of the campaign, Resurrection City, as the cluster of canvas and plywood shanties came to be called, would be the base for activists of all races and would have the facilities and services of a small city. The campers would remain as long as it was required to get Congress to enact their program.

The scheme failed. Neither Congress nor the administration was in a mood to augment the War on Poverty programs of the past few years. If anything, the nation's attitude had turned sour on the poor. Nor did the American people feel flush in the spring of 1968, as they had in 1964–65. Marches, sit-ins, and confrontations with federal officials during the weeks of the campaign extracted airy promises but achieved little more. Meanwhile, things at Resurrection City fell apart. The rains came in late May, turning the paths and streets of the shanty community into open streams of water and goo. Sanitation facilities collapsed; health problems developed. Ethnic dissension soon appeared as well, with the tensions between Hispanics and blacks becoming particularly disruptive.

From the public relations viewpoint, the worst problem of Resurrection City was crime and violence. The organizers had imported members of urban street gangs to keep the peace, on the principle, apparently, of "set a thief to catch a thief." The hoodlums quickly became predators on the many good folk of the community. The encampment also attracted toughs from Washington itself who joined in the robbery, rape, and intimidation.

This June 21, 1968, newspaper story by two Washington Post *reporters describes the crime and violence of the spring. Two days after these events occurred, District of Columbia police—a thousand strong—appeared at West Potomac Park and shut the encampment down. The Poor People's Campaign was over, and with it, many would say, the civil rights revolution passed into history.*

[*David A. Jewell and Paul W. Valentine, "The Troubles of Resurrection City,"* **Washington Post,** *June 21, 1968, pp. A1, A6. Reprinted with permission.*]

THE TROUBLES OF RESURRECTION CITY

"The reason the population of this city is going down is not mud, poor food, rain or lousy homes. . . . The reason they leave is that men are getting tired of coming home from a day's picketing to find their belongings stolen or their wife raped."

These are the words of Alvin Jackson, 35, a Washington TV repairman, who until his resignation yesterday afternoon was the chief security marshal at Resurrection City.

"If the leaders don't do something soon, this is going to be known as Blood City instead of Resurrection City."

Jackson's resignation—some marshals say he was fired—came as tension reached new heights in the wake of a growing number of violent incidents that have police and city officials worried.

The Reverend Ralph Abernathy, leader of the Poor People's Campaign, said yesterday that reports of assaults and robberies in the encampment indicate "restlessness" among some residents.

"We do have some people in the city who have not adequately gone through the stage of self-purification to my satisfaction," he said.

He said he believed policemen provoke some incidents by their presence.

Park Police Acting Chief Grant Wright estimates that about one hundred assaults and other violent incidents have occurred inside Resurrection City since it was built in mid-May and that at least twenty visitors have been robbed, beaten, or stabbed by residents outside the snow fence surrounding the encampment.

Jackson, a Negro who gave up two weeks of vacation, a week's leave of absence, and all his nights to help out at the troubled city said:

"Please, mister, if you put this in your newspaper, don't just put the bad things. Put in all the good things, too.

"This is a great Campaign and a just one, and it has just goals."

In a rare instance of candor by a Resurrection City official, Jackson unburdened himself early yesterday after he had calmed down a band of Negro youths who almost precipitated a serious fight with police.

Disorder Denied

Later yesterday, the Reverend James Bevel, director of nonviolent action for the Southern Christian Leadership Conference, denied that the youths taunted police—or threw bottles at them.

The incident was witnessed from beginning to end by reporters from the *Washington Post* and *Washington Evening Star* and was reported in yesterday's editions of both newspapers.

"There are rape, robbery and cuttings every day, and there is nothing we can do about it even when we catch the guys who did it," Jackson said.

At another point he said, "There are about twenty guns in Resurrection City. There are lead pipes, knives, and Molotov cocktails in there."

He said he has tried desperately to gain an audience with Mr. Abernathy or other SCLC leaders to plead with them for some form of discipline inside the city.

Discipline Lacking

"My bosses are (Chief Marshal Albert) Spencer and Mr. (The Reverend James) Orange (an SCLC official). They are both fine men, but they just won't allow any kind of discipline in the camp.

"Today one white guy burned his shanty down. He has been a real hard worker around here and spent all day in the march, but when he got back, every stick of clothing and furniture he had, right down to his bed, had been stolen. I guess he was just so frustrated that he burned his shanty down to relieve his feelings.

"And he was just about ready to cry, he felt so bad. I guess we're going to have to punish him. I can hardly blame him though. I know how he must feel."

Since Jackson was put in charge of the security marshals, Park Police officials say he has been the only official of Resurrection City with whom they had decent liaison.

"Always Peacemaker"

"We could always talk to him, and he would keep us informed if anything serious happened, and we knew we could trust and deal responsibly with him. He was always the peacemaker if any young hotheads would blow up," said one police source.

"I'll give you an example of the problems we have here," said Jackson during the interview.

"Earlier today one of my marshals caught a resident in the act of punching a white woman in the nose and stealing her camera. All we could do was paddle his rear with a tent stick and put him on a bus home.

"When I finish talking to you, I got to go back and handle three more cases, one stabbing, one assault with a tree branch, and one robbery.

"The reason the population of this city is going down is not mud and poor food, rain, or lousy homes. Most of these people come from places that would make this city look good.

Thrive on Donations

"The reason they leave is that men are tired of coming home from a day's picketing to find their belongings stolen or their wife raped.

"I am ashamed to say this, but the only thing that keeps this camp going is donations of goods and work from the white people.

"If it were left to us, it just wouldn't last. I just can't understand my black brothers. Many of them are able to cause trouble at night because they sleep around all day while the white residents work.

"Almost all the whites here are dedicated, but they take a real hard time from some of the blacks. I just can't understand my black brothers who will take things from the whites and then spit on them.

"I ask some of these guys if they hate whites so much, why do they come up here and take things from them. Why don't they stay in Marks,

Miss[issippi], where the man puts his foot on your back and you dare not move.

"Get Away With More"

"They answer that they are needed here, but that's not the answer. The answer is that they can get away with more up here.

"There are all kinds of guys on soapboxes in there saying 'we don't need discipline,' but they are the ones who are going to do wrong. Hell, man, you can't run a cat show without some kind of discipline, but I just can't get through to the leaders to tell them this."

At the end of the interview Jackson was almost crying as he recounted what he felt were the frustrations of trying to keep order without discipline.

"I'm only afraid that one of these days it's going to blow up, and in thirty years your grandchildren and mine will only know about the bad things and not the good."

Youths Hostile

Jackson's comments came as new incidents occurred at Resurrection City.

Though most residents went about their business yesterday ignoring visitors and newsmen in the area, individual Negro youths kept up a continual barrage of hostile comments and threats.

One youth brandished a saw blade and cursed an NBC camera crew filming residents. Other young toughs surrounded the crew, and it withdrew.

Later, the crew attempted filming the city from beyond the snow fence boundary. A youth hurled a pair of roller skates at them. No one was injured.

At the main gate, a husky Negro cursed two white men dressed in business suits when they said they were looking for a white girl in the city. The Negro ordered the pair to leave. They retreated and spoke to a marshal, who entered the city and returned escorting a white girl who appeared to be in her teens.

Tensions Increase

Tensions rose during the day as idle residents loitered about the front gate, some arguing among themselves, others grumbling about the Park and District policemen on patrol nearby.

Chief Grant said marshals and residents generally refuse to cooperate with police authorities when incidents occur inside the city.

Marshals say the incidents are "internal matters" and do not require police intervention, and the residents say they don't trust the police.

A complicating factor is that the organizational structure of the marshals has been changed at least once. Originally, many marshals were recruited from tough urban street gangs in a deliberate effort by SCLC to involve disadvantaged youths in leadership functions.

These younger marshals attended to routine matters while an older, elite group called Tent City Rangers provided major security measures and attempted, not always successfully, to maintain discipline among their younger colleagues.

The Tent City Rangers were recently augmented, and many of the young marshals refuse to recognize them and now operate independently of them.

Park Police say that the several gangs from Chicago, Milwaukee, Detroit, and Memphis are also vying for power in the city and that one of their weapons is simple terror.

Police patrolling the area say they are frequently threatened and are the targets of stones and bottles.

Passing Cars Stoned

Youths have also periodically stoned cars passing the city on Independence Avenue. Police closed the street for several hours after one rash of stone-throwing about two weeks ago.

Numerous residents of the city say their cameras, sleeping bags, and other personal equipment have been stolen. Police say none of the cameras has yet turned up in any local pawnshops.

Hosea Williams, chief of direct action for the Campaign, said yesterday he suspects much of the trouble is instigated by "outsiders."

Bevel compared the situation to infiltration by strike breakers in the labor movement and Vietcong "peasants" in South Vietnam.

6

The Counterculture

Political and racial orthodoxies were not the only targets for protest during the Sixties. The traditional values, behavior, and personal relationships of most Americans also came under attack. Those holding radical views in these areas came to be collectively called the counterculture.

Cultural revolt has been an accompaniment of urban society in the West for a century and a half. It began in midnineteenth-century Paris, when groups of students, artists, writers, and social misfits repudiated the dominant middle-class morals and manners of their society and adopted a more spontaneous, relaxed, and hedonistic way of living. The rebels lived in garrets, wore flamboyant clothes, flaunted the traditional moral code, played at art and literature, and often had no visible means of support. They were called bohemians.

In the United States, bohemia surfaced before World War I, when New York's Greenwich Village and San Francisco's Barbary Coast became havens for an assortment of cultural mavericks who deplored the materialistic, philistine, bourgeois world that surrounded them. In the prosperous and fearful 1950s, America was not fertile soil for bohemia, but even in that repressed decade the Beat poets, musicians, painters, and philosophers captured the attention of the media with their argot, their odd dress, their casual pursuit of pleasure, and their professed commitment to aesthetic values.

The Beats represented a thin layer of creative men and women floating on a sea of 1950s conformity. Though they had their hangers-on and disciples among the young, they never had a mass following, perhaps because admission to their circle required a level of devotion to the arts that few could claim. In the counterculture that appeared in the following decade, standards were lower. It was consumer oriented. You needed only to dress, eat, listen, decorate, and speak in special ways to qualify as a hippie.

Thousands of young men and women—and adults who found the ways of youth irresistible—could meet the requirements. Many found that being a hippie could even be managed on weekends, part time.

"Beats + LSD = Counterculture" is a formula often endorsed by critics and historians, and it contains much truth. The new bohemia of the Sixties was drenched in psychedelics, starting with marijuana, then magic mushrooms, and progressing to lysergic acid diethylamide, LSD, an artificial substance developed by a Swiss pharmaceutical firm in the 1930s and then forgotten. Unlike previous mood-altering substances, LSD—"acid," in the contemporary jargon—left its users with a transformed sense of the world's qualities and possibilities sufficient to build a *Zeitgeist* on.

At the core of the counterculture spirit, as it evolved from about 1966 on, was liberation from instinctual restraints. Borrowing from Freud and from Wilhelm Reich, a refugee psychotherapist influenced by Freud and Marx alike, it called pleasure good and denial bad. Hippies—the young members of the counterculture—took visual delight in colorful dress and poster designs and illustrations derived from "acid dreams." They were emotional, passionate people who renounced square taboos against physical contact. They were enthusiasts of thunderous acid rock music, often combined with brilliant flashing lights. They imbibed mood-altering substances of every imaginable kind, though pot and LSD were probably the most popular. Inspired by Tantric Buddhism, Freud, and Norman O. Brown, they practiced sexual liberation, condoning not only a wider range of heterosexual acts but also homosexual behavior. The gay liberation movement that emerged abruptly in 1969 was in part only a creature of the counterculture. It also borrowed from the civil rights movement. But it was clearly encouraged by the new sexual tolerance that insisted: "If it feels good, do it!"

The counterculture, even more than the political New Left, was the child of prosperity. Hippies renounced the bourgeois rat race of nine-to-five jobs, manicured suburban lawns, and prudent lives. Some professed to despise private property and possessions generally, but most of them came from this very milieu. Almost all were white suburban dropouts who lived off the surplus and cast-offs of an affluent society. Some were straight remittance men and women who survived on checks sent by Dad or Mom from home.

It is easy to find fault with the counterculture. It was naive, dogmatic, and self-deceived. But it was also vastly influential. Its outward symbols and cultural preferences—long hair, beards, acid rock, pot, sexual permissiveness, gentleness, short time horizons—diffused through to adults and to working-class youths who had not been originally susceptible to the hippie appeal. It gave rise, in turn, to movements that borrowed its sexual tolerance and its professed love of nature. Not only did it contribute to the gay liberation movement, it also left its mark on the new ecological movement of the 1970s. Conservatives today would say that it can also be blamed for the collapse of reasonable sexual prudence and the resulting medical scourges of AIDS, hepatitis, and herpes as well as the breakdown of sexual restraint among the young and the explosion of illegitimacy and one-parent families that followed. Whenever we hear the remark "blame it on the Sixties," we can be sure it is the excesses of the counterculture to which the speaker is referring.

Whether for good or ill, then, it transformed our perceptions and values and left an indelible mark on our own times.

Rock 'n' Roll

Rock music helped define the counterculture. Rock 'n' roll began as the music of teenagers—it expressed their passion, raging hormones, delight in excess, and contempt for authority. It broke away from the teen culture with the music of the Beatles, a band of four working-class Liverpool youths, who created a sensation in February 1963, when they appeared on the popular Ed Sullivan Show *on TV. The next year, another British rock group, the Rolling Stones—tougher, harder-driving, and more sexual than the Beatles—made their first American appearance. For the rest of the decade, rock 'n' roll totally dominated the popular music scene. Even folk music transmuted into a hybrid, for which rock often supplied the dominant parentage. Marking a milestone, in 1965, folk hero Bob Dylan abandoned the acoustic guitar for the electric guitar, to the outrage of his followers.*

During the Sixties, the Bay Area contributed LSD—acid—to the rock music environment. It was the novelist Ken Kesey, allied with Bill Graham, manager of the San Francisco Mime Troup, who thought of merging hard-driving, blasting rock music with psychedelics at concert performances where both audience and performers were stoned. Out of this brew emerged acid rock, informed by LSD fantasies and dreams. The practitioners of acid rock—the Jefferson Airplane, Quicksilver Messenger Service, Family Dog, Big Brother and the Holding Company, Country Joe and the Fish, and the Grateful Dead—often lived the lives they sang about. Unlike the successful rockers elsewhere, who lived in mansions surrounded by servants, many resided in communal houses in the raffish Haight-Ashbury district of San Francisco, which they helped to make into the hippie capital of the world.

If there was ever a culminating moment for the counterculture, it took place from August 15 to 17, 1969, at the rock festival in Bethel, New York, known as

Woodstock. *The festival's promoters were two rich kids, John Roberts and Joel Rosenman, both at the point in their lives when they had finished with higher education but did not yet know what they wanted to do when they grew up. In early 1967, they placed an ad in* The New York Times: *"Young men with Unlimited Capital looking for interesting, legitimate investment opportunities and business propositions."*

In early 1969, Michael Lang and Artie Kornfield, two young men of the hippie persuasion, arrived at the office with a proposal to create a recording studio for rock musicians in Woodstock, New York, to be launched with a big rock festival. Roberts and Rosenman liked the festival idea and agreed to put up seed money for it. The contract split the profits of Woodstock Ventures four ways.

Rock festivals were not new. The Monterey Pop Festival on the West Coast and the Newport Jazz Festival in Rhode Island had attracted thousands of people and made money. Woodstock would be bigger and better. Besides the price of admission, the promoters would get revenue from concessions, a film about the event, and other peripherals. They would make money if they could attract just 25,000 rock lovers to buy six-dollar one-day admission tickets; they would be rich if they could get 75,000.

Serious problems intervened before the festival opened. The town of Woodstock itself was too small for the crowds expected. After some hectic months of looking for a suitable tract of open land, they struck a deal with Max Yasgur, a local dairy farmer in Bethel, to lease his acres for $50,000, with another $75,000 in escrow against damage and liabilities. The anxious quest for big-name groups to perform was solved with offers of $7,500 to $15,000 an appearance—money that the promoters stretched hard to get. By the eve of the festival, some of the biggest names in Sixties pop music— Creedence Clearwater Revival, the Jefferson Airplane, Janis Joplin, Jimi Hendrix, the Grateful Dead, The Who, Santana, Richie Havens, Joan Baez, Joe Cocker, and Arlo Guthrie—had signed up.

There were also formidable hurdles on the technical and logistical sides: lighting, sound equipment, electrical power, sanitation facilities, food, clean water, a stage, and garbage disposal. Security people and a medical team would be essential. And then there was the question of publicity. Here the massive network of the underground press that had sprouted since 1965 proved a boon. One unexpected expense was Abbie Hoffman, the bad boy of the counterculture, who threatened to bad-mouth the festival on the street and create chaos at Woodstock if he and his friends were not given payola. The promoters sent $10,000 to Hoffman and associates on the Lower East Side.

The festival was three frenzied days of music, pot, acid, grooving, skinny-dipping, and lovemaking, along with rain, mud, garbage, broken limbs, dysentery, freak-outs, two deaths, and one birth. Attendance far exceeded the promoters' wildest dreams.

More than 400,000 people came: they overwhelmed the latrines, the food stands, the ticket booths. A majority of the audience in the end got in free. About $800,000 in tickets were sold, not enough to cover expenses, but the returns from the film Woodstock *kept the promoters from taking a major loss.*

If the promoters got less than they hoped, the audience got more. Despite their discomfort, Woodstock was an experience that most never forgot. As an event, it would take on a mythic quality, like a major battle in a war. In later years, it would seem a transforming experience, as the moment in time when thousands of young people were merged into a distinct "nation," the Woodstock Nation, a symbolic representation of the counterculture world that was soon to dissolve into the gray mist of the 1970s.

The document excerpted here is the "Prologue" from an oral history of Woodstock. It summarizes, through the voices of four young men and one young woman, the Woodstock experience.

[*Excerpted from* Woodstock: The Oral History, *by Joel Makower (Doubleday, 1989). Copyright © 1989 by Tilden Press, Inc.*]

PROLOGUE

Diana Warshawsky: I was living in San Francisco in the Haight-Ashbury area . . . and I heard that there was going to be some kind of gathering of music . . . in a place called Woodstock and had something to do with a ranch owned by Bob Dylan. That's what I heard, that's what . . . the rumor had it. And some of the people from the area were thinking of going. . . . It . . . sounded pretty interesting. And so I made arrangements to go. . . .

Joseph Coakley: I was reading a copy of *Ramparts* magazine, flying back from Denver to Cleveland. . . . I saw this little ad in the back of the magazine that had this rather interesting-looking music festival that was going to be happening. . . . I decided that this could be a lot of fun. I ended up calling up my cousin Jim, and he knew a few people that were going, and we ended up going together. . . .

Rick Gavras: I was living in Montreal. . . . I was nineteen years old and had moved to Montreal with my family in '67. . . . I was very kind of collegiate. And when I got to Montreal, I was quite shocked at everything that was going on, because it was a big cosmopolitan East Coast city and there were people with real long hair and I was still wearing Weejuns. . . . It was scary for me. I didn't know quite what was going on. But I learned quickly, and I became involved in it. I suppose it was a combination of just what was going on at the time—acceptance from peers, getting involved with LSD and smoking marijuana, getting involved in kind of Eastern approaches to life. I don't remember exactly how I heard about Woodstock, except it was being, I'm sure, broadcast on the radio and stuff like that. And since Montreal was only a three- or four-hour drive from Woodstock, it just seemed to fall into place to drive to Woodstock. . . .

Alan Green: It was right after my freshman year of college. I was working at the Department of Public Works in Teaneck. . . . I had this girlfriend, Eve, who lived out in Long Island. . . . Towards the end of the summer, I remember Woodstock sort of slipping in and out of my consciousness. . . . But I didn't remember any kind of great electricity. . . . But as it got closer to the day, there started to be a little more excitement and I remember saying to Eve . . . and I said, "Well, we should go to Woodstock," which really thrilled her parents. . . . I was going to buy a car—a Volkswagen—from my brother that day to take to Woodstock. . . . I had never driven a stick before, and I figured I would learn on my way to Woodstock. . . .

Joe Tinkelman: I had dropped out of college, but all my college friends were home for the summer in Poughkeepsie, New York. . . . And I had been spending a lot of time with my friend Larry Woodside. . . . We happened to see ads in the *Times* that there was going to be a concert and that originally it was scheduled for Woodstock and that now it was going to be near Monticello. . . .

Joseph Coakley: It's kind of interesting. I look at this festival as a very definite—not to sound trite—but it had significant meaning to my life in the sense that I had been busted by my parents the night before for smoking pot and my mom had flushed all of my stuff down the toilet. It made me feel like I was a reject to society and all these other things. Anyways, it was really funny because I remember going up in the car, and this one guy had some hash with him and I wouldn't have anything to do with it. . . . I made it as far as somewhere between the general store of White Lake and the festival site before I decided to break down and buy something.

Rick Gavras: We all jumped in the car. . . . I was supposed to meet my girlfriend. . . . I was supposed to meet her at Woodstock and, of course, little did we know that there was going to be a few hundred thousand people there. So I never did meet her. I suppose we thought there was some sort of front gate or something of that sort. . . . When I got there, it was just, well, there was a lot of land. I don't know how many acres it was, but there was no front entrance at that point. I think everybody was pretty much being allowed just to go in. It was just kind of like a long field and just people sort of en masse kind of converging on the spot, and I realized right away I wasn't going to meet Mimi.

Alan Green: There was no idea of how big the thing could possibly be. . . . So we packed up a little bit of food, some dope, a jacket—once again, there was no planning at all, unlike a lot of people who seemed to arrive with all sorts of provisions. . . . I think we started out around noon and picked up someone hitchhiking, and as we started getting closer . . . up the Thruway . . . there were people all of a sudden appearing with signs: WOODSTOCK. And as it got closer, it was really obvious that something was happening, and there was this—it was sort of weird. . . .

Rick Gavras: It was overwhelming because there were so many people. It was like something kind of colossal. There was a stage. And the stage from where I was for the first couple of days was real far away because I was way, way in back. I was busy kind of strolling all over the place. And I never really got up close to the stage until the third day, the very last day.

I pretty much stayed with my friends most of the time, or at least a couple of them. And, of course, we were all taking LSD twenty-four hours a day and smoking twenty-four hours a day, which I guess most people were doing. And so everything was very surreal.

Alan Green: There were long, long lines of cars—I guess miles already at that point—but when you got onto Yasgur's farm, there was still no idea to sort of understand what was going on because there were people milling around. . . . We looked around and thought, "Well, this should be fun. We'll camp out here for two days or three days, and there will probably be a lot of people around." So we found a spot in the woods and we decided maybe we should smoke a joint and we were very paranoid that someone would know that we were getting high so we sort of went way back in the woods because there just weren't that many people around. There was nothing happening. There weren't mobs of people, and there was no reason to expect what would ultimately happen. . . .

We [finally] figured it must be time for the music to start, and we walked down to the hill and, once again, it did not seem like there were that many people. But the amazing thing, as we were sitting off in the woods before we went in to see the music, there was this parade of people that just seemed to never stop, and it kept getting deeper and wider. . . .

Joe Tinkelman: We drove past Monticello Raceway, and within a very few miles the road just became filled with cars stopped on both sides. The state highway became a parking lot. . . . We were really sort of puzzled by it all. . . . [But] this was parking for the concert. . . . And we got out of the car and started walking in the direction of White Lake. Then, as we walked five to ten car lengths in front of our car, we started to see people setting up lawn chairs on their front lawns—the houses that fronted on the highway—to watch this spectacle. And the feeling sort of changed over to a sense of exhilaration that all these people had gotten together. . . .

Diana Warshawsky: We had to park pretty far away, and we had sleeping bags and duffel bags and walked for a long time to get there . . . following streams of other people all walking with their sleeping bags and duffel bags, and hot, humid. We finally arrived at the area and it was a very strange scene. It was muddy and there was some grass. It was all in browns and grays, you know, from the sky and the overcast and the humidity, and there was a huge—like a big mud puddle is all I can call it—that was as big as a small swimming pool. And all these people had their clothes off and thought they were swimming or something, I don't know. They were all bathing in this muddy water, and I remember—I'll never forget this—all these muddy brown bodies, you know, bathing and sort of frolicking in this water hole. It didn't look appealing at all to me. I thought, "Boy, who knows, some people will jump at the chance to do anything." The field was huge and it was surrounded . . . by barbed wire, this area that the concert was taking place in. And we eventually found, with our stuff with us, you know, found a spot in this field. . . . We just walked in, I guess. I don't know what the story was. Were they selling tickets? Were there supposed to be tickets?

Joseph Coakley: I can remember, having my ticket, looking for someplace to give my ticket as we walked to the gate, which turns out had been busted, I guess, wide open. And there was a rumor going around that there was this very left-wing political group from New York called Up Against the Wall* that had apparently threatened to have some sort of political event and had stormed the gate, and I don't know if they collected tickets early or what, but the place was wide open when we got there in the early afternoon.

*Actually, the group, which combined radical politics with guerrilla theater, was called Up Against the Wall, Motherfuckers—ed.

Rick Gavras: There was just so much stuff going on that looking back on it now it seems as though it was some sort of episode out of maybe a Fellini movie or something. Just so bizarre and so weird, and yet there I was, experiencing a lot of personal conflict too. Having discussions and arguments about the [Vietnam] war. . . . There were talks about the nature of the war and why America was there. . . . Here I was in the midst of this experience that was so overwhelming. And all the visual stuff—just adding large doses of hallucinogens. I mean, it was a very powerful experience.

Alan Green: We found a spot in the woods where we originally had been when we came in Friday afternoon to sleep, and it was sort of well behind the hill. . . . And when I woke up in the morning, this stream of people was still moving through the road. . . . We walked from where we were in the woods to the stage and looked out, and all of a sudden what had . . . seemed to me a few thousand people had become this half million people. . . .

Diana Warshawsky: It wasn't ever an out-of-control situation. I know they had emergency stands . . . in case somebody was flipping out or sick or hurt or anything, and it was a very peaceful group of people. People were just happy, you know, getting stoned and just being happy to be there. But I found it very unnerving to be with this many people inside a barbed wire. And there was a helicopter flying over . . . I felt like I was trapped. . . . I was having a good time because of, you know, being with my friends, the person I was with, and I remember, in terms of music, I have almost no recollection of the music except that the only performer that I remember is Richie Havens. I remember him and I remember really liking that, and that's it. I don't know who else performed that night. Actually, I'd be curious to know.

I do remember that when the music was over for that evening, we sort of trudged down a road and found a relatively hospitable place to unroll sleeping bags off the side of the road, and slept that night. . . . I wanted to leave the next morning. And so we ended up hitchhiking out of the area back into New York City. . . .

Joseph Coakley: I remember how incredibly crowded it was. I can remember putting my hand somewhere and then not being able to move it for two hours. . . . It was just incredibly cramped. . . .

I remember it rained that night. I can remember we were hungry, and there were some concession stands at the top of the bowl that for all intents and purposes were the only places I knew of to eat, and these political people, you know, that were wandering around the area—you didn't see them or whatever, but I understand that some of the concessions got torched that night due to their high prices or whatever, which further burdened the whole problem of what to eat. But as I remember waking up the next morning, it was a sea of mud. That bowl was just incredible. Everybody was cold and wet. Just a very unpleasant camping experience out there in the bowl. But as I remember, the music stopped Friday night; I don't think they played all night Friday night. I don't remember if they did or not.

Rick Gavras: As far as the music goes, what I remember mostly was they had two stages set up on the sides of the main stage. I remember one night at the main stage real vividly, but most of my memories of music were on the side stages. And there was where you could kind of lay in the grass, and it wasn't real crowded. The Grateful Dead played there a lot. That was good. They were really into relating with the people. I remember seeing them a lot and sitting on the stage and how wonderful they were at that time. And the music I remember the most out of everything was on one night, and that was basically the people that stand out mostly in my mind: Santana and Sly and the Family Stone. I think they all played on one night. Janis Joplin. That was kind of the most connected night I had. I was just totally enveloped in the music. . . . The music was real important but there was just so much stuff going on. . . .

I think maybe a lot of it had to do with kind of maintaining a sense of sanity for me, especially when you're tripping twenty-four hours a day. A lot of stuff sure appeared weird. Maybe a lot of that had to do with how people looked. . . . Just seeing so many strange, strangely adorned people and all the costumes and just the intensity of how the people were relating to each other in a lot of ways. Not so much through speaking and everything, but just through the experience and the being there and people kind of smiling and dancing. People were giving away drugs, LSD and stuff like that. . . .

Alan Green: It was almost like being in an Army unit and going out to do reconnaissance to hear someone play music. I remember we were laying on the tarp and someone would say, "Hey, Canned Heat is playing," and people would go out. . . . I remember going back to the Hog Farm because we figured that's where we would get our food. They had this just horrible rice with raisins or something, and it was just the most disgusting thing. But I don't even remember hearing a lot of music after that. We could hear the music from where we were, and every now and then we'd sort of head out to the crowd and stand up and look out from the top of the hill on everything and then go back to the tarp.

Then it started with people climbing on the light towers and all the announcements. When they first started, they were mostly the things you would hear at an airport: "Meet your friend at so-and-so." And then they seemed to take on sort of odder proportions almost, and they gravitated from "Meet your friend" to "Your friend is ill" to "Your friend took bad acid" to—anything imaginable. . . .

Joseph Coakley: I can remember having to go to the bathroom really badly, and I was afraid of losing my cousin Jim. I remember finally I had to do something about it and I had to leave this little sanctuary that I'd been guarding or calling home for the last eight to ten hours or whatever, and Creedence Clearwater was playing and I decided to venture out into the unknown . . . and try to find a toilet. This was Saturday night, and I remember going out there and finding a bathroom and wandering around. Coming back, I looked out there and I was lost. I mean, I had no idea. . . . I was just looking at this huge mass and there were no ushers, no seats, nobody there with a flashlight to help you out, and miraculously, after I wandered around for . . . a long time . . . I remember tripping over this body, and it ended up being my cousin Jim. . . .

Rick Gavras: Seeing the emphasis on people being concerned with helping other people in a sense of like doing it for free . . . I think that was important to me because in those days I kind of considered myself a hippie, but in retrospect, I wasn't. I mean, I was involved in a lot of drug dealing and I always had a significant chunk of money, so it was easy to call myself a hippie and all that. Especially when you have money in your pockets. A lot of the principles and everything, although they sounded good to me, I don't know how fond of them I would have been if I really had to live them. . . . I think that would have been pretty scary for me in those younger years to be in that kind of condition, to be on the streets, or to be living a life like that. My life was very drug-oriented. And I'm one of the ones who continued down that path for many years . . . and eventually ending up a heroin addict. . . .

It was a very, very moving and powerful time because I think it was that night when I was so connected with the music and with everything that was going on around me . . . that's when I seemed to have a sense that it was all kind of a oneness of experience, that everybody was there together and enjoying themselves and celebrating in that sense of togetherness. . . . The way I see it, those were the days when that whole thing was flowering and opening up. Because it was so dependent on drugs, it had a lot of illusory qualities to it.

Alan Green: The most bizarre kinds of people started floating through the woods. . . . I remember we were just sitting around while people were cutting down limbs or something, pulling branches off trees and some guy coming through and standing and talking about how we should all stare up at the sun—I mean, just all kinds of odd people began filtering through this little enclave that we had back in the woods. And, for a while it was almost like there was no festival because you couldn't see anything. You could hear the music and people would be filtering through the woods on their way to the Hog Farm. . . .

I was not a nerd who happened to end up at Woodstock because his friends dragged him along, but I think it was pretty clear that there were all these people who were really far out there. . . . It was sort of a great shock to see that many freaky people in one place and people who seemed to have been doing this kind of stuff . . . for years, because it looked like their hair had been growing for years. . . . They had years' worth of counterculture apparatus and stories and weirdness, and I think there were a lot of people who were on the fringes of that that maybe got catapulted towards that after that summer. . . .

I was one of those people who had to call home to assure my parents that everything was okay. . . . And I remember talking to my mother, who kept saying, "Well, what is it like there? What is it like?" And I was saying, "It's nothing like you're probably hearing about. It's just a rock festival."

Doctor HIPpocrates

Every movement needs its intellectual public squares to exchange opinions, news, ideas, and programs among its followers. The counterculture forum was the underground press, an efflorescence of publications that touched every major campus and every major city by 1967. The prototype of these papers was New York's Village Voice, *started in 1955 by a group of dissident Democrats and cultural dissenters to express their advanced liberal politics and their avant-garde tastes. Not until the first issue of* The Berkeley Barb *a decade later, however, was the form perfected.*

A crudely printed weekly that looked as if it were assembled by enterprising high school seniors, the Barb *was a mirror of the emerging radical politics and liberated culture of the Berkeley scene. It reported on radical campus politics, the Bay Area antiwar movement, the emerging sexual revolution, and acid rock music. One of its more interesting functions was to provide medical advice to the hippie community taking root in the Telegraph Avenue neighborhood near the UC campus and in Haight-Ashbury, across the bay in San Francisco.*

This community of predominantly young people had diseases aplenty. Drugs, poor hygiene, and free and easy sex, created a plague of medical problems that had to be addressed. The Barb *met the challenge through the services of Dr. Eugene Schoenfeld, a young Bay Area M.D. who began a syndicated column in 1965. Calling himself "Dr. HIPpocrates"—a wordplay on both the father of Western medicine and the hippie culture—his weekly column for the* Barb *was so popular, it ran in many other underground newspapers.*

The following document, combining parts of two HIPpocrates columns from the Barb *of 1967, suggests the quality of hippie life better than a direct description. In it, the good doctor adds a dash of humor to sound and sober advice to his hippie clientele. Dr. Schoenfeld was no prude. He did not condemn the lifestyles of his young correspondents, but he also felt compelled to keep them from hurting themselves.*

[**Eugene Schoenfeld, M.D., M.P.H., "HIPpocrates," Berkeley Barb, September 7, 1967, and October 5, 1967. With permission of Dr. Eugene Schoenfeld.**]

*HIP*POCRATES

QUESTION: I have heard that marijuana usage causes vitamin deficiencies. Can you tell me if this is so, and if so what vitamins?

ANSWER: There are no known harmful effects from the use of marijuana in normal individuals. A vitamin deficiency coincident with the use of marijuana is probably the result of an inadequate diet, such as some of the Zen macrobiotic diets, which are low in protein and devoid of such essentials as ascorbic acid or vitamin C.

QUESTION: Is it possible to get a venereal disease in the bathroom?

ANSWER: It is certainly possible to get a venereal disease in the bathroom, but the floors are usually cold and hard. In other words, only in the rarest of circumstances could one contract a venereal disease other than by intimate physical contact.

QUESTION: What are the effects of sniffing airplane glue?

ANSWER: When I was gluing model airplanes, we thought it a great kick to squeeze out ten-foot-long strips of glue, put a match to them, and watch the fire race along the fuselike glue strips. But like the mind-affecting properties of LSD, the use of airplane glue to get high must have been found accidentally, perhaps by a preteen innocently working on his models in a poorly ventilated garage. No one really knows the prevalence of glue sniffing, but police records show thousands of arrests yearly in some large cities.

The behavioral effects of glue sniffing are usually described as imitating those of alcohol intoxication though there are reports of hallucinations and body image distortions.

At least ten deaths by suffocation have resulted from the practice of sniffing glue from a plastic sack. Direct toxic effects have included two deaths in young adult males, both of whom had been drinking alcohol; one, in addition, had a history of sniffing gasoline. . . .

QUESTION: Two of my roommates are in the hospital with hepatitis. Their doctor says they have serum hepatitis. Is there more than one type? Could I have caught it from them?

ANSWER: There are two types of viral hepatitis: serum and infectious. Infectious is thought to be spread by fecal or, rarely, urinary contamination. Recently, an outbreak of hepatitis at San Quentin Prison was traced to a pissed-off inmate urinating into a huge soup pot.

Your roommates, however, have the type spread through contaminated blood. Users of narcotics and methedrine who share inadequately sterilized needles and syringes have a very high rate of hepatitis. Hepatitis is a most disabling and often fatal disease, and I would guess that those who use needles for their highs become ill or die more often from contaminated needles or syringes than from overdose of drugs.

Symptoms of viral hepatitis are dark-colored urine, light-colored stools, and jaundice or yellowing of the eyes and skin.

QUESTION: My boyfriend had a discharge from his penis, saw a doctor, and was treated for gonorrhea. I haven't noticed any symptoms in myself. Is it necessary to get a checkup? If so, where can I go? I have very little money and no regular doctor.

ANSWER: Gonorrhea in the male usually makes itself known by a penile discharge, itching, and burning on urination. In the female, however, there may be less obvious symptoms or no symptoms at all. If your boyfriend had gonorrhea (and I assume you two are friendly), there is a good chance you may have it also, even though you may feel perfectly well. Most cities of any size operate clinics where you may receive treatment of venereal diseases free of charge. If you are a college student, you may go to your student health service. . . .

QUESTION: Can infectious hepatitis be contracted through cunnilingus?

ANSWER: This is an excellent way—if the recipient of your affection has the disease. . . .

The Stonewall Riot

The Sixties insurgency not only empowered outsiders, it also reduced the ability of the conventional moral code to penalize cultural nonconformists. Together the two trends enabled sexual rebels whose preferences were abhorred by mainstream society to find their voices and assert their rights. The largest contingent of these dissenters were gays and lesbians.

As the Sixties opened, gays and lesbians were outlaw groups. In virtually every legal jurisdiction, their sexual preferences were illegal and, if detected, they could be arrested and punished. Beyond this, the larger society held them in contempt and discriminated against them in jobs, housing, and social contact. In only a very few areas, mostly connected with the arts, fashion, and interior design, could homosexuals freely acknowledge their identity. But in almost every other realm of life, they had to hide who they were to avoid paying an exorbitant price in personal regard and career advancement.

Homosexuals created enclaves where they could associate with each other and pursue their preferences. There were gay and lesbian bars, social clubs, baths, and gyms. In some of the more permissive communities, such as San Francisco and New York, gays sponsored carnivals or balls where they could openly display their cultural sensibilities. These often attracted straights who came to gawk at the "freaks."

But homosexual meeting places generally remained illegal and flourished only by sufferance of the authorities. Gay promoters or straight entrepreneurs catering to gays often had to pay large bribes to the police to keep their establishments open. The police, however, were subject to pressure by the custodians of conventional morality and their sufferance was often erratic.

The Stonewall Inn was a Greenwich Village bar that catered to gay men. On Friday, June 27, 1969, New York police from the sixth precinct raided it for lack of a liquor license and arrested the bartender, the bouncer, and a number of cross-dresser drag queens. The rest of the patrons were let out one by one. But instead of dispersing, the men, as well as sympathetic spectators, hurled bottles, cans, and cobblestones at the cops. Reinforcements rescued the police and ended the disorder. But it resumed the next night and spread through the Village. Many of the angry people chanted a new war cry: "Gay power."

The Stonewall riot was the Boston Tea Party of the gay community. The courageous defiance of the police by the New York homosexual community electrified gays everywhere in America and ignited a full-fledged liberation movement. In a half dozen years the forces unleashed in 1969 would reduce the isolation and segregation of gays and lesbians and dismantle most of the legal repression that cast a dark shadow over their lives.

The piece below is from The Village Voice, *the parent of the underground press. It is an eyewitness account by a* Voice *reporter, the later novelist Lucian Truscott, who was not gay and who had a somewhat dismissive attitude toward the participants, though in the end he cheers the new liberation movement that Stonewall stirred to life.*

[**Lucian Truscott IV, "Gay Power Comes to Sheridan Square," Village Voice, July 3, 1969.**]

GAY POWER COMES TO SHERIDAN SQUARE

Sheridan Square this weekend looked like something from a William Burroughs novel as the sudden specter of "gay power" erected its brazen head and spat out a fairy tale the likes of which the area has never seen.

The forces of faggotry, spurred by a Friday night raid on one of the city's largest, most popular, and longest-lived gay bars, the Stonewall Inn, rallied Saturday night in an unprecedented protest against the raid and continued Sunday night to assert presence, possibility, and pride until the early hours of Monday morning. "I'm a faggot, and I'm proud of it!" "Gay power!" "I like boys!"—these and many other slogans were heard all three nights as the show of force by the city's finery met the force of the city's finest. The result was a kind of liberation, as the gay brigade emerged from the bars, back rooms, and bedrooms of the Village and became street people.

• • •

Cops entered the Stonewall for the second time in a week just before midnight on Friday. It began as a small raid—only two patrolmen, two detectives, and two policewomen were involved. But as the patrons trapped inside were released one by one, a crowd started to gather on the street. It was initially a festive gathering, composed mostly of Stonewall boys who were waiting around for friends still inside or to see what was going to happen. Cheers would go up as favorites would emerge from the door, strike a pose, and swish by the detective with a "Hello there, fella." The stars were in their element. Wrists were limp, hair was primped, and reactions to the applause were classic. "I gave them the gay power bit, and they loved it, girls." "Have you seen Maxine? Where *is* my wife—I told her not to go far."

Suddenly the paddywagon arrived and the mood of the crowd changed. Three of the more blatant queens—in full drag—were loaded inside, along with the bartender and doorman, to a chorus of catcalls and boos from the crowd. A cry went up to push the paddywagon over, but it drove away before anything could happen. With its exit, the action waned momentarily. The next person to come out was a dyke, and she put up a struggle—from car to door to car again. It was at that moment that the scene became explosive. Limp wrists were forgotten. Beer cans and bottles were heaved at the windows, and a rain of coins descended on the cops. At the height of the action a bearded figure was plucked from the crowd and dragged inside. It was Dave Van Ronk, who had come from the Lion's Head to see what was going on. He was later charged with having thrown an object at the police.

Three cops were necessary to get Van Ronk away from the crowd and into the Stonewall. The exit left no cops on the street, and almost by signal the crowd erupted into cobblestone and bottle heaving. The reaction was total; they were pissed. The trash can I was standing on was nearly yanked out from under me as a kid tried to grab it for use in the window-smashing melee. From nowhere came an uprooted parking meter—used as a battering ram on the Stonewall door. I heard several cries of "Let's get some gas," but the blaze of flame which soon appeared in the window of the Stonewall was still a shock. As the wood barrier behind the glass was beaten open, the cops inside turned their hose on the crowd. Several kids took the opportunity to cavort in the spray, and their momentary glee served to stave off what was rapidly becoming a full-scale attack. By the time the fags were able to regroup forces and come up with another assault, several carloads of police reinforcements had arrived, and in minutes the streets were clear.

A visit to the Sixth Precinct revealed that thirteen persons had been arrested on charges that ranged from Van Ronk's felonious assault of a police officer to the owners' illegal sale and storage of alcoholic beverages without a license. Two police officers had been injured in the battle with the crowd. By the time the last cop was off the street Saturday morning, a sign was going up that the Stonewall would reopen that night. It did.

●   ●   ●

Protest set the tone for the "gay power" activities on Saturday. The afternoon was spent boarding up the windows of the Stonewall and chalking them with signs of the new revolution: "We are open," "There is all college boys and girls in here," "Support Gay Power—C'mon in girls," "Insp. Smyth looted our money, jukebox, cigarette mach., telephones, safe, cash register, and the boys' tips." Among the slogans were two carefully clipped and bordered copies of the *Daily News* story about the previous night's events, which was anything but kind to the gay cause.

The real action Saturday was that night on the street. Friday night's crowd had returned and was being led in "gay power" cheers by a group of gay cheerleaders. "We are the Stonewall girls/We wear our hair in curls/We have no underwear/We show our pubic hairs!" The crowd was gathered across the street from the Stonewall and was growing with additions of onlookers, Eastsiders, and rough street people who saw a chance for a little action. Though dress had changed from Friday night's gayery to

Saturday night street clothes, the scene was a command performance for queers. If Friday night had been pick-up night, Saturday was date night. Hand-holding, kissing, and posing accented each of the cheers with a homosexual liberation that had appeared only fleetingly on the street before. One-liners were as practiced as if they had been used for years. "I just want you to all know," quipped a platinum blond with obvious glee, "that sometimes being a homosexual is a big pain in the ass." Another allowed as how he had become a "left-deviationist." And on and on.

The quasi-political tone of the street scene was looked upon with disdain by some, for radio news announcements about the previous night's "gay power" chaos had brought half of Fire Island's Cherry Grove* running back to home base to see what they had left behind. The generation gap existed even here. Older boys had strained looks on their faces and talked in concerned whispers as they watched the up-and-coming generation take being gay and flaunting it before the masses.

As the "gay power" chants on the street rose in frequency and volume, the crowd grew restless. The front of the Stonewall was losing its attraction, despite efforts by the owners to talk the crowd back into the club. "C'mon in and see what da pigs done to us," they growled. "We're honest business-men here. We're American-born boys. We run a legitimate joint here. There ain't nuttin bein' done wrong in dis place. Everybody come and see."

The people on the street were not to be coerced. "Let's go down the street and see what's happening, girls," someone yelled. And down the street went the crowd; smack into the Tactical Patrol Force, who had been called earlier to disperse the crowd and were walking west on Christopher from Sixth Avenue. Formed in a line, the TPF swept the crowd back to Waverly Place, where they stopped. A stagnant situation there brought on some gay tomfoolery in the form of a chorus line facing the line of hel-meted and club-carrying cops, and as the line got into full kick routine, the TPF advanced again and cleared the crowd of screaming gay powerites down Christopher to Seventh Avenue. The street and park were then held from both ends and no one was allowed to enter—naturally causing a fall off in normal Saturday night business at the straight Lion's Head. . . . The TPF positions in and around the park were held with only minor inci-dent—one busted head and a number of scattered arrests—while the cops amused themselves by arbitrarily breaking up small groups of people up and down the avenue. The crowd finally dispersed around 3:30 A.M. The

*Fire Island, on the south shore of Long Island, was a major summer beach resort for New York. It had several gay communities, including Cherry Grove—ed.

TPF had come and they had conquered, but Sunday was already there, and it was to be another story.

•   •   •

Sunday night was a time for watching and rapping. Gone were the "gay power" chants of Saturday, but not the new and open brand of exhibition-ism. Steps, curbs, and the park provided props for what amounted to the Sunday fag follies as returning stars from the previous night's perfor-mances stopped by to close the show for the weekend.

It was slow going. Around one A.M. a nonhelmeted version of the TPF arrived and made a controlled and very cool sweep of the area, getting everyone moving and out of the park. That put a damper on posing and primping, and as the last buses were leaving Jerseyward, the crowd grew thin. Allen Ginsberg* . . . walked by to see what was happening and . . . [was] filled in on the previous evenings' activities by some of the gay activists. "Gay power! Isn't that great!" Allen said. "We're one of the largest minorities in the country—ten percent, you know. It's about time we did something to assert ourselves."

Ginsberg expressed a desire to visit the Stonewall. "You know, I've never been there"—and ambled on down the street flashing peace signs and hal-loing the TPF. It was a relief and a kind of joy to see him on the street. He lent an extra umbrella of serenity to the scene with his laughter and quiet commentary on consciousness, "gay power" as a new movement, and the various implications of what had happened. I followed him into the Stonewall, where rock music blared from speakers all around the room that might have come right from a Hollywood set of a gay bar. He was immediately bouncing and dancing wherever he moved.

He left, and I walked east with him. Along the way, he described how things used to be. "You know, the guys there were so beautiful—they've lost that wonderful look that fags all had ten years ago." It was the first time I had heard that crowd described as beautiful.

We reached Cooper Square, and as Ginsberg turned his head toward home, he waved and yelled, "Defend the fairies!" and bounced on across the square. He enjoyed the prospect of "gay power" and is probably work-ing on a manifesto for the movement right now. Watch out. The liberation is under way.

*The famous Beat poet, author of *Howl*. Ginsberg had made the transition from 1950s bohemia to the antiwar counterculture movements of the Sixties—ed.

The Psychedelic Revolution

The chief apostle of a world transformed through LSD was a young Harvard psychology instructor, Timothy Leary. Already a dabbler with mind-altering substances, Leary first took LSD in 1962, when it was known only to a sliver of artists and cultural adventurers. The encounter was the "most shattering experience in my life," he later said. He soon became a regular "tripper" and, with another young Harvard psychologist, Richard Alpert, began to experiment with LSD on prison inmates and students to alter consciousness and change behavior.

Leary and Alpert were both fired from Harvard in 1963 for their psychedelic zealotry and became international missionaries for LSD as the key to a new ecstatic religion. Eventually, like many cultural explorers during the Sixties, Alpert turned to Eastern religion, becoming reincarnated as Baba Ram Dass, a Buddhist guru. Leary created IFIF (International Foundation for Internal Freedom), sited first in Newton, Massachusetts, and then at Millbrook, New York. Here Leary's acolytes could imbibe LSD in controlled situations and absorb the philosophical teachings their leader extracted from the psychedelic experience. IFIF's high priest, like an old-time Methodist minister, also went circuit-riding to spread the gospel of "Turn on, tune in, drop out." Despite Leary's zeal (or because of it), in 1965 Congress made unlicensed manufacture and sale of LSD a federal crime.

In this selection—a talk he gave at the University of California in June 1966—Leary describes the "psychedelic revolution" as it was unfolding. Before this university audience his tone is that of the rational scientist, but he was also a shameless publicity hound and a carnival showman who staged light and sound spectacles to pay the bills. In May 1996, Leary turned his final act, death from prostate cancer, into a public spectacle. His last words, reputedly, were "Why not?"

THE POLITICS OF ECSTASY

This mention of good, right, and legal brings me to the final part of my essay, the politics of ecstasy.

To understand the current controversy over LSD and marijuana, I think you have to realize that we are right in the middle of that most amazing social phenomenon, a religious renaissance. The LSD experience is, and the marijuana experience can be, a deeply spiritual event. The LSD kick is a spiritual ecstasy. The LSD trip is a religious pilgrimage. The LSD gamble is that risk that men have faced for thousands of years if they wished to pursue what lay beyond their minds. The LSD psychosis is a religious confusion, an ontological confusion, a spiritual crisis. What is real? Who am I? Where do I belong? What's the real level of energy? Can I go back? Should I go back? Should I go on? How many of you can answer those questions?

When you hear about or read about a lurid account of an LSD psychosis, keep this hypothesis in mind. It may be pathology, but it might be divine madness.

Turn On, Tune In, Drop Out

My advice to people in America today is as follows: If you take the game of life seriously, if you take your nervous system seriously, if you take your sense organs seriously, if you take the energy process seriously, you must turn on, tune in, and drop out.

Turning On

By "turn on" I mean get in touch, first of all, with your sense organs (not as instruments to be used in some secular game, but as cameras to put you in touch with the vibrant energies around you). Get in touch with your cellular wisdom. Get in touch with the universe within. The only way out is in. And the way to find the wisdom within is to turn on.

Now turning on is not an easy thing to do. In the first place, it takes courage to go out beyond your mind. The psychedelic yoga is the toughest, most demanding yoga of all. The easy thing to do is to stay with your addiction, stay with the symbol system you have. As you expand your symbol system from year to year by building up a few conditioned reflexes, you learn a few new words, a few new techniques each year. You will say, "Well, I'm growing. I'm learning." But you are still caught in symbols. The psychedelic road to divinity is neither a royal nor an easy one. As I said earlier, to learn how to use your sense organs with the help of marijuana is a very exacting discipline. The discipline of LSD is without doubt the most complex and demanding task that man on this planet has yet confronted. I often tell college students, "If you want to get a Ph.D., count on four years after you graduate. If you want to get an M.D., count on six or eight after your A.B. But for your LSD, count on thirty years at least."

Tuning In

By "tune in" I mean harness your internal revelations to the external world around you. I am not suggesting that we all find a desert island and curl up under a palm tree and take LSD and study our navels. As I look around at the people who have taken LSD, far from being inactive, lazy, and passive, I see them in every walk of life and in every age group, struggling to express what they are learning. The hippie movement, the psychedelic style, involves a revolution in our concepts of art and creativity which is occurring right before our eyes. The new music, the new poetry, the new visual art, the new film.

Dropping Out

"Dropping out" is the toughest pill to swallow. Whenever I give a lecture and tell people to drop out, invariably I alarm many listeners, including my friends, who say, "Now listen, Timothy, tone it down. You can't go around telling students to drop out of school, telling middle-class men with mortgage payments to drop out of their jobs. That's just too much! You can't do that in a technological society like this!" Of course, this message, *turn on, tune in, and drop out,* just happens to be the oldest message around—the old refrain that has been passed on for thousands of years by every person who has studied the energy process and man's place in it. Find the wisdom within, hook it up in a new way, but above all, detach yourself. Unhook the ambitions and the symbolic drives and the mental connections which keep you addicted and tied to the immediate tribal game.

Is our American society so insecure that it cannot tolerate our young people taking a year or two off, growing beards, wandering around the country, fooling with new forms of consciousness? This is one of the oldest traditions in civilized society. Take a voyage! Take the adventure! Before you settle down to the tribal game, try out self-exile. Your coming back will be much enriched.

The Psychedelic Migration

Today we face a problem which is unique in man's history. Due to the population explosion, there is no place for people like us to go. During the summer of 1963 a group of us were deported from three countries to which we had gone to find a quiet place where we could teach ourselves and a small group of other people how to use our nervous systems. We made no demands on these countries. We actually brought money into these shaky economies, but we were barred. So as we looked around this planet, pored over maps and atlases that summer, it dawned on us that today, for the first time in human history, there was no place for people like us to go.

A hundred years ago, people who believed as we do in the spiritual life would get into covered wagons and move across the prairie. The Mormons did it. Or three hundred years ago, people like us got into leaky boats and sailed for Plymouth Rock. And the fact of the matter is, there are many more people today who wish to follow a psychedelic way of life than there were Puritans in England who colonized this country. There are probably more in the city of San Francisco.

External migration as a way of finding a place where you can drop out and turn on and then tune in to the environment is no longer possible. The only place to go is in. And that's the fascinating thing about this new and indigenous religious movement which is springing up in this country today. It is interesting, too, that the psychedelic religious movement uses the same chemical aids or sacraments as the first American religion—the peyote religion of the native American Indians. I wonder if this is an accident or rather, perhaps, a curious game of the DNA code.

The characteristics of the psychedelic-spiritual quest are these: it's highly individual, highly personal. You will find no temples, you will find no organized dogmas; you will find instead small groups of people, usually centered on families, making these voyages together. We have discovered, as men have discovered for thousands of years, that the only temple is the human body and the place of worship is the shrine within your own home, prepared and lovingly designed for your spiritual procedure. The growth of LSD use in this country in the last few years is, if I dare say so, a minor miracle in itself. It has grown without any institutional backing or even recognition or approval. For the first three or four years it grew silently, person by person, cell by cell, husband and wife, you and your friends. My cells tell me that that's how everything durable grows. That's how it's always been.

When I say that the LSD movement is highly individual, I do not want you to think that I am talking about individuality in the personality sense. John Doe. Or Timothy Leary. I am saying rather that it's all located inside.

My Nervous System and Yours Is the Hinge of Evolution

From the genetic point of view, your nervous system and my nervous system is a hinge, a curious cellular hinge on which all of evolutionary history pivots. The cosmic Fox Movietone newsreel camera. Turn your nervous system on and focus it outside, and you're tuning in on all sorts of messages and energy constellations that are out there, here and now. But if you focus your nervous system within, you will decode the cellular script and discover that the entire string of evolution on this planet is writ in protein molecules inside the nucleus of every cell in your body.

Be God and the Universe

Now here is the challenge. And it's the toughest and the most exciting challenge that I can think of. It is possible for you (in a way, you might say it is your duty) to recapitulate personally the entire evolutionary sequence. In other words, you can flash through the whole cycle yourself because the whole thing is buried inside your body.

Every generation lives the old drama out over and over again. Every person can. The challenge is for you to become your own priest. For you to become your own doctor. For you to become your own researcher on consciousness. Researcher. Now there's a tricky symbol. Research. The cop-out cliché is to say that research is needed in LSD. Who dares to say he is against research in LSD? Should LSD be turned over to the research scientists to study the implication and possibility of the experience? Nope. You cannot get off that easy. No government research project, no medically controlled scientific study, is going to solve your spiritual or emotional problems. And remember: the textbooks only tell you what you have to discover yourself. Have you ever personally experienced that the world is round and whirls around the sun? Please do not wait around in the hope that others will do it for you. The medical profession has had LSD for twenty-three years. And it has not come up with a use for it yet. And I do not blame the doctors. The psychedelic chemicals which expand consciousness are just not medical problems. LSD has nothing to do with disease or sickness.

When people talk about research on LSD, I have a little formula I go through in my mind. Talking about LSD is like talking about sex. Now I am not against research on LSD and I am not against research on sex. If some scientists want to hook people up and study the external manifestations of their internal experiences and if some people are willing to be hooked up and be studied by scientists during sexual or psychedelic moments, fine. But the psychedelic experience is an intimate, personal, and sacred one. And you, and you, and you, the individual man and woman, are the only one to do this research. And we cannot wait around, dealing with energies which are so insistent and important, until scientists or government agencies tell us that we can take that risk.

Drop Out into What?

Turn on, tune in, and drop out. I want to be very clear about the term "drop out." I don't mean external dropping out. I certainly don't mean acts of rebellion or irresponsibility to any social situation you are involved in. But I urge any of you who are serious about life, who are serious about your nervous system or your spiritual future, to start right now planning how you can harmoniously, sequentially, lovingly, and gracefully detach yourself from the social commitments to which you are addicted.

Well, what do you do after you drop out? This question was asked. A young man in the audience said, "Well, it's all right for you older, middle-aged fellows to go around lecturing on LSD, but what do we young people do?" There's so much you can do that it makes me dizzy to think about it. First of all, if you are serious about this business, you should find a spiritual teacher. Find someone that knows more about consciousness than you, and study with him. And if he is a good teacher, he will teach you all he knows and tell you when he cannot teach you anymore, and then maybe you can start teaching him or you will both go on your separate ways. But there's a tremendous amount of information which has been stored up for the last three or four thousand years by men who have been making this voyage and who have left landmarks, guidebooks, footsteps in the sand, symbols, and rituals which can be learned from and used.

Another thing you can do is to be careful with whom you spend your time. Every human interaction is an incredible confrontation of several levels of consciousness. The average civilized human confrontation is, "I bring my checkerboard to you, and you bring your chessboard to me, and we start moving pieces around. If we are cultured and civilized, I will let you make a few moves on your board, and then you will watch me play for a while. If we get very, very intimate and have a deep relationship, we might get to the point where I'll put some of my symbols on your board and you will put some of your symbols on my board."

Anyone you meet is automatically going to come on to you with a fierce symbol system. And tremendous neurological inertia takes over. There is a conditioned-reflex training which pulls you into the other person's game at the same time that you are pulling him into your game. The more I study the neurology of the psychedelic experience, the more awed and amazed I am at what we do with and to each other's nervous systems.

Only a Tiny Bit of You Is Policeman

Well, what happens if you drop out and leave school and leave your jobs? (And by the way, I address here not just the young people, but the researchers and the doctors and the police investigators here in the audience. You know, only a tiny bit of you is policeman, only a tiny bit of you is doctor.) If you want to drop out of your nonlove game and tune in to life and take some of these questions seriously, you do not have to go on welfare or go around with a begging bowl. The odd thing about our society today is that in the mad lemminglike rush to the urban, antilove power centers and the mad rush toward mechanical conformity, our fellow citizens are leaving tremendous gaps and gulfs which make economic bartering very simple. For the first thing, consider moving out of the city. You'll find ghost towns empty and deserted three or four hours from San Francisco where people can live in harmony with nature, using their sense organs as two billion years of evolution had trained them to.

To make a living these days for a psychedelic person is really quite easy. How? There's one thing that our mechanized society cannot do and that is, delight the senses. Machines can make things go faster and move more efficiently, but machine-made objects make no sense to your cells or your senses. Our countrymen are fed up with plastic and starved for direct, natural sensory stimulation. As you begin to drop out, you will find yourself much less reliant on artifactual symbols. You will start throwing things out of your house. And you won't need as much mechanical money to buy as many mechanical objects. When you go home tonight, try a psychedelic exercise. Look around your living room and your study and dining room and ask yourself the question which might be asked by a man who lived three thousand years ago, or a man from another planet: "What sort of a fellow is this who lives in a room like this?" Because the artifacts you surround yourself with are external representations of your state of consciousness.

It's All Going to Work Out All Right

And now, a final word of good cheer, directed especially to those who are concerned about the psychedelic revolution. This revolution has just begun. For every turned-on person today I predict that there will be two or three next year. And I'm not at all embarrassed about making this prophecy because for the last six years Dr. Alpert and Dr. Metzner and I have been making predictions about the growth of the new race, and we have always been too conservative. Let no one be concerned about the growth and the use of psychedelic chemicals. Trust your young people. You gotta trust your young people. You had better trust your young people. Trust your creative minority. The fact of the matter is that those of us who use LSD wish society well. In our way we are doing what seems best and right to make this a peaceful and happy planet. Be very careful how you treat your creative minority, because if we are crushed, you will end up with a robot society. Trust your sense organs and your nervous system. Your divine body has been around a long, long time. Much longer than any of the social games you play. Trust the evolutionary process. It's all going to work out all right.

Summer of Love

Even in the repressed decade of the 1950s the "Beat" poets, musicians, painters, and philosophers captured the attention of the media with their defiant clothes, their free and easy lifestyle, their commitment to aesthetic values.

The new bohemia of the 1960s, unlike the old, was drenched in psychedelics start-
ing with magic mushrooms and progressing to LSD. Unlike previous chemical mood-
altering substances, LSD left its users with a transformed sense of the world's
qualities and possibilities sufficient to build a Zeitgeist *on.*

The new drug-drenched culture migrated in the early 1960s to New York and San
Francisco. Its denizens were called hippies, after "hip," a jazz term meaning "with
it" or "in tune." In New York, their locale was the East Village. In San Francisco,
it was Haight-Ashbury, near Golden Gate Park. There, attracted by the low rents,
students, artists, and younger college faculty gathered in the first years of the decade,
and their presence soon attracted a corps of attuned shopkeepers and entrepreneurs
willing to supply their needs in food, music, art, clothes, and drugs. Establishments
with names like Psychedelic Shop, I/Thou Coffee Shop, and Print Mint, with their
mysterious drug paraphernalia, their eye-blast posters, their fragrant marijuana
smoke, and their aura of the forbidden, began to attract curiosity seekers and
tourists. Tour buses were soon running through the Haight bringing "squares" by
the thousands.

The climax came in 1967. That spring the media announced that Haight-
Ashbury would be the mecca for all who shared the new consciousness. A popular
song announced: "If you are going to San Francisco be sure to wear a flower in your
hair." All told 75,000 hippies and would-be hippies heeded the call to share the
Summer of Love.

Two of the documents here are accounts from local San Francisco counterculture
*newspapers—*The Oracle *and* The Haight-Ashbury Maverick*—of the Summer*
of Love. The third is a guide for the tourists who flocked to the Haight between May
and September 1967 to observe the hippie phenomenon. It reads like a tour guide for
visitors to some exotic Amazonian tribe.

[*"The Summer Solstice,"* **Haight-Ashbury Maverick**, *August 1967; Richard Honigman, "Flowers*
from the Street," San Francisco **Oracle**, *August 1967; "Notes to Tourists,"* **Haight-Ashbury**
Maverick, *August 1967.*]

THE SUMMER SOLSTICE

San Francisco enjoyed the Summer Solstice as a community should enjoy
the beginning of a new season of growing blooming and planting.

The Summer Solstice celebration was held in a long valley leading to the
Polo Fields in Golden Gate Park. It brought together beautiful people
from all over the world with every type, every emotion, and each was on
their own trip with everything to make that experience one of great and
lasting joy.

The music was provided by name groups. One group was stationed in
the valley and played to the crowds playing with a huge ball and hungrily

watching the food being prepared over a twenty-foot trench of glowing fires. Another group played at the entrance to the polo grounds and then one group at each side of the grounds.

Probably never before had so many people smiled, spoken, and enjoyed the sheer beauty and joy of being free in the sun for a few hours. For the summers in San Francisco are not noted for being sunny. But Saint Francis smiled on his favorite flower children and provided the first sunlight in several days for the celebration.

A brisk breeze came down through the valley, and the scantily clad hovered closely to their lovers, and this was in itself a beautiful thing.

The Indian Dancers were a poem of indescribable music. They performed in several areas of the area.

Before the festivities began in Golden Gate Park the celebration of the rising sun was held by Khrisna atop Twin Peaks, this high point of San Francisco looking down Market Street. The sun barely peeked out from under the fog before it was obscured from view, but the chimes and the horns announced the beginning of the Summer Solstice and the early risers (or late retirers) trouped down the hill to the nearby Haight-Ashbury where the coffee and doughnuts of Tracy's and the big breakfast at the Drogstore Cafe got undivided attention until the trek at noon to the meadow in the park got underway.

It was definitely a mixed bag in the park. We saw some of the media there. They are still able to blow their minds at some of the costumes of the Love Generation, and a beautiful girl offering a simple flower to a hard-bitten TV cameraman still makes the camera go astray from time to time. The assemblyman from San Diego who was attending a conference of Democrats in San Francisco drifted out into the meadow. . . . He is shaking his head and wondering what happened to him that enjoyment was the order for him rather than the condemnation that he was prepared to level against the hippies—those people he had heard so much about but had only seen from the seat of an automobile in his native San Diego. He enjoyed the Grateful Dead. When he found out the name of the group, he frowned disapprovingly, but his foot kept in motion.

The visitor from Decatur, Illinois, kept thinking what would happen if such a celebration was held there.

The New Yorker, who still had his leg in a cast from the Be-In there, was out of his mind with the beauty of the grounds and the complete lack of law officers. He kept looking over his shoulder to see if they were lurking in the bushes with night sticks. But the police apparently enjoyed the day in their own way somewhere else. A few narcotics agents in plain clothes were there. And they could not reveal their cover merely to make a bust for using.

The meat on the spit never got completely done before it was consumed by the hungry people.

The sun went through its daily path and started sinking at the foot of the Park, and the Flower Children and the Love Generation and the Political Activists, and the Christians and the Buddhists, and the Atheists and the musicians, and the dancers and the beautiful people from all over these United States followed the sun down to the beach in a straggling herd to the end of a day that will live in thousands of memories for many many years.

This was the day that we reaffirmed our faith in the goodness of mankind and the hope of a continuing future filled with an abundance of Summer Solstices, Winter Solstices, and a hope for the future of mankind.

How many people were there? Who gives a damn—there were thousands. How many people met new friends and renewed old knowledges? This is the important thing—and thousands did this. The joy of free men associating in a free sun did wonders for the soul of San Francisco, and it will be working as a force all summer long.

The Summer of Love called for a reawakening of true values of life, and the celebration of the Summer Solstice was the first of the celebrations of that Season of Love. It was a reawakening, a celebration of the beginning of such a personal-intimate closeness that those who were there could feel the vibrations and responded to them as rarely before.

San Francisco, the West Coast, and America awaits the other celebrations of the Summer of Love and its great spiritual experience. The beginning has come, and the celebrations of the future cannot fail but have a profound effect on the future of America.

FLOWERS FROM THE STREET

"Hui Tzu said to Chuang Tzu, 'Your teachings are of no practical use.' Chuang Tzu said, 'Only those who already know the value of the useless can be talked to about the useful. This earth we walk upon is of vast extent, yet in order to walk a man uses no more of it than the soles of his two feet will cover. But suppose one cut away the ground around his feet till one reached the Yellow Springs (the world of the Dead). Would his patches of ground still be of any use to him for walking?' Hui Tzu said, 'They would be of no use.' Chuang Tzu said, 'So then the usefulness of the useless is evident.'"

Walking barefoot with hair askew, hand-made robes over torn blue jeans, the young people wander from noon until early two. Wandering aimlessly up Haight Street, over to the free store at Carl and Cole, then back to Masonic for a cream pie and Coke or to the Panhandle for Digger stew. Hundreds of young people, refugees from suburban interment camps, are making the scene (or duplications in kind) in several dozen cities around the country. Most streets, like Haight Street in San Francisco, were once local shopping districts now turned into an abstract vortex for an indefinable pilgrimage. An admixture of home-made spiritual group theory and actors in life theater which turns the participants into celebrants.

The street scene has become an entrance into a phenomenon to which we all have been invited. The word has been passed throughout the country, compliments of the aboveground media, that there is a scene going down on Haight Street. The most receptive to the call are from middle-class urbia. They leave jobs, armies, and schools to turn their lives and psyches inside out, all looking for some material to build a life with. All of us started to realize, even in 17 or 20 short years, that the game of life played in school and the supermarket U. leads only to styrofoam coffins and oblivious servitude. Most of us have been on the threshold of jumping into the accepted swim, but stop and ask for time, having already seen enough instinctively, if not intellectually. Few have talents or skills developed enough for personal satisfaction or for the marketplace; all are well trained towards indiscriminate consumption. Yet the feeling persists—there must be something greater than this!

The street becomes where it's at. It is easy to get laid there, cop dope, find a friend or a mate. Books and ideas, acid and pot, the nearby park, or a pad full of music from a surreal montage of the constant weekend.

How else in America today can the Protestant Ethic be wrung out? To learn the reality of fantasy and the fantasy of reality? It is a process of steady deculturalization, to clear your head of the Mustang Pledge and the nonsense of a chicken in every Dodge Rebellion. Running in opposite directions of childhood conditioning, looking for perspective by playing roles, wearing costumes, and dropping acid. LSD becomes a sacrificial deconditioner expanding consciousness, allowing each person to actually experience the adventure of self-discovery. It has also led to the widespread interest in Eastern thought and the meditative religions, besides opening the doors to precedents and conditions upon which the world now finds itself. The street scene and its extensions into the art and living patterns that are being developed is in large part due to what is first envisioned and then consciously applied through the use of LSD and other drugs. To get high and look around in the now, towards the before, and to the possibilities in the future, almost inevitably removes a person from the transitory superficial machinations of western society . . . a society which consciously strives to prevent this sort of looking around.

It takes time and experience to reintegrate these new forms of knowledge and personality into a comfortable living pattern. In the meantime some people use the limbo of street life and drop practically every material possession to live solely by their wits. They sleep in parks, on doorsteps when the commune is full, live at night and rest by day. Scrounge food, shoot meth, hustle college kids coming to gawk and get laid, just as their fathers went to Fillmore when *nigger* wasn't spelled *negro*. Work as a last resort but better to play or hitch to Big Sur. Bohemia is no longer refuge for a few, the third V.P.'s daughter wants in too. Hepatitis, hunger, crabs, and clap, freak out, then on to the next scene. Frantic searching, then slow growth, learn to let go, live only on what you need. How long does it take to dig where you're at and catch on to the scene? There is no one to tell you now, but only file cabinets can lie.

The street can be a classroom, a zoo, a stage, an asphalt padded cell, a whorehouse, a folksong, or the traverse of Scorpio. Fashions develop for brown rice and the *I Ching*, for farms and Indians, '47 panel trucks, beads and books. Most of us have gone through something like it, possibly they are at first only bourgeois allusions of freedom, in attempting to find what is real for ourselves or at least comfortable. The street is there and some must run its course, called doing their thing, going through changes. Others less mangled are able to deculturalize or find themselves easier, but the educational conformist pressures stack higher against them. It can be done anywhere, but our society tends to produce exaggerations of itself and only extremity seems to break through its accompanying neurosis. Thus the phenomenon of street life, a clearing house spontaneously formed to break the conditioning of the perpetual motion machine. People running away from disaster without a place to go, only an idea of where it might be found.

This phenomenon has been going on for perhaps ten years (with roots going back much further), but it has only been noticed as having importance in the past year or two. The numbers of young people dropping out and seeking new lifestyles at a tangent or opposed to the majority of the country has caught the attention of almost everyone, including the lower income groups. But attention is turning it into a "Hippie Problem" added to the multitude of hypocrisies America finds adding pressure against its fantasy-laden bubble of affluence. What's coming in the next year or two that will affect the scene is hard to determine, but we must start making considerations and plans now for future developments.

What has developed already is exciting and positive. An explosion of creative energies directly related to the scene is deeply affecting all the arts in this country and revitalizing once dormant ones like poster art. Even more important, however, are the people on the street who have committed themselves to a creative life based on cultivating life and art, without a professional intent towards the latter, and a humane, spiritual, or revolutionary orientation to society. Extended families, communes and small tribes are being formed amongst small groups who find they can work and groove well together. Some stay in the city and take an active part in the scene, maintaining crash pads, pitching in on various projects, turning on, stringing beads, making music. Others are forming small communities in the country, developing their lives and environments along aesthetic guidelines. Grinding guilt and glut into the pavement, finding the beauty of environment, pure food, a good high and a good lay.

An answer is being found to the seemingly overwhelming forces in this bureauocratized technocracy which are trying to remove life from the individual's own hands, preventing the marvel of a person's individual destiny. No matter what happens, this is a good extension of the scene to work on. There are enough people involved in the scene, and enough dissatisfaction with life in America, to build parallel, exemplary demi-societies of our own. More communal houses in the city are desperately needed, but land and farms are an even greater necessity at this point.

Everyone should be prepared for our government's flirtation with disaster.

Back packs, sleeping bags, rifles, and a knowledge of edible plants and animals found in the wilderness is the next logical step. We have found out what it is like to be free men in a servile society attuned to the time clock. Sticking to what has been learned, building it up, and helping others along the way must be viewed with a knowledge of the eventualities that lie ahead. No matter what happens, to be self-sufficient of other men and of the machine is an enviable position for anyone to be in. Life can be a three-dimensional mixed bag of forest and city stimuli, building new structures and making the old more livable and humane.

All the while, as we think of the infinite possibilities ahead, psychedelic scavengers zero in on their prey. People are spilling their guts out on the street looking for some sanity while the Pizza Parlors and security guards move in. Montgomery Street licks its chops on war profits during the week, then clogs Haight Street on Sunday. Through three layers of safety glass, they photograph the neighbor's kid and buy native handicrafts from "quaint" shops along the way. Suburbia sucks in the music and bright baubles which came from the street, then flicks the dial to see the latest war footage, while their niece and son cry "no, not me." The slums get worse, long haired girls turn tricks. The government encourages double think and psychedelic entrepreneurs hustle the new kids coming to play in the Haight Street school yard.

Where is it at? Is community and brotherhood being built here? Is Haight Street going to take off before it is absorbed into the grade B movie of the American Mainstream, which is likely to turn into another bad Nazi flick? America is cracking open at the seams; joy and flowers are always groovy, but crops would be better still. The phenomenon is slowly evolving into an alternative life, but now it is only beating the system by living off of the outdated waste of mass production. Name your poison: methedrine and chocolate pie, watch the *Lucy* show and get high. The scene is yours, laugh and groove, but don't tell anyone there is a revolution going on. What are you going to do when the deal goes down?

NOTES TO TOURISTS

Please remember as you approach Haight Street that you are about to see one of the most wondrous sights yet to come to the attention of mankind. It is far from perfect, but the mere fact that hundreds of thousands of tourists have spent many hours in traffic jams to see if there is any truth in the Love Generation testifies to the fact that all of us would like to find a better way of life. You may well be one of those wondering if it is truly possible to love your fellow man. Take it from *Maverick*, it is not only possible, but it is being done every day.

First let us apologize for the long hour that you have spent in the traffic jam. The San Francisco traffic engineers are mostly refugees from various loony bins. They are also handicapped by the San Francisco Police Department—who have made no attempt to control traffic in The Haight. It is understandable—they are far too busy chasing pot-users (that is slang for marijuana), keeping the kids from sitting on the sidewalks, and passing out parking tickets. On that last note let us give you a warning: Be sure you know all the laws regarding parking . . . tickets are passed out here like you have never seen before. As many as three parking-meter minders are at work in this twelve-block area at any one time. If you have not yet entered the Haight area, be sure and check to see if all your stoplights are working, your windshield wipers are working, your brakes working, etc. This is because if you are stopped for anything, you will be checked out minutely. It will help if you are cleanly shaven, have your Rotary Sticker on the bumper, and most of all have a Saint Christopher statuette on the dashboard. The latter is recommended throughout San Francisco.

Roll Down Your Windows

Many tourists upon seeing the unshaven, unconventionally clothed Love Generation roll up their car windows and lock the doors. This is not necessary and can be mightily inconvenient. Some of the hippies do bite, but all of them have taken their rabies shots so their bite is not too bad. Honestly though, you must consider that the unconventional attire would make it easy to describe your assailant to the police. By the way, if it appears to you that there are no police in the area, have no fears—probably one out of every twenty males that you see between the ages of 25 and 35 is an officer of some kind or the other.

Brands of Hippies

Just like your normal folk, there are many brands of hippies. . . . Some of you are vitally interested in politics . . . so are some of the hippies. . . . We call that particular brand "activists." Probably you won't notice an activist on Haight since most of them stick pretty close to the home base— Berkeley. The activists run the gamut from a middle of the road (very rare) to the anarchist (not so rare).

Then there are the Flower Children. . . . These are the most lovable of all the hippies. Early in the summer it was quite common to have them going down the streets passing out flowers and wearing garlands of flowers. But flowers are rather expensive to come by, and even a small bunch of flowers is getting beyond the reach of those of moderate (or less) means.

Then there are the bikeriders. When you see them on the street, they just plain look rough. And they damn well can be. But since they want the right to live their own life—as they choose—they respect the right of the others to do likewise. And they might well be the ones who defend in acts the rights of those who are unprepared to do so. The riders primarily keep to a certain area but mix well in all the other areas of Haight Street.

And there are many many other tribes of hippies.

The Drug Scene

We failed to warn you when we were talking about getting parking tickets that there are other areas of personal conduct that you must be careful about in the Haight-Ashbury area. If you have any unlabeled medicines or if you are a diabetic and must carry a hypodermic with you—we strongly suggest that you pass through the Haight with as much speed as possible.

(However, if you are a ballet star you need not worry because if you get arrested the police will apologize most resoundingly.)

But the ordinary person must be careful because the police cannot tell a hippie by just looking and those who have any drugs of any kind must be careful.

If you have come to the Haight looking for grass, then we suggest that you give up that long drive for these six blocks. There just isn't any around. Acid is also very scarce. Most tourists assume that they can pick up some for their private uses back in Oshkosh and Dallas. Sorry, it is just not so. Besides every nark (narcotics agent) in California is here, and if there is any grass about, it will be in their hands shortly. We strongly urge, however, that you might be able to get some in your home town, and we further strongly urge that you smoke a joint before retiring and throw away those patent-medicine Nytol, Sleepeze, and so forth. Grass is so much better for relaxing. Try it instead of that martini before dinner; be sure, be safe, and use pot instead of gin.

The Dress for the Haight

We would warn the tourists that our police department is highly uptight about dress here. Again they cannot tell a hippie from a straightie, and those miniskirts are strictly out for the Haight. One girl was arrested for wearing a traditional Indian costume that came well below the midpoint of the upper leg. Some of the tourists who have ambled down Haight Street recently have caused consternation among the hippies (who you will admit are accustomed to wild dress), but those two-ax-handle-broad broads in phosphorescent orange slacks are a little much. Now if, on the other hand, if you have a burning desire to take that Indian blanket on the back seat and drape it over your shoulders and walk down the street, then you must do so. If you have a burning desire to take off your shirt (men only—there is a double standard here) and walk down the street bare breasted (chested), then do so, for that is called "doing your thing." But if you see a cop scowling at you, then retire back to your Mustang and drive off. That is, unless you are prepared to defend your American right to do so. However, you will find that American rights are largely disregarded by the municipal courts here. The one who dares to defy the mores (not the laws) here is bound to have a big legal bill to pay. All this is done in the name of "order."

Free Love

If you have come to the Haight looking for "free" love, then we suggest that you turn around and leave—for you are wasting your time. This is of course assuming that our readers are males. If you are a female, then sex is highly likely—for free even.

The mass media has played up big the idea that there is a lot of free nookey here! The ratio of male to female is about 5 to 1. As in other areas, the females are tied up with permanent partners to a large degree. Some cats up for kicks from the oil fields of Texas and the Movie Moguls from Hollywood with sixteen credit cards and a Hertz rented automobile have tried to impress the local chicks. It was a waste of time and money, but we do thank them for feeding the chicks. In this case money won't buy anything at all.

7

The New Feminism

The assault on hierarchy and privilege during the Sixties started with the struggle of blacks to tear down segregation and dismantle white supremacy. It soon evolved into a campaign for personal liberation waged by thousands of Americans who deemed themselves outside the circle of power. The discontents were not primarily those of class. Factory workers in the Sixties were too prosperous, the poor were in the end too disorganized to challenge the status quo. But virtually every group defined by race and gender—Native Americans, Hispanics, Asians, and women—rushed to confront white male dominance and the values associated with it.

Of all these "liberation movements," the New Feminism was the most significant. As the Sixties opened, traditional feminism appeared moribund, its last great victory dating to the suffrage amendment of 1920. The period following World War II, with its massive retreat to family life, had not encouraged feminism. Many women, recalling the insecurities of the Great Depression and the global war, were satisfied with the comfort and safety of family and the suburban daily round. But as the hard, frightening years receded in memory, domesticity often became a lifeless trap. By the early Sixties a growing number of American women, especially college-educated women, began to examine their lives and find them wanting.

Meanwhile, the civil rights movement was providing an older group of feminists—survivors of the 1920s and 1930s—with the tools and the moral claim to enlist government in their unfinished agenda. In 1961, to placate leading Democratic women, John Kennedy created a Commission on the Status of Women and appointed Eleanor Roosevelt to chair it. The commission's report, in the spirit of the earlier women's rights movement, demanded an end to job and legal discrimination but acknowledged "the fundamental responsibility" of women to remain "mothers and housewives." Though a moderate group, the commission helped to recharge the feminist movement. Congress soon gave a further lift to the reemerging feminist impulse by proscribing, almost as an afterthought, job discrimination against women in the 1964 Civil Rights Act, a measure designed primarily to fight racial bias.

Johnson appointed only one woman, Aileen Hernandez, to the Equal Employment Opportunity Commission established by the new law. Women activists soon found that the commission did not take gender discrimination very seriously. In fact, as one commissioner said, they considered its inclusion in the law "a fluke . . . conceived out of wedlock." By 1966, they were prepared to stage a revolt. At the grassroots level, meanwhile, the festering discontents of educated suburban women were finding their voice. In 1963, a forty-two-year-old Long Island housewife, Betty Friedan, published *The Feminine Mystique,* which described the quiet desperation that afflicted so many suburban middle-class women. The book almost overnight crystallized the dissatisfactions that many women only vaguely felt and became a runaway best seller.

The creation in 1966 of the National Organization for Women (NOW) in Washington, D.C., brought together these strands of reemerging feminism and expressed the growing sense that women remained a disadvantaged group. NOW was a liberal reform organization run predominantly by middle-aged women. It demanded equal treatment within the existing social structures of the nation. By 1967 or 1968 there had appeared a number of radical feminist organizations, led by younger women, making *liberation,* rather than reform, their core demand.

Women's liberation organizations had roots in the radical mood of the mid- and late Sixties. Some were inspired by a class analysis that saw women, as well as blacks, as a "superexploited" proletariat whose oppression could be attributed to capitalism: Destroy capitalism, and sexism would vanish. A larger group of liberationists preferred a cultural analysis that emphasized the dominance and exploitative nature of males generally. Here the villain was not capitalism but "patriarchy." Abolish capitalism, but retain male supremacy, and women would remain oppressed.

The liberationists had a far more radical vision and agenda than the reformers of NOW. They were skeptical of men qua men, though they acknowledged that a few might be willing to surrender their male privilege. Women, they even suggested at times, could well do without the male sex. Some of the more militant liberationists were acknowledged lesbians whose influence in the movement spread beyond their relatively small numbers. The liberationists did not focus on winning equality for women in the job market or in family law. That was too superficial. Rather, they challenged the very existence of the traditional family as male-dominated and inherently unequal. Many denied the existence of significant innate physical and psychological differences between men and women and insisted that the apparent disparities in performance were overwhelmingly cultural in origin. Women, they claimed, even when they appeared privileged, were systematically subordinated by an all-encompassing patriarchy that defined the fundamental nature of Western societies.

The first radical feminists—Casey Hayden, Heather Booth, Naomi Weisstein, for example—were members of male-dominated radical groups like SDS and SNCC who found themselves relegated to second-class status and ridiculed when they tried to get the leaders to acknowledge their bias. The chauvinist reactions of the movement "heavies"—men presumably committed to class equality—made it apparent that sexism, rather than capitalism, was the chief oppressive force in America.

The first clusters of distinctive radical feminist groups emerged in Chicago, San Francisco, Boston, and New York in 1967 and 1968. At about the same time, the first radical feminist writings and journals began to appear. Nineteen sixty-eight also marked the debut of consciousness-raising (CR), a technique owing much to old-fashioned group therapy. First introduced by New York Radical Women, CR sought to make the merely latent manifest. A truly open-ended consciousness-raising process might have revealed many kinds of buried resentments, including those against mothers, daughters, sisters, and female colleagues. But inevitably, the radical feminist version focused on the wrongs that men—all men—committed against women. Consciousness-raising would become a powerful weapon in the battles to change the relations of the sexes in the years ahead.

The New Feminism was a flowering of the late Sixties. Not until the next decade would it reach full strength. When it did, it would alter the underlying relations of American life more fundamentally than any other movement that came to life during the volcanic decade of revolt.

The Feminine Mystique

Betty Friedan's book The Feminine Mystique, *published in 1963, brought into focus the frustrations and dissatisfactions that seemed to afflict educated suburban women as the Sixties began. Like Michael Harrington's* The Other America, *the work marked the end of the complacent 1950s equilibrium and the beginning of a new social realignment.*

Friedan's subject was the "problem that has no name," the post–World War II cult of domesticity that enveloped women. Perhaps, after 1945, seeking safety and certi-

*tude, women had welcomed the new suburban life that centered on children, hus-
bands, and houses. But as the Sixties began, she wrote, the pattern had to be sustained by an ideology, a "feminine mystique," that coerced women into a narrow
round, diminishing them and leading to boredom and despair. Friedan brilliantly
analyzed the plight of her subjects, but she said little to guide them in their liberation. That, presumably, was a separate matter. What was important, at this point,
was to acknowledge the problem and describe it, allowing other women to recognize
it in their own lives.*

*The appeal of The Feminine Mystique was not universal. Like the movement
it helped to launch, the book spoke primarily to educated suburban women. Here
Friedan was no outside observer. A graduate of prestigious Smith College and a resident of Rockland County, an exurb of New York City, she understood the women she
surveyed, although, as a magazine writer, she herself presumably was not caught in
the same trap. The New Feminism was class specific. Working-class women, black
women, and Hispanic women would be too busy fighting for survival to worry about
fulfillment. But as in most reform movements, it was the articulate, educated, and
affluent whose discontents counted, and with these women the book was a powerful
catalyst that justified the title the movement would give Friedan: "The Founding
Mother."*

THE PROBLEM THAT HAS NO NAME

The problem lay buried, unspoken, for many years in the minds of
American women. It was a strange stirring, a sense of dissatisfaction, a
yearning that women suffered in the middle of the twentieth century in the
United States. Each suburban wife struggled with it alone. As she made the
beds, shopped for groceries, matched slipcover material, ate peanut butter
sandwiches with her children, chauffeured Cub Scouts and Brownies, lay
beside her husband at night—she was afraid to ask even of herself the
silent question—"Is this all?"

For over fifteen years there was no word of this yearning in the millions
of words written about women, for women, in all the columns, books, and
articles by experts telling women their role was to seek fulfillment as wives
and mothers. Over and over women heard in voices of tradition and of
Freudian sophistication that they could desire no greater destiny than to
glory in their own femininity. Experts told them how to catch a man and
keep him, how to breastfeed children and handle their toilet training,
how to cope with sibling rivalry and adolescent rebellion; how to buy a

dishwasher, bake bread, cook gourmet snails, and build a swimming pool with their own hands; how to dress, look, and act more feminine and make marriage more exciting; how to keep their husbands from dying young and their sons from growing into delinquents. They were taught to pity the neurotic, unfeminine, unhappy women who wanted to be poets or physicists or presidents. They learned that truly feminine women do not want careers, higher education, political rights—the independence and the opportunities that the old-fashioned feminists fought for. Some women, in their forties and fifties, still remembered painfully giving up those dreams, but most of the younger women no longer even thought about them. A thousand expert voices applauded their femininity, their adjustment, their new maturity. All they had to do was devote their lives from earliest girlhood to finding a husband and bearing children.

By the end of the nineteen-fifties, the average marriage age of women in America dropped to 20, and was still dropping into the teens. Fourteen million girls were engaged by 17. The proportion of women attending college in comparison with men dropped from 47 percent in 1920 to 35 percent in 1958. A century earlier, women had fought for higher education; now girls went to college to get a husband. . . .

Then American girls began getting married in high school. And the women's magazines, deploring the unhappy statistics about these young marriages, urged that courses on marriage, and marriage counselors, be installed in the high schools. . . . Manufacturers put out brassieres with false bosoms of foam rubber for little girls of ten. An advertisement for a child's dress . . . in *The New York Times* in the fall of 1960, said: "She Too Can Join the Man-Trap Set."

By the end of the fifties, the United States birthrate was overtaking India's. The birth-control movement, renamed Planned Parenthood, was asked to find a method whereby women who had been advised that a third or fourth baby would be born dead or defective might have it anyhow. Statisticians were especially astounded at the fantastic increase in the number of babies among college women. Where once they had two children, now they had four, five, six. Women who had once wanted careers were now making careers out of having babies. . . .

Interior decorators were designing kitchens with mosaic murals and original paintings, for kitchens were once again the center of women's lives. Home sewing became a million-dollar industry. Many women no longer left their homes except to shop, chauffeur their children, or attend a social engagement with their husbands. Girls were growing up in America without ever having jobs outside the home. In the late fifties, a sociological phenomenon was suddenly remarked: a third of American women worked, but most were no longer young and very few were pursuing careers. They were married women who held part-time jobs, selling or secretarial, to put their husbands through school, their sons through college, or to help pay the mortgage. Or they were widows supporting families. Fewer and fewer women were entering professional work. . . .

The suburban housewife—she was the dream image of the young American women and the envy, it was said, of women all over the world. The American housewife—freed by science and labor-saving appliances from drudgery, the dangers of childbirth, and the illnesses of her grandmother. She was healthy, beautiful, educated, concerned only about her husband, her children, her home. She had found true feminine fulfillment. As a housewife and mother, she was respected as a full and equal partner to man in his world. She was free to choose automobiles, clothes, appliances, supermarkets; she had everything that women ever dreamed of.

In the fifteen years after World War II, this mystique of feminine fulfillment became the cherished and self-perpetuating core of contemporary American culture. Millions of women lived their lives in the image of those pretty pictures of the American suburban housewife, kissing their husbands goodbye in front of the picture window, depositing their station-wagonsful of children at school, and smiling as they ran the new electric waxer over the spotless kitchen floor. . . . Their only dream was to be perfect wives and mothers; their highest ambition to have five children and a beautiful house, their only fight to get and keep their husbands. They had no thought for the unfeminine problems of the world outside the home; they wanted the men to make the major decisions. . . .

If a woman had a problem in the 1950s and 1960s, she knew that something must be wrong with her marriage, or with herself. Other women were satisfied with their lives, she thought. What kind of woman was she if she did not feel this mysterious fulfillment waxing the kitchen floor. She was so ashamed to admit her dissatisfaction that she never knew how many other women shared it. If she tried to tell her husband, he didn't understand what she was talking about. She did not really understand it herself. For over fifteen years women in America found it harder to talk about this problem than sex. Even the psychoanalysts had no name for it. When a woman went to a psychiatrist for help, as many women did, she would say, "I'm so ashamed," or "I must be hopelessly neurotic." "I don't know what's wrong with women today," a suburban psychiatrist said uneasily. "I only know something is wrong because most of my patients happen to be women. And their problem isn't sexual." Most women with this problem did not go to see a psychoanalyst, however. "There's nothing wrong really," they kept telling themselves. "There isn't any problem."

But on an April morning in 1959, I heard a mother of four, having coffee with four other mothers in a suburban development fifteen miles from New York, say in a tone of quiet desperation, "the problem." And the others knew, without words, that she was not talking about a problem with her husband, or her children, or her home. Suddenly they realized they all shared the same problem, the problem that has no name. They began, hesitantly, to talk about it. Later, after they had picked up their children at nursery school and taken them home to nap, two of the women cried, in sheer relief, just to know they were not alone. . . .

Gradually I came to realize that the problem that has no name was shared by countless women in America. As a magazine writer I often interviewed women about problems with their children, or their marriages, or their houses, or their communities. But after a while I began to recognize the telltale signs of this other problem. I saw the same signs in suburban ranch houses and split-levels on Long Island and New Jersey and Westchester County; in colonial houses in a small Massachusetts town; on patios in Memphis; in suburban and city apartments; in living rooms in the Midwest. Sometimes I sensed the problem, not as a reporter, but as a suburban housewife, for during this time I was also bringing up my three children in Rockland County, New York. . . . The groping words I heard from other women, on quiet afternoons when children were at school or on quiet evenings when husbands worked late, I think I understood first as a woman before I understood their larger social and psychological implications.

Just what was this problem that has no name? What were the words women used when they tried to express it? Sometimes a woman would say, "I feel empty somehow . . . incomplete." Or she would say, "I feel as if I don't exist." Sometimes she blotted out the feeling with a tranquilizer. Sometimes she thought the problem was with her husband, or her children, or that what she really needed was to redecorate her house, or move to a better neighborhood, or have an affair, or another baby. Sometimes she went to a doctor with symptoms she could hardly describe: "A tired feeling. . . . I get so angry with the children it scares me. . . . I feel like crying without reason." (A Cleveland doctor called it "the housewife's syndrome.") . . .

Sometimes a woman would tell me that the feeling gets so strong she runs out of the house and walks through the streets. Or she stays inside her house and cries. Or her children tell her a joke, and she doesn't laugh because she doesn't hear it. . . .

In 1960 the problem that has no name burst like a boil through the image of the happy American housewife. In the television commercials the pretty housewives still beamed over their foaming dishpans and *Time*'s cover story on "The Suburban Housewife, an American Phenomenon" protested: "Having too good a time . . . to believe they should be unhappy." But the actual unhappiness of the American housewife was suddenly being reported—from *The New York Times* and *Newsweek* to *Good Housekeeping* and CBS Television. . . .

It is my thesis that the core of the problem for women today is not sexual but a problem of identity—a stunting or evasion of growth that is perpetuated by the feminine mystique. It is my thesis that as the Victorian culture did not permit women to accept or gratify their basic sexual needs, our culture does not permit women to accept or gratify their basic need to grow and fulfill their personalities as human beings, a need which is not solely defined by their sexual role. . . .

There have been identity crises for man at all the crucial turning points in human history, though those who lived through them did not give them that name. It is only in recent years that the theorists of psychology, sociology, and theology have isolated the problem and given it a name. But it is considered a man's problem. It is defined, for man, as the crisis of growing up, of choosing his identity, "the decision as to what one is and is going to be," in the words of the brilliant psychoanalyst Erik H. Erikson. . . .

But why have the theorists not recognized this same identity crisis in women? In terms of the old conventions and the new feminine mystique, women are not expected to grow up to find out who they are, to choose their human identity. Anatomy is woman's destiny, say the theorists of femininity; the identity of woman is determined by her biology.

But is it? More and more women are asking themselves this question. As if they are waking from a coma, they ask, "Where am I . . . what am I doing here?" For the first time in their history, women are becoming aware of an identity crisis in their own lives, a crisis which began many generations ago, has grown worse with each succeeding generation, and will not end until they or their daughters turn an unknown corner and make of themselves and their lives the new image that so many women so desperately need.

In a sense this goes beyond any one woman's life. I think this is the crisis of women growing up—a turning point from an immaturity that has been called femininity to full human identity. I think women had to suffer this crisis of identity, which began a hundred years ago, and have to suffer it still today, simply to become fully human. . . .

The National Organization for Women
"Bill of Rights"

Betty Friedan and other activists came to the June 1966 meeting of the state status-of-women commissions to express their anger at the Equal Employment Opportunity Commission (EEOC) for failing to enforce the sex-discrimination clause of the Civil Rights Act of 1964. When the conference organizers refused to allow a resolution demanding enforcement of Title VII on the grounds that delegates were there only to exchange information, not take action, twenty-seven outraged women decided on the spot to form a new feminist group.

The National Organization for Women (NOW) held its founding conference in late October 1966 in the nation's capital. The new organization initially emphasized equal job opportunity, and in its early months, its leaders spent much time in Washington lobbying the attorney general, the secretary of labor, and the director of the EEOC to apply Title VII. Bowing to pressure by the NOW leaders, the EEOC finally held public hearings on sex discrimination in the job market in May 1967. That October, President Johnson signed Executive Order 11375 forbidding sex discrimination by federal contractors.

The document here is the Bill of Rights for women adopted at NOW's first national conference in November 1967.* The meeting confirmed that in one short year the organization had become more militant. At its founding meeting NOW had emphasized equal job opportunity. Now three hundred activists engaged in "stormy" debate over an Equal Rights Amendment (ERA) to the Constitution, child-care centers for working mothers, and abortion rights. NOW endorsed the ERA, long a staple of feminist activists, and demanded repeal of anti-abortion laws which limited "the right of women to control their own reproductive lives." The turn to the left dismayed some members, who seceded to form the Women's Equity Action League, which was devoted to ending discrimination in jobs and education. But it put NOW, for a time, at the crest of the fast-moving new feminist wave and helped make it into the largest feminist group in the world.

[With permission of the National Organization for Women.]

NOW BILL OF RIGHTS

I. Equal Rights Constitutional Amendment
II. Enforce Law Banning Sex Discrimination in Employment
III. Maternity Leave Rights in Employment and in Social Security Benefits
IV. Tax Deduction for Home and Child Care Expenses for Working Parents

---

*As distinct from its 1966 organizing meeting.

V. Child Day Care Centers

VI. Equal and Unsegregated Education

VII. Equal Job Training Opportunities and Allowances for Women in Poverty

VIII. The Right of Women to Control Their Reproductive Lives

WE DEMAND:

I. That the U.S. Congress immediately pass the Equal Rights Amendment to the Constitution to provide that "Equality of rights under the law shall not be denied or abridged by the United States or by any state on account of sex," and that such then be immediately ratified by the several states.

II. That equal employment opportunity be guaranteed to all women, as well as men, by insisting that the Equal Employment Opportunity Commission enforces the prohibitions against racial discrimination.

III. That women be protected by law to ensure their rights to return to their jobs within a reasonable time after childbirth without loss of seniority or other accrued benefits, and be paid maternity leave as a form of social security and/or employee benefit.

IV. Immediate revision of tax laws to permit the deduction of home and child-care expenses for working parents.

V. That child-care facilities be established by law on the same basis as parks, libraries, and public schools, adequate to the needs of children from the pre-school years through adolescence, as a community resource to be used by all citizens from all income levels.

VI. That the right of women to be educated to their full potential equally with men be secured by federal and state legislation, eliminating all discrimination and segregation by sex, written and unwritten, at all levels of education, including colleges, graduate and professional schools, loans and fellowships, and federal and state training programs such as the Job Corps.

VII. The right of women in poverty to secure job training, housing, and family allowances on equal terms with men, but without prejudice to a parent's right to remain at home to care for his or her children; revision of welfare legislation and poverty programs which deny women dignity, privacy, and self-respect.

VIII. The right of women to control their own reproductive lives by removing from the penal code laws limiting access to contraceptive information and devices, and by repealing penal laws governing abortion.

The Myth of the Vaginal Orgasm

The daily discrimination and condescension that women experienced were the primary issues of the New Feminists. But they also took aim at more exalted targets. Behind the daily slurs and rebuffs, they detected a framework of ideas and concepts that relegated females to the status of the "second sex" and accorded full humanity only to men.

No set of ideas did so much to condone female subordination as Freudian psychology, radical feminists held. A man of his times, Sigmund Freud, the father of psychoanalysis and the discoverer of the unconscious, seemed to consider women unfinished human beings. He surmised that lacking a penis, women sought completion by attaching themselves to males and through motherhood. Women's healthy sexual functioning, moreover, depended on males since their satisfaction, achieved only through vaginal orgasm, required penetration. Men could live full lives without women, presumably. But with women, "biology was destiny," and that was incontrovertible.

In this essay, Anne Koedt, a founder of New York Radical Feminists and New York Radical Women, confronts the Freudian theory of the vaginal orgasm. Koedt is clearly not discussing an obscure issue in anatomy. She is questioning the way the Freudians "construct the female," as psychologist Naomi Weisstein called it in a famous feminist article. There is also a subtext in the essay: If penetration is not needed for women's sexual satisfaction, if the clitoris is the real site of female sexual satisfaction, then other women are as competent sexual partners for women as men. In fact, since they understand feminine responses better than men, perhaps they make superior sexual partners. Written as a paper for the first national women's liberation conference in Chicago in 1968, the essay's sexual frankness and its glancing lesbian aperçu gave it a notoriety that led to its wide distribution and republication.

[*With permission of Anne Koedt.*]

THE MYTH OF THE VAGINAL ORGASM

Whenever female orgasm and frigidity are discussed, a false distinction is made between the vaginal and the clitoral orgasm. Frigidity has generally been defined by men as the failure of women to have vaginal orgasms. Actually the vagina is not a highly sensitive area and is not constructed to achieve orgasm. It is the clitoris which is the center of sexual sensitivity and which is the female equivalent of the penis.

I think this explains a great many things: First of all, the fact that the so-called frigidity rate among women is phenomenally high. Rather than tracing female frigidity to the false assumptions about female anatomy, our "experts" have declared frigidity a psychological problem of women. Those women who complained about it were recommended psychiatrists, so that they might discover their "problem"—diagnosed generally as a failure to adjust to their role as women.

The facts of female anatomy and sexual response tell a different story. Although there are many areas for sexual arousal, there is only one area for sexual climax; that area is the clitoris. All orgasms are extensions of sensation from this area. Since the clitoris is not necessarily stimulated sufficiently in the conventional sexual positions, we are left "frigid."

Aside from physical stimulation, which is the common cause of orgasm for most people, there is also stimulation through primarily mental processes. Some women, for example, may achieve orgasm through sexual fantasies, or through fetishes. However, while the stimulation may be psychological, the orgasm manifests itself physically. Thus, while the cause is psychological, the *effect* is still physical, and the orgasm necessarily takes place in the sexual organ equipped for sexual climax—the clitoris. The orgasm experience may also differ in degree of intensity—some more localized, and some more diffuse and sensitive. But they are all clitoral orgasms.

All this leads to some interesting questions about conventional sex and our role in it. Men have orgasms essentially by friction with the vagina, not the clitoral area, which is external and not able to cause friction the way penetration does. Women have thus been defined sexually in terms of what pleases men; our own biology has not been properly analyzed. Instead, we are fed the myth of the liberated woman and her vaginal orgasm—an orgasm which in fact does not exist.

What we must do is redefine our sexuality. We must discard the "normal" concepts of sex and create new guidelines which take into account mutual sexual enjoyment. While the idea of mutual enjoyment is liberally applauded in marriage manuals, it is not followed to its logical conclusion. We must begin to demand that if certain sexual positions now defined as "standard" are not mutually conducive to orgasm, they no longer be defined as standard. New techniques must be used or devised which transform this particular aspect of our current sexual exploitation.

Freud—A Father of the Vaginal Orgasm

Freud contended that the clitoral orgasm was adolescent, and that upon puberty, when women began having intercourse with men, women should transfer the center of orgasm to the vagina. The vagina, it was assumed, was able to produce a parallel, but more mature, orgasm than the clitoris. Much work was done to elaborate on this theory, but little was done to challenge the basic assumptions.

To fully appreciate this incredible invention, perhaps Freud's general attitude about women should first be recalled. Mary Ellman, in *Thinking About Women,* summed it up this way:

> *Everything in Freud's patronizing and fearful attitude toward women follows from their lack of a penis, but it is only in his essay* The Psychology of Women *that Freud makes explicit . . . the deprecations of women which are implicit in his work. He then prescribes for them the abandonment of the life of the mind, which will interfere with their sexual function. When the psycho-analyzed patient is male, the analyst sets himself the task of developing the man's capacities; but with women patients, the job is to resign them to the limits of their sexuality. As Mr. Rieff puts it: For Freud, "Analysis cannot encourage in women new energies for success and achievement, but only teach them the lesson of rational resignation."*

It was Freud's feelings about women's secondary and inferior relationship to men that formed the basis for his theories on female sexuality.

Once having laid down the law about the nature of our sexuality, Freud not so strangely discovered a tremendous problem of frigidity in women. His recommended cure for a woman who was frigid was psychiatric care. She was suffering from failure to mentally adjust to her "natural" role as a woman. Frank S. Caprio, a contemporary follower of these ideas, states:

> *. . . whenever a woman is incapable of achieving an orgasm via coitus, provided the husband is an adequate partner, and prefers clitoral stimulation to any other form of sexual activity, she can be regarded as suffering from frigidity and requires psychiatric assistance.* (The Sexually Adequate Female, *p. 64.*)

The explanation given was that women were envious of men—"renunciation of womanhood." Thus it was diagnosed as an antimale phenomenon.

It is important to emphasize that Freud did not base his theory upon a study of woman's anatomy, but rather upon his assumptions of woman as an inferior appendage to man, and her consequent social and psychological role. In their attempts to deal with the ensuing problem of mass frigidity, Freudians embarked on elaborate mental gymnastics. Marie Bonaparte, in *Female Sexuality,* goes so far as to suggest surgery to help women back on their rightful path. Having discovered a strange connection between the nonfrigid woman and the location of the clitoris near the vagina,

> it then occurred to me that where, in certain women, this gap was excessive, and clitoridal fixation obdurate, a clitoridal-vaginal reconciliation might be effected by surgical means, which would then benefit the normal erotic function. Professor Halban, of Vienna, as much a biologist as surgeon, became interested in the problem and worked out a simple operative technique. In this, the suspensory ligament of the clitoris was severed and the clitoris secured to the underlying structures, thus fixing it in a lower position, with eventual reduction of the labia minora. (p. 148.)

But the severest damage was not in the area of surgery, where Freudians ran around absurdly trying to change female anatomy to fit their basic assumptions. The worst damage was done to the mental health of women, who either suffered silently with self-blame, or flocked to psychiatrists looking desperately for the hidden and terrible repression that had kept from them their vaginal destiny.

Lack of Evidence

One may perhaps at first claim that these are unknown and unexplored areas, but upon closer examination this is certainly not true today, nor was it true even in the past. For example, men have known that women suffered from frigidity often during intercourse. So the problem was there. Also, there is much specific evidence. Men knew that the clitoris was and is the essential organ for masturbation, whether in children or adult women. So obviously women made it clear where *they* thought their sexuality was located. Men also seem suspiciously aware of the clitoral powers during "foreplay," when they want to arouse women and produce the necessary lubrication for penetration. Foreplay is a concept created for male purposes, but works to the disadvantage of many women, since as soon as the woman is aroused, the man changes to vaginal stimulation, leaving her both aroused and unsatisfied.

It has also been known that women need no anesthesia inside the vagina during surgery, thus pointing to the fact that the vagina is in fact not a highly sensitive area.

Today, with extensive knowledge of anatomy, with Kelly, Kinsey, and Masters and Johnson, to mention just a few sources, there is no ignorance on the subject. There are, however, social reasons why this knowledge has not been popularized. We are living in a male society which has not sought change in women's role.

Anatomical Evidence

Rather than starting with what women *ought* to feel, it would seem logical to start out with the anatomical facts regarding the clitoris and vagina.

The Clitoris is a small equivalent of the penis, except for the fact that the urethra does not go through it as in the man's penis. Its erection is similar to the male erection, and the head of the clitoris has the same type of structure and function as the head of the penis. G. Lombard Kelly, in *Sexual Feeling in Married Men and Women*, says:

> *The head of the clitoris is also composed of erectile tissue, and it possesses a very sensitive epithelium or surface covering, supplied with special nerve endings called genital corpuscles, which are peculiarly adapted for sensory stimulation that under proper mental conditions terminates in the sexual orgasm. No other part of the female generative tract has such corpuscles. (Pocketbooks; p. 35.)*

The clitoris has no other function than that of sexual pleasure.

The Vagina—Its functions are related to the reproductive function. Principally, (1) menstruation, (2) receive penis, (3) hold semen, and (4) birth passage. The interior of the vagina, which according to the defenders of the vaginally caused orgasm is the center and producer of the orgasm, is:

> *like nearly all other internal body structures, poorly supplied with end organs of touch. The internal entodermal origin of the lining of the vagina makes it similar in this respect to the rectum and other parts of the digestive tract.* (Kinsey, Sexual Behavior in the Human Female, *p. 580.*)

The degree of insensitivity inside the vagina is so high that "Among the women who were tested in our gynecologic sample, less than 14% were at all conscious that they had been touched" (Kinsey, p. 580).

Even the importance of the vagina as an *erotic* center (as opposed to an orgasmic center) has been found to be minor.

Other Areas—Labia minora and the vestibule of the vagina. These two sensitive areas may trigger off a clitoral orgasm. Because they can be effectively stimulated during "normal" coitus, though infrequently, this kind of stimulation is incorrectly thought to be vaginal orgasm. However, it is important to distinguish between areas which can stimulate the clitoris, incapable of producing the orgasm themselves, and the clitoris:

Regardless of what means of excitation is used to bring the individual to the state of sexual climax, the sensation is perceived by the genital corpuscles and is localized where they are situated: in the head of the clitoris or penis. (Kelly, p. 49.)

Psychologically Stimulated Orgasm—Aside from the above mentioned direct and indirect stimulations of the clitoris, there is a third way an orgasm may be triggered. This is through mental (cortical) stimulation, where the imagination stimulates the brain, which in turn stimulates the genital corpuscles of the glans to set off an orgasm.

Women Who Say They Have Vaginal Orgasms

Confusion—Because of the lack of knowledge of their own anatomy, some women accept the idea that an orgasm felt during "normal" intercourse was vaginally caused. This confusion is caused by a combination of two factors. One, failing to locate the center of the orgasm, and two, by a desire to fit her experience to the male-defined idea of sexual normalcy. Considering that women know little about their anatomy, it is easy to be confused.

Deception—The vast majority of women who pretend vaginal orgasm to their men are faking it to "get the job." In a new best-selling Danish book, *I Accuse*, Mette Ejlersen specifically deals with this common problem, which she calls the "sex comedy." This comedy has many causes. First of all, the man brings a great deal of pressure to bear on the woman, because he considers his ability as a lover at stake. So as not to offend his ego, the woman will comply with the prescribed role and go through simulated ecstasy. In some of the other Danish women mentioned, women who were left frigid were turned off to sex, and pretended vaginal orgasm to hurry up the sex act. Others admitted that they had faked vaginal orgasm to catch a man. In one case, the woman pretended vaginal orgasm to get him to leave his first wife, who admitted being vaginally frigid. Later she was forced to continue the deception, since obviously she couldn't tell him to stimulate her clitorally.

Many more women were simply afraid to establish their right to equal enjoyment, seeing the sexual act as being primarily for the man's benefit, and any pleasure that the woman got as an added extra.

Other women, with just enough ego to reject the man's idea that they needed psychiatric care, refused to admit their frigidity. They wouldn't accept self-blame, but they didn't know how to solve the problem, not knowing the physiological facts about themselves. So they were left in a peculiar limbo.

Again, perhaps one of the most infuriating and damaging results of this whole charade has been that women who were perfectly healthy sexually were taught that they were not. So in addition to being sexually deprived, these women were told to blame themselves when they deserved no blame. Looking for a cure to a problem that has none can lead a woman on an endless path of self-hatred and insecurity. For she is told by her analyst that not even in her one role allowed in a male society—the role of a woman—is she successful. She is put on the defensive, with phony data as evidence that she'd better try to be even more feminine, think more feminine, and reject her envy of men. That is, shuffle even harder, baby.

Why Men Maintain the Myth

1. *Sexual Penetration Is Preferred*—The best physical stimulant for the penis is the woman's vagina. It supplies the necessary friction and lubrication. From a strictly technical point of view, this position offers the best physical conditions, even though the man may try other positions for variation.

2. *The Invisible Woman*—One of the elements of male chauvinism is the refusal or inability to see women as total, separate human beings. Rather, men have chosen to define women only in terms of how they benefited men's lives. Sexually, a woman was not seen as an individual wanting to share equally in the sexual act, any more than she was seen as a person with independent desires when she did anything else in society. Thus, it was easy to make up what was convenient about women; for on top of that, society has been a function of male interests, and women were not organized to form even a vocal opposition to the male experts.

3. *The Penis as Epitome of Masculinity*—Men define their lives primarily in terms of masculinity. It is a universal form of ego-boosting. That is, in every society, however homogeneous (i.e., with the absence of racial, ethnic, or major economic differences), there is always a group, women, to oppress.

The essence of male chauvinism is in the psychological superiority men exercise over women. This kind of superior-inferior definition of self, rather than positive definition based upon one's own achievements and development, has of course chained victim and oppressor both. But by far the most brutalized of the two is the victim.

An analogy is racism, where the white racist compensates for his feelings of unworthiness by creating an image of the black man (it is primarily a male struggle) as biologically inferior to him. Because of his position in a white male power structure, the white man can socially enforce this mythical division.

To the extent that men try to rationalize and justify male superiority through physical differentiation, masculinity may be symbolized by being the *most* muscular, the most hairy; having the deepest voice, and the biggest penis. Women, on the other hand, are approved of (i.e., called feminine) if they are weak, petite; shave their legs; have high soft voices.

Since the clitoris is almost identical to the penis, one finds a great deal of evidence of men in various societies trying to either ignore the clitoris and emphasize the vagina (as did Freud) or, as in some places in the Mideast, actually performing clitoridectomy. Freud saw this ancient and still practiced custom as a way of further "feminizing" the female by removing this cardinal vestige of her masculinity. It should be noted also that a big clitoris is considered ugly and masculine. Some cultures engage in the practice of pouring a chemical on the clitoris to make it shrivel up into "proper" size.

It seems clear to me that men in fact fear the clitoris as a threat to masculinity.

4. *Sexually Expendable Male*—Men fear that they will become sexually expendable if the clitoris is substituted for the vagina as the center of pleasure for women. Actually this has a great deal of validity if one considers *only* the anatomy. The position of the penis inside the vagina, while perfect for reproduction, does not necessarily stimulate an orgasm in women because the clitoris is located externally and higher up. Women must rely upon indirect stimulation in the "normal" position.

Lesbian sexuality could make an excellent case, based upon anatomical data, for the irrelevancy of the male organ. Albert Ellis says something to the effect that a man without a penis can make a woman an excellent lover.

Considering that the vagina is very desirable from a man's point of view, purely on physical grounds, one begins to see the dilemma for men. And it forces us as well to discard many "physical" arguments explaining why women go to bed with men. What is left, it seems to me, are primarily psychological reasons why women select men at the exclusion of women as sexual partners.

5. *Control of Women*—One reason given to explain the Mideastern practice of clitoridectomy is that it will keep the women from straying. By

removing the sexual organ capable of orgasm, it must be assumed that her sexual drive will diminish. Considering how men look upon their women as property, particularly in very backward nations, we should begin to consider a great deal more why it is not in men's interest to have women totally free sexually. The double standard, as practiced for example in Latin America, is set up to keep the woman as total property of the husband, while he is free to have affairs as he wishes.

6. *Lesbianism and Bisexuality*—Aside from the strictly anatomical reasons why women might equally seek other women as lovers, there is a fear on men's part that women will seek the company of other women on a full, human basis. The recognition of clitoral orgasm as fact would threaten the heterosexual *institution*. For it would indicate that sexual pleasure was obtainable from either men *or* women, thus making heterosexuality not an absolute, but an option. It would thus open up the whole question of *human* sexual relationships beyond the confines of the present male-female role system.

No More Miss America!

One theme of the Sixties women's liberation movement was the evil effects of gender stereotyping. Defining some personal attributes and characteristics as feminine and others as masculine served to limit or degrade women because almost always the niches into which they were placed were inferior to the masculine equivalent. Even stereotypes that seemed outwardly benign were often oppressive, designed to force women to accept subordinate positions and rewards in life.

Denoting women the "fair sex" was one such denigrating stereotype. The custom was meant to compliment women, but it really reinforced their position as sex objects whose value to men and to the world derived primarily from their physical attractiveness. From this, it was said, flowed all sorts of evils: prostitution, low female self-esteem, consumerism, oppressive domesticity, masculine supremacy, and disrespect for women who did not meet conventional male standards.

No ritual epitomized this male-derived beauty cult so vividly as the annual fall Miss America Pageant in Atlantic City. In 1968, a group of militant feminists, New York Radical Women, decided to challenge this ceremony of female inferiority. Arriving by bus, several hundred women lugged "freedom ashcans" to the New Jersey resort to strike their blow against patriarchy. They were refused admission to Convention Hall, where the crowning ceremony was being held. So they picketed outside and dumped symbols of their female enslavement into the ashcans: high-heeled shoes, kitchen detergent, girdles, and brassieres. (No bra was ever burned.)

Patriarchy of course survived—so did the pageant, for that matter—but the media loved the event and Life *magazine,* Time, Newsweek, *and many daily papers gave it generous space. As the promoters hoped, the demonstration put radical feminism on the map. This document is the manifesto that the protesters printed up and handed out to the media and to spectators on the city's famous boardwalk.*

[*"No More Miss America!" from* **Sisterhood Is Powerful: An Anthology of Writings from the Women's Liberation Movement,** *edited by Robin Morgan. Copyright © 1970 by Robin Morgan. By permission of Edite Kroll Literary Agency, Inc.*]

NO MORE MISS AMERICA!

On September 7 in Atlantic City, the Annual Miss America Pageant will again crown "your ideal." But this year, reality will liberate the contest auction-block in the guise of "genyooine" de-plasticized, breathing women. Women's Liberation Groups, black women, high-school and college women, women's peace groups, women's welfare and social-work groups, women's job-equality groups, pro-birth control and pro-abortion groups—women of every political persuasion—all are invited to join us in a day-long boardwalk-theater event, starting at 1:00 P.M. on the Boardwalk in front of Atlantic City's Convention Hall. We will protest the image of Miss America, an image that oppresses women in every area in which it purports to represent us. There will be: Picket Lines; Guerrilla Theater; Leafleting; Lobbying Visits to the contestants urging our sisters to reject the Pageant Farce and join us; a huge Freedom Trash Can (into which we will throw bras, girdles, curlers, false eyelashes, wigs, and representative issues of *Cosmopolitan, Ladies' Home Journal, Family Circle,* etc.—bring any such woman-garbage you have around the house); we will also announce a Boycott of all those commercial products related to the Pageant, and the day will end with a Women's Liberation rally at midnight when Miss America is crowned on live television. Lots of other surprises are being planned (come and add your own!) but we do not plan heavy disruptive tactics and so do not expect a bad police scene. It should be a groovy day on the Boardwalk in the sun with our sisters. In case of arrests, however, we plan to reject all male authority and demand to be busted by policewomen only. (In Atlantic City, women cops are not permitted to make arrests—dig that!)

Male chauvinist-reactionaries on this issue had best stay away, nor are male liberals welcome in the demonstrations. But sympathetic men can donate money as well as cars and drivers.

Male reporters will be refused interviews. We reject patronizing reportage. *Only newswomen will be recognized.*

The Ten Points

We Protest:

1. *The Degrading Mindless-Boob-Girlie Symbol.* The Pageant contestants epitomize the roles we are all forced to play as women. The parade down the runway blares the metaphor of the 4-H Club county fair, where the nervous animals are judged for teeth, fleece, etc., and where the best "specimen" gets the blue ribbon. So are women in our society forced daily to compete for male approval, enslaved by ludicrous "beauty" standards we ourselves are conditioned to take seriously.

2. *Racism with Roses.* Since its inception in 1921, the Pageant has not had one Black finalist, and this has not been for a lack of test-case contestants. There has never been a Puerto Rican, Alaskan, Hawaiian, or Mexican-American winner. Nor has there ever been a *true* Miss America—an American Indian.

3. *Miss America as Military Death Mascot.* The highlight of her reign each year is a cheerleader-tour of American troops abroad—last year she went to Vietnam to pep-talk our husbands, fathers, sons and boyfriends into dying and killing with a better spirit. She personifies the "unstained patriotic American womanhood our boys are fighting for." The Living Bra and the Dead Soldier. We refuse to be used as Mascots for Murder.

4. *The Consumer Con-Game.* Miss America is a walking commercial for the Pageant's sponsors. Wind her up and she plugs your product on promotion tours and TV—all in an "honest, objective" endorsement. What a shill.

5. *Competition Rigged and Unrigged.* We deplore the encouragement of an American myth that oppresses men as well as women: the win-or-you're-worthless competive disease. The "beauty contest" creates only one winner to be "used" and forty-nine losers who are "useless."

6. *The Woman as Pop Culture Obsolescent Theme.* Spindle, mutilate, and then discard tomorrow. What is so ignored as last year's Miss America? This only reflects the gospel of our society, according to Saint Male: women must be young, juicy, malleable—hence age discrimination and the cult of youth. And we women are brainwashed into believing this ourselves!

7. *The Unbeatable Madonna-Whore Combination.* Miss America and Playboy's centerfold are sisters over the skin. To win approval, we must be both sexy and wholesome, delicate but able to cope, demure yet titillatingly bitchy. Deviation of any sort brings, we are told, disaster: "You won't get a man!!"

8. *The Irrelevant Crown on the Throne of Mediocrity.* Miss America represents what women are supposed to be: unoffensive, bland, apolitical. If you are tall, short, over or under what weight The Man prescribes you should be, forget it. Personality, articulateness, intelligence, commitment—unwise. Conformity is the key to the crown—and, by extension, to success in our society.

9. *Miss America as Dream Equivalent To—?* In this reputedly democratic society, where every little boy supposedly can grow up to be President, what can every little girl hope to grow to be? Miss America. That's where it's at. Real power to control our own lives is restricted to men, while women get patronizing pseudo-power, an ermine cloak, and a bunch of flowers; men are judged by their actions, women by their appearance.

10. *Miss America as Big Sister Watching You.* The Pageant exercises Thought Control, attempts to sear the Image onto our minds, to further make women oppressed and men oppressors; to enslave us all the more in high-heeled, low-status roles; to inculcate false values in young girls; to use women as beasts of buying; to seduce us to prostitute ourselves before our own oppression.

NO MORE MISS AMERICA

The Redstockings Manifesto

Redstockings was founded in early 1969 by a small group of activists including Ellen Willis, Shulamith Firestone, and Kathie Sarachild, a feminist who had changed her last name from Amatniek to favor her female over her male parent. Redstockings came to public attention when it interrupted the hearings of a New York State legislative committee to demand that the lawmakers move beyond "reform" to total abolition of the state's anti-abortion laws. Thereafter Redstockings conducted several "speakouts" where aggrieved women told receptive audiences of their experiences with abortion, rape, incest, and sexual harrassment. By the spring of 1969, however, Redstockings began to emphasize consciousness-raising as a feminist device.

CR was designed to overcome the self-abasement that male society imposed on women and, through self-awareness, release them from oppression. But consciousness-raising would be more than a means for personal salvation. Women whose consciousness had been fully raised would then begin to fight for equality and autonomy.

Redstockings denied that, through brainwashing, women unconsciously became what men wanted them to be. Rather, they deliberately chose the roles they played. Many of the attributes and attitudes in women that other feminists deplored, they said, could be seen as rational survival tactics. Referred to as a "pro-woman" position, this view was denounced by other new feminists as an implicit defense of traditional female sex roles.

The document here, dated July 7, 1969, expresses the pro-woman position. Even more clearly, however, it voices an anti-man position. Though it does not use the term, it condemns patriarchy. "All men have oppressed women," it says. No male can claim innocence of the crime.

[*"Redstockings Manifesto," in Robin Morgan, ed.,* **Sisterhood Is Powerful** *(New York: Vintage Books, 1970), pp. 533–36.*]

REDSTOCKINGS MANIFESTO

I. After centuries of individual and preliminary political struggle, women are uniting to achieve their final liberation from male supremacy. Redstockings is dedicated to building this unity and winning our freedom.

II. Women are an oppressed class. Our oppression is total, affecting every facet of our lives. We are exploited as sex objects, breeders, domestic servants, and cheap labor. We are considered inferior beings, whose only purpose is to enhance men's lives. Our humanity is denied. Our prescribed behavior is enforced by the threat of physical violence.

Because we have lived so intimately with our oppressors, in isolation from each other, we have been kept from seeing our personal suffering as a political condition. This creates the illusion that a woman's relationship with her man is a matter of interplay between two unique personalities, and can be worked out individually. In reality, every such relationship is a *class* relationship, and the conflicts between individual men and women are *political* conflicts that can only be solved collectively.

III. We identify the agents of our oppression as men. Male supremacy is the oldest, most basic form of domination. All other forms of exploitation and oppression (racism, capitalism, imperialism, etc.) are extensions of male supremacy: men dominate women, a few men dominate the rest. All power structures throughout history have been male-dominated and male-oriented. Men have controlled all political, economic, and cultural institutions and backed up this control with physical force. They have used their power to keep women in an inferior position. *All men* receive economic, sexual, and psychological benefits from male supremacy. *All men* have oppressed women.

IV. Attempts have been made to shift the burden of responsibility from men to institutions or to women themselves. We condemn these arguments as evasions. Institutions alone do not oppress; they are merely tools of the oppressor. To blame institutions implies that men and women are equally victimized, obscures the fact that men benefit from the subordination of women, and gives men the excuse that they are forced to be oppressors. On the contrary, any man is free to renounce his superior position provided that he is willing to be treated like a woman by other men.

We also reject the idea that women consent to or are to blame for their own oppression. Women's submission is not the result of brainwashing, stupidity, or mental illness but of continual, daily pressure from men. We do not need to change ourselves, but to change men.

The most slanderous evasion of all is that women can oppress men. The basis for this illusion is the isolation of individual relationships from their political context and the tendency of men to see any legitimate challenge to their privileges as persecution.

V. We regard our personal experience, and our feelings about that experience, as the basis for an analysis of our common situation. We cannot rely on existing ideologies as they are all products of male supremacist culture. We question every generalization and accept none that are not confirmed by our experience.

Our chief task at present is to develop female class consciousness through sharing experience and publicly exposing the sexist foundation of all our institutions. Consciousness-raising is not "therapy," which implies the existence of individual solutions and falsely assumes that the male-female relationship is purely personal, but the only method by which we can ensure that our program for liberation is based on the concrete realities of our lives.

The first requirement for raising class consciousness is honesty, in private and in public, with ourselves and other women.

VI. We identify with all women. We define our best interest as that of the poorest, most brutally exploited woman.

We repudiate all economic, racial, educational or status privileges that divide us from other women. We are determined to recognize and eliminate any prejudices we may hold against other women.

We are committed to achieving internal democracy. We will do whatever is necessary to ensure that every woman in our movement has an equal chance to participate, assume responsibility, and develop her political potential.

VII. We call on all our sisters to unite with us in struggle.

We call on all men to give up their male privileges and support women's liberation in the interest of our humanity and their own.

In fighting for our liberation we will always take the side of women against their oppressors. We will not ask what is "revolutionary" or "reformist," only what is good for women.

The time for individual skirmishes has passed. This time we are going all the way.

8

Judicial Activism

The United States Supreme Court is unique. No other judicial body in the world has the same power to alter the basic constitutional processes of a nation and affect in such fundamental ways how ordinary citizens relate to their society and go about their lives.

Much of the Supreme Court's power comes from precedent rather than express legal provision. Nowhere in the Constitution, for example, is there any mention of the Court's most potent prerogative: the right to determine the constitutionality of acts of Congress and the state legislatures. It was only in 1803, in *Marbury v. Madison,* that the Court ruled a federal law unconstitutional. And not until 1857, in the *Dred Scott* decision, did the Court void another act of Congress. This self-limitation was often joined with a reluctance to bend the express words of legislation to make them fit new circumstances. Together, these have been called judicial restraint. It is a principle that enjoins the courts to interpret the Constitution narrowly and limits the urge to seek in that document justification for remedying wrongs or altering practices that Congress and the legislatures have not expressly addressed.

In our own century, the justices have varied widely in their assertion of judicial restraint. In the last third of the nineteenth century, the Supreme Court handed down a raft of decisions invalidating, on constitutional grounds, state and federal regulation of business practices. During the 1920s, the justices avoided cases that challenged the validity of federal and state laws. In the 1930s, however, they resumed their activist approach and disallowed much early New Deal legislation, leading to a major counterattack by FDR—the "court-packing plan" to replace justices over seventy by new appointees—that threatened the Court's integrity and independence. For a time thereafter the justices assumed a low profile once again.

But the Court has not only varied in its degree of activism; it has also run the ideological gamut. Though insulated by express design of the Founders from the direct impact of politics, the justices have not been totally protected from outside influence. Roosevelt's 1937 court-packing plan failed to be enacted, but his attack on the obstructionist "nine old men" shifted enough votes among them to save most of the New Deal's social programs. Nor are the justices kept from contact with the overall ideological climate. In some ultimate sense, even the dignified, black-robed men and women who listen to the pleas of high state officials and private attorneys each October term cannot completely ignore the deep-running social and economic currents of their day. Though lawyers, they are also citizens of the turbulent republic.

In the post–World War II era, new moderate-to-liberal nominations by Truman and Eisenhower moved the Court further left and at the same time ended the period of relative passivity that followed Roosevelt's attack. Under Eisenhower's appointee, Chief Justice Earl Warren, a former Republican governor of California, the Court became the active champion of "fairness" and individual freedom in American life. The Warren Court, though composed of mature men and seasoned lawyers, registered the new liberated consciousness of the post–World War II era. This liberated consciousness had penetrated the major law schools and influenced the entire legal profession. Beyond this, especially after the departure in the early 1960s of Justice Felix Frankfurter, a judicial conservative, the Supreme Court was dominated by activists who sought to shape the rules and laws vital to the conduct by which Americans led their lives and performed their public functions.

The Chief Justice and his close allies on the Court during his tenure— William O. Douglas, Hugo Black, William Brennan, Arthur Goldberg, Abe Fortas, and Thurgood Marshall—were indifferent to the original intent of legislators when they passed laws. They also cared little about constitutional theory, legal precedent, or traditional judicial reasoning that so often seemed to reinforce the biased status quo. Their end was a fairer, freer, more just and more equal society, one that protected individual rights, and if the legislative process failed to achieve these goals, they would find ways, in the course of judicial interpretation, to attain them.

During the sixteen years of the Warren Court, the combination of activism and liberalism produced an avalanche of major judicial decisions that changed the quality of American life indelibly. Starting with the landmark *Brown v. Board of Education of Topeka* (1954), which struck down segregated schools in the South, the Court took on controversial political, social, and intellectual issues that had long seemed untouchable through normal legislative action, and resolved them in a liberal direction. In *Mapp v. Ohio* (1961), the Court voted to exclude evidence illegally acquired by the police from consideration in criminal cases before state courts. In *Engel v. Vitale* (1962), it disallowed school prayer as contrary to "separation of church and state." In *Gideon v. Wainright* (1963), it mandated court-appointed lawyers for indigent defendants in felony cases. In *Reynolds v. Sims* (1964), it required that states periodically reapportion voting districts to guarantee "one person, one vote." In *Griswold v. Connecticut* (1965), it overturned a state statute that forbade the use of contraceptive methods on the gounds that it violated the inherent right of privacy. In *Miranda v. Arizona* (1966), it required police to warn suspects of their possible self-incrimination and inform them of their right to an attorney. Other decisions defined an "obscene" book as a work "utterly without redeeming social value," struck down state laws making interracial marriage illegal, and mandated busing of students for the sake of interracial balance.

The Warren Court's work dismayed conservatives and even, at times, liberals. Its opponents charged that, rather than applying the law as courts were supposed to do, the liberal judges were making law. Moreover, the effects of their decisions were deplorable in substance and worse in their effects. In their view, the federal courts during the Sixties seemed as determined as the hippies, the radical students, and the antiwar protesters to shred the fabric of American life, unleashing immorality, crime, irreligion, and contempt for legitimate authority. One of the right-wing icons of the decade was the ubiquitous "Impeach Earl Warren" billboards, sponsored by the far right John Birch Society and displayed across Dixie and in parts of the North.

Warren retired in 1968, but the activist current continued under his successor, Warren Burger. The judicial activisim of the Warren Court, in many ways, reached its apogee in *Roe v. Wade* (1973), in which the court decided that no state could deny a woman the right to an abortion during the first trimester of pregnancy.

No one can doubt that the Warren Court was a vital component of the Sixties. Indeed, it can be argued that its assault on the political, cultural, and legal rigidities of the day went deeper and had more long-lasting effects than all the decade's rallies, protests, marches, and elections laid end to end.

Engel v. Vitale

Engel v. Vitale *denied the right of the New York Board of Regents to prescribe a period of prayer in the state schools. Few decisions of the Warren Court offended Americans of traditional religious views as much as this one.*

In the Bill of Rights, the Founders forbade Congress to make a law "respecting an establishment of religion." Their purpose was to prevent government from giving special, favored status to one religious denomination, a universal practice in Christian lands since the days of the late Roman empire. Preferential treatment had been carried to America by the early colonists, and such religious "establishments" had not been finally eliminated in the states until a generation after the Revolution. The First Amendment to the Constitution applied the "separation of church and state" doctrine to the federal government.

In the twentieth century, no state gave special advantages to a particular religious denomination, but this did not mean that government did not acknowledge the importance of religion in the lives of citizens or seek to encourage it in various ways. Few Americans objected to putting "In God We Trust" on U.S. coins, opening Congress with a chaplain's prayer, giving religious institutions a property tax exemption, or closing government offices on Christmas Day. But what about school prayer?

Secularists, "humanists," atheists, and agnostics believed that "separation of church and state" must be absolute: government should have nothing to do with religion in any form. They often objected to the many pragmatic compromises with religion that Americans had evolved in the public realm. At the other extreme, ultraconservatives sought a federal law or constitutional amendment to declare the United States "a Christian nation." Less dogmatic Christians, mainstream social conservatives and traditionalists, for their part, saw nothing wrong with the state encouraging piety, at least of a nondenominational sort, through school prayer and other means.

The Warren Court, with Engel v. Vitale, would be the means for striking down state policies deemed by liberals to be reactionary and obscurantist. Holding that the due process clause of the 1868 Fourteenth Amendment "incorporated" all the Bill of Rights guarantees, the justices held that states could not allow prayer in the publicly supported schools.

The 1962 decision fired up a chorus of protest. Many ordinary churchgoers were dismayed. Why not allow children to say a brief prayer in school, as long as it avoided sectarianism? It could only encourage reverence and respect, and that was all to the good. In Congress, Representative George Anderson of Alabama announced: "They put the Negroes in the schools, and now they've driven God out." Mendel Rivers of South Carolina declared: "I know of nothing in my lifetime that could give more aid and comfort to Moscow than this bold, malicious, atheistic and sacrilegious twist by this unpredictable group of uncontrolled despots." Chief Justice Warren, a religious man, was dismayed by the reaction and denied that he was opposed to God. But the decision was a red flag for the religious right and has remained so to this day.

[Engel v. Vitale, 370 Supreme Court Reporter, 421.]

ENGEL V. VITALE

Mr. Justice BLACK delivered the opinion of the Court.

• • •

The respondent Board of Education of Union Free School District No. 9, New Hyde Park, New York, acting in its official capacity under state law, directed the School District's principal to cause the following prayer to be said aloud by each class in the presence of a teacher at the beginning of each school day:

> *"Almighty God, we acknowledge our dependence upon Thee, and we beg Thy blessings upon us, our parents, our teachers, and our Country."*

This daily procedure was adopted on the recommendation of the State Board of Regents, a government agency created by the state constitution to which the New York legislature has granted broad supervisory, executive, and legislative powers over the state's public school system. These state officials composed the prayer which they recommended and published as part of their "Statement on Moral and Spiritual Training in the Schools," saying: "We believe that this Statement will be subscribed to by all men and women of good will, and we call upon all of them to aid in giving life to our program."

• • •

[1] Shortly after the practice of reciting the Regents' prayer was adopted by the School District, the parents of ten pupils brought this action in a New York State Court insisting that use of this official prayer in the public schools was contrary to the beliefs, religions, or religious practices of both themselves and their children. Among other things, these parents challenged the constitutionality of both the state law authorizing the School District to direct the use of prayer in public schools and the School District's regulation ordering the recitation of this particular prayer on the ground that these actions of official governmental agencies violate that part of the First Amendment of the Federal Constitution which commands that "Congress shall make no law respecting an establishment of religion"—a command which was made "applicable to the State of New York by the Fourteenth Amendment of the said Constitution." . . .

• • •

[2] We think that by using the public school system to encourage recitation of the Regents' prayer, the State of New York has adopted a practice wholly inconsistent with the Establishment Clause. There can, of course, be no doubt that New York's program of daily classroom invocation of God's blessings is a religious activity. It is a solemn avowal of divine faith and supplication for the blessings of the Almighty. The nature of such a prayer has always been religious, none of the respondents has denied this and the trial court expressly so found. . . .

• • •

[3] The petitioners contend among other things that the state laws requiring or permitting use of the Regents' prayer must be struck down as a violation of the Establishment Clause because that prayer was composed by governmental officials as part of a governmental program to further religious beliefs. For this reason, petitioners argue, the state's use of the Regents' prayer in the public school system breaches the constitutional wall of separation between Church and State. We agree with that contention since we think that the constitutional prohibition against laws respecting an establishment of religion must at least mean that in this country it is no part of the business of government to compose official prayers for any group of the American people to recite as a part of a religious program carried on by government. . . .

• • •

[4,5] By the time of the adoption of the Constitution, our history shows that there was a widespread awareness among many Americans of the dangers of a union of Church and State. These people knew . . . that one of the greatest dangers to the freedom of the individual to worship in his own way lay in the government's placing its official stamp of approval upon one particular form of prayer or one particular form of religious services. . . . The First Amendment was added to the Constitution as a guarantee that neither the power nor the prestige of the federal government would be used to control, support, or influence the kinds of prayer the American people can say—that the people's religions must not be subjected to the

pressure of government for each time a new political administration is elected to office. Under that Amendment's prohibition against governmental establishment of religion, as reinforced by the provisions of the Fourteenth Amendment, government in this country, be it state or federal, is without power to prescribe by law any particular form of prayer which is to be used as an official prayer in carrying on any program of governmentally sponsored religious activity.

• • •

[6–12] There can be no doubt that New York's state prayer program officially establishes the religious beliefs embodied in the Regents' prayer. The respondents' argument to the contrary, which is largely based upon the contention that the Regents' prayer is "nondenominational" and the fact that the program, as modified and approved by the state courts, does not require all pupils to recite the prayer but permits those who wish to do so to remain silent or be excused from the room, ignores the essential nature of the program's constitutional defects. Neither the fact that the program may be denominationally neutral nor the fact that its observance on the part of the students is voluntary can serve to free it from the limitations of the Establishment Clause, as it might from the Free Exercise Clause of the First Amendment, both of which are operative against the states by virtue of the Fourteenth Amendment. . . .

It has been argued that to apply the Constitution in such a way as to prohibit state laws respecting an establishment of religious services in public schools is to indicate hostility toward religion or toward prayer. Nothing, of course, could be more wrong. The history of man is inseparable from the history of religion. And perhaps it is not too much to say that since the beginning of that history many people have devoutly believed that "More things are wrought by prayer than this world dreams of. . . ." And there were men of this same faith in the power of prayer who led the fight for adoption of our Constitution and also for our Bill of Rights with the very guarantees of religious freedom that forbid the sort of governmental activity which New York has attempted here. These men knew that the First Amendment, which tried to put an end to governmental control of religion and of prayer, was not written to destroy either. They knew rather that it was written to quiet well-justified fears which nearly all of them felt arising out of an awareness that governments of the past had shackled men's tongues to make them speak only the religious thoughts that government wanted them to speak and to pray only to the God that government wanted them to pray to. It is neither sacrilegious nor antireligious to say that each separate government in this country should stay out of the business of writing or sanctioning official prayers and leave the purely religious function to the people themselves and to those the people choose to look to for religious guidance. . . .

The judgment of the Court of Appeals of New York is reversed and the cause remanded for further proceedings not inconsistent with this opinion.

Reversed and remanded.

Griswold v. State of Connecticut

In its drive to expand the individual's area of freedom against government intrusion, the Warren Court discovered the constitutional right to privacy. In fact, nowhere in the Constitution does the word privacy *appear. Neither in the Bill of Rights nor in the post–Civil War amendments is the concept mentioned. It was only as an echo, as it were, from existing constitutional rights that the right of privacy could be deduced.*

Justice William Douglas, one of the Court's most committed activists, first enunciated the doctrine in 1961. But it was not until 1965 that a majority decision of the Court proclaimed it the law of the land.

The case in question was Griswold v. State of Connecticut, *which was an appeal by two birth-control activists convicted of violating the Connecticut state law forbidding the use and dissemination of contraceptive devices or instruction in their use. The law expressed the view, strongly backed by the state's powerful Catholic diocese, that preventing conception, except by "natural means," was sinful. Passed many years before by a legislature dominated by pious Protestants, the state law was widely ignored, but it could be, and was, used to prevent wider acceptance and knowledge of how to restrict births by means deemed "artificial." To liberal activists, like the Warren Court majority, its continued existence was an affront to personal freedom.*

Warren assigned the task of writing the majority decision to William O. Douglas who, at the urging of his liberal colleague William J. Brennan, Jr., made the opinion hinge on the right of privacy. It was his claim in the Griswold *ruling that a right of privacy existed as "a penumbra" from other, better established rights, that made the decision memorable. This right would justify major Court decisions in the next ten years. Culminating in the 1973 decision in* Roe v. Wade, *it would divide the nation and set off a major political war that has lasted to this day.*

[Griswold v. State of Connecticut, *381* Supreme Court Reporter, *479.*]

GRISWOLD V. STATE OF CONNECTICUT

Defendants were convicted of violating the Connecticut birth control law. The Circuit Court in the Sixth Circuit, Connecticut, rendered judgements and the defendants appealed. . . .

• • •

Mr. Justice DOUGLAS delivered the opinion of the Court.

• • •

Appellant [Estelle T.] Griswold is Executive Director of the Planned Parenthood League of Connecticut. Appellant Buxton is a licensed physician and a professor at the Yale Medical School who served as medical director for the League at its center in New Haven—a center open and operating from November 1 to November 10, 1961, when appellants were arrested.

They gave information, instruction, and medical advice to *married persons* as to the means of preventing conception. They examined the wife and prescribed the best contraceptive device or material for her use. . . .

The statutes whose constitutionality is involved in this appeal are §§ 53-32 and 54-196 of the General Statutes of Connecticut. . . . The former provides:

> *"any person who uses any drug, medicinal article, or instrument for the purpose of preventing conception shall be fined not less than fifty dollars or imprisoned not less than sixty days nor more than one year or both fined and imprisoned."*

Section 54-196 provides:

> *"Any person who assists, abets, counsels, causes, hires or commands another to commit any offense may be prosecuted and punished as if he were the principal offender."*

• • •

[1] We think that appellants have standing to raise the constitutional rights of the married people with whom they had a professional relationship. . . .

•　•　•

[2] Coming to the merits, we are met with a wide range of questions that implicate the Due Process Clause of the Fourteenth Amendment. [Here follows a discussion of a number of cases in which the Court defended people's right of "association," as a form "of expression of opinion."]

•　•　•

[8] The foregoing cases suggest that specific guarantees in the Bill of Rights have penumbras, formed by emanations from those guarantees that help give them life and substance. . . . Various guarantees create zones of privacy. The right of association contained in the penumbra of the First Amendment [protecting freedom of speech, press, assembly, and petition from congressional interference] is one. . . . The Third Amendment in its prohibition against the quartering of soldiers "in any house" in time of peace without the consent of the owner is another facet of that privacy. The Fourth Amendment explicitly affirms the "right of the people to be secure in their persons, houses, papers, and effects, against unreasonable searches and seizures." The Fifth Amendment in its Self-Incrimination Clause enables the citizen to create a zone of privacy which government may not force him to surrender to his detriment. The Ninth Amendment provides: "The enumeration in the Constitution of certain rights, shall not be construed to deny or disparage others retained by the people. . . ."

•　•　•

[9, 10] The present case, then, concerns a relationship lying within the zone of privacy created by several fundamental constitutional guarantees. And it concerns a law which, in forbidding the *use* of contraceptives rather than regulating their manufacture or sale, seeks to achieve its goals by means having a maximum destructive impact upon that relationship. Such a law cannot stand in light of the familiar principle, so often applied by this Court, that a "government purpose to control or prevent activities constitutionally subject to state regulation may not be achieved by means which sweep unnecessarily broadly and thereby invade the area of protected freedoms. . . ." Would we allow the police to search the sacred precincts of marital bedrooms for telltale signs of the use of contracep-

tives? The very idea is repulsive to notions of privacy surrounding the marriage relationship.

We deal with a right of privacy older than the Bill of Rights—older than our political parties, older than our school system. Marriage is a coming together for better or for worse, hopefully enduring, and intimate to the degree of being sacred. It is an association that promotes a way of life, not causes; a harmony in living, not political faiths; a bilateral loyalty, not commercial or social projects. Yet it is an association for as noble a purpose and any involved in our prior decisions.

Reversed.

Mapp v. Ohio, Gideon v. Wainright, *and* Miranda v. Arizona

Three decisions of the Warren Court profoundly affected American criminal procedure: Mapp v. Ohio *(1961),* Gideon v. Wainright *(1962), and* Miranda v. Arizona *(1966). All sought to protect defendants in criminal trials against "overbearing" practices of police and district attorneys who ignored their rights under the Constitution.*

Mapp *is the least familiar of these decisions by name, yet every viewer of TV police dramas has seen the "exclusionary" principle it established at work. That's when the judge throws out vital incriminating evidence against an accused murderer, rapist, or drug dealer because it was gathered in a way that fails to meet constitutional guidelines.*

Dollree Mapp had been arrested for possessing obscene material after the Cleveland police searched her house without a legal warrant. Despite this illegal action, the Ohio courts had convicted her and the state supreme court had upheld the conviction. In its 1961 decision, the Court extended the principle, long established in federal criminal cases, that evidence gathered in ways that violated the constitutional rights of individuals under the "unreasonable searches and seizures" clause of the Fourth Amendment to the Constitution, applied to state courts as well. Here we must remember that the Fourth Amendment applied solely to the federal government. Once more the question of whether the due process clause of the Fourteenth Amendment "incorporated" most of the Bill of Rights was raised. The Supreme Court was reluctant, even under the activists' domination, to fold the entire Bill of Rights into the post–Civil War amendment, but in Mapp, *it came close to doing so.*

The more familiar Gideon *(1963) became part of our folklore after Anthony Lewis, the* New York Times *columnist, wrote a best-selling account (*Gideon's Trumpet*) of Clarence Earl Gideon,* arrested for breaking into the Bay Harbor*

---

*It has been widely assumed that Gideon was black. In fact, he was a fifty-year-old white man with a record of indigence and petty crime.

Poolroom in Panama City, Florida, allegedly with the intent to burglarize the premises. Too poor to retain a lawyer and forced, under protest, to conduct his own defense, Gideon was convicted and sentenced to a term in the Florida state prison. From his cell, he block-printed in pencil a petition to the Supreme Court claiming he had been denied a constitutional right to counsel in a criminal trial. The Court, which accepted few petitions in forma pauperis *(that is, from indigent petitioners), agreed to hear the plea. The case resembled* Mapp *in that it turned on whether the Fourteenth Amendment due process clause applied to the states, in this case requiring counsel in criminal proceedings to meet the due process test. The Court decided that the all-purpose 1868 amendment in fact did apply, and Gideon was given a new trial with court-appointed attorneys and acquitted.*

Miranda *did not involve extending an already-recognized principle of federal practice to the states. Rather, it established for* both *federal and local governments formal procedures to protect accused criminals in police custody against self-incrimination.*

Ernesto Miranda was a Phoenix resident who was arrested for kidnapping and rape and interrogated at the police station, where he was not advised that he had the right to have a lawyer present. After two hours of police grilling, the accused man signed a confession, which was then admitted over his protest as evidence at his trial. The Court had already declared in a previous decision that the right of counsel in criminal cases started at the interrogation process. In Miranda *it reiterated this right of counsel during questioning, but it also underlined the accused's right to avoid self-incrimination by requiring the police to inform him clearly of his rights, including the right to remain silent. Chief Justice Warren then went on to prescribe a warning formula for police use that would meet the Court's concerns. To this day, the formula is referred to as an accused felon's "Miranda rights."*

Conservatives, predictably, denounced the Warren Court's campaign to limit the power of the police. Mapp, Gideon, *and* Miranda *appeared to be instances of legal nitpicking that seemingly frustrated true justice while allowing criminals to escape proper punishment. In the view of law-and-order conservatives, the chief justice and his liberal colleagues had sanctioned the coddling of criminals, and their actions had abetted the nationwide surge in crimes against persons and property that marked the later Sixties.*

The surge was real. The statistics show that crime soared and felony rates remained high for a generation. But no one is certain why it occurred, and few historians today would blame it on the Court's campaign to preserve and extend the Bill of Rights.

[Mapp v. Ohio, *367* Supreme Court Reporter, *643;* Gideon v. Wainright Corrections Director, *372* Supreme Court Reporter, *335; and* Miranda v. Arizona, *384* Supreme Court Reporter, *436.*]

Mapp v. Ohio

Mr. Justice CLARK delivered the opinion of the Court.

• • •

Appellant stands convicted of knowingly having had in her possession . . . certain lewd and lascivious books, pictures, and photographs in violation of §2905.34 of Ohio's Revised Code. . . . [T]he Supreme Court of Ohio found her conviction was valid "based primarily upon the introduction in evidence of lewd and lascivious books and pictures unlawfully seized during an unlawful search of defendant's home. . . ."

On May 23, 1957, three Cleveland police officers arrived at appellant's residence . . . pursuant to information that "a person [was] hiding out in the home, who was wanted for questioning in connection with a recent bombing, and that there was a large amount of policy paraphernalia [i.e., material connected with 'numbers' gambling] being hidden in the home." . . . Upon their arrival at that house, the officers knocked on the door and demanded entrance but appellant, after telephoning her attorney, refused to admit them without a search warrant. They advised their headquarters of the situation and undertook a surveillance of the house.

The officers again sought entrance some three hours later when four or more additional officers arrived on the scene. When Miss Mapp did not come to the door immediately, at least one of the several doors to the house was forcibly opened and the policemen gained admittance. Meanwhile Miss Mapp's attorney arrived, but the officers having secured their own entry, and continuing in their defiance of the law, would permit him neither to see Miss Mapp nor to enter the house. . . . She demanded to see the search warrant. A paper, claimed to be the warrant, was held up by one of the officers. She grabbed the "warrant" and placed it in her bosom. A struggle ensued in which the officers recovered the piece of paper and as a result of which they handcuffed appellant because she was "belligerent" in resisting their official rescue of the "warrant" from her person. . . . Appellant, in handcuffs, was then forcibly taken upstairs to her bedroom where the officers searched a dresser, a chest of drawers, and some suitcases. . . . The search spread to the rest of the second floor. . . . The obscene materials for possession of which she was ultimately convicted were discovered in the course of that widespread search.

At the trial no search warrant was produced by the prosecution, nor was the failure to produce one explained or accounted for. . . . The Ohio

Supreme Court believed a "reasonable argument" could be made that the conviction should be reversed "because the 'methods' employed to obtain the [evidence] . . . were such to 'offend "a sense of justice,"'" but the court found determinative the fact that the evidence had not been taken "from defendant's person by the use of brutal or offensive physical force against defendant." . . .

The state says that even if the search were made without authority, or otherwise unreasonably, it is not prevented from using the unconstitutionally seized evidence at trial, citing *Wolf v. Colorado* . . . in which this Court did indeed hold "that in a prosecution in a State court for a State crime the Fourteenth Amendment does not forbid the admission of evidence by an unreasonable search and seizure." On this appeal . . . it is urged that we review that holding.

I.

Seventy-five years ago, in *Boyd v. United States* . . . considering the Fourth and Fifth Amendments . . . this Court held that the doctrines of these Amendments

> *"apply to all invasions on the part of the government and its employés of the sanctity of a man's home and the privacies of life. . . . Any forcible and compulsory extortion of a man's own testimony or of his private papers to be used as evidence to convict him of a crime or to forfeit his goods, is within the condemnation [of these Amendments]." . . .*

Less than 30 years after *Boyd,* this Court, in *Weeks v. United States* . . . stated that

> *"The Fourth Amendment . . . put the courts of the United States and Federal officials, in the exercise of their power and authority, under limitations and restraints [and] . . . forever secure[d] the people, their persons, houses, papers, and effects against all unreasonable searches and seizures under the guise of law. . . ."*

[I]n the *Weeks* case, this Court, "for the first time" held that "in a federal prosecution the Fourth Amendment barred the use of evidence secured through an illegal search and seizure." . . . This Court has ever since required of federal law officers a strict adherence to that command which this Court has held to be a clear, specific, and constitutionally required . . . deterrent safeguard without insistence upon which the Fourth Amendment would have been reduced to "a form of words. . . ."

This Court has not hesitated to enforce as strictly against the states as it does against the federal government the rights of free speech and of a free press. . . . Why should not the same rule apply to what is tantamount to coerced testimony by way of unconstitutional seizure of goods, papers, effects, documents, etc.? We find that as to the federal government, the Fourth and Fifth Amendments and as to the states, the freedom from unconscionable invasions of privacy and the freedom from convictions based upon coerced confessions do enjoy an "intimate relation" in their perpetuation of "principles of humanity and civil liberty [secured] . . . only after years of struggle." . . .

IV.

Since the Fourth Amendment's right of privacy has been declared enforceable against the states through the Due Process Clause of the Fourteenth, it is enforceable against them by the same sanction of exclusion as is used against the federal government. Were it otherwise, then . . . without that rule the freedom from state invasions of privacy would be so ephemeral and so neatly severed from its conceptual nexus with the freedom from all brutish means of coercing evidence as not to merit this Court's high regard as a freedom "implicit in the concept of ordered liberty." . . .

V.

Moreover, our holding that the exclusionary rule is an essential part of both the Fourth and Fourteenth Amendments is not only a logical dictate of prior cases, but it also makes very good sense. There is no war between the Constitution and common sense. Presently, a federal prosecutor may make no use of evidence legally seized, but a state's attorney across the street may, though he supposedly is operating under the enforcement prohibitions of the same Amendment. Thus the state, by admitting evidence unlawfully seized, serves to encourage disobedience to the Federal Constitution which it is bound to uphold. . . .

The ignoble shortcut to conviction left open to the state tends to destroy the entire system of constitutional restraints on which the liberties of the people rest. Having once recognized that the right of privacy embodied in the Fourth Amendment is enforceable against the states, and that the right to be secure against rude invasions of privacy against state officers is therefore constitutional in origin, we can no longer permit that right to remain an empty promise. Because it is enforceable in the same manner and to like effect as other basic rights secured by the Due Process Clause, we can no longer permit it to be revocable at the whim of any police officer who, in the name of law enforcement itself, chooses to suspend its enjoyment. Our decision, founded on reason and truth, gives to the individual no more than that which the Constitution guarantees him, to the police officer no less than that to which honest law enforcement is entitled, and, to the courts, that judicial integrity so necessary in the true administration of justice.

The judgment of the Supreme Court of Ohio is reversed and the cause remanded for further proceedings not inconsistent with this opinion.

Reversed and remanded.

GIDEON V. WAINRIGHT CORRECTIONS DIRECTOR

Mr. Justice BLACK delivered the opinion of the Court.

• • •

Petitioner was charged in a Florida state court with having broken and entered a poolroom with intent to commit a misdemeanor. This offense is a felony under Florida law. Appearing in court without funds and without a lawyer, petitioner asked the court to appoint counsel for him, whereupon the following colloquy took place:

> *"The Court: Mr. Gideon, I am sorry, but I cannot appoint Counsel to represent you in this case. Under the laws of the state of Florida, the only time the Court can appoint Counsel to represent a defendant is when that person is charged with a capital offense. I am sorry, but I will have to deny your request to appoint Counsel to defend you in this case.*
> *"The Defendant: The United States Supreme Court says I am entitled to be represented by Counsel."*

Put to a trial before a jury, Gideon conducted his defense about as well as could be expected from a layman. He made an opening statement to the jury, cross-examined the state's witnesses, presented witnesses in his own defense, declined to testify himself, and made a short argument "emphasizing his innocence to the charge contained in the information filed in this case." The jury returned a verdict of guilty, and petitioner was sentenced to serve five years in the state prison. Later, petitioner filed in the Florida Supreme Court this habeas corpus petition attacking his conviction and sentence on the ground that the trial court's refusal to appoint counsel for him denied him rights "guaranteed by the Constitution and the Bill of Rights by the United States Government." Treating the petition for habeas corpus as properly before it, the State Supreme Court, "upon consideration thereof" but without opinion, denied all relief. Since 1942, when *Betts v. Brady* . . . was decided by a divided Court, the problem of a defendant's federal constitutional right to counsel in a state court has been a continuing source of controversy and litigation in both state and federal courts. To give this problem another review here we granted certiorari [i.e., the Supreme Court agreed to hear the case]. . . .

I.

The facts upon which Betts claimed he had been unconstitutionally denied the right to have counsel appointed to assist him are strikingly like the facts upon which Gideon here bases his federal constitutional claim. Betts was indicted for robbery in a Maryland state court. On arraignment, he told the trial judge of his lack of funds to hire a lawyer and asked the court to appoint one for him. Betts was advised that it was not the practice in that county to appoint counsel for indigent defendants except in murder and rape cases. He then pleaded not guilty, had witnesses summoned, cross-examined the state's witnesses, examined his own, and chose not to testify himself. He was found guilty by the judge, sitting without a jury, and sentenced to eight years in prison. Like Gideon, Betts sought release by habeas corpus, alleging that he had been denied the right to assistance of counsel in violation of the Fourteenth Amendment. Betts was denied any relief, and on review the Court affirmed. It was held that a refusal to appoint counsel for an indigent defendant charged with a felony did not necessarily violate the Due Process Clause of the Fourteenth Amendment, which for reasons given, the Court deemed to be the only applicable provision. . . .

Treating due process as "a concept less rigid and more fluid than those envisaged in other specific and particular provisions of the Bill of Rights," the Court held that the refusal to appoint counsel under the particular facts and circumstances of the *Betts* case was not so "offensive to the common and fundamental ideas of fairness" as to amount to a denial of due process. Since the facts and circumstances of the two cases are so nearly indistinguishable, we think the *Betts v. Brady* holding if left standing would require us to reject Gideon's claim that the Constitution guarantees him the assistance of counsel. Upon full reconsideration we conclude that *Betts v. Brady* should be overruled.

II.

The Sixth Amendment provides, "In all criminal prosecutions, the accused shall enjoy the right . . . to have the Assistance of Counsel for his defence." We have construed this to mean that in federal courts counsel must be provided for defendants unable to employ counsel unless the right is competently and intelligently waived. Betts argued that this right is extended to indigent defendants in state courts by the Fourteenth Amendment. In response the Court stated that, while the Sixth Amendment laid down "no rule for the conduct of the States, the question recurs whether the constraint laid by the Amendment upon the national courts expresses a rule so fundamental and essential to a fair trial, and so, to due process of law, that it is made obligatory upon the States by the Fourteenth Amendment." . . .

The fact is that in deciding as it did—that "appointment of counsel is not a fundamental right, essential to a fair trial"—the Court in *Betts v. Brady* made an abrupt break with its own well-considered precedents. In returning to these old precedents, sounder we believe than the new, we but restore constitutional principles established to achieve a fair system of justice. Not only these precedents but also reason and reflection require us to recognize that in our adversary system of criminal justice, any person haled into court, who is too poor to hire a lawyer, cannot be assured a fair trial unless counsel is provided for him. This seems to us to be an obvious truth. Governments, both state and federal, quite properly spend vast sums of money to establish machinery to try defendants accused of crime. Lawyers to prosecute are everywhere deemed essential to protect the public's interest in an orderly society. Similarly, there are few defendants charged with crime . . . who fail to hire the best lawyers they can get to prepare and present their defenses. . . . The right of one charged with crime to counsel may not be deemed fundamental and essential to fair trials in some countries, but it is in ours. From the very beginning, our state and national constitutions and laws have laid great emphasis on procedural and substantive safeguards designed to assure fair trials before impartial tribunals in which every defendant stands equal before the law. This noble idea cannot be realized if the poor man charged with a crime has to face his accusers without a lawyer to assist him. . . .

The Court in *Betts v. Brady* departed from . . . sound wisdom. . . . Florida, supported by two other states, has asked that *Betts v. Brady* be left intact. Twenty-two states, as friends of the Court, argue that it should now be overruled. We agree.

The judgment is reversed and the cause is remanded to the Supreme Court of Florida for further action not inconsistent with this opinion.

Reversed.

Miranda v. Arizona

Mr. Chief Justice WARREN delivered the opinion of the Court.

• • •

The cases before us* raise questions which go to the roots of our concepts of American criminal jurisprudence: the restraints society must observe consistent with the Federal Constitution in prosecuting individuals for crime. More specifically, we deal with the admissibility of statements obtained from an individual who is subjected to custodial police interrogation and the necessity for procedures which assure that the individual is accorded his privilege under the Fifth Amendment to the Constitution not to be compelled to incriminate himself.

We dealt with certain phases of this problem recently in *Escobedo v. Illinois*. . . . There, as in the four cases before us, law enforcement officials took the defendant into custody and interrogated him in a police station for the purpose of obtaining a confession. The police did not effectively advise him of his right to remain silent or of his right to consult with his attorney. Rather, they confronted him with an alleged accomplice who accused him of having perpetrated a murder. When the defendant denied the accusation and said "I didn't shoot Manuel, you did it," they handcuffed him and took him to an interrogation room. There, while handcuffed and standing, he was questioned for four hours until he confessed. During this interrogation, the police denied his request to speak to his attorney, and they prevented his retained attorney, who had come to the

---

*That is, *Vignera v. New York*, *Westover v. United States*, and *California v. Stewart*—as well as *Miranda v. Arizona*—ed.

police station, from consulting with him. At his trial, the state, over his objection, introduced the confession against him. We held that the statements thus made were constitutionally inadmissible. . . .

We granted certiorari in these cases . . . in order further to explore some facets of the problems thus exposed, of applying the privilege against self-incrimination to in-custody interrogation, and to give concrete constitutional guidelines for law enforcement agencies and courts to follow.

We start here, as we did in *Escobedo,* with the premise that our holding is not an innovation in our jurisprudence, but is an application of principles long recognized and applied in other settings. We have undertaken a thorough re-examination of the *Escobedo* decision and the principles it announced and we reaffirm it. That case was but an explication of basic rights that are enshrined in our Constitution—that "No person . . . shall be compelled in any criminal case to be a witness against himself," and that "the accused shall . . . have the Assistance of Counsel"—rights which were put in jeopardy in that case through official overbearing. These precious rights were fixed in our Constitution only after centuries of persecution and struggle. And in the words of Chief Justice Marshall, they were secured "for ages to come, and . . . designed to approach immortality as nearly as human institutions can approach it." . . .

Our holding will be spelled out with some specificity in the pages which follow but briefly stated it is this: the prosecution may not use statements, whether exculpatory or inculpatory, stemming from custodial interrogation of the defendant unless it demonstrates the use of procedural safeguards effective to secure the privilege against self-incrimination. By custodial interrogation, we mean questioning initiated by law enforcement officers after a person has been taken into custody or otherwise deprived of his freedom of action in any significant way. As for the procedural safeguards to be employed, unless other fully effective means are devised to inform accused persons of their right of silence and to assure a continuous opportunity to exercise it, the following measures are required. Prior to any questioning, the person must be warned that he has a right to remain silent, that any statement he does make may be used as evidence against him, and that he has a right to the presence of an attorney, either retained or appointed. The defendant may waive effectuation of these rights, provided the waiver is made voluntarily, knowingly, and intelligently. If, however, he indicates in any manner and at any stage of the process that he wishes to consult with an attorney before speaking there can be no questioning. Likewise, if the individual is alone and indicates in any manner that he does not wish to be interrogated, the police may not question him.

The mere fact that he may have answered some questions or volunteered some statements on his own does not deprive him of the right to refrain from answering any further inquiries until he has consulted with an attorney and thereafter consents to be questioned.

I.

The constitutional issue we decide in each of these cases is the admissibility of statements obtained from a defendant questioned while in custody or otherwise deprived of his freedom of action in any significant way. In each, the defendant was questioned by police officers, detectives, or a prosecuting attorney in a room where he was cut off from the outside world. In none of these cases was the defendant given a full and effective warning of his rights at the outset of the interrogation process. In all the cases, the questioning elicited oral admissions, and in three of them, signed statements as well which were admitted at their trials. They all thus share salient features—incommunicado interrogation of individuals in a police-dominated atmosphere, resulting in self-incriminating statements without full warnings of constitutional rights. . . .

[The text here provides examples of coercive and deceptive police questioning methods, as actually practiced and as described in standard police manuals.]

From these representative examples of interrogation techniques, the setting . . . becomes clear. In essence, it is this: To be alone with the subject is essential to prevent distraction and to deprive him of any outside support. The aura of confidence in his guilt undermines his will to resist. He merely confirms the preconceived story the police seek to have him describe. . . .

Even without employing brutality, the "third degree" or the specific stratagems described above, the very fact of custodial interrogation exacts a heavy toll on individual liberty and trades on the weakness of individuals. . . .

It is obvious that such an interrogation environment is created for no purpose other than to subjugate the individual to the will of his examiner. This atmosphere carries its own badge of intimidation. To be sure, this is not physical intimidation, but it is equally destructive of human dignity. The current practice of incommunicado interrogation is at odds with one of our nation's most cherished principles—that the individual may not be compelled to incriminate himself. Unless adequate protective devices are employed to dispel the compulsion inherent in custodial surroundings, no statement obtained from the defendant can truly be the product of his free choice. . . .

V.

To summarize, we hold that when an individual is taken into custody or otherwise deprived of his freedom by the authorities in any significant way and is subjected to questioning, the privilege against self-incrimination is jeopardized. Procedural safeguards must be employed to protect the privilege, and unless other fully effective means are adopted to notify the person of his right of silence and to assure that the exercise of the right will be scrupulously honored, the following measures are required. He must be warned prior to any questioning that he has the right to remain silent, that anything he says can be used against him in a court of law, that he has the right to the presence of an attorney, and that if he cannot afford an attorney one will be appointed for him prior to any questioning if he so desires. Opportunity to exercise these rights must be afforded to him throughout the interrogation. After such warnings have been given and such opportunity afforded him, the individual may knowingly and intelligently waive these rights and agree to answer questions or make a statement. But unless and until such warnings and waiver are demonstrated by the prosecution at trial, no evidence obtained as a result of interrogation can be used against him.

9

Foreign Affairs and Vietnam

We Americans are an insular people; what happens in other countries often seems remote and marginal to our lives. Yet events abroad sometimes become so urgent that they dominate the domestic dialogue. The Sixties was one such time. A stretch of the larger cold war era that began soon after 1945 and lasted until the 1990s, the decade witnessed, as a central feature, American entrapment in a seemingly interminable conflict in Southeast Asia that aroused deep and divisive passions and distorted the shape of domestic events.

The young man whose presidency ushered in the Sixties seemed to view the superpower rivalry we call the cold war as his chief concern. Kennedy's inaugural address devoted far more attention to the U.S.–Soviet world confrontation than to domestic affairs. It was appropriate, then, that in a matter of weeks, foreign policy eclipsed domestic policy in the new administration. In April 1961, Kennedy gave the green light to an ill-planned invasion of Fidel Castro's Cuba by CIA-trained exiles that ended in disaster when the United States refused to come to their rescue. The Bay of Pigs fiasco made the young man in the White House seem maladroit and callow.

This dismissive estimate tempted the Soviet leader, Nikita Khrushchev, into bullying his American rival. At a summit meeting of the two leaders in Vienna that June, he threatened to approve a final Soviet treaty with Communist satellite East Germany that promised, as in 1948, to cut off Western-occupied Berlin from the German Federal Republic. In August, the Communist East German authorities built a wall across Berlin to prevent the escape of people to the western sectors from the repressive Communist regime in the rest of the city. Soon after, the Soviet Union resumed atmospheric nuclear testing and the United States retaliated in kind. The cold war had warmed up appreciably.

The most dangerous U.S.–Soviet confrontation, however, came in the early fall of 1962 over Cuba. The Bay of Pigs had cemented relations between the Cubans and the Soviet Union. In return for Soviet protection, Castro allowed the Russians to deploy missiles on Cuban soil capable of conveying nuclear warheads deep into the American heartland. Designed to trump America's strategic military advantage, the Soviet move triggered a frightening international crisis. Kennedy declared a naval blockade around Cuba to prevent further missile deliveries, and he threatened to retaliate against the USSR itself if missiles were actually launched at the United States from Cuba. Facing the prospect of nuclear doom, the Russians retreated. People everywhere heaved a sigh of relief.

Thereafter, U.S.–Soviet relations improved. In mid-1963, the two countries established a telephone hotline to improve communications in future crises. The following month, they signed an agreement pledging to stop further nuclear weapons testing in the atmosphere and underwater. During the remainder of the decade, U.S.–Soviet relations remained relatively calm despite the 1968 Soviet invasion of its satellite, Czechoslovakia, to put down a revolt against the repressive Communist puppet regime.

Diminished tensions between the superpowers themselves did not end the cold war, however. The confrontation between liberal capitalism and authoritarian socialism continued through superpower client states and allies, with its most bitter fruit in Vietnam.

In January 1961, the Soviet premier had declared his country's "unlimited support" for "peoples fighting for their liberation." The Soviet Union, in effect, was prepared to subsidize any revolution or uprising that challenged regimes friendly to the West. The Kennedy administration reacted with a new policy of "flexible response." Instead of the Eisenhower-Dulles "massive retaliation"—nuclear attack to stop every Communist probe and thrust—America would employ counterinsurgency tactics and conventional arms, except in response to direct Soviet attacks on our NATO European allies. This new policy reduced the danger that "wars of national liberation" would turn into nuclear holocausts, but it increased the chances that marginal cold war entanglements all around the world would become violent confrontations.

It was in Vietnam that the hazards of the flexible response policy became apparent. Part of the French colony of Indochina before World War II, Vietnam resisted the return to colonial status after 1945. The French, however, refused to surrender their empire and the United States, embracing the "domino theory" that Communist victory in Vietnam endangered the other pro-Western countries of Southeast Asia, provided money and supplies to help the French. American aid was not enough. Led by the Communist-trained Ho Chi Minh, in 1954, after defeating the colonialists at Dien Bien Phu, the insurgents (Vietminh) forced the French to sign a treaty at Geneva partitioning Vietnam between the Communists and non-Communists along the seventeenth parallel, pending an election to unite the entire country.

The Communists had no intention of allowing the division to persist. South Vietnam quickly became a battleground between local Communist guerrillas (Vietcong) supplied by Hanoi, and supporters of a pro-Western government in Saigon. After the French defeat and withdrawal, Washington came to the direct aid of the Saigon regime, determined to keep South Vietnam from falling to the Communists.

Under Kennedy, American help was limited to money, arms, and military and political advice. But by the time he died in late 1963, some 15,000 Americans were in South Vietnam advising the South Vietnamese government and helping to train its troops to resist the insurgents.

Lyndon Johnson retained Kennedy's chief foreign policy advisers and, with their guidance, marched the country straight into the quagmire of a major land war in Asia. Johnson hated the war as a distraction from the Great Society, but at the outset he did not believe an extended war likely. The enemy lacked modern technology and fought with small arms. How could they resist for very long the awesome military might of the United States?

Johnson soon found the Communists in Vietnam more than he had bargained for. Following North Vietnamese attacks on American naval vessels in August 1964, to deflect charges of weakness as the presidential election approached, he secured the Tonkin Gulf Resolution from Congress, authorizing him to "take all necessary measures to repel any armed attack" against the United States. So equipped, Johnson gradually increased the American military commitment. In January 1965, in retaliation for a Vietcong attack on an American airbase at Pleiku, he ordered American planes to bomb North Vietnam. In April, he dispatched the first American combat troops. At the end of the year, there were almost 200,000 American military personnel in Vietnam fighting the Communist enemy.

The war that unfolded over the next eight years took the lives of 46,000 Americans and several million Vietnamese. It was an especially dirty war. There were few pitched battles between matched military forces. The United States and its South Vietnamese ally deployed jet bombers, helicopters, heavy artillery, and forms of chemical warfare* to destroy the

---

*Though not poison gas.

enemy. The Vietcong and the North Vietnamese army relied on rifles, mines, mortars, and even pointed bamboo stakes tipped with poison. They used infiltration, hit-and-run tactics, and ambushes to wear down their superior enemy. In the countryside, Vietcong guerrillas moved among the people "like fish in the water" and won converts to their cause by persuasion as well as intimidation.

With each passing month, the United States augmented its military investment. At the end of 1966, there were 375,000 U.S. military personnel in Vietnam. By mid-1968, there were 540,000. Many of these were draftees, predominantly of working-class background, often black or Hispanic.

Vietnam was not a popular war. Many Americans could not see what vital stake their nation had in events in a backward country in remotest Asia. The war, moreover, was never an "unlimited" conflict. Unlike World War II, the United States never fully mobilized its resources; nor did it use every weapon in its arsenal for fear of tripping off World War III. This response confused many Americans. And then there was its sheer duration: the war seemed to go on forever, stretching over three administrations.

Yet despite misgivings, until 1968, a majority of Americans still supported their nation's Vietnam policies. Then came the Tet Offensive, a concerted Vietcong attack on scores of cities and provincial capitals in South Vietnam. One of these sallies penetrated the American embassy compound in Saigon, the symbolic heart of the American anti-Communist effort. Although the Vietcong were decimated by U.S. and ARVN (South Vietnam Army) troops, the unexpected assault convinced many Americans that little if any progress was being made in winning the war and it would be wise for the United States to cut its losses and leave. Opponents of the war had by now mounted a major campaign to dump Johnson and nominate a "dove" on the Democratic ticket to end the war.

Johnson tried several times between 1965 and 1968 to bring the Communists to the bargaining table. But the North Vietnamese had no intention of accepting any solution that did not reunite all of Vietnam under their sole rule, and the Americans, for their part, resisted abandoning their South Vietnamese ally. The Communists paid dearly in lives and wealth for their goal, but they felt that time was on their side. They could not expect to defeat the "capitalists" in the military field, but they doubted the resolution of the United States. If only they held on, they could count on the antiwar movement to force the Americans to back out.

Soon after Tet, the president's closest advisers refused to endorse the generals' requests for still further reinforcements of the U.S. military in

Vietnam. Deescalation had begun. In late March 1968, on national TV, the president called again for peace talks and offered as inducement a bombing halt. He also announced that to show his sincerity in pursuit of peace, he would not run for reelection in November.

Johnson's initiative brought the North Vietnamese to the bargaining table in Paris. But it failed to end the war. The meetings bogged down over seemingly endless symbolic minutiae but actually because neither side felt it could give the other what it really wanted. Peace was not at hand when Richard Nixon took office in 1969. But Nixon initiated a policy of Vietnamization that steadily reduced the number of American troops, the last of which left in 1973, following a peace agreement that provided for little more than "a decent interval" before a Communist takeover. In the spring of 1975, the North Vietnamese marched into Saigon and quickly imposed a brutal and rigid Marxist regime on the South. They had won the war.

Vietnam made Americans deeply skeptical of foreign entanglements. Never again would the voters permit their leaders to send American troops abroad without a clear view of goals and means. The country would not again accept war in a fit of absentmindedness as it had in the mid-1960s.

The Vietnam War is often considered the core event of the Sixties. One scholar has called it "the engine of the Sixties." Without the war, he writes, "the decade would have remained a liberal reform era, not a radical decade."* On a layman's level, the antiwar movement is considered the prototype of dissent during the decade.

These conclusions are exaggerated. Undoubtedly Vietnam lit a fire under the cauldron of discontent and outrage, especially among the young. The antiwar movement was more than an exercise in "expressive politics" that functioned primarily to give its adherents emotional satisfaction. It was also instrumental—oriented toward concrete goals—and reasonably successful in achieving them. But hatred of the war was also only part of what moved the era. In other parts of the forest, other tensions had grown—over race, gender, sexuality, drugs, culture, class—and these too would pour their passions into the general stream we call the Sixties.

The Bay of Pigs Invasion

Most Americans applauded the overthrow in early 1959 of the corrupt Cuban strongman Fulgencio Batista by the magnetic young rebel Fidel Castro. Castro called himself a democrat and a friend of the United States and promised to bring freedom and prosperity to the beautiful island just ninety miles from Key West, Florida.

*Terry H. Anderson, *The Movement and the Sixties* (New York: Oxford University Press, 1995), p. 135.

It did not take long, however, for him to establish his own dictatorship in Havana, suspending habeas corpus, establishing punitive military tribunals to try his enemies, and sending idealistic former followers to jail. Thousands of Cubans—supporters of Batista and disillusioned Fidelistas alike—fled the country for south Florida and parts of Latin America. Worse yet, from the point of view of American policy makers, Castro renounced Cuba's military pact with the United States, gave diplomatic recognition to the People's Republic of China, and called the United States a "vulture . . . feeding on humanity." Cuba soon became a source of revolutionary propaganda and anti-American agitation throughout the Western Hemisphere.

In early 1960, the United States and a group of Cuban exiles began to plan the overthrow of the Castro regime by invading Cuba. Under the tutelage of the CIA, Cuban exiles were trained in guerrilla tactics in various spots around the Caribbean and in Guatemala. The anti-Castro brigade never numbered more than some twelve hundred, far too few to defeat Castro's army, but from the outset the CIA and the exiles assumed that once the Cuban people learned that the insurgents had landed, they would rise up against the tyrant. Little thought was given to the possibility of failure. At worst, if the Cuban people did not revolt, the invaders could escape into the hills.

From the outset, the operation was a limited American commitment. The exiles assumed that they would be backstopped by American military might. But the CIA and the Eisenhower administration had no intention of deeply entangling the United States in the enterprise. If the invaders did not topple the dictator by themselves, they could not count on the United States. Kennedy learned of the planned operation within a week of assuming office and had serious doubts. He consulted Allen Dulles of the CIA and the Joint Chiefs of Staff, and sent a valued Marine Corps colonel to evaluate the exiles at their training camp. All the "experts" pronounced the operation practical, and he gave his reluctant approval.

The operation was in trouble from the outset. On April 15, exile-manned World War II planes from Nicaragua bombed Cuban airfields to eliminate the small Castro air force. They were themselves eliminated, and the Cubans retained air superiority over the landing place. That place, the Bay of Pigs on Cuba's south coast, was supposedly a deserted area, but in fact it had become a major beach resort since the CIA had last checked. It was well connected to the rest of the country by roads and telephone, and rather than achieving surprise, the invaders, when they landed on April 17, were detected immediately and surrounded by Castro's troops. Heavily armed with Soviet guns and tanks, the Fidelistas pounded the invaders on the beach. Meanwhile, the Cuban air force sank the vessels carrying most of the invaders' ammunition and supplies.

The invaders and their superiors in the Frente, the exiles' political arm, pleaded for U.S. air support. From the beachhead itself came desperate radio messages: "Send all available aircraft. Out of ammo. Enemy closing in. Help must arrive in next hour." Help never did arrive. Kennedy refused to act. The United States did not intend to invest anything more in a lost cause, not at the expense of starting a major war. In less than seventy-two hours, all the invaders had been killed or captured. The survivors were tried and sentenced to long prison terms. At Christmas 1962, American officials, using private contributions, finally ransomed them.

The Bay of Pigs fiasco had major consequences for the administration. It convinced the president that he could not rely on the experts in responding to foreign policy issues. More significant, it solidified Castro's alliance with the Soviet Union and sent the mistaken message to the Soviets that America was being led by a weak man who could be bullied. That, in turn, prepared the ground for Soviet intransigence at the summit meeting at Vienna in June and for the missile crisis of the following year.

This document is from a report of the Cuban Study Group led by General Maxwell D. Taylor, the trusted officer assigned the job of extracting the lessons "from recent events in Cuba." The document refers to the invasion operation by its CIA code name, "Zapata."

[Maxwell Taylor, "Report and Testimony of the Cuban Study Group on the Bay of Pigs" (Washington, DC: U.S. Government Printing Office, 1981), pp. 122–135, passim.]

MEMORANDUM NO. 3: CONCLUSIONS OF THE CUBAN STUDY GROUP

1. It is concluded that:
   a. A paramilitary operation of the magnitude of Zapata could not be prepared and conducted in such a way that all U.S. support of it and connection with it could be plausibly disclaimed. Accordingly, this operation did not fit within the limited scope of NSC 5412/2.* By about November 1960, the impossibility of running Zapata as a covert operation under CIA should have been recognized and the situation reviewed. The subsequent decision might then have been made to limit the efforts to attain covertness to the degree and nature of U.S. participation, and to assign responsibility for the amphibious operation to the Department of Defense. In this case, the CIA would have assisted in concealing the participation of Defense. Failing such a reorientation, the project should have been abandoned.
   b. Once the need for the operation was established, its success should have had the primary consideration of all agencies in the government. Operational restrictions designed to protect its covert character should have been accepted only if they did not impair the

---

*The directive of the National Security Council authorizing the operation—ed.

chance of success. As it was, the leaders of the operation were obliged to fit their plan inside changing ground rules laid down for nonmilitary considerations, which often had serious operational disadvantages.

c. The leaders of the operation did not always present their case with sufficient force and clarity to the senior officials of the government to allow the latter to appreciate the consequences of some of their decisions. This remark applies in particular to the circumstances surrounding the cancellation of the D-Day strikes.

d. There was a marginal character to the operation which increased with each additional limitation and cast a serious doubt over its ultimate success. The landing force was small in relation to its 36-mile beachhead and to the probable enemy reaction. The air support was short of pilots if the beach was to require cover for a long period. There were no fighters to keep off such Castro airplanes as might escape the initial air strikes. There were few Cuban replacements for the battle losses which were certain to occur on the ground and in the air. It is felt that the approval of so marginal an operation by many officials was influenced by the feeling that the Cuban Brigade was a waning asset which had to be used quickly as time was against us, and that this operation was the best way to realize the most from it. Also, the consequences of demobilizing the Brigade and the return of the trainees to the USA, with its implication that the United States had lost interest in the fight against Castro, played a part in the final decision.

e. The Cuban Expeditionary Force achieved tactical surprise in its landing and, as we have said, fought well and inflicted heavy casualties on the enemy. Although there had been considerable evidence of strong pockets of resistance against Castro throughout Cuba, the short life of the beachhead was not sufficient to trigger an immediate popular reaction, and Castro's repressive measures following the landing made coordinated uprisings of the populace impossible. The effectiveness of the Castro military forces, as well as that of his police measures, was not entirely anticipated or foreseen.

f. In approving the operation, the President and senior officials had been greatly influenced by the understanding that the landing force could pass to guerrilla status, if unable to hold the beachhead. These officials were informed on many occasions that the Zapata area was guerrilla territory, and that the entire force, in an emergency, could operate as guerrillas. With this alternative to fall back on, the view was held that a sudden or disastrous defeat was most improbable. As we have indicated before, the guerrilla alternative as it had been described was not in fact available to this force in the situation which developed.

g. The operation suffered from being run from the distance of Washington. At that range and with the limited reporting which was inevitable on the part of field commanders absorbed in combat, it was not possible to have a clear understanding in Washington of events taking place in the field. This was particularly the case on the night of D+1 when an appreciation of the ammunition situation would have resulted in an appeal for U.S. air cover and an all-out effort to supply the beach by all available means.

h. The Joint Chiefs of Staff had the important responsibility of examining into the military feasibility of this operation. By acquiescing in the Zapata Plan, they gave the impression to others of approving it although they had expressed their preference for Trinidad at the outset, a point which apparently never reached the senior civilian officials. As a body they reviewed the successive changes of the plan piecemeal and only within a limited context, a procedure which was inadequate for a proper examination of all the military ramifications. Individually, they had differing understandings of important features of the operation apparently arising from oral briefings in the absence of written documents.

i. Although the intelligence was not perfect, particularly as to the evaluation of the effectiveness of the T-33s, we do not feel that any failure of intelligence contributed significantly to the defeat.

j. The planning and conduct of the operation would have been improved if there had been an initial statement of governmental policy, assigning the mission and setting the guidelines within which it was to develop. Thereafter, there was a need for a formalized procedure for interdepartmental coordination and follow-up with adequate record-keeping of decisions.

2. In the light of the foregoing considerations, we are of the opinion that the preparations and execution of paramilitary operations such as Zapata are a form of Cold War action in which the country must be prepared to engage. If it does so, it must engage in it with a maximum chance of success. Such operations should be planned and executed by a governmental mechanism capable of bringing into play, in addition to military and covert techniques, all other forces, political, economic,

ideological, and intelligence, which can contribute to its success. No such mechanism presently exists but should be created to plan, coordinate, and further a national Cold War strategy capable of including paramilitary operations.

Cuban Missile Crisis

John Kennedy became president when the cold war was at its apex. Stalin, the brutal Soviet dictator, was dead, but his successor, Nikita Khrushchev, though a less ruthless man, was a dogged defender of his country's interests around the world. Indeed, it was Khrushchev who proclaimed Soviet intentions to provide "unlimited support" to "peoples fighting for their liberation," in effect making the whole Third World a stage for the U.S.–Soviet cold war rivalry.

The Soviet leader, in the wake of the Bay of Pigs fiasco, judged Kennedy a feeble leader. Pushed by Fidel Castro, who feared renewed American efforts to topple his regime, Khrushchev decided in mid-1962 to test American mettle by emplacing intermediate-range Soviet missiles, capable of delivering a nuclear warhead as far as Montana, on Cuban soil. On October 14, American U-2 spy planes detected and photographed the construction of Soviet missile sites on the island. On the morning of October 16, National Security Adviser McGeorge Bundy informed the president of the report. Kennedy immediately called key members of the administration into emergency meeting.

For the next two weeks, while Ex Com* met daily to consider the U.S. response, the nation and the world hovered on the edge of disaster. Whether the aim was to repel a frightening military threat to the nation or primarily to protect its prestige, the administration could not allow the missiles to remain. But how could it end the peril without precipitating World War III? In Ex Com, presided over by Attorney General Robert Kennedy, the president's brother, opinion was divided. A majority initially favored a massive air strike to destroy the weapons. But this would assure a heavy loss of life in Cuba, including hundreds of casualties among the Soviet technicians installing them. Nuclear war with the USSR seemed a possible outcome. An alternative was a blockade of Cuba. That would be an act of war, it was true, but it would avoid immediate bloodshed. As the administration foreign policy experts pondered their options, the blockade plan seemed to be the wiser move.

Until Monday, October 22, the public did not know what was afoot, though with all the hush-hush around the White House, Americans suspected something. That evening, after briefing congressional leaders and diplomats from friendly nations, Kennedy appeared on national television to inform Americans of the Soviet missile

*The Executive Committee of the National Security Council.

installations and to tell them that he intended to impose a naval blockade of Cuba to prevent the delivery of additional offensive weapons.

The quarantine worked. It took thirteen hours for the Soviet leaders to respond to the note laying out America's terms. Khrushchev initially denied that the missiles were weapons and called Kennedy's act "piracy." Meanwhile, as a flotilla of Soviet merchantmen approached the blockading American naval vessels, the world waited in fear. Many Europeans accused the United States of reckless gambling with mankind's survival. On Cuba itself, the technicians and workmen labored furiously to prepare the launch sites for action in the event the unthinkable should occur.

Then came the break. On the morning of the twenty-fourth, twenty Russian ships heading west heaved to; soon twelve of them reversed course and steamed away from Cuba. At the ongoing Ex Comm meeting, Bundy remarked: "We're eyeball to eyeball, and I think the other fellow just blinked." Two days later, the Soviets proposed that in exchange for removing the missiles and a promise by Castro of no further offensive weapons on Cuban soil, the United States would pledge not to invade Cuba. A later note from Khrushchev tried to add the proviso that the United States would dismantle its missile bases in Turkey. The president chose to ignore it and accept the original formula, while privately assuring the Soviets that the Turkish-based missiles would be removed later. On Sunday, October 28, Radio Moscow announced that the Soviet Union had agreed to dismantle the missiles. After thirteen agonizing days, the crisis was over.

The document below is the text of the president's TV address of October 22, when the outcome was still in perilous doubt.

[*John F. Kennedy, "Radio and Television Report to the American People on the Soviet Arms Buildup in Cuba,"* **Public Papers of the Presidents of the United States: John F. Kennedy, 1962** *(Washington, DC: U.S. Government Printing Office, 1963), pp. 806–809.*]

KENNEDY REPORTS ON THE MISSILES IN CUBA

Good evening, my fellow citizens:

This government, as promised, has maintained the closest surveillance of the Soviet military buildup on the island of Cuba. Within the past week, unmistakable evidence has established the fact that a series of offensive missile sites is now in preparation on that imprisoned island. The purpose of these bases can be none other than to provide a nuclear strike capability against the Western Hemisphere.

Upon receiving the first preliminary hard information of this nature last Tuesday morning at nine A.M., I directed that our surveillance be stepped up. And having now confirmed and completed our evaluation of the evidence and our decision on a course of action, this government feels obliged to report this new crisis to you in fullest detail.

The characteristics of these new missile sites indicate two distinct types of installations. Several of them include medium range ballistic missiles, capable of carrying a nuclear warhead for a distance of more than one thousand nautical miles. Each of these missiles, in short, is capable of striking Washington, D.C., the Panama Canal, Cape Canaveral, Mexico City, or any other city in the southeastern part of the United States, in Central America, or in the Caribbean area.

Additional sites not yet completed appear to be designed for intermediate range ballistic missiles—capable of traveling more than twice as far—and thus capable of striking most of the major cities in the Western Hemisphere, ranging as far north as Hudson Bay, Canada, and as far south as Lima, Peru. In addition, jet bombers, capable of carrying nuclear weapons, are now being uncrated and assembled in Cuba, while the necessary air bases are being prepared.

This urgent transformation of Cuba into an important strategic base—by the presence of these large, long-range, and clearly offensive weapons of sudden mass destruction—constitutes an explicit threat to the peace and security of all the Americas, in flagrant and deliberate defiance of the Rio Pact of 1947, the traditions of this nation and hemisphere, the joint resolution of the 87th Congress, the Charter of the United Nations, and my own public warnings to the Soviets on September 4 and 13. This action also contradicts the repeated assurances of Soviet spokesmen, both publicly and privately delivered, that the arms buildup in Cuba would retain its original defensive character, and that the Soviet Union had no need or desire to station strategic missiles on the territory of any other nation.

The size of this undertaking makes clear that it has been planned for some months. Yet only last month, after I had made clear the distinction between any introduction of ground-to-ground missiles and the existence of defensive antiaircraft missiles, the Soviet government publicly stated on September 11 that, and I quote, "the armaments and military equipment sent to Cuba are designed exclusively for defensive purposes," that, and I quote the Soviet government, "there is no need for the Soviet government to shift its weapons . . . for a retaliatory blow to any other country, for instance Cuba," and that, and I quote their government, "the Soviet Union has so powerful rockets to carry these nuclear warheads that there is no need to search for sites for them beyond the boundaries of the Soviet Union." That statement was false.

Only last Thursday, as evidence of this rapid offensive buildup was already in my hand, Soviet Foreign Minister Gromyko told me in my office that he was instructed to make it clear once again, as he said his government had already done, that Soviet assistance to Cuba, and I quote, "pursued solely the purpose of contributing to the defense capabilities of Cuba," that, and I quote him, "training by Soviet specialists of Cuban nationals in handling defensive armaments was by no means offensive, and if it were otherwise," Mr. Gromyko went on, "the Soviet government would never become involved in rendering such assistance." That statement also was false.

Neither the United States of America nor the world community of nations can tolerate deliberate deception and offensive threats on the part of any nation, large or small. We no longer live in a world where only the actual firing of weapons represents a sufficient challenge to a nation's security to constitute maximum peril. Nuclear weapons are so destructive and ballistic missiles are so swift, that any substantially increased possibility of their use or any sudden change in their deployment may well be regarded as a definite threat to peace.

For many years, both the Soviet Union and the United States, recognizing this fact, have deployed strategic nuclear weapons with great care, never upsetting the precarious status quo which insured that these weapons would not be used in the absence of some vital challenge. Our own strategic missiles have never been transferred to the territory of any other nation under a cloak of secrecy and deception; and our history—unlike that of the Soviets since the end of World War II—demonstrates that we have no desire to dominate or conquer any other nation or impose our system upon its people. Nevertheless, American citizens have become adjusted to living daily on the bull's-eye of Soviet missiles located inside the USSR or in submarines.

In that sense, missiles in Cuba add to an already clear and present danger—although it should be noted the nations of Latin America have never previously been subjected to a potential nuclear threat.

But this secret, swift, and extraordinary buildup of Communist missiles—in an area well known to have a special and historical relationship to the United States and the nations of the Western Hemisphere, in violation of Soviet assurances, and in defiance of American and hemispheric policy—this sudden, clandestine decision to station strategic weapons for the first time outside of Soviet soil—is a deliberately provocative and unjustified change in the status quo which cannot be accepted by this country, if our courage and our commitments are ever to be trusted again by either friend or foe.

The 1930s taught us a clear lesson: aggressive conduct, if allowed to go unchecked and unchallenged, ultimately leads to war. This nation is opposed to war. We are also true to our word. Our unswerving objective, therefore, must be to prevent the use of these missiles against this or any other country, and to secure their withdrawal or elimination from the Western Hemisphere.

Our policy has been one of patience and restraint, as befits a peaceful and powerful nation, which leads a worldwide alliance. We have been determined not to be diverted from our central concerns by mere irritants and fanatics. But now further action is required—and it is under way; and these actions may only be the beginning. We will not prematurely or unnecessarily risk the costs of worldwide nuclear war in which even the fruits of victory would be ashes in our mouth—but neither will we shrink from that risk at any time it must be faced.

Acting, therefore, in the defense of our own security and of the entire Western Hemisphere, and under the authority entrusted to me by the Constitution as endorsed by the resolution of the Congress, I have directed that the following *initial* steps be taken immediately:

First: To halt this offensive buildup, a strict quarantine on all offensive military equipment under shipment to Cuba is being initiated. All ships of any kind bound for Cuba from whatever nation or port will, if found to contain cargoes of offensive weapons, be turned back. This quarantine will be extended, if needed, to other types of cargo and carriers. We are not at this time, however, denying the necessities of life as the Soviets attempted to do in their Berlin blockade of 1948.

Second: I have directed the continued and increased close surveillance of Cuba and its military buildup. The foreign ministers of the OAS, in their communiqué of October 6, rejected secrecy on such matters in this hemisphere. Should these offensive military preparations continue, thus increasing the threat to the hemisphere, further action will be justified. I have directed the Armed Forces to prepare for any eventualities; and I trust that in the interest of both the Cuban people and the Soviet technicians at the sites, the hazards to all concerned of continuing this threat will be recognized.

Third: It shall be the policy of this Nation to regard any nuclear missile launched from Cuba against any nation in the Western Hemisphere as an attack by the Soviet Union on the United States, requiring a full retaliatory response upon the Soviet Union.

Fourth: As a necessary military precaution, I have reinforced our base at Guantanamo, evacuated today the dependents of our personnel there, and ordered additional military units to be on a standby alert basis.

Fifth: We are calling tonight for an immediate meeting of the Organ of Consultation under the Organization of American States, to consider this threat to hemispheric security and to invoke articles 6 and 8 of the Rio Treaty in support of all necessary action. The United Nations Charter allows for regional security arrangements—and the nations of this hemisphere decided long ago against the military presence of outside powers. Our other allies around the world have also been alerted.

Sixth: Under the Charter of the United Nations, we are asking tonight that an emergency meeting of the Security Council be convoked without delay to take action against this latest Soviet threat to world peace. Our resolution will call for the prompt dismantling and withdrawal of all offensive weapons in Cuba, under the supervision of UN observers, before the quarantine can be lifted.

Seventh and finally: I call upon Chairman Khrushchev to halt and eliminate this clandestine, reckless, and provocative threat to world peace and to stable relations between our two nations. I call upon him further to abandon this course of world domination, and to join in an historic effort to end the perilous arms race and to transform the history of man. He has an opportunity now to move the world back from the abyss of destruction—by returning to his government's own words that it had no need to station missiles outside its own territory, and withdrawing these weapons from Cuba—by refraining from any action which will widen or deepen the present crisis—and then by participating in a search for peaceful and permanent solutions.

This nation is prepared to present its case against the Soviet threat to peace, and our own proposals for a peaceful world, at any time and in any forum—in the OAS, in the United Nations, or in any other meeting that could be useful—without limiting our freedom of action. We have in the past made strenuous efforts to limit the spread of nuclear weapons. We have proposed the elimination of all arms and military bases in a fair and effective disarmament treaty. We are prepared to discuss new proposals for the removal of tensions on both sides—including the possibilities of a genuinely independent Cuba, free to determine its own destiny. We have no wish to war with the Soviet Union—for we are a peaceful people who desire to live in peace with all other peoples.

But it is difficult to settle or even discuss these problems in an atmosphere of intimidation. That is why this latest Soviet threat—or any other threat which is made either independently or in response to our actions this week—must and will be met with determination. Any hostile move anywhere in the world against the safety and freedom of peoples to whom we are committed—including in particular the brave people of West Berlin—will be met by whatever action is needed.

Finally, I want to say a few words to the captive people of Cuba, to whom this speech is being directly carried by special radio facilities. I speak to you as a friend, as one who knows of your deep attachment to your fatherland, as one who shares your aspirations for liberty and justice for all. And I have watched and the American people have watched with deep sorrow how your nationalist revolution was betrayed—and how your fatherland fell under foreign domination. Now your leaders are no longer Cuban leaders inspired by Cuban ideals. They are puppets and agents of an international conspiracy which has turned Cuba against your friends and neighbors in the Americas—and turned it into the first Latin American country to become a target for nuclear war—the first Latin American country to have these weapons on its soil.

These new weapons are not in your interest. They contribute nothing to your peace and well-being. They can only undermine it. But this country has no wish to cause you to suffer or to impose any system upon you. We know that your lives and land are being used as pawns by those who deny your freedom.

Many times in the past, the Cuban people have risen to throw out tyrants who destroyed their liberty. And I have no doubt that most Cubans today look forward to the time when they will be truly free—free from foreign domination, free to choose their own leaders, free to select their own system, free to own their own land, free to speak and write and worship without fear or degradation. And then shall Cuba be welcomed back to the society of free nations and to the associations of this hemisphere.

My fellow citizens: let no one doubt that this is a difficult and dangerous effort on which we have set out. No one can foresee precisely what course it will take or what costs or casualties will be incurred. Many months of sacrifice and self-discipline lie ahead—months in which both our patience and our will will be tested—months in which many threats and denunciations will keep us aware of our dangers. But the greatest danger of all would be to do nothing.

The path we have chosen for the present is full of hazards, as all paths are—but it is the one most consistent with our character and courage as a nation and our commitments around the world. The cost of freedom is always high—but Americans have always paid it. And one path we shall never choose, and that is the path of surrender or submission.

Our goal is not the victory of might, but the vindication of right—not peace at the expense of freedom, but both peace *and* freedom, here in this hemisphere, and, we hope, around the world. God willing, that goal will be achieved.

Thank you and good night.

The Tonkin Gulf Resolution

On August 5, 1964, as the presidential campaign opened, President Johnson asked Congress for a joint resolution giving him powers to wage war against the North Vietnamese. In a matter of hours and with only two dissenting votes, Congress complied. In later months the administration would call the Tonkin Gulf Resolution the legal equivalent of a declaration of war.

The president claimed to be responding to unprovoked attacks by Communist forces on American naval units engaged in legal surveillance actions along the North Vietnamese coast. In two separate exchanges, American officials insisted, U.S. destroyers had been fired on and had fired back, sinking several hostile Communist vessels. As a further retaliatory measure, Johnson had ordered U.S. naval jets to attack North Vietnamese patrol boat bases and a Communist oil storage depot.

Historians have been skeptical of the president's story. Many doubt that the second North Vietnamese attack ever occurred. They also question the innocence and legitimacy of the American naval patrols. It seems clear that the American vessels were helping the South Vietnamese, and the Communist attacks can be considered legitimate self-defense.

In the summer of 1964, Johnson obviously did not anticipate the full-scale war that would unfold over the next two years. He was not lying when he claimed in the message to Congress proposing the resolution that he sought "no wider war." He probably did not plan to use the resolution as the equivalent of a war declaration. But he feared that the Republican presidential candidate, Barry Goldwater, a hard-line cold warrior, would, during the campaign ahead, accuse him of timidity in fighting Communism if he did not respond vigorously to the North Vietnamese attack.

Whatever his intentions, Johnson would in fact use the Tonkin Gulf Resolution to provide legal cover to America's massive military intrusion into Vietnam. His opponents would deny that it was so intended and seek to have it repealed. They finally succeeded in early 1971, but by that time vast damage had been done. Thirty thousand Americans had died in Southeast Asia.

[*Tonkin Gulf Resolution*, **Congressional Record**, *August 5, 1964, pp. 18, 132–33.*]

TONKIN GULF RESOLUTION

Resolved by the Senate and House of Representatives of the United States of America in Congress assembled.

Whereas naval units of the Communist regime in Vietnam, in violation of the principles of the Charter of the United Nations and of international law, have deliberately and repeatedly attacked United States naval vessels lawfully present in international waters, and have thereby created a serious threat to international peace;

Whereas these attacks are part of a deliberate and systematic campaign of aggression that the Communist regime in North Vietnam has been waging against its neighbors and the nations joined with them in the collective defense of their freedom;

Whereas the United States is assisting the peoples of Southeast Asia to protect their freedom and has no territorial, military, or political ambitions in that area, but desires only that these peoples should be left in peace to work out their own destinies in their own way;

Now, therefore, be it resolved by the Senate and the House of Representatives of the United States of America in Congress assembled:

Section 1—The Congress approves and supports the determination of the President as Commander in Chief, to take all necessary measures to repel any armed attack against the forces of the United States and to prevent further aggression.

Section 2—The United States regards as vital to its national interest and to world peace the maintenance of international peace and security in Southeast Asia. Consonant with the Constitution of the United States and the Charter of the United Nations and in accordance with its obligations under the Southeast Asia Collective Defense Treaty,* the United States is, therefore, prepared, as the President determines, to take all necessary steps, including the use of armed force, to assist any member . . . of the Southeast Asia Collective Defense Treaty requesting assistance in defense of its freedom.

Section 3—This resolution shall expire when the President shall determine that the peace and security of the area is reasonably assured by international conditions created by action of the United Nations, or otherwise, except that it may be terminated earlier by concurrent resolution of the Congress.

Approved August 10, 1964

McNamara Proposes Vietnam Escalation

Mid-1965 was the defining moment of U.S. involvement in Vietnam. In the wake of Vietcong attacks on the American airbase at Pleiku in February, the United States had begun to bomb targets in North Vietnam, triggering major antiwar protests on college campuses. The first American combat troops, a contingent of marines, were dispatched to South Vietnam in April 1965. By summer, the administration faced a major decision on whether to commit still more fighting men to the war, in a process

---

*This collective defense treaty, negotiated in 1954 with eight Asian nations and Britain and France, was intended to check Communist expansion in the western Pacific region—ed.

that came to be called "escalation." The investment of more and more combat personnel by small increments eventually became a Chinese water torture that drove the country to madness.

In this selection, written in July 1965 after a whirlwind trip to Vietnam, Secretary of Defense Robert McNamara reviews the prospects in Vietnam and lays out the American options as he then perceived them. McNamara favors option C— sending the first large contingent of army personnel to join the "advisers" to the South Vietnamese military and the marines. This new force is to be assigned the specific task of engaging the Vietcong in what came to be called "search and destroy" missions.

The administration accepted this proposal as a balanced action. Hanoi would be kept from achieving its goal of conquering the South, while at the same time it would not incite direct military intervention by the Soviets and the Chinese Communists. Soon after the McNamara memo, the president approved the deployment of an additional 50,000 American troops with an equal number for later in the year. The United States was now on the slippery slope to full immersion in the Vietnam swamp. In fact, McNamara had anticipated this possibility. As he noted under "Option" 3, accepting his advice "would make any later decision to withdraw even more difficult and more costly than would be the case today."

[Manuscripts in the Lyndon Baines Johnson Library, Austin, Texas, Country file: Vietnam.]

MEMORANDUM FOR THE PRESIDENT

SUBJECT: Recommendations of additional deployments to Vietnam

1. *Introduction.* Our object in Vietnam is to create conditions for a favorable outcome by demonstrating to the VC/DRV [Vietcong/ Democratic Republic of Vietnam, i.e., North Vietnam] that the odds are against their winning. We want to create these conditions, if possible, without causing the war to expand into one with China or the Soviet Union and in a way which preserves [the] support of the American people and, hopefully, of our allies and friends. The following assessments, . . . following my trip to Vietnam . . . are addressed to the achievement of that object. My specific recommendations appear in paragraph 5. . . .

2. *Favorable outcome.* To my view, a "favorable outcome" for purposes of these assessments and recommendations has nine fundamental elements.

    a. VC [Vietcong] stop attacks and drastically reduce incidents of terror and sabotage.

b. DRV [Democratic Republic of Vietnam, i.e., North Vietnam] reduces infiltration to a trickle, with some reasonably reliable method of our obtaining confirmation of this fact.

c. US/GVN [United States/Government of Vietnam, i.e., South Vietnam] stops bombing of North Vietnam.

d. GVN stays independent (hopefully pro-U.S., but possibly genuinely neutral).

e. GVN exercising governmental functions over substantially all of South Vietnam.

f. Communists remain quiescent in Laos and Thailand.

g. DRV withdraw PAVN [People's Army of Vietnam, i.e., North Vietnamese military infiltrators into South Vietnam] and other North Vietnamese infiltration . . . from South Vietnam.

h. VC/NLF [Vietcong/National Liberation Front, i.e. all the Communist guerrilla forces in South Vietnam] transform from a military to a purely political organization.

i. U.S. combat forces (not advisers . . .) withdraw.

A favorable outcome could also include arrangements regarding relations between North and South Vietnam, participation in peace-keeping by international forces, membership for North and South Vietnam in the UN, and so on. The nine fundamental elements can evolve with or without an express agreement and, except for what might be negotiated incidental to a cease-fire, are more likely to evolve without an express agreement than with one. We do not need now to address the question whether ultimately we would settle for something less than the nine fundamentals; because deployment of the forces recommended in paragraph 5 is prerequisite to the achievement of *any* acceptable settlement, and a decision can be made later, when bargaining becomes a reality, whether to compromise in any particular.

3. *Estimate of the situation.* The situation in South Vietnam is worse than a year ago (when it was worse than a year before that). After a few months of stalemate, the tempo of the war has quickened. A hard VC push is now on to dismember the nation and to maul the army. The VC main and local forces, reinforced by militia and guerrillas, have the initiative and, with large attacks (some in regimental strength), are hurting ARVN [Army of the Republic of Vietnam] forces badly. . . . [T]he government is able to provide security to fewer and fewer people in less and less territory as terrorism increases. Cities and towns are being isolated as fewer and fewer roads and railroads are usable and power and communications lines are cut.

The economy is deteriorating—the war is disrupting rubber production, rice distribution, . . . vegetable production, and the coastal fishing industry, causing the loss of jobs and income, displacement of people and frequent breakdown or suspension of vital means of transportation and communication; foreign exchange earnings have fallen; and severe inflation is threatened.

The odds are less than even that the Ky [Nguyen Cao Ky, the prime minister at Saigon] government will last out the year. Ky is "executive agent" for a directorate of generals. His government is youthful and inexperienced. . . . His tenure depends upon unity of the armed forces behind him. . . .

Rural reconstruction (pacification) even in the . . . area around Saigon is making little progress. Gains in the IV Corps are being held, but in I and II Corps and adjacent III Corps areas it has lost ground fast since the end of the VC monsoon offensive (300,000 people have been lost to the VC and tens of thousands of refugees have poured out of these areas).

The Government-to-VC ratio overall is now only a little better than 3-to-1, and in combat battalions little better than 0.5-to-1. Some ARVN units have been mauled; many are under strength. . . . Desertions are at a high rate, and force buildup has slipped badly. . . .

There are no signs that we have throttled the inflow of supplies for the VC or can throttle the flow while their material needs are as low as they are: indeed, more and better weapons have been observed in VC hands, and it is probable that there has been a further buildup of North Vietnamese regular units in the I and II Corps area. . . . The DRV/VC seems to believe that South Vietnam is now on the run and near collapse; they show no signs of settling for less than a complete takeover.

4. *Options open to us.* We must choose among three courses of action with respect to Vietnam, all of which involve different probabilities, outcomes, and costs:

   a. Cut our losses and withdraw under the best conditions that can be arranged—almost certainly conditions humiliating to the United States and very damaging to our future effectiveness on the world scene.

   b. Continue at about the present level, with U.S. forces limited to say 75,000, holding on and playing for the breaks—a course of action which, because our position would grow weaker, almost certainly would confront us later with a choice between withdrawal and an emergency expansion of forces, perhaps too late to do any good.

c. Expand promptly and substantially the U.S. military pressure against the Vietcong in the South and maintain the military pressure against the North Vietnamese in the North while launching a vigorous effort on the political side to lay the groundwork for a favorable outcome by clarifying our objectives and establishing channels of communication. This alternative would stave off defeat in the short run and offer a good chance of producing a favorable settlement in the longer run; at the same time it would imply casualties and material and would make any later decision to withdraw even more difficult and more costly than would be the case today.

My recommendations in paragraph 5 below are based on the choice of the third alternative (Option c) as the course of action involving the best odds of the best outcome with the most acceptable cost to the United States.

5. *Military recommendations.* There are now 15 U.S. (and 1 Australian) combat battalions in Vietnam; they, together with other combat personnel and noncombat personnel, bring the total U.S. personnel to approximately 75,000.

a. I recommend that the deployment of U.S. ground troops in Vietnam be increased by October to 34 maneuver battalions (or, if the Koreans fail to provide the expected 9 battalions promptly, to 43 battalions). The battalions, together with increases in helicopter lift, air squadrons, naval units, air defense combat support, and miscellaneous log support and advisory personnel which I also recommend—would bring the total U.S. personnel in Vietnam to approximately 175,000 (200,000 if we must make up for the Korean failure). It should be understood that the deployment of more men (perhaps 100,000) may be necessary in early 1966, and that the deployment of additional forces thereafter is possible but will depend on developments.

b. I recommend that Congress be requested to authorize the call-up of approximately 235,000 men in the Reserve and National Guard (Deleted).

The call-up would be for a two-year period; but the intention would be to release them after one year, by which time they will be relieved by regular forces if conditions permitted.

c. I recommend that the regular armed forces be increased by approximately 375,000 men. . . . (Deleted)*

*This item was, in effect, withdrawn—ed.

d. I recommend that a supplemental appropriation of approximately $X [*sic*] for FY [fiscal year] 1966 be sought from the Congress to cover the first part of the added cost attributable to the buildup in and for the war in Vietnam. A further supplemental appropriation might be required later in the fiscal year. . . .

6. *Use of forces.* The forces will be used however they can be brought to bear most effectively. The U.S./third country [i.e., other nations besides the United States and South Vietnam] ground forces will operate in coordination with South Vietnamese forces. They will defend their own bases; they will assist in providing security in neighboring areas; they will augment Vietnamese forces, assuring retention of key logistic areas and population centers. Also, in the initial phase, they will maintain a small reserve-reaction force, conducting nuisance raids and spoiling attacks, and opening and securing selected lines of communication; as in-country ground strength increases to a level permitting extended U.S. and third-country forces, by aggressive exploitation of superior military forces, they are to gain and hold the initiative—keeping the enemy at a disadvantage, maintaining a tempo such as to deny them time to recuperate or regain their balance, and pressing the fight against VC/DRV main force units in South Vietnam to run them to ground and destroy them. The operations should combine to compel the VC/DRV to fight at a higher and more sustained intensity with resulting higher logistical consumption and, at the same time, to limit his capability to resupply forces in combat at that scale. . . .

7. *Action against North Vietnam.* We should continue the program of bombing military targets in North Vietnam. While avoiding striking population and industrial targets not closely related to the DRV's supply of war material to the VC, we should announce to Hanoi and carry out actions to destroy such supplies and interdict their flow. The number of strike sorties against North Vietnam . . . should increase slowly from the present level of 2,500 a month to 4,000 or more a month. . . .

North Vietnamese Official Explains Communist Negotiating Tactics

While steadily expanding the American military presence in Vietnam after early 1965, the Johnson administration sought to bring the Communists to the negotiating table. As early as May 1965, the United States agreed to a bombing pause to help end the war through diplomacy. This move was probably not sincere. The American position in South Vietnam was still too weak for the administration to expect that the goal of keeping South Vietnam independent could be realized. Its primary purpose was to ease antiwar pressure at home, and in the end, of course, the initiative came to nothing.

But there would be other American-inspired peace feelers. Johnson launched a major "peace offensive" in early 1966, which included another bombing pause. This time he dispatched several close advisers, including Vice President Humphrey, on a world tour to inform neutral nations and America's friends of our sincerity. Again, nothing significant followed. Still another bombing pause and peace initiative took place a year later, with similar results. In all there would be literally scores of peace feelers during the war years and a half-dozen bombing pauses during Johnson's time in the White House.

Americans opposed to the Vietnam War often grew impatient with their country's negotiating approach, accusing the administration of rigidity or duplicity or, usually, both. There was some truth in this view, but it also left out of account the Communists' hard-line attitude toward negotiations. In this document we get a glimpse of that attitude. It is an excerpt from a 1966 letter by Le Duan, a high official of the North Vietnamese Communist Party, to the commander of the People's Liberation Armed Forces, one component of the National Liberation Front—the Vietcong, in American parlance. Note the Communist view that negotiation was not designed to produce a compromise but was another tactic to defeat the enemy and produce complete victory for the Communist side in the shape of "national reunification and socialism."

[Le Duan, Letter to Commander-in-Chief of the People's Liberation Armed Forces, Nguyen Chi Thanh, March 1966, in Gareth Porter, ed., Vietnam: The Definitive Documentation of Human Decisions, vol. 2 (Stanfordville, NY: Earl M. Coleman, 1979), p. 416.]

THE NORTH VIETNAMESE AND A NEGOTIATED PEACE

When speaking of defeating the U.S. imperialists, we mean we are advocating the policy of destroying as much of their potential as possible, checking their military purpose, crushing their aggressive scheme, thus preventing them from enlarging and protracting the war of aggression, and forcing them into submission on specific conditions and finally getting them out of South Vietnam. . . .

But the basic problem is to defeat the imperialists on the battlefield to foil their political and military plan, to destroy as much of their potential as possible, and undermine the puppet army. Only when we comply with the above requirements can we break up their plan of aggression.

As far as the general strategy is concerned, we are advocating that the revolution in South Vietnam has to pass through several transitional phases prior to advancing toward national reunification and socialism. With regard to struggle, we stand for joint political and armed struggle, that is to say, the armed struggle must be simultaneously conducted with the political one. Heavy emphasis is to be placed on the political struggle, which includes the diplomatic struggle, which is of prime importance. As a consequence, the strategy on war and negotiation must be properly used to efficiently serve the political and military aims of our strategy on pitting the weak against the strong.

The problem of war and negotiation is not quite new in the history of our country. Nguyen Trai had once used such a strategy to defeat the feudalist elements of Ming's dynasty. Our comrades in China had also adopted the "fight-and-negotiation" policy in their struggle against the U.S. and Chiang (Kai-Shek). The same strategy was used in the Korean war.

However, this problem is very complicated considering that, at present, when speaking of negotiations, the views are quite divergent. The U.S. views hold that negotiation is to be conducted from a strong position. Some countries sincerely support our struggle but, in view of diplomatic reasons and their domestic administration and misunderstanding of the situation in our country, want to see us at the conference table in order to forestall aimless sacrifice on our part. There are those who hold the view that the political struggle is of major importance, but such a view is different from ours as to degree and time to use this strategy.

At present, the U.S. imperialists, on the one hand, are attempting to widen the war in a move to save them from the said predicament and quagmire but, on the other hand, are trying to force us to the negotiation table for some concessions. As for us, we must constantly take the initiative, our strategy on negotiation must serve in a practical manner our concrete political aims. For this reason, the Party Central Committee has unanimously entrusted the Politburo with the task of carrying out the above strategy in conformity with the policy of our Party and on the basis of the situation between us and the enemy whenever necessary. . . .

The Tet Offensive

By the summer of 1967, there were 450,000 American soldiers, airmen, and marines fighting in the swamps, mountains, and jungles of Vietnam. Thirteen thousand men had died in that distant, tropical land.

As the war dragged on and opposition at home grew, the Johnson administration struggled to put the best face on events. During the last part of the year, the president sponsored programs to send distinguished visitors to South Vietnam to see American "nation building" for themselves, and he ordered the embassy and U.S.

military command in Saigon to find "occasions to present sound evidence of progress in Viet Nam." Johnson also brought home William Westmoreland, the U.S. commander in South Vietnam, to brief the American people on the war. The obliging general told the American public that "we have reached an important point where the end begins to come into view."

And then came the Tet Offensive. Tet was the Lunar New Year, a week-long holiday when the Vietnamese bought new clothes, visited their families, prepared special foods, and draped their houses with flowers. During previous years, both sides had observed a truce during Tet, and now, in January 1968, they again promised to suspend the fighting for a week.

The Communists had no intention of observing their agreement. While the South Vietnamese, civilians and military, were preparing for the festivities, Vietcong troops began to infiltrate the cities and towns, preparing for a major offensive that would, they hoped, trigger a general uprising of the South Vietnamese masses. Within twenty-four hours of Tet's start, Vietcong fighters attacked South Vietnamese government headquarters in 36 of 44 provincial capitals, five of the six major cities, and 64 district capitals. The boldest stroke was in Saigon itself, where the airport, the presidential palace, and the headquarters of the ARVN general staff came under attack.

No act was as brazen, however, as the assault on the American embassy, the very embodiment of American power in South Vietnam. Though the small contingent of Vietcong sappers occupied the embassy grounds for some six hours, they were never able to shoot their way into the embassy itself. The botch of the embassy attack was matched by military failure elsewhere. The Vietcong lost thousands of soldiers and held on to none of their initial gains. But it was a Communist victory nonetheless. The Tet Offensive shook the confidence of the American public in their Vietnam policy and led to a serious reappraisal of the U.S. role there.

The embassy attack is described here by CBS-TV reporter Mike Wallace soon after it ended.

[CBS News Special Report, "Saigon Under Fire," January 31, 1968, CBS, Inc.]

SAIGON UNDER FIRE

WALLACE: Good evening. I'm Mike Wallace.

With a bold series of raids during the last three days, the enemy in Vietnam has demolished the myth that Allied military strength controls that country. The Communists hit the very heart of Saigon, the capital of South Vietnam, and at least ten cities which correspond to state capitals here in the United States. And then, as if to demonstrate that no place in that war-torn nation is secure, they struck at least nine American military strongholds and unnumbered field positions. Tonight the magnitude of those raids became apparent in the U.S. Command's report on casualties. The Communists paid a heavy toll for their strikes, almost 5,000 dead, including 660 in Saigon alone, and almost 2,000 captured. But Allied casualties also are high: 232 Americans killed, 929 wounded; 300 South Vietnamese killed, 747 wounded, and that toll is expected to climb.

The enemy's well-coordinated attacks occurred throughout South Vietnam, but the most dramatic demonstration of his boldness and capability came at the very symbol of America's presence in Vietnam, the brand new U.S. Embassy building there. CBS News Correspondent Robert Schakne reports.

SCHAKNE: The American Embassy is under siege; only the besiegers are Americans. Inside, in part of the building, are the Vietcong terror squads that charged in during the night. Military Police got back into the compound of the $2.5 million Embassy complex at dawn. Before that a platoon of Vietcong were in control. The Communist raiders never got into the main chancery building; a handful of Marines had it blocked and kept them out. But the raiders were everywhere else. By daylight (voice drowned out by gunfire). No one, unless identified, was allowed in the street. An Australian Military Policeman was standing guard, firing warning shots to keep the street clear.

Outside the building knots of Military Policemen held positions. There were bursts of wild shooting in the streets, perhaps snipers in other buildings and there had been casualties. The bodies of two Military Policemen who died as they tried to assault the compound lay near their jeep across the boulevard. But even after the Military Police fought their way back inside, there was more fighting to do. The raiders were still about the compound. They may have been a suicide cadre. In the end none of them were to surrender.

This is where the Vietcong raiders broke in. They sneaked up and blasted a hole in the reinforced concrete fence surrounding the compound. They were inside before anyone knew it. They had the big Embassy wall to protect them. But none of the raiders lived to tell of their exploit. By eight o'clock, five hours after they first broke in, almost all of them were dead. Nineteen bodies were counted. All in civilian clothes, they had been armed with American M-16 rifles and also rocket-launchers and rockets. They had explosives, their purpose apparently to destroy the Embassy. In that purpose they did not succeed.

The fighting went on for a total of six hours before the last known Vietcong raider was killed. They were rooted out of bushes, from outlying buildings, and then the last one, the nineteenth, from the small residence of the Embassy's Mission Coordinator, George Jacobson, who had been hiding out all alone, all morning. . . .

Saigon had been on the alert for Vietcong terror attacks during the night, but for some reason the Embassy guard was not increased. Just two Military Policemen at one gate, a handful of Marines inside. There wasn't anyone to stop the Vietcong when they came. General William Westmoreland came by soon after. His version was that all this represented a Vietcong defeat.

WESTMORELAND: In some way the enemy's well-laid plans went afoul. Some superficial damage was done to the building. All of the enemy that entered the compound as far as I can determine were killed. Nineteen bodies have been found on the premises—enemy bodies. Nineteen enemy bodies have been found on the premises.

SCHAKNE: General, how would you assess yesterday's activities and today's? What is the enemy doing? Are these major attacks?

(Sound of explosions)

WESTMORELAND: That's POD setting off a couple of M-79 duds, I believe.

SCHAKNE: General, how would you assess the enemy's purposes yesterday and today?

WESTMORELAND: The enemy very deceitfully has taken advantage of the Tet truce in order to create maximum consternation within South Vietnam, particularly in the populated areas. In my opinion this is diversionary to his main effort, which he had planned to take place in Quang Tri Province, from Laos, toward Khesanh and across the Demilitarized Zone. This attack has not yet materialized; his schedule has probably been thrown off balance because of our very effective air strikes.

Now yesterday the enemy exposed himself by virtue of this strategy, and he suffered great casualties. When I left my office late yesterday, approximately eight o'clock, we—we had accounted for almost 700 enemy killed in action. Now we had suffered some casualties ourselves, but they were small by comparison. My guess is, based on my conversations with my field commanders, that there were probably—there were probably far more than 700 that were killed. Now by virtue of this audacious action by the enemy, he has exposed himself, he has become more vulnerable. As soon as President Thieu, with our agreement, called off the truce, U.S. and American [ARVN?] troops went on the offensive and pursued the enemy aggressively.

SCHAKNE: When they built this Embassy, it was first to be a secure building. This Embassy was designed as a bomb-proof, attack-proof building, but it turned out, when the VC hit us, it wasn't attack-proof enough. Robert Schakne, CBS News, Saigon.

WALLACE: Washington regards the enemy raids as the first step in a strategy aimed at strengthening their hand for any peace talks which may develop, and captured Communist documents lend weight to the theory.

CBS News White House Correspondent Dan Rather reports.

RATHER: We knew this was coming—a well-coordinated series of enemy raids against South Vietnamese cities. Our intelligence even pinpointed the exact day it would happen. What we did not know was where. This is the official story, as given out by White House news secretary George Christian, who went on to say there was no way to completely insulate yourself against this kind of thing if the enemy is willing to sacrifice large numbers of men.

But if we knew it was coming, even to the exact day, Christian was asked, why wasn't extra protection placed around such an obvious place as the Saigon Embassy? The White House spokesman paused, then said, "I just don't know." At the Pentagon a high-ranking source said, "There simply were more of them and they were better than we expected."

Washington is startled but not panicked by the latest series of events. President Johnson privately is warning Congressmen that intelligence reports indicate the whole month of February will be rough in Southeast Asia. Mr. Johnson is emphasizing that the enemy's winter offensive is only beginning. Dan Rather, CBS News, Washington.

WALLACE: The drama of the battle for Saigon captured most attention, but the South Vietnamese capital was only one of the Communist targets. In a moment we'll return with battle film from another city.

(Announcement)

WALLACE: The U.S. Command's battle communiqué indicates that the Allies repulsed most of the enemy's attacks, but this success was not universal. In an assault today the Communists captured half of the Central Highlands city of Kontum and the Vietcong flag flies in the center of the northern city of Hue. The enemy claims also to control Quang Tri City, also in I Corps in the north, a claim as yet unconfirmed by the Allies.

But one place where American and South Vietnamese troops turned back the enemy was at Nhatrang, a coastal city about 190 miles northeast of Saigon. In peacetime a pleasant resort city, now Nhatrang is the headquarters for the Fifth Special Forces, the Green Berets; and the Green Berets were in the thick of the fighting. The Communist attack there had begun around midnight, and it developed into a street fight which, as you see here, carried over into the daylight hours. The enemy's apparent goal in this fight, down the street, was a provincial prison where many important Vietcong were held. During this battle many innocent civilians, friendly to the Allies, were trapped in their homes between the lines of fire between VC and the Green Berets. It was only after twelve hours of battle that the area was secure enough to call those civilians out to safety.

The Communist raids had a stunning impact, all of them, around the world, and the question is, what is it that the enemy is after in these attacks. Certainly he does not believe that these suicide assaults by terrorists squads are going to radically change the course of the war in Vietnam; but there can be no doubt that these attacks are calculated to impress indelibly on public opinion in North and South Vietnam and in the United States the resourcefulness and the determination of the Vietcong and his ability to strike almost at will any place in South Vietnam if he is willing to pay the price.

The story of the past three days, with heavy emphasis, of course, on American and South Vietnamese casualties will be trumpeted throughout Vietnam and around the world by Hanoi. Whether all of this is a prelude to an expression that Hanoi is willing now to go to the negotiation table remains to be seen, but there is little doubt that there will be more such stories from Khesanh and elsewhere in South Vietnam in the bitter month of February that lies ahead.

Mike Wallace, CBS News, New York.

ANNOUNCER: This has been a CBS News Special Report: "Saigon Under Fire."

My Lai

One of the most shameful incidents of a war that produced more than its share of atrocities was the massacre in mid-March 1968 of Vietnamese civilians by a company of American soldiers at the hamlet of My Lai in coastal Quang Ngai province.

The men were members of Task Force Barker, a unit of the Americal Division, who had been sent to destroy a Vietcong base supposedly located at Son My village, of which My Lai was a subhamlet. Many of the men, like a large proportion of "grunts" in Vietnam, were young and poorly educated. Few of them were churchgoers. As we know, neither a college education nor church attendance guarantees elevated moral principles, but they do, perhaps, serve as some deterrent to savagery. And deterrents were needed. The Vietcong were guerrillas. They fought by ambush, by stealth. They disguised themselves as civilians. They used booby traps and hidden pits with poisoned stakes to maim and kill their enemies. We admire irregular fighters when we judge their cause to be good. But they are seldom beloved by their victims.

The men of Charlie Company ("C/1–20," in this document), commanded by Captain Ernest Medina, with Lieutenant William Calley, Jr., in charge of the First Platoon, were the most deeply implicated in what ensued at My Lai. They were completely indiscriminate in their murderous rampage. Before the bloody work was fin-

ished, they had slaughtered more than a hundred Vietnamese, mostly old men, women, and children, and put the torch to most of the hamlet's dwellings. First Platoon was the most savage, but another eighty or so Vietnamese were killed by Second and Third Platoons as well. Few, if any, of these people were members of the Vietcong.

There was a whistle-blower: Hugh Thompson, a helicopter pilot who observed the operation from the air. Thompson reported the massacre to his superiors, who gave it perfunctory attention. When reports persisted, Colonel Oran Henderson undertook an investigation that the commission headed by Lieutenant General William R. Peers, created by the secretary of the army, called "little more than a pretense . . . [that had as its] goal the suppression of the true facts."

After revelations in the press by reporter Seymour Hersh, Calley was tried by a military court in 1971 and convicted of twenty-two murders. Sentenced to life imprisonment, he was befriended by President Nixon, who substituted house arrest for time in the stockade. In the end, Calley served almost no jail time for his crimes.

The document that follows is an excerpt from the Peers report summarizing the crimes committed by the American troops.

[*Joseph Goldstein, Burke Marshall, and Jack Schwartz,* **The My Lai Massacre and Its Cover-up: Beyond the Reach of Law. The Peers Commission Report** *(New York: The Free Press, 1976), pp. 44–56.*]

THE PEERS REPORT

A. The Son My Village Incident

During the period 16–19 March 1968, a tactical operation was conducted into Son My Village, Son Tinh District, Quang Ngai Province, Republic of Vietnam, by Task Force (TF) Barker, a battalion-size unit of the Americal Division.

TF Barker was an interim organization of the 11th Brigade, created to fill a tactical void resulting from the withdrawal of a Republic of Korea Marine Brigade from the Quang Ngai area. The Task Force was composed of a rifle company from each of the 11th Brigade's three organic infantry battalions—A/3–1 Inf, B/4–3 Inf, C/1–20 Inf. The commander was LTC Frank A. Barker (now deceased).

The plans for the operation were never reduced to writing, but it was reportedly aimed at destroying the 48th VC Local Force (LF) Battalion, thought to be located in Son My Village, which also served as a VC staging and logistical support base. On two previous operations in the area, units of TF Barker had received casualties from enemy fire, mines, and booby-traps and had not been able to close effectively with the enemy.

On 15 March 1968, the new 11th Brigade commander, COL Oran K. Henderson, visited the TF Barker command post at Landing Zone (LZ) Dottie and talked to the assembled staff and commanders. He urged them to press forward aggressively and eliminate the 48th LF Battalion. Following these remarks, LTC Barker and his staff gave an intelligence briefing and issued an operations order. The company commanders were told that most of the population of Son My were "VC or VC sympathizers" and were advised that most of the civilian inhabitants would be away from Son My and on their way to market by 0700 hours. The operation was to commence at 0725 hours on 16 March 1968 with a short artillery preparation, following which C/1–20 Inf was to combat assault into an LZ immediately west of My Lai and then sweep east through the subhamlet. Following C Company's landing, B/4–3 Inf was to reinforce C/1–20 Inf, or to conduct a second combat assault to the east of My Lai into an LZ south of the subhamlet of My Lai or "Pinkville." A/3–1 Inf was to move from its field location to blocking positions north of Son My.

During or subsequent to the briefing, LTC Barker ordered the commanders of C/1–20 Inf, and possibly B/4–3 Inf, to burn the houses, kill the livestock, destroy foodstuffs, and perhaps to close the wells. No instructions were issued as to the safeguarding of noncombatants found there.

During a subsequent briefing by CPT Medina to his men, LTC Barker's orders were embellished, a revenge element was added, and the men of C/1–20 Inf were given to understand that only the enemy would be present in My Lai on 16 March and that the enemy was to be destroyed. In CPT Michles' briefing to his platoon leaders, mention was also apparently made of the burning of dwellings.

On the morning of 16 March 1968, the operation began as planned. A/3–1 Inf was reported in blocking positions at 0725 hours. At about that same time the artillery preparation and fires of the supporting helicopter gunship were placed on the C/1–20 Inf LZ and a part of My Lai. LTC Barker controlled the artillery preparation and combat assault from his helicopter. COL Henderson and his command group also arrived overhead at approximately this time.

By 0750 hours all elements of C/1–20 Inf were on the ground. Before entering My Lai, they killed several Vietnamese fleeing the area in the rice paddies around the subhamlet and along Route 521 to the south of the subhamlet. No resistance was encountered at this time or later in the day.

The infantry assault on My Lai began a few minutes before 0800 hours. During the 1st Platoon's movement through the southern half of the subhamlet, its members were involved in widespread killing of Vietnamese inhabitants (comprised almost exclusively of old men, women, and children) and also in property destruction. Most of the inhabitants who were not killed immediately were rounded up into two groups. The first group, consisting of about 70–80 Vietnamese, was taken to a large ditch east of My Lai and later shot. A second group, consisting of 20–50 Vietnamese, was taken south of the hamlet and shot there on a trail. Similar killings of smaller groups took place within the subhamlet.

Members of the 2d Platoon killed at least 60–70 Vietnamese men, women, and children, as they swept through the northern half of My Lai and through Binh Tay, a small subhamlet about 400 meters north of My Lai. They also committed several rapes.

The 3d Platoon, having secured the LZ, followed behind the 1st and 2d and burned and destroyed what remained of the houses in My Lai and killed most of the remaining livestock. Its members also rounded up and killed a group of 7–12 women and children.

There was considerable testimony that orders to stop the killing were issued two or three times during the morning. The 2d Platoon received such an order around 0920 hours and promptly complied. The 1st Platoon continued the killings until perhaps 1030 hours, when the order was repeated. By this time the 1st Platoon had completed its sweep through the subhamlet.

By the time C/1–20 Inf departed My Lai in the early afternoon, moving to the northeast for link-up with B/4–3 Inf, its members had killed at least 175–200 Vietnamese men, women, and children.* The evidence indicates that only three or four were confirmed as Viet Cong, although there were undoubtedly several unarmed VC (men, women, and children) among them and many more active supporters and sympathizers. One man from the company was reported as wounded from the accidental discharge of his weapon.

Since C Company had encountered no enemy opposition, B/4–3 Inf was air-landed in its LZ between 0815 and 0830 hours, following a short artillery preparation. Little if any resistance was encountered, although the 2d Platoon suffered 1 KIA and 7 WIA from mines and/or boobytraps. The 1st Platoon moved eastward separately from the rest of B Company to cross and secure a bridge over the Song My Khe (My Khe River). After crossing the bridge and approaching the outskirts of the subhamlet of My Khe, elements

*Casualty figures cited for My Lai were developed by this Inquiry solely on the basis of statements and testimony of U.S. personnel. Separate estimates by the Criminal Investigation Division (CID) agency together with other evidence, indicate the number of Vietnamese killed in the overall area of Son My Village may have exceeded 400.

of the platoon opened fire on the subhamlet with an M-60 machinegun and M-16 rifles. The fire continued for approximately five minutes, during which time some inhabitants of My Khe, mostly women and children, were killed. The lead elements of the platoon then entered the subhamlet, firing into the houses and throwing demolitions into shelters. Many noncombatants apparently were killed in the process.

It is believed that only ten men in B/4–3 Inf directly participated in the killings and destruction in My Khe; two of these are dead and the remaining eight have either refused to testify or claim no recollection of the event. As a result, it has not been possible to reconstruct the events with certainty. It appears, however, that the number of noncombatants killed by B/4–3 Inf on 16 March 1968 may have been as high as 90. The company reported a total of 38 VC KIA on 16 March, but it is likely that few if any were Viet Cong.

On the evening of 16 March 1968, after C/1–20 Inf and B/4–3 Inf had linked up in a night defensive position, a Viet Cong suspect was apparently tortured and maimed by a U.S. officer. He was subsequently killed along with some additional suspects by Vietnamese National Police in the presence of U.S. personnel.

During the period 17–19 March 1968 both C/1–20 Inf and B/4–3 Inf were involved in additional burning and destruction of dwellings, and in the mistreatment of Vietnamese detainees.

B. Reports of the Incident

1. Reports of Civilian Casualties

Commencing early in the operation, commanders began receiving reports of civilian casualties in My Lai. At about 0930 hours, MG Koster was advised by COL Henderson that he had observed six to eight such casualties. The figure was increased when LTC Barker reported to Henderson during the afternoon that the total was 12 to 14, and was further increased to 20 in a report Barker made that evening. This last report was relayed to MG Koster at about 1900 hours. None of these reports was entered in unit journals or reported outside the Americal Division.

2. Observations and Complaints by Aviation Personnel

One element which provided combat support to TF Barker on 16 March was an aero-scout team from Company B, 123d Aviation Battalion. A pilot of this team, WO1 (now 1LT) Hugh Thompson, had been flying at a low altitude over My Lai during the morning hours and had observed the actions of C/1–20 Inf. He became greatly concerned over the "needless and unnecessary killings" he had witnessed. He landed his helicopter several times to aid the inhabitants and in an attempt to stop the killing.

Shortly before noon, WO1 Thompson returned to LZ Dottie and reported his observations to his company commander, MAJ Frederic Watke. The complaints of WO1 Thompson were confirmed by other pilots and crewmen who had also been over My Lai. The complaints were expressed in most serious terms; those who were present heard the terms "killing" and "murder" used freely, with estimates of the dead in My Lai running over 100. Upon receipt of this report, MAJ Watke went to the commander of TF Barker and advised him of the allegations. Watke stated that Barker then left for his helicopter, presumably to visit C/1–20 Inf. Watke considered the matter was "in the hands of the man who could do something about it" and took no further action at that time. Later that day, he again encountered Barker who advised him that he could find nothing to substantiate Thompson's allegations. While Watke testified that he was convinced at the time that LTC Barker was lying, he took no further action until 2200 hours that night, when he reported to his battalion commander, LTC Holladay, and related for the second time the substance of what is hereafter referred to as the "Thompson Report."

3. The Order to Return to My Lai
At about 1530 hours on 16 March, after receiving a second report of civilian casualties, COL Henderson stated he became suspicious and directed TF Barker to send a company back through My Lai to ascertain the exact number of casualties and the cause of death. As the order was being transmitted to C/1–20 Inf by TF Barker, it was monitored by MG Koster, the commander of the Americal Division, who inquired concerning the reasons. After a brief explanation by the CO of C/1–20 Inf, during which time MG Koster was advised that 20–28 noncombatants had been killed, MG Koster countermanded the order and directed that COL Henderson be notified. There were no further efforts to make an on-site determination of the cause or extent of the civilian casualties.

4. The Thompson Report Reaches Division Headquarters
Because of the late hour at which LTC Holladay received the report from MAJ Watke, they waited until the following morning before reporting to BG Young, an Assistant Division Commander. Watke repeated his story, which both he and LTC Holladay agree contained the allegations that there had been "lots of unnecessary killing . . . mostly women, children, and old men" and that a confrontation had taken place between personnel of aviation and

ground units; however, there is conflict as to the number of casualties mentioned. LTC Holladay and MAJ Watke also agree that BG Young was advised that the complaints made by Thompson had been confirmed by other aviation unit personnel.

At about noon on the 17th, BG Young reported to MG Koster the information he had received from MAJ Watke and LTC Holladay. There is substantive disagreement in testimony between what BG Young testified he received from Watke and Holladay and what the latter two state they reported. BG Young stated he was not apprised of any charge of indiscriminate or unnecessary killing of noncombatants. He further stated that it was his impression the matter of major concern was that there had been a confrontation between the ground forces and an aviation unit, resulting from an incident in which noncombatants had been caught in a cross fire between U.S. and enemy forces.

BG Young contends that it was this lesser charge he brought to MG Koster, who directed BG Young to instruct COL Henderson to conduct a thorough investigation of the incident. MG Koster has confirmed parts of BG Young's account of this conversation, but in a previous statement before the Criminal Investigation Division (CID), MG Koster stated that he had been advised of some indiscriminate shooting of civilians.

The Inquiry has concluded that the two general officers received a muted version of the Thompson Report from Watke and Holladay, but one that included the allegation that noncombatants had been indiscriminately killed. Upon receipt of the report, it seems most likely that they related it to the information MG Koster had received from TF Barker the previous day, that 20–28 noncombatants had been inadvertently killed. The information concerning noncombatant casualties had not been forwarded outside of the Division, although MACV and III MAF regulations required such action, nor were the new allegations reported to higher headquarters. Adopting a "close hold" attitude concerning all information relating to this matter, MG Koster directed BG Young to have COL Henderson investigate the incident.

C. Investigation of the Incident and Review
1. COL Henderson's "Investigation"
BG Young made arrangements for a meeting which was held on 18 March at 0900 hours at LZ Dottie. The meeting was attended by five officers: BG Young, COL Henderson, LTC Barker, LTC Holladay, and MAJ Watke. BG Young told the group of the Division Commander's instructions concerning the investigation, and MAJ Watke repeated his account of the complaints. When the meeting terminated, COL Henderson commenced his

"investigation" with an interview of WO1 Thompson and two other aviation unit personnel. (While Henderson states he talked only with Thompson and for only a few minutes, the testimony of others indicates that he talked individually with three persons for almost an hour.) These interviews, together with the information already possessed by Henderson from personal observation and conversations with TF Barker personnel, should have provided a full awareness of the nature and extent of the incident at My Lai. From at least this point forward, Henderson's actions appear to have been little more than a pretense of an investigation and had as their goal the suppression of the true facts concerning the events of 16 March.

Following his interview with aviation personnel, Henderson questioned CPT Medina, whose explanation concerning civilian casualties left him "suspicious." The remainder of Henderson's "investigation" was without substance; his "interview with a substantial number of C Company personnel" consisted of a discussion on the afternoon of 18 March with a group which, COL Henderson claims, numbered from 30 to 40 personnel. After complimenting them on their performance in the operation, he asked them collectively if they had witnessed any atrocities. Henderson stated that the response he received was negative. While COL Henderson claims he spoke with other individuals and responsible commanders, available evidence indicates that his so-called investigative actions ended after a brief flight which he stated he made over the area of operation on 18 March.

Commencing on 19 March, COL Henderson is said to have made a series of oral reports to BG Young and MG Koster in which he was purported to have related to them the results of his "investigation." It seems clear that in his reports Henderson deliberately misrepresented both the scope of his investigation and the information he had obtained. He reported that while 20 civilians had been killed by artillery and/or gunships, there was no basis in fact to the allegations made by WO1 Thompson. Henderson's final oral report was accepted by MG Koster as adequately responding to the charges made by WO1 Thompson. The matter appears to have rested there until about mid-April 1968, when information was received at Division Headquarters from Vietnamese sources. . . .

D. Suppression and Withholding of Information

Within the Americal Division, at every command level from company to division, actions were taken or omitted which together effectively concealed the Son My incident. Outside the division, advisory teams at Province, District, and possibly the 2d ARVN Division also contributed to this end. Some of the acts and omissions that resulted in concealment of the incident were inadvertent while others constituted deliberate suppression or withholding of information.

Efforts initiated in 1968 deliberately to withhold information continue to this day. Six officers who occupied key positions at the time of the incident exercised their right to remain silent before this Inquiry, others gave false or misleading testimony or withheld information, and key documents relating to the incident have not been found in U.S. files.

1. At Company Level

No reports of the crimes committed by C/1–20 Inf and B/4–3 Inf during the operation were made by members of the units, although there were many men in both companies who had not participated in any criminal acts. The commander of C/1–20 Inf assembled his men after the operation and advised them not to discuss the incident because an investigation was being conducted, and he advised one individual not to write to his Congressman about the incident. He also made a false report that only 20–28 noncombatants had been killed and attributed the cause of death to artillery and gunships.

The commander of B/4–3 Inf submitted false reports (possibly without knowing they were false) that 38 VC had been killed by his 1st Platoon and that none of them were women and children.

2. At Task Force and Brigade Levels

Significant information concerning irregularities in the operation and the commission of war crimes by C/1–20 Inf was known to the commanders and staff officers of both TF Barker and the 11th Brigade on 16 March but was never transmitted to the American Division. Reports of VC killed by C/1–20 Inf on 16 March terminated at 0840 hours when the total reached 90, although the killing continued. In addition to withholding information, the 11th Brigade headquarters submitted false and misleading reports to Division. One instance concerned a C/1–20 Inf VC body count report of 69, which was changed to attribute the cause of death to artillery and to move the location at which the purported VC were killed from inside the hamlet of My Lai to a site 600 meters away. A second false report involved an interrogation report from C/1–20 Inf that 30–40 VC had departed the hamlet immediately prior to the combat assault. The record of this interrogation report as received at the American Division on 16 March stated that there were many VC in the C/1–20 Inf area of operation.

A reporter and photographer attached to the 11th Brigade Information Office accompanied TF Barker on 16 March and observed many war crimes committed by C/1–20 Inf. Both individuals failed to report what they had seen, the reporter wrote a false and misleading account of the operation, and the photographer withheld and suppressed from proper authorities the photographic evidence of atrocities he had obtained.

In response to a routine division requirement, LTC Barker submitted a Combat Action Report, dated 28 March 1968, concerning his unit's operations on 16 March. The report significantly omitted any reference to non-combatant casualties and other irregularities, falsely depicted a hotly contested combat action, and appears to have been an outright effort to suppress and mislead.

Perhaps the most significant action taken to suppress the true facts of the Son My operation was the deception employed by COL Henderson to mislead his commander as to the scope and findings of his investigation of the Thompson allegations. His later submission—the so-called Report of Investigation, dated 24 April 1968, which dismissed the allegations from Vietnamese sources as baseless propaganda and restated the fiction that 20 noncombatants had been inadvertently killed—continued the original deception practiced upon his commander.

3. At Division Level

A. Within Aviation Units

There is no evidence to suggest that there were deliberate attempts within the division aviation unit to conceal information concerning the Son My incident. However, there were acts and omissions by the commanders of the 123d Aviation Battalion, and of Company B of that unit, which contributed to concealment of the facts. One of the principal reasons why the full import of the Thompson Report was probably not appreciated at the division command level can be attributed to these two commanders and their failure to verify or document the serious charges made by WO1 Thompson and others. Neither took action to obtain documentary substantiation, to conduct a low-level aerial reconnaissance or otherwise to verify the allegations, or to confirm in writing what they reported orally to BG Young. The initial delay in reporting the matter through command channels needlessly prevented the report from reaching the Americal Division command group until approximately 24 hours after the incident had occurred.

A second serious charge against both of these two commanders is that they failed to take any action when they became convinced that the investigation of the incident was a "cover-up." An admonition was issued by the B Company Commander to his unit to halt further discussion of the incident while it was being investigated. This action was not taken to conceal information, but it probably had the unfortunate, although unintended, result of aiding in the suppression of the facts.

B. Within Headquarters, American Division

American Division Headquarters was the recipient of much information concerning the Son My operation from both US and GVN sources. Except for routine operational data forwarded on 16 March, none of the reports or allegations concerning irregularities at Son My were transmitted to higher headquarters, although directives from III MAF and MACV clearly required such action. As previously indicated, the Inquiry has concluded that on 17 March, when they received a muted version of the Thompson Report, MG Koster and BG Young may have viewed the report in relation to information previously received that 20–28 noncombatant casualties had been caused by artillery and gunships. While COL Henderson's later reports were false, and the general officers were negligent in having accepted them, they probably believed they were withholding information concerning a much less serious incident than the one that had actually occurred.

Additional information from Vietnamese sources reaching the American Division sometime in April implied that a far more serious event had taken place at Son My. The command response to this information was so inadequate to the situation and so inconsistent with what would ordinarily be expected of officers of the ability and experience of MG Koster and BG Young that it can only be explained as a refusal or an inability to give credence to information or reports which were not consistent with their original, and erroneous, conclusions.

In summary form, the following are the significant acts done or omitted at the American Division headquarters which contributed to the concealment of the true facts concerning Son My:

1. There was a failure to report information concerning noncombatant casualties and allegations for war crimes known to be of particular interest to COMUSMACV and required to be reported by directives of both III MAF and MACV;
2. Having decided to withhold from higher headquarters information concerning civilian casualties, MG Koster directed that the matter be investigated by COL Henderson. However, he did not insure that a thorough investigation was conducted nor did he subject COL Henderson's reports to adequate review, thereby nullifying his efforts to determine the true facts;

3. The Division command group acted to control closely all information regarding the Son My incident. Information regarding the incident was not included in daily briefings or provided the General or Special Staff, and the investigative resources of the staff were not employed.

4. By Persons Outside the Americal Division

Among the Vietnamese officials who came in contact with information concerning possible war crimes in Son My during the period 16–19 March, there was a natural reluctance to confront their American counterparts with such serious allegations and to insist upon inquiry into the matter. Such information as did reach U.S. advisory personnel was not forwarded through advisory channels, but referred only to the Americal Division and its 11th Brigade. In addition, there is evidence that at the Quang Ngai Province and Son Tinh District levels and probably at the 2d ARVN Division, the senior U.S. military advisors aided in suppressing information concerning the incident.

10

The Antiwar Movement

The philosophy of nonviolence first came to America with the "peace churches"—the Quakers, Brethren, and Mennonites—during the colonial era. The secular movement against war dates from the pre–Civil War reform wave that also begat the temperance, antislavery, and women's rights crusades. It was in the wake of World War I, however, that the modern American peace movement was born. The Great War of 1914–18 inspired a profound disillusionment with patriotic chauvinism and fostered a score of organizations dedicated to preventing another mass slaughter on the battlefield.

World War II damaged the peace movement of the 1920s and 1930s. A "good war," fought to defeat one of the most monstrous tyrannies in history, it validated organized violence to fight evil and protect civilized values. Nonetheless, thousands of young American men refused either to enter the military service or to accept combat duty. Twelve thousand conscientious objectors (COs) served in Civilian Public Service (CPS) camps between 1941 and 1945, where they helped in asylums, hospitals, national parks, and forests and volunteered as guinea pigs in medical experiments. Several of the radical prewar pacifist organizations, the War Resisters League and the Fellowship of Reconciliation, actually gained recruits during the war from among draft-age young men seeking moral and legal support for their pacifist convictions. In many of the CPS camps, as well as in federal prisons where other conscientious objectors were confined, harsh treatment of inmates created a cadre of radicals, antagonistic to all coercive government and inequalities of wealth and power. These radicalized pacifists would contribute disproportionately to the Sixties peace movement as well as to the New Left.

After V-J Day, the cold war and the danger of nuclear annihilation revived and refocused pacifism and the antiwar movement. Fear of a collision between the Soviet Union and the United States, both now equipped with nuclear weapons, provided fuel for a new campaign against the use of violence as the way to settle international disputes. In 1945, radical pacifists, many of them newly released COs, organized the Committee for Non-Violent Revolution (CNVR), a nonviolent civil disobedience group, dedicated to achieving peace and equality alike. CNVR and successor groups organized a number of cooperative living communities and established several listener-supported FM radio stations in the San Francisco Bay Area to disseminate their views and expose the injustices of the larger society. Meanwhile, groups of socially conscious scientists, appalled by the horrors of Hiroshima and Nagasaki and the urgent danger of "the bomb," formed the Federation of American Scientists. Its motto was "The arms race must be stopped."

The peace movement flagged in the mid-1950s but then revived following the extensive American H-bomb testing in the Pacific. The National Committee for a Sane Nuclear Policy (SANE), formed in 1957, expressed the growing fear of damage to health and the environment caused by radioactive fallout from nuclear testing. From 1959 on, SANE activists lobbied for an international test-ban treaty that would end the fallout danger and provide a first step toward nuclear disarmament.

The revived adversarial mood of the late 1950s inevitably invaded the peace movement. The Committee for Non-Violent Action (CNVA), organized in 1958, took a more aggressive civil disobedience approach to nuclear issues than SANE. Women Strike for Peace, organized by Washington-area housewives in 1960, was another antibomb group. Simultaneously, on campuses, the new Student Peace Union denounced "militarism" and pledged to seek "new and creative means of achieving a free and peaceful society."

By the early Sixties a broad-spectrum peace coalition had come into existence ready to target the accelerating American involvement in Vietnam. Poised to join them were Old Leftists, especially Trotskyists and Maoists, and new political radicals affiliated with Students for a Democratic Society. These groups were nonpacifist; they would oppose Vietnam primarily because it seemed an extension of America's aggressive imperialist foreign policy.

The first anti-Vietnam rally was a small affair of fifteen hundred protesters in New York in late 1964. But the anti-Vietnam movement took off in early 1965, when Johnson ordered the first bombing raids on North Vietnamese targets. At the University of Michigan, liberal faculty organized a teach-in against U.S. Vietnam policy that inspired scores of similar events on campuses all across the nation. In April, SDS attracted 25,000 marchers for the first anti-Vietnam protest rally in Washington. Later that year, after the first American combat troops arrived in Vietnam, peace activists and civil rights leaders formed the National Committee to End the War in Vietnam. From this group came the International Days of Protest, which mounted a major antiwar parade down New York's Fifth Avenue. Meanwhile, in the Bay Area, the Vietnam Day Committee, composed of Berkeley Free Speech activists, pacifists, and assorted radicals, tried to shut down the Oakland Army Terminal, the departure point for men and matériel going to Vietnam.

Over the next three years, the antiwar movement became more inventive in attracting media attention and raising the level of confrontation with the "war makers." Protesters burned their draft cards for the first time in mid-1965 and Congress quickly made the practice a crime. The following year saw the first antiwar organizing among soldiers on active duty and the first demonstrations against campus recruiters for Dow Chemical, maker of napalm, an incendiary substance that destroyed the flesh of its victims. In 1967, at the Spring Mobilization's New York demonstration, Martin Luther King, Jr., broke publicly with the Johnson administration's foreign policy and demanded that the United States get out of Vietnam. That fall, the MOBE (the National Mobilization to End the War in Vietnam) arranged a massive march on the Pentagon in Washington led by two counterculture jesters, Abbie Hoffman and Jerry Rubin.

A considerable segment of the American public, especially before 1968, disagreed with the protesters. Many of the nation's "hawks" considered the antiwar movement a first cousin of treason, a feeling apparently confirmed by the defiant use by some protesters of Vietcong and North Vietnamese flags and anti-American slogans at marches and rallies. Yet constant exposure to the war rapidly eroded public support for American policy. Vietnam, unlike its predecessors, was a "living room" war where every night civilians at home could see the smoldering villages, the disfigured civilians, the dead and wounded American soldiers on their TV screens. The public found the images sickening and recoiled from the war that produced them.

At the end of 1967, Allard Lowenstein, a left-liberal activist for civil rights and other causes, talked "dovish" Wisconsin Senator Eugene McCarthy into challenging Johnson on a peace plank for the 1968 Democratic presidential nomination. McCarthy's near victory in the March New Hampshire primary, followed soon after by the entrance into the campaign of Robert Kennedy, helped convince Johnson that he should not run again. In August, the peace activists made a shambles of the Democratic National Convention and helped, with some malice aforethought, to elect Nixon the thirty-seventh president.

Nixon as president also had to contend with a militant peace movement. In 1970, ostensibly to "interdict" Communist supplies and men slipping into South Vietnam, he dispatched several thousand U.S. troops from Vietnam into neutral Cambodia. The campuses erupted with passionate demonstrations. At Kent State in Ohio, the state National Guard fired on student demonstrators, killing four. Five hundred campuses shut down in protest, fifty for the remainder of the semester.

This was the peak of anti-Vietnam protest. As Nixon's new Vietnamization policy reduced the number of U.S. troops in Southeast Asia, the demonstrations inevitably dwindled. A small remnant of young men and women who had lost their faith in America over Vietnam continued to fight "the system," some from underground, but the peace movement itself had evaporated.

To the thousands of Americans who had joined or supported the antiwar movement its success seemed clear: it had ended the war. But had it?

Neither Johnson nor Nixon was willing to admit that the antiwar protests influenced their decisions. To concede otherwise would have encouraged the demonstrators and allowed foreign policy to be made on the streets. Yet they deeply feared the movement. The policy makers in Washington were certain that the protests and demonstrations reinforced the Vietnamese Communists' refusal to accept a peace compromise. And they were partly right. The Hanoi government counted on domestic opposition in America, more than on its own military prowess, to compel American withdrawal from Vietnam.

And Hanoi's calculations were on target. With the passing months, many moderate, mainstream Americans, whatever they thought of the war itself, grew fearful of the violence and defiance that was tearing the nation's social fabric to tatters. Their defection could not be ignored by the political leaders in Washington. By 1970 or 1971, moreover, draft resistance, conscientious objection, and escape by young men to Canada had virtually made the draft inoperative.

And despite the denials, the policy makers themselves did not have skins thick enough to ignore the chaos that the war was creating on the streets and campuses of the nation. Several of Johnson's closest advisers, especially those with adult children, found their domestic lives disrupted by passionate hatred of the war at their own dinner tables. The resignation of Secretary of Defense Robert McNamara in early 1968 was influenced by the antiwar commitment of his son.

Both Johnson and Nixon tried to weaken the antiwar movement through federal prosecutions for undermining the draft and by "dirty tricks"—rumormongering to damage the antiwar leaders' reputations and IRS investigations to tie them up in tax litigation. These moves undoubtedly made the lives of antiwar leaders difficult. But they failed to seriously blunt their efforts. And in the end, these efforts succeeded: For good or ill, the antiwar movement helped defeat the United States in Vietnam.

SDS and Vietnam

In April 1965, SDS led the first anti-Vietnam march on Washington. The demonstration, conceived the previous December, excited wide interest among the emerging and reemerging left. All the existing peace-movement groups pledged their support, as did several liberal unions and even the New York Reform Democrats, liberal challengers to the city's Tammany machine. To the dismay of liberals and democratic socialists, the SDS leaders—long impatient with the anti-Communism of their parent organization, the League for Industrial Democracy—refused to exclude from the march outright Marxist groups like the Communist DuBois Clubs, the Maoist May 2nd Movement, and the Trotskyists. Money for the rally came from folk singer Joan Baez and radical troubadour Pete Seeger, as well as from Martin Peretz, a young Harvard professor married to heiress Anne Farnsworth.

The weather was glorious as 25,000 opponents of the war converged on the nation's capital. The largest contingent consisted of college students, many recently converted to antiwar positions by the campus teach-ins. The rally began outside the White House and then moved on to the Mall. The format of the demonstration was the mixture that would become standard at peace rallies: protest songs, chants, speeches by organizers and celebrities or semicelebrities, and visits to politicians' offices to present petitions.

This excerpt is from the talk, at the rally's end, by Paul Potter, SDS's president. A farm boy from Illinois, the twenty-five-year-old Potter had acquired his radical politics at the University of Michigan, birthplace of SDS, where he had been a graduate student. It is a fine example of the affecting rhetoric that the young SDS idealists and the student rebels would master in their battle against the system. At its end, Potter received an ovation that exceeded any other speaker's.

One rhetorical device that proved especially effective was Potter's play on the theme of "the system." Until now SDS had avoided Marxist terminology in its polemics. But now, its president was prodding his audience to identify the villain in Vietnam as capitalism. The speech marks a small step along SDS's road to the far left.

[*Paul Potter, speech to the April 17, 1965, march on Washington,* **National Guardian,** *April 29, 1965; excerpted in Massimo Teodori, ed.,* **The New Left: A Documentary History** *(Indianapolis and New York: Bobbs-Merrill, 1969), pp. 246–48.*]

THE INCREDIBLE WAR

The incredible war in Vietnam has provided the razor, the terrifying sharp cutting edge that has finally severed the last vestiges of illusion that morality and democracy are the guiding principles of American foreign policy. The saccharine, self-righteous moralism that promises the Vietnamese a billion dollars of economic aid at the very moment we are delivering billions for economic and social destruction and political repression is rapidly losing what power it might ever have had to reassure us about the decency of our foreign policy. The further we explore the reality of what this country is doing and planning in Vietnam, the more we are driven toward the conclusion of Senator Morse that the U.S. may well be the greatest threat to peace in the world today. . . .

The President says that we are defending freedom in Vietnam. Whose freedom? Not the freedom of the Vietnamese. The first act of the first dictator (Diem) the U.S. installed in Vietnam was to systematically begin the persecution of all political opposition, non-Communist as well as Communist. . . .

The pattern of repression and destruction that we have developed and justified in the war is so thorough that it can only be called "cultural genocide." I am not simply talking about napalm or gas or crop destruction or torture hurled indiscriminately on women and children, insurgent and neutral, upon the first suspicion of rebel activity. That in itself is horrendous and incredible beyond belief. But it is only part of a large pattern of destruction to the very fabric of the country. We have uprooted the people from the land and imprisoned them in concentration camps called "sunrise villages." Through conscription and direct political intervention and control we have broken or destroyed local customs and traditions, trampled upon those things of value which give dignity and purpose to life. . . .

Not even the President can say that this is war to defend the freedom of the Vietnamese people. Perhaps what the President means when he speaks of freedom is the freedom of the Americans.

What in fact has the war done for freedom in America? It has led to even more vigorous governmental efforts to control information, manipulate the press, and pressure and persuade the public through distorted or downright dishonest documents such as the White Paper on Vietnam. . . .

In many ways this is an unusual march, because the large majority of the people here are not involved in a peace movement as their primary basis of concern. What is exciting about the participants in this march is that so many of us view ourselves consciously as participants as well in a movement to build a more decent society. There are students here who have been involved in protest over the quality and kind of education they are receiving in growingly bureaucratized, depersonalized institutions called universities; there are Negroes from Mississippi and Alabama who are struggling against the tyranny and repression of those states; there are poor people here—Negro and white—from Northern urban areas who are attempting to build movements that abolish poverty and secure democracy; there are faculty who are beginning to question the relevance of their institutions to the critical problems facing the society. . . .

The President mocks freedom if he insists that the war in Vietnam is a defense of American freedom. Perhaps the only freedom that this war protects is the freedom of the warhawks in the Pentagon and the State Department to "experiment" with "counter-insurgency" and guerrilla warfare in Vietnam. Vietnam, we may say, is a "laboratory" run by a new breed of gamesmen who approach war as a kind of rational exercise in international power politics. . . .

Thus far the war in Vietnam has only dramatized the demand of ordinary people to have some opportunity to make their own lives, and of their unwillingness, even under incredible odds, to give up the struggle against external domination. We are told however that that struggle can be legitimately suppressed since it might lead to the development of a Communist system—and before that menace, all criticism is supposed to melt.

This is a critical point, and there are several things that must be said here—not by way of celebration, but because I think they are the truth. First, if this country were serious about giving the people of Vietnam some alternative to a Communist social revolution, that opportunity was sacrificed in 1954 when we helped to install Diem and his repression of non-Communist movements. There is no indication that we were serious about that goal—that we were ever willing to contemplate the risks of allowing the Vietnamese to choose their own destinies. Second, those people who insist now that Vietnam can be neutralized are for the most part looking for a sugar coating to cover the bitter pill. We must accept the consequences that calling for an end of the war in Vietnam is in fact allowing for the likelihood that a Vietnam without war will be a self-styled Communist Vietnam. Third, this country must come to understand that the creation of a Communist country in the world today is not an ultimate defeat. If people are given the opportunity to choose their own lives, it is likely that some of them will choose what we have called "Communist systems." . . . And yet the war that we are creating and escalating in Southeast Asia is rapidly eroding the base of independence of North Vietnam as it is forced to turn to China and the Soviet Union.

But the war goes on; the freedom to conduct that war depends on the dehumanization not only of Vietnamese people but of Americans as well: it depends on the construction of a system of premises and thinking that insulates the President and his advisers thoroughly and completely from the human consequences of the decisions they make. I do not believe that the President or Mr. Rusk or Mr. McNamara or even McGeorge Bundy are particularly evil men. If asked to throw napalm on the back of a ten-year-old child, they would shrink in horror—but their decisions have led to mutilation and death of thousands and thousands of people.

What kind of system is it that allows "good" men to make those kinds of decisions? What kind of system is it that justifies the U.S. or any country seizing the destinies of the Vietnamese people and using them callously for our own purpose? What kind of system is it that disenfranchises people in the South, leaves millions upon millions of people throughout the country impoverished and excluded from the mainstream and promise of American society, that creates faceless and terrible bureaucracies and makes those the place where people spend their lives and do their work, that consistently puts material values before human values—and still persists in calling itself free and still persists in finding itself fit to police the world? . . .

We must name that system. We must name it, describe it, analyze it, understand it, and change it. For it is only when that system is changed and brought under control that there can be any hope for stopping the forces that create a war in Vietnam today or a murder in the South tomorrow. . . .

If the people of this country are to end the war in Vietnam, and to change the institutions which create it, then, the people of this country must create a massive social movement—and if that can be built around the issue of Vietnam, then that is what we must do. . . .

But that means that we build a movement that works not simply in Washington but in communities and with the problems that face people throughout the society. That means that we build a movement that understands Vietnam, in all its horror, as but a symptom of a deeper malaise, that we build a movement that makes possible the implementation of the values that would have prevented Vietnam, a movement based on the integrity of man and a belief in man's capacity to determine his own life; a movement that does not exclude people because they are too poor or have been held down; a movement that has the capacity to tolerate all of the formulations of society that men may choose to strive for; a movement that will build on the new and creative forms of protest that are beginning to emerge, such as the teach-in, and extend their efforts and intensify them; a movement that will not tolerate the escalation or prolongation of this war but will, if necessary, respond to the Administration war effort with massive civil disobedience all over the country that will wrench the country into a confrontation with the issues of the war; a movement that must of necessity reach out to all those people in Vietnam or elsewhere who are struggling to find decency and control for their lives.

For in a strange way the people of Vietnam and the people on this demonstration are united in much more than a common concern that the war be ended. In both countries there are people struggling to build a movement that has the power to change their condition. The system that frustrates these movements is the same. All our lives, our destinies, our very hopes to live depend on our ability to overcome that system. . . .

SANE

SANE *was not an acronym like* NOW *or* RADAR—*a word derived from the first letters of a longer phrase. It stood for National Committee for a Sane Nuclear Policy. The full name expresses its origins: it began as a "ban the bomb" organization in 1957, at a time when nuclear testing and the nuclear arms race seemed to many the most urgent dangers of the cold war.*

SANE's founders were liberals and moderate pacifists who had long been active as fighters for peace and for worthy social causes. Many were "one-worlders," members of the United World Federalists who believed in some sort of world government. Mostly well-educated professionals, they feared nuclear war and the accruing dangers of atmospheric pollution from nuclear testing. Few were wealthy, but many were famous or influential. Among the founders were Norman Cousins, editor of the Saturday Review; *Erich Fromm, the famous psychiatrist; theologian Paul Tillich; novelists James Jones and John Hersey; Edward Sparling, president of Roosevelt University; Walter Reuther, head of the powerful United Automobile Workers; Norman Thomas, the venerable socialist leader; biologist Linus Pauling; and Lewis Mumford, the prominent architecture critic and social philosopher. The new organization would devote its energies to alerting the American public to the dangers of the Soviet–U.S. nuclear rivalry and serve as an organizer and coordinator of protest and propaganda against "the bomb."*

SANE's campaign touched a chord in the American people. Membership leaped to 25,000 in 130 local chapters within a few months. But it also offended hardened cold warriors and militant anti-Communists, who suspected the movement was controlled by "reds." In May 1960, Senator Thomas Dodd of Connecticut accused SANE of playing into Soviet hands by supporting a test ban treaty. He soon dragged SANE leader Harry Abrams before his Senate Internal Security Subcommittee and demanded that he reveal whether he had been a member of the Communist Party. Abrams refused to answer on the grounds of self-incrimination, and co-chairman Cousins fired him. Fearing that SANE would be tagged as a fellow-traveling group, the SANE board of directors soon after excluded anyone from policy-making positions who could not apply the same standards to both the United States and the Soviet Union. Many of SANE's more radical leaders considered this red-baiting and resigned from the organization.

SANE recovered and went on to lead the test ban movement. In July 1963, its efforts were rewarded with the signing of a partial test ban treaty, between the Soviet Union and the United States, that prohibited atmospheric testing of nuclear weapons but allowed underground detonations. The nuclear arms race continued, but at least the world's air and water would not be further contaminated with radioactive fall-out. SANE continued to oppose the arms race and later joined the anti-Vietnam coali-tion as part of its moderate wing.

This selection is from a SANE pamphlet of 1961 or 1962. Its wealth of technical detail may seem inappropriate for a propaganda document. But the cold statistics by themselves conveyed to readers the ominous quality of nuclear fallout that the test ban advocates desired.

[SANE, "Facts You Should Know About Nuclear Fallout," pamphlet in Tamiment Library, New York University.]

FACTS YOU SHOULD KNOW ABOUT NUCLEAR FALLOUT

What is fallout?

Fallout consists of tiny particles of radioactive elements which are created by nuclear explosions. These are carried aloft by the blast, dispersed around the globe, and gradually "fall out" to earth.

Is fallout uniform throughout the world?

No. Twice as much falls in the north temperate zone as elsewhere—the zone where we live. It is apparently heavier in the dairy and wheat states of the United States than anywhere else in the world, according to Dr. Willard F. Libby, former AEC scientist.

Is fallout all Strontium-90?

Fallout consists of many elements which remain radioactive for varying lengths of time. We have been most concerned about Sr-90 because it is similar to calcium and gets involved in the same biological processes. Sr-90 falls on the leaves of plants and on the soil and is picked up by the roots, is eaten by animals or man, and finds its way into the bone structure of men and animals just as calcium does.

Other radioactive nucleides which present known dangers to humans are: Cesium-137 / Iodine-131 / Carbon-14 / Strontium-89 / Barium-140 / Cesium-144 / Zirconium-95. (The number is the atomic weight.)

What do these fallout particles do?

Whether they find their way into bone as does Sr-90, into muscles and tissues as do Cesium-137 and Carbon-14, or into the thyroid gland as does Iodine-131, they act like little X-ray machines emitting a continuous bombardment of high energy particles.

Strontium-90 can cause leukemia and bone cancer / *Iodine-131* can cause cancer of the thyroid / *Cesium-137* and *Carbon-14* can cause *genetic* damage, changing the characteristics we pass on to our children, and resulting in stillbirths, neonatal deaths, and malformations of various kinds.

Is there any proof that these elements cause severe damage?

There is proof that *all* radiation causes damage of this kind. We should add life-shortening effects and lowered resistance to diseases as well. There is no proof that any *particular* case is caused by fallout, by radiation from another source or from some other cause. Such cases won't come tagged "this one died from fallout." But we do have some very well-educated estimates of what the damage will be:

> *"An estimated total of 25,000 to 150,000 cases of leukemia will ultimately occur, if tests are stopped in 1958, from tests already held."*

(These figures apply only if there is no "threshold" below which no effect is observable. Most recent evidence from the survivors at Hiroshima indicates that this is the case.)

> *"An estimated total of 2,500 to 100,000 genetic defects will occur over subsequent years from tests already held."*—Table II, page 42, United Nations Report on Radiation.

The heaviest tests came after these estimates were made.

As regards Carbon-14, a report prepared by the Atomic Energy Commission, *The Biological Hazard to Man of Carbon-14 from Nuclear Weapons,* concludes that bomb tests to September 1958 would cause 100,000 gross physical or mental defects, 360,000 cases of stillbirths and childhood deaths, and 900,000 cases of embryonic and neonatal deaths from this cause alone.

Why do many people say the effects of fallout are negligible?

If you are concerned about what happens to people, they are not negligible, for, as you can see, large absolute numbers of people are involved. Apologists for testing feel that these people represent a "negligible" percentage of the world's population.

Why is it said that a luminous wrist watch dial is more dangerous than fallout?

It has been said, all right, but it doesn't mean much. Don't scrape the radium off the dial and eat it, as you do fallout. It is not harmless when it settles in bones. Radium dial painters have a history of dying from bone cancer. You may also be interested to know that wrist watches painted with Strontium-90 have been forbidden by the AEC as being too dangerous.

Another argument we hear is that exposure from fallout is no more dangerous than moving from San Francisco to Denver.

Old fables die hard. The basis for this story is that radiation from cosmic rays increases with altitude. The same sort of thing has been said about localities where natural radioactivity in drinking water is higher than usual, or about high altitude localities like Tibet.

It is true that no undesirable effects have been noted from such changes of location. This may be only because no one has yet studied them sufficiently to know. One place a study was made that does bear on this: In New York, Dr. William T. Gentry of the New York Board of Health in Syracuse found that where natural radioactivity was higher, the number of malformed births increased consistently. Coincidence? Not likely.

But the fact is that the cosmic-ray and watch-dial stories, and others of a similar nature, have been based on poor estimates of the amount of radiation due to fallout. Most such estimates are based on "total body *external* dose" and ignore the fact that the intensest radiation comes from concentrations of fallout at tiny spots *within the body*, magnifying the effect, and *not* from fallout on the ground.

Isn't it true that fallout is less dangerous than X-rays?

X-rays are not harmless. Remember that when you submit to massive irradiation from X-rays, you do so at a risk and for a specific purpose. You should know, for instance, that pelvic X-rays given in pregnancy double the chances of your child's having cancer in the first ten years of his life, according to Dr. Jack Schubert, formerly of Argonne National Laboratory. In the case of fallout, you are giving *whole populations* a slight X-ray over and above any other radiation that they receive, and one that they didn't ask for. This adds up to a tremendous effect, as we have seen from the figures quoted above.

Is natural radiation more powerful in its effect than fallout?

Natural or background radiation has always been with us. But it hasn't been harmless. It is thought to cause hundreds of thousands of mutations a year, and probably also a certain percentage of the cases of leukemia. Any *added* radiation causes *added* cases. The effects of fallout will cause radiation equal to or surpassing background radiation in a large segment of the population, according to AEC testimony. And whatever is received from fallout is *in addition* to what was already there, so that if you add an amount equal to background, you double the amount received.

Is there a level below which no damage is done by radiation?

This is the "threshold" idea. There is no threshold for genetic effects. A proportional number of mutations occur for any amount of radiation, big or small. For somatic effects, including those causing cancer, there is apparently no threshold either. The most recent results from Hiroshima (not included in the Congressional hearings of May 1959) show that the incidence of leukemia was exactly proportional to the radiation received even to the lowest levels.

Have safe standards been established?

So-called "maximum permissible" doses have been set. Basically, there is no safe dose, since any amount of radiation causes damage. The question really is, how much additional danger do you want to allow? And this is a political, philosophical, or moral question, not a scientific one.

What are the "permissible" doses now in use?

Only recently have any levels been suggested for general populations. Formerly the suggestions referred basically to atomic workers. The

International Commission on Radiological Protection has suggested that the level be 33 strontium units in foodstuffs. A strontium unit is equal to one micromicrocurie of strontium per gram of calcium. This suggested level will probably create a bone burden about equal to natural background, or, in other words, double the amount to which we would otherwise be a subject. Older levels of 100 and 200 strontium units were used by the AEC.

More recently, the Federal Radiation Council has set the following standards:

| | *Micromicrocuries per day* | | |
	Range I	Range II	Range III
Radium-226	0–2	2–20	20–200
Iodine-131	0–10	10–100	100–1,000
Strontium-90	0–20	20–200	200–2,000
Strontium-89	0–200	200–2,000	2,000–20,000

Range I calls for "periodic confirmatory surveillance as necessary," Range II for "quantitative surveillance and routine control," and Range III for "evaluation and application of additional control measures as necessary."

Who is responsible for protecting the public?

The Federal Radiation Council is merely an interagency committee consisting of the secretaries of Defense, Commerce, Labor, and Health, Education and Welfare, and the chairman of the Atomic Energy Commission. This hardly inspires confidence that the public welfare is foremost.

The Federal Radiation Council standards are only a guide for government agencies, and no one knows what the phrase "control measures" means. In the past, the government has been more interested in reassuring the public than in protecting it.

Have all reports shown food to be well below the danger levels?

No. The level of radioactive iodine in milk reached high into Range III for several months in 1958 and again in September and October of 1961. Strontium-90 in many wheat samples ranged from 100 to 200 strontium units in 1958 and 1959. The high for milk was reached in Mandan, North Dakota—47.5 strontium units—well above the levels recommended by the International Commission on Radiological Protection. With renewed testing, these levels will be equaled or surpassed.

Why is the strontium unit count higher in other foods than in milk?

The strontium-to-calcium ratio is more favorable in milk, and then, too, the cows screen out a proportion of the strontium from the milk they produce. So do nursing mothers. This is a new argument for breast feeding!

Can the dangerous Strontium-90 be removed from milk?

Yes. However, milk is not now being decontaminated. The Department of Agriculture and other agencies have developed methods which seem practical on a commercial scale. Unfortunately, Strontium-90 cannot be extracted from other foods.

What can I do to protect my children?

From Iodine-131: This decays by one-half each eight days, and is therefore only dangerous during and shortly after atmospheric testing. During these times, use powdered or canned milk. Ask your doctor for instructions on adding nonradioactive iodine to the diets of children or expectant mothers. A small amount will reduce the accumulation of radioactive iodine 100 times.

From Strontium-90: Do not give up the use of milk. It is still the safest food we have. There is a possibility that the uptake of Strontium-90 can be reduced by adding uncontaminated calcium to the diet. Again, this should be done only under medical guidance. In addition, clean foods thoroughly, especially leafy vegetables. Wash or peel fruits. This will reduce greatly the surface contamination, but not that which was taken up by the roots.

Unfortunately, whole grains are particularly high in radioactivity. White flour and white rice contain much less. We have the unhappy choice of selecting poorer foods or more strontium.

What else can I do?

You can demand the decontamination of milk. Ask the government to subsidize the equipment. You can urge dairies to feed cows uncontaminated food during times of high Iodine-131 activity, and to set aside current milk production until the iodine has had time to decay, or use it for butter, cheese, powdered milk, which will allow time for decay. You can ask dairies to feed uncontaminated calcium to the cows, which will reduce the amount of Strontium-90 in the milk. You can urge full and frank information from the government, and ask that the jurisdiction of radiation be given to the Public Health Service entirely.

But more important, you can join with those who are working to end permanently all nuclear tests by all nations. You can both safeguard your children's health now and help to head off the nuclear catastrophe which threatens the world.

The Mobe

The anti-Vietnam movement spawned a bewildering array of organizations. Some of these represented professional groups (like Clergy Concerned About Vietnam, and the Lawyers Committee on American Policy Toward Vietnam). Others spoke to women (Women Strike for Peace) or students (Student Peace Union). Several of the small Marxist splinters formed their own anti-Vietnam fronts or sought to dominate existing ones (the Trotskyist Student Mobilization Committee; the Maoist May 2nd Movement). But several umbrella oganizations, usually called the "mobilization" (Mobe), were also created to coordinate the diverse groups for major demonstrations. Following the longtime practice of American pacifists, the various mobilizations, beginning in 1967, mounted demonstrations in San Francisco, New York, and Washington in the spring and fall of each year. These protests did not cease with the end of the Johnson administration. If anything, the antiwar protesters trusted Richard Nixon even less than Lyndon Johnson, and through Nixon's first term the antiwar protests expanded and deepened.

This flier was distributed by the New Mobilization, the coordinating group for a major march on Washington in November 1969. The rally was a joint demonstration with the Moratorium, a student organization that preferred local "actions" to the large, nationally visible marches preferred by the Mobe. In all, the demonstration brought as many as a half a million men and women to Washington for the usual round of speeches, songs, and ceremonies, the latter including a solemn March Against Death to commemorate the men who had lost their lives in the interminable war. At a few spots during the three-day event, violence erupted, deliberately provoked by zealots and crazies. But on the whole, it was an impressive political assembly. According to columnist Nicholas von Hoffman, "It was the best, it was the biggest, it was the last of the antiwar [mass] demonstrations."

[New Mobilization Committee to End the War in Vietnam, "March Against Death—A Vietnam Memorial," November 13–15, 1969, pamphlet in Tamiment Library, New York University.]

MARCH AGAINST DEATH—A VIETNAM MEMORIAL

The New Mobilization Committee to End the War in Vietnam is calling the American people to Washington, D.C. to March Against Death in Vietnam, and to demonstrate for life; for an immediate and unconditional withdrawal of all U.S. troops from Vietnam; for self-determination for Vietnam and black America; for an end to poverty and racism.

The Fall Offensive of the New Mobilization incorporates a variety of antiwar activities taking place all over the United States. It will culminate with the massing of many thousands of people in Washington, D.C. for the March Against Death (Nov. 13–15) and finally end on Nov. 15 with a mass march and rally—the most significant and possibly the largest antiwar action this country has ever seen.

March Against Death

At midnight, Nov. 13, the first of fifty state delegations totaling 43,000–45,000 persons will begin walking from Arlington National Cemetery in a solemn single-file procession past the White House to the steps of the Capitol. There will be at least as many people in each state delegation as the number of slaughtered G.I.s from that state; there will be additional people representing the cities and towns of Vietnam that have been destroyed. The marchers will all be wearing placards with the name of either a dead G.I. or a Vietnamese city or town, and as he passes the White House, each person will call out the name on his placard.

The March Against Death will conclude thirty-six hours later with a memorial service at the Capitol steps on the morning of Nov. 15, preceding the mass march and rally. The placards deposited on the Capitol steps will later be taken by representative parents of dead G.I.s, antiwar veterans and G.I. groups, clergy and Congressmen to the White House as part of the mass march and rally.

Organizing the Project

The principal resources lending strength to the March Against Death are organizations which have sponsored readings of the names of the war dead in various parts of the country: A Quaker Action Group, American Friends Service Committee, SANE, War Resisters League, Women Strike for Peace, Women's International League for Peace and Freedom, Fellowship of Reconciliation, the Resistance, Resist, Clergy and Laymen Concerned About Vietnam, and others, combined with newer groups such as the Vietnam Moratorium, veterans and G.I. groups, the next of kin of G.I.s who have been killed in Vietnam, and others that will join in.

Individual sponsors of the November actions of the New Mobilization Committee to End the War in Vietnam include: the Rev. William Sloane Coffin, Jr., Dave Dellinger, Douglas Dowd, Donald Kalish, Mrs. Martin Luther King, Jr., Sid Lens, Stewart Meacham, Sid Peck, Dr. Benjamin Spock, Cora Weiss.

What You Can Do

1. Contact the New Mobilization Washington Action Office, 1029 Vermont Ave., N.W., Washington, D.C. 20005 (phone: 202-737-8600) for the name and address of the March Against Death committee which is organizing in your area.

2. If your area has not yet had a meeting to mobilize for the March Against Death as part of its Fall Offensive to end the war, contact the Washington Action Office for speakers and literature.

3. Plan local and statewide activities focusing attention on the human and political toll of Vietnam. Reading the names of the war dead from your area and local death marches are possible activities.

4. Write your Congressmen to ask if they will participate in the March Against Death. Send the Washington office a copy of your letter. If they will not, ask how many more deaths it will take before they will publicly call for U.S. withdrawal from Vietnam.

5. The Washington Action Office for the March Against Death has leaflets for distribution and buttons and posters for sale. It is suggested that local organizing committees sell these materials as part of their own fund-raising campaign and arrange that a percentage of the profits be contributed to the New Mobilization Committee to End the War in Vietnam. Quantity price list available on request.

6. Individual contributions are, of course, especially welcome.

The Resistance

The Vietnam War was fought largely by an army of draftees. In past eras—the Civil War excepted—the draft had created a citizens' army in which all male youths, except for those in a few exempt classes, had served alike. Not so during the Sixties. Middle-class white youths could avoid military service by gaining a college deferment or a medical or mental health exemption, or by winning conscientious-objector status. Those caught by the Selective Service system were predominantly working class and disproportionately black and brown.

But however adeptly the prosperous white youths could manipulate the system, they always ran the risk of getting tangled in its web, and beyond this, pangs of conscience sometimes beset the successful draft evader. Many conscientious young men who themselves could avoid being inducted could not accept the class privilege that spared them the pain and danger of fighting while placing the burden on the poor and minorities. These considerations made the draft the natural target of the antiwar movement. But by 1967, resisting the draft also seemed a way to defeat the war machine: Deprive it of the needed manpower, and it would cease to run.

In the fall of 1967, a group calling itself the Resistance appeared on the anti-Vietnam scene. Formed in March by Stanford University undergraduates, it sought to create such extreme obstacles to the draft that Selective Service would break down. The war itself would inevitably break down soon after.

Young men of military age had already protested by burning their draft cards or returning them to the Selective Service system. Though both practices were illegal, they did not seem sufficiently militant, and in 1967, the Resistance pledged to pursue a policy of "total noncooperation with the military establishment."

This document, "We Refuse to Serve," describes the goals and tactics of the Resistance. It was handed out as a handbill to participants at the Spring (1967) Mobilization, held in April in San Francisco.

[*Resistance, "We Refuse to Serve," in Alice Lynd, ed.,* **The Resistance** *pamphlet in Tamiment Library, New York University.*]

WE REFUSE TO SERVE

I. We Refuse to Serve

In the past few months, in many parts of the country, a resistance has been forming. . . . A resistance of young men—joined together in their commitment against the war. . . .

We will renounce all deferments and refuse to cooperate with the draft in any manner, at any level. We have taken this stand for varied reasons:

opposition to conscription
opposition only to the Vietnam war
opposition to all wars and to all American military adventures.

We all agree on one point: the war in Vietnam is criminal and we must act together, at great individual risk, to stop it. Those involved must lead the American people, by their example, to understand the enormity of what their government is doing . . . that the government cannot be allowed to continue with its daily crimes. . . .

There are many ways to avoid the draft, to stay clear of this war. Most of us now have deferments . . . but all these individual outs can have no effect on the draft, the war, or the consciousness of this country. To cooperate with conscription is to perpetuate its existence, without which, the government could not wage war. We have chosen to openly defy the draft and confront the government and its war directly.

This is no small decision in a person's life. Each one realizes that refusing to cooperate with Selective Service may mean prison. Again we agree that to do anything but this is to effectively abet the war. The government will not be permitted to use us on its way to greater crimes and destruction. We prefer to resist.

The organization is an action committee, composed of those who make this commitment. We stand all-for-one, one-for-all. We are prepared to act together to support anyone singled out for arrest by every means possible, including civil disobedience and unified, public violations of the Selective Service Act. As the resistance grows, the government will either have to allow the draft noncooperators to go free and thereby swell our ranks, or fill the jails. . . .

II. The Politics of Resistance

. . . The government's success in countering the challenge of the antiwar movement is directly related to its ability to co-opt the ideals and strategy of the movement. . . . The challenge presented by the peace movement has become assimilated into the dominant structure of power, and hence transformed into an integral part of that structure. . . . To accept the bounds of the established structure of authority and to define the political action of the movement in terms of that structure, means to accept political emasculation and the inevitable co-optation of the movement's spirit and energies.

The stance of resistance is active rather than passive, offensive rather than defensive. The aim of resistance is to provoke continual confrontations with the governmental institutions linked to the war. The resistance confronts the government with an unresolvable dilemma; to prosecute and imprison us, which will generate new waves of protest and dissent of unsurpassed intensity; or to set us free, which will provide greater impetus for the expansion of the movement. . . .

III. Going Beyond Prayers to an Unjust King

. . . It is becoming increasingly clear that peace cannot be attained unless some fundamental change is first effected within American society, that there is something about the functioning of the American "system" that does not permit it to respond other than violently to the yearnings of the people it oppresses. . . . One cannot appeal to a repository of justice that does not exist. The incantation of protest must become resistance if we are to avoid the co-optation, invisibility, and sheer impotence that have, up to now, been our experience with regard to the war and the whole issue of the garrison society in America. There is, however, one potential repository of justice, and that is "the people."

... If the normal day-to-day pattern of American life were sufficiently disrupted, people in large numbers would have to begin thinking about the nature of their lives and the society around them. ... People and societies have a hard time existing out of equilibrium. If we can succeed in breaking the emptiness of the current equilibrium of American society (and it is already being severely threatened by a monstrously confusing war, and by bewildering revolt in our own cities) a new equilibrium will have to be found. ...

... Noncooperation must be seen in its larger context: a seizing of control of our own lives and a conscious effort to redirect the movement of American society.

... If all the issues can be clarified and tied together by competent community organizers, if viable courses of action can then be charted by an organized people, we will again see America moving in the direction of justice and democracy. ...

IV. The Resistance

Since the United States is engaged in criminal activity in Vietnam,

Since the major instrument of that criminal activity is the American military establishment,

Since the machinery of the military cannot effectively function without the acquiescence of the people it is supposed to represent,

Since we are young Americans who still believe in the ideals our country once stood for,

The RESISTANCE has been formed to organize and encourage resistance to, disruption of, and noncooperation with all the war-making machinery of the United States.

The RESISTANCE is a nationwide movement with organizations in New York, Illinois, Massachusetts, Iowa, Ohio, Wisconsin, Michigan, Oregon, and California.

ON OCTOBER 16, 1967, WE WILL PUBLICLY AND COLLECTIVELY RETURN OUR DRAFT CARDS TO THE SELECTIVE SERVICE SYSTEM IN MAJOR CITIES THROUGHOUT THE COUNTRY. We will clearly challenge the government's right to use any young lives for its own nefarious purposes. Our challenge will continue, and we will openly confront the Selective Service System, until the government is forced to deal with our collective action. After October 16, we will organize campuses and communities for similar waves of resistance in December, March, etc. We have gone beyond the "We Won't Go" statements in that we are renouncing all deferments, joining the forces of those who can and those who cannot afford deferments, and forcing an immediate confrontation by practicing total noncooperation with the military establishment. By turning in rather than burning our draft cards, we will be proudly giving our names to the public at large, and to the powers that be. Our hope is that upon our example, every young man in America will realize that *he* must decide whether to resist or acquiesce to the draft and the war. We are confident that many will resist. . . .

11

The Moon Race

While some Americans struggled to change the world, others were trying to escape it entirely. History will view the Sixties not only as the era of the civil rights movement, the Great Society, Vietnam, and the counterculture, but also as the decade when men first walked on the moon.

The space program was, in part, a cold war artifact. The leaders of the Soviet Union at first saw long-distance rockets primarily as devices to offset American superiority in atomic weapons and target the inaccessible American heartland in the event of war. Later, the conquest of space became a way to forge ahead of the Americans in rocket technology and demonstrate Communism's superiority over capitalism. The motives of Americans were the mirror image of the Soviets': to counter the missile threat and to prove how capitalism must inevitably win the world competition with Communism.

But both countries were also moved by more admirable motives than cold war rivalry. For thousands of years, humans have dreamed of going to the stars, of shaking off the trammels of gravity and exploring new worlds beyond our own. In the late nineteenth and early twentieth centuries, in each of the major industrial nations, visionary scientists and technicians experimented with chemically propelled rockets, the only devices that offered hope of success in finding a means to travel in space. World War II enormously advanced rocketry, as the belligerents sought new ways to destroy their enemies. The push culminated with the infamous V-2, launched by Germany against Britain in the closing months of the war. In the space race that lay ahead, both sides would employ former German rocket engineers who had worked for Adolf Hitler.

On October 4, 1957, the Russians established a clear lead when they put a sphere the size of a beach ball into orbit around the earth. Sputnik, as the Soviets called their small satellite, was not a scientific breakthrough; it was based on elementary and well-known principles. But it was an immense propaganda triumph, amplified several weeks later when they managed to put a dog into earth orbit. Today, when the USSR and the cold war are both gone, it is difficult to remember how much seemed at stake in the Soviet-American rivalry and how close the contest appeared to be in the early postwar years. For two societies dedicated alike to this-worldly success, Sputnik was an extraordinary validation of one system over the other.

Sputnik deeply wounded Americans' self-esteem. Proud of their technological prowess, they insisted on catching up and surpassing their rivals. The Eisenhower administration's initial response was dismissive, but it found it impossible to resist public pressure and soon launched a drive to equal and exceed the Soviets in space. It also endorsed the National Defense Education Act, providing generous federal support to upgrade the teaching of engineering, science, mathematics, and languages in American colleges and universities.

In December 1957, the United States was finally ready to launch a small sphere into orbit. With the whole world watching on TV, the Vanguard rocket rose four feet and then exploded on the launch pad. The media quickly labeled it "flopnik." The Soviets chortled that the United States should apply for technical assistance under the UN program of aid to backward nations.

The United States finally got its first satellite, Explorer 1, into orbit in January 1958. Later that year, strongly backed by Senate Majority Leader Lyndon Johnson, Congress established the National Aeronautics and Space Administration (NASA) to plan and administer a massive American space program. But for the remainder of the 1950s, Soviet missile and space achievements outstripped the American. In April 1961, the Soviet cosmonaut Yuri Gagarin became the first man to orbit the earth and return. In truth, the Soviet Union was starving its overall economy by pouring scarce resources into the space race, but the rest of the world perceived only the humiliation of capitalism by Communism.

It is not surprising that Kennedy accepted the space challenge with gusto. Had he not proclaimed in his inaugural address that Americans would "pay any price, bear any burden, meet any hardship, support any friend, oppose any foe, to assure the . . . success of liberty"? But beyond the cold war jingoism, he and his party were free of Eisenhower's prejudice against ambitious, expensive federal programs. During the 1960 presidential campaign, Kennedy had chided the Republicans for putting frugality before national prestige and national security. After the inauguration, he decided to put his money where his mouth was. On May 25, 1961, he appeared before Congress and, in a speech on "urgent national needs," stated that the

United States "should commit itself to achieving the goal, before this decade is out, of landing a man on the moon and returning him safely to earth."

The Apollo program under NASA was the response to Kennedy's mandate. In five years, the agency would grow tenfold in personnel and fivefold in budget. Thousands more would work for private space industry contractors. That summer, NASA chose Cape Canaveral, on Florida's east coast, as the launch site for the moon shot. Later in the year, the Army Corps of Engineers broke ground near Houston for the Manned Spaceflight Center where planning for the moon launches would be conducted and the "missions" monitored. NASA would eventually spread around the federal largess through lucrative contracts to firms and universities scattered strategically across the American landscape.

By this time, riding a Mercury rocket, astronaut Alan Shepard had soared high over the Atlantic in ballistic flight and returned safely to earth. In February 1962, John Glenn became the first American to be put into orbit around the earth. America was clearly catching up. But the technical problems of an actual moon landing were immense and the means to achieve it uncertain. In the end, NASA chose a compromise mode called LOR—lunar-orbit rendezvous—to make the trip. A three-stage rocket from earth would travel to the moon and then enter its orbit. While two astronauts descended to the surface in a special landing vehicle, a third would remain behind in the command module circling the earth's satellite. The moon crew would perform their experiments, raise a flag, collect lunar rocks and so forth, and return to the orbiting command module in the landing vehicle. The module, with the crew aboard, would break out of moon orbit, and all three astronauts would depart for earth.

The country followed the Apollo program with enormous interest. The media, abetted by NASA officials eager to sustain public support for a costly program, made the panel of Apollo astronauts into all-American heroes. Meanwhile, James Webb, NASA head, assured the public that the engineering and scientific knowledge acquired in the course of the project would be useful for solving practical and even social problems on earth. But despite the public relations effort, the moon race had its enemies among social activists and purists in the scientific community. Fortunately for the program, after November 1963, the man in the White House was Lyndon Johnson, one of the creators of NASA and a man-on-the-moon enthusiast who had no intention of abandoning the program of his predecessor.

The Apollo launch series, using the newly developed Saturn rockets, began in tragedy. In the late afternoon of January 27, 1967, three astronauts, Virgil Grissom, Edward White, and Roger Chaffee, strapped into the spacecraft to test it for launch the following month, became the first American casualties of the moon race when a spark ignited some combustible materials and raced through the craft in the pure oxygen atmosphere. When the hatches were finally pried off, all three men were dead. After the Apollo 1 disaster, there were inevitable calls to discontinue the project. But NASA rallied, and after changes in equipment and procedures, the Apollo program regained momentum.

Apollo 8, the first successful manned launch using the Saturn, blasted off from the Kennedy Space Center on December 21, 1968. Designed as a lunar orbital trip, the mission enabled men for the first time to break the bounds of earth. On Monday afternoon of the twenty-third, the astronauts passed the earth's gravitational dominance; early the next morning, they whipped behind the moon, the side no human had ever seen.

There were two more missions before the moon landing. Apollo 9, in March 1969, tested the deployment in earth orbit of the lunar module, the vehicle designed to actually touch the moon's surface. Apollo 10, in May, was the dress rehearsal before the landing. The moon-landing launch itself, the culmination of eight years of effort, came on July 16. John Kennedy was now dead and Lyndon Johnson had retired. Richard Nixon, no great friend of the moon-landing program, would be the political beneficiary of his Democratic predecessors' faith and work.

Neil Armstrong, Edwin ("Buzz") Aldrin, and Michael Collins, the three brave, young high achievers from the Apollo roster who held the winning numbers, blasted off in Apollo 11 in a letter-perfect launch from the Space Center at 9:32 A.M. They went into low lunar orbit on July 19. At 4:17 Eastern Daylight Time the following day, the lunar module *Eagle* touched the moon's surface. Three hours later, Neil Armstrong became the first human to walk on another planetary body. The astronauts returned to earth to heroes' welcomes on July 24.

Apollo 11 was followed by five more successful moon landings through late 1972. The program was then discontinued. It had cost $25 billion dollars and the lives of at least three men to prove that the "American way" was better than the alternative. But the project was also a monument to human bravery and genius and a giant boost to the human imagination.

John F. Kennedy Pledges to Reach the Moon

Few presidents in this century have been as conscious of the need to preserve and augment America's prestige in the world as John F. Kennedy. The Kennedys had been raised in a competitive family circle where coming in first—at sailing, at touch football, at argument—was the way to please the family patriarch, Joseph Kennedy. John, the second son, had been relieved of some of this burden by his physical afflictions, but he never entirely escaped the need to win. As president, he projected this urge onto the nation he led.

In May 1961, President John Kennedy felt particularly insecure. The invasion of Castro's Cuba by American-sponsored Cuban exiles had just failed spectacularly and left him looking indecisive and weak. At the recent summit meeting in Vienna, Khrushchev had bullied him by blustering and threatening war over Berlin. The untried president, then, could not ignore recent Soviet successes in space and the relative lag in America's performance.

But his interest in surpassing the Soviets in space was not solely an extension of his inner needs. America's role as chief defender of the liberal capitalist world made a major response to Sputnik unavoidable. The United States could not have ducked the Soviet challenge. We know today that the Soviet command economy was a dead end that even the Russians would repudiate. But in the early 1960s, the Soviet model of development had great appeal to many new nations. Without the American display of technical and scientific prowess that the moon race demonstrated, how many more nations might have succumbed to the Soviet illusion?

Nor was Kennedy indifferent to the adventurous side of landing a man on the moon. He always admired courage, and what better arena for its display than the unknown, unchartered domain of space?

The document below is an excerpt from the special message in which Kennedy proposed landing a man on the moon before the decade ended. It is significant that the proposal was part of a request to Congress for funds to augment American military power against the Soviet rival.

[*John F. Kennedy, May 25, 1961,* **Public Papers of the Presidents of the United States, John F. Kennedy, 1961** *(Washington, DC: U.S. Government Printing Office, 1962), pp. 403–405.*]

JOHN F. KENNEDY PROPOSES SENDING A MAN TO THE MOON

... [I]f we are to win the battle that is now going on around the world between freedom and tyranny, the dramatic achievements in space which occurred in recent weeks should have made it clear to us all, as did the Sputnik in 1957, the impact of this adventure on the minds of men everywhere, who are attempting to make a determination of which road they should take. Since early in my term, our efforts in space have been under review. With the advice of the Vice President [Lyndon Johnson], who is chairman of the National Space Council, we have examined where we are strong and where we are not, where we may succeed and where we may not. Now it is time to take longer strides—time for a great new American enterprise—time for this nation to take a clearly leading role in space achievement, which in many ways may hold the key to our future on earth.

I believe we possess all the resources and talents necessary. But the facts of the matter are that we have never made the national decisions or marshaled the resources required for such leadership. We have never specified long-range goals on an urgent time schedule, or managed our resources and our time so as to insure their fulfillment.

Recognizing the head start obtained by the Soviets with their large rocket engines, which gives them many months of lead-time, and recognizing the likelihood that they will exploit this lead for some time to come in still more impressive successes, we nevertheless are required to make new efforts of our own. For while we cannot guarantee that we shall one day be first, we can guarantee that any failure to make this effort will make us last. We take an additional risk by making it in full view of the world, but as shown by the feat of astronaut [Alan] Shepard,* this very risk enhances our stature when we are successful. But this is not merely a race. Space is open to us now; and our eagerness to share its meaning is not governed by the efforts of others. We go into space because whatever mankind must undertake, free men must fully share.

I therefore ask the Congress, above and beyond the increases I have earlier requested for space activities, to provide the funds which are needed to meet the following national goals:

First, I believe this nation should commit itself to achieving the goal, before this decade is out, of landing a man on the moon and returning him safely to the earth. No single space project in this period will be more impressive to mankind, or more important for the long-range exploration of space; and none will be so difficult or expensive to accomplish. We propose to accelerate the development of the appropriate lunar space craft. We propose to develop alternate liquid and solid fuel boosters, much larger than any now being developed, until certain which is superior. We propose additional funds for other engine development and for unmanned explorations—explorations which are particularly important for one purpose which this nation will never overlook: the survival of the man who first makes this daring flight. But in a very real sense, it will not be one man going to the moon—if we make the judgment affirmatively, it will be an entire nation. For all of us must work to put him there.

*Some weeks earlier, navy commander Shepard had been successfully sent aloft on a fifteen-minute suborbital flight. Americans had cheered—ed.

Secondly, an additional 23 million dollars, together with 7 million dollars already available, will accelerate development of the Rover nuclear rocket. . . .

Third, an additional 75 million dollars . . . will help give us at the earliest possible time a satellite system for world-wide weather observation.

Let it be clear . . . that I am asking the Congress and the country to accept a firm commitment to a new course of action—a course which will last for many years and carry very heavy costs: 531 million dollars in fiscal '62—an estimated seven to nine billion dollars additional over the next five years. . . .

Now this is a choice which this country must make, and I am confident that under the leadership of the Space Committees of Congress, and the Appropriating Committees, that you will consider the matter carefully.

It is a most important decision we make as a nation. But all of you have lived through the last four years and have seen the significance of space and the adventures in space, and no one can predict with certainty what the ultimate meaning will be of mastery of space.

I believe we should go to the moon. But I think every citizen of this country as well as the members of Congress should consider the matter carefully in making their judgment. . . .

This decision demands a major national commitment of scientific and technical manpower, materiel, and facilities, and the possibility of diversion from other important activities where they are already thinly spread. It means a degree of dedication, organization, and discipline which have not always characterized our research and development efforts. It means that we cannot afford undue work stoppages, inflated costs of materiel or talent, wasteful interagency rivalries, or high turnover of key personnel.

New objectives and new money cannot solve these problems. They could, in fact, aggravate them further—unless every scientist, every engineer, every serviceman, every technician, contractor, and civil servant gives his personal pledge that this nation will move forward with the full speed of freedom, in the exciting adventure of space.

Moonwalk

More than half a billion TV viewers watched Neil Armstrong place his foot on the "fine and powdery" surface of the moon. The Columbia, *the command vessel that had carried the three astronauts from the earth, had gone into lunar orbit on July 20, 1969, after its four-day, 240,000-mile journey from Cape Kennedy. Now came the critical part. Donning a bulky spacesuit and support backpack, Edwin ("Buzz") Aldrin and Armstrong squeezed into* Eagle, *the insectlike lander, for descent to the moon's surface. Moving both laterally and downward,* Eagle *felt its way to the ground, touching the lunar surface at the Sea of Tranquillity just short of a dangerous crater and with less than two minutes of fuel left. At 4:18 P.M. Armstrong radioed Mission Control in Houston: "The Eagle has landed!"*

Six hours later, the astronauts opened Eagle's hatch, and Armstrong* backed down the ladder to the surface, pulling the cord of the TV camera aimed at him as he went. As 600 million earthlings watched, he intoned: "That's one small step for man, one giant leap for mankind."† Fourteen minutes later, Aldrin joined Armstrong on the moon's dusty surface. Both were soon leaping about exuberantly like kangaroos in the one-sixth gravity.

The two astronauts collected forty-five pounds of moon rock, set up an American flag, and planted a plaque inscribed: "HERE MEN FROM THE PLANET EARTH FIRST SET FOOT UPON THE MOON JULY 1969, A.D. / WE CAME IN PEACE FOR ALL MANKIND." Soon after, they returned to the Eagle, and after jettisoning their cumbersome boots and backpacks and detaching the Eagle's descent stage, they lifted off the moon. Four hours later, they docked with the Columbia, the orbiting command module. At 12:51 on July 24, after an uneventful sixty-four-hour journey, they reached earth and splashed down in the Pacific near the aircraft carrier Hornet. After spending eighteen days in quarantine to guard against potential moon germs, they were welcomed as heroes by their fellow Americans with the traditional New York ticker tape parade, a state dinner in Los Angeles, and medals of freedom. In late September, the government sent them on a world tour to advertise the American triumph to those who had managed not to hear of it in July.

This document is from the transcript of the conversations that crackled back and forth between NASA mission control director Bruce McCandless in Houston and the two men in the Eagle after it had landed at Tranquillity Base. In the flat tones of the semimilitary delivery imposed by radio technology, it conveys the excitement of the moment when the first man walked on the moon.

[National Aeronautics and Space Administration, Apollo II, Technical Air-to-Ground Voice Transcription (GOSS Net 1), pp. 370 et seq.]

HOUSTON TO EAGLE

HOUSTON (McCandless): Neil, this is Houston. What's your status on hatch open? Over.

EAGLE (Armstrong): Everything is go here. We're just waiting for the cabin pressure to bleed so—to blow enough pressure to open the hatch. It's about 0.1 on our gauge now.

---

*Aldrin was dismayed by the decision that Armstrong would be the first to walk on the moon's surface. The two had words over it, but Aldrin soon accepted the inevitable.

†Armstrong, apparently, meant to put "a," the indefinite article, before "man."

EAGLE (Aldrin): Sure hate to tug on that thing [the hatch handle]. Alternative would be to open the overhead hatch too. . . .

HOUSTON (McCandless): We're showing a relatively static pressure on your cabin. Do you think you can open the hatch at this pressure?

EAGLE (Armstrong): We're going to try it.

EAGLE (Aldrin): The hatch is opening.

EAGLE (Armstrong): The hatch is open!

ARMSTRONG: Is my antenna out? Okay, now we're ready to hook up the LEC here.

ALDRIN: Now that should go down. . . . [static] Put the bag up this way. That's even. Neil, are you hooked up to it?

ARMSTRONG: Yes, okay. Now we need to hook this.

ALDRIN: Leave that up there.

ARMSTRONG: Yes.

ALDRIN: Okay, your visor down? Your back is up against the . . . [static]. All right, it's now on top of the DSKY. Forward and up, now you're there, over toward me, straight down, relax a little bit. . . . Neil, you're lined up nicely. Toward me a little bit. Okay, down. Okay, made it clear. . . . [static]

ALDRIN: Move. Here roll to the left. Okay, now you're clear. You're lined up with the platform. Put your left foot to the right a little bit.

ARMSTRONG: Okay, now I'm going to check the ingress here.

ALDRIN: Okay, not quite squared away. Roll to the—roll right a little. Now you're even.

ARMSTRONG: That's okay?

ALDRIN: That's good. You've got plenty of room.

ARMSTRONG: How am I doing?

ALDRIN: You're doing fine. . . . Okay, do you want these bags?

ARMSTRONG: Yes. Got it. . . . Okay, Houston, I'm on the porch. . . .

HOUSTON (McCandless): Roger, Neil. . . . Columbia, Columbia, this is Houston. One minute and thirty seconds to LOS. All systems go. Over. . . .

ARMSTRONG: You need more slack, Buzz?

ALDRIN: No, hold it just a minute.

ARMSTRONG: Okay.

ALDRIN: Okay, everything's nice and straight in here.

ARMSTRONG: Okay, can you pull the door open a little more?

ALDRIN: Did you get the MESA out?

ARMSTRONG: I'm going to pull it now.

ARMSTRONG: Houston, the MESA came down all right.

HOUSTON (McCandless): Roger, we copy, and we're standing by for your TV.

HOUSTON (McCandless): Neil, this is Houston. You're loud and clear. Break, break. Buzz, this is Houston. Radio check and verify TV circuit breaker in.

EAGLE (Aldrin): Roger. TV circuit breaker's in. LMP reads loud and clear.

HOUSTON (McCandless): And we're getting a picture on TV.

EAGLE (Aldrin): Oh, you got a good picture. Huh?

HOUSTON (McCandless): Okay, Neil, we can see you coming down the ladder now.

EAGLE (Armstrong): Okay, I just checked it—getting back up to that first step, Buzz, it's not even collapsed too far, but it's adequate to get back up. . . . It makes a pretty good little jump. . . . I'm at the foot of the ladder. The LM footpads are only depressed in the surface about one or two inches. Although the surface appears to be very, very fine-grained, as you get close to it. It's almost like a powder. Now and then, it's very fine. . . . I'm going to step off the LM now. . . .

That's one small step for man, one giant leap for mankind.

12

Election '68

Seldom has the American nation approached a presidential election year with such foreboding as it did in 1968. The incumbent president, once popular, was losing support for his management of the war in Southeast Asia. The economy was faltering; for the first time in twenty years consumer prices were creeping upward. In Washington, Congress was becoming impatient at rubber-stamping the president's social programs, and these programs were losing their sheen as their beneficiaries often responded not with gratitude but with rage. Meanwhile, an expanding cohort of voters, many of them Democrats, were recoiling from the turmoil on the campuses, the assault on traditional values, and the soaring statistics for murder, robbery, and rape on the cities' streets.

As early as November 1967, a full year before Election Day, leading Democrats were beginning to consider challenging Lyndon Johnson for renomination. The defectors were primarily from the left of the party spectrum; their argument with Johnson was over the interminable war in Vietnam, not the Great Society. Johnson would have to be replaced if America was to extricate itself from the Vietnam morass; his reputation and ego were unalterably tied to the damnable war, and he would never budge.

The author of the "dump Johnson" movement was Allard Lowenstein, a thirty-eight-year-old dynamo of liberal causes. Lowenstein had spent a decade organizing campus protests against apartheid, against racial segregation, against Franco's Spain, and for world peace. In 1964, he had mobilized northern white students for the Freedom Summer project in Mississippi. Lowenstein despised the war, and in August 1967, he set the "Dump Johnson" movement in motion.

Johnson could be successfully denied a second nomination if a prominent Democratic "dove" could be found to oppose him. But who? Lowenstein first approached Robert Kennedy, now U.S. senator from New

York, who turned him down. He then asked Senator George McGovern of South Dakota and the dovish general, James Gavin. They both said no. His last stop was Eugene McCarthy. The Minnesota senator was skeptical but did not reject the overture outright. On November 30, at a press conference in Washington, McCarthy announced his candidacy. Shortly after the new year, Blair Clark, the campaign head, announced that McCarthy would run against the president in the New Hampshire primary in mid-March.

Presidential politics during the next nine weeks were dominated by the famous "Children's Crusade." Clark brought to the Granite State a large contingent of young anti-Vietnam enthusiasts, mostly undergraduates from eastern colleges. For those who expected to ring doorbells and solicit the votes of New Hampshire's registered Democrats, the orders were "Clean for Gene." The die-hard hippies could work at headquarters.

On March 12, McCarthy won a stunning near-upset. After all the votes were counted, the president had received only 230 more than his challenger. But the euphoria did not last. On March 16, Robert Kennedy announced that he too would challenge Lyndon Johnson in the remaining primary states.

With the Wisconsin primary on April 2 promising to be a McCarthy landslide, and with Kennedy now in the race, the president's prospects for renomination were fading. It was at this point of imminent humiliation that Johnson allowed his fears, doubts, and discouragements to overwhelm his ambition and pride. With the knowledge only of his family and Vice President Humphrey, he inserted a coda into a major address on Vietnam that he delivered on March 31. With millions watching on TV, he described new peace initiatives in Vietnam, and then at the end, he changed his bearing and voice. He briefly recalled his public career and the tragic circumstances of his elevation to the presidency. He had united the country in that moment of fear, he noted. Now he did not want the presidency to "become involved in the partisan divisions that are developing in this political year. . . . Accordingly, I shall not seek and I will not accept the nomination of my party for another term as your president."

As expected, McCarthy swept the Wisconsin primary and took all the state's delegates. For the next twelve weeks, the two senators squared off in a dozen primaries across the country. Kennedy's passion and charisma appealed to blue-collar whites and inner-city minorities. McCarthy drew to his side the liberal professional middle class and affluent suburbanites. The climax came in California on June 3. Kennedy edged out his rival and won the state's 174 delegates, but shortly after his victory speech, while exiting the campaign hotel through a back corridor, he was shot and killed by Sirhan Sirhan, a disgruntled Arab-American who resented Kennedy's pro-Israel positions.

Vice President Humphrey had entered the race in April after Johnson's withdrawal. Too late for the primaries, he expected to win the delegates chosen by the party regulars—the local Democratic politicians, the big-city Democratic bosses, the trade union leaders. Though the McCarthy enthusiasts would not concede after Kennedy's assassination, Humphrey could now count on winning easily in Chicago.

By the time the delegates assembled in Chicago, the Democrats were facing new dangers. The antiwar activists, the radicalized student left, and the enthusiasts of political apocalypse did not intend to allow the party pros to have it their own way. The most determined insurgents were the Yippies, a band of politicized counterculture folk led by Abbie Hoffman and Jerry Rubin, two impish rebels who had moved from political radicalism to hippiehood and sought to combine the two. They would go to Chicago and confront the establishment's festival of death with their own "Festival of Life" that would mock the regular convention and create turmoil.

It is distinctly possible that the election in November was decided by the events in Chicago during the Democratic convention. Fears of mayhem reduced the number of celebrators at the Festival of Life to well below expected levels. But the 2,500 or so who did come to the Windy City were not there solely for fun and games. Years later, Jerry Rubin admitted, "We were not just innocent people who were victimized by the police. We came to plan a confrontation."* And their plans were ably abetted by Mayor Daley and the Chicago police. Hizzoner not only refused to permit park rallies; he also announced an eleven P.M. curfew on demonstrations and strict enforcement of the pot laws.

Trouble began even before the convention officially opened when, on August 23, the police attempted to break up the Yippie pig-nomination ceremony. On Sunday, August 25, the police and demonstrators mixed it up in Lincoln Park. The convention opened the next day and took its predictable course. The delegates rejected the dovish McCarthyite Vietnam plank in favor of the harder-line statement of the administration and the Humphrey forces.

Meanwhile, in the streets surrounding the delegates' hotels, the police and the protesters were turning the city into a war zone. Each day saw vio-

*Quoted in Abe Peck, *Uncovering the Sixties: The Life and Times of the Underground Press* (New York: Pantheon, 1985), p. 118.

lent encounters between quick-tempered police and foul-mouthed demonstrators. The nadir came on Wednesday evening, August 28, just as the convention was getting down to the business of officially nominating a presidential candidate. A crowd of demonstrators, sponsored by the Mobe, marched out of Grant Park across from the Democratic headquarters in the Hilton Hotel, intending to push on to the amphitheater. The police charged, clubbing them and dragging protesters into waiting patrol wagons. Fleeing demonstrators, as well as reporters and spectators, were caught between the police and the hotel and pressed up against the plate glass of the street-level cocktail lounge. It shattered, hurling people into the lounge, many of them badly cut.

All the ugliness was captured on the TV cameras and transmitted to a stunned audience of citizens from every corner of the land. Liberals, with some reason, called the events a "police riot" and denounced Daley and the "hawk" establishment. But to millions of traditional voters, it seemed that the Democrats had reaped the whirlwind of violence they themselves had created by their social legislation and at the same time were incapable of managing their affairs. Many voters would remember the disgrace of Chicago on Election Day.

Meanwhile, as the furies gathered around the Windy City, Richard Nixon had been nominated by the Republicans in Miami Beach. Nixon had loyally supported Goldwater in 1964, when many liberal Republican leaders deserted the ticket. Having earned the respect of the party regulars and successfully courted the southern delegations, he fended off his competitors—George Romney of Michigan, Nelson Rockefeller of New York, and the new governor of California, Ronald Reagan—and easily won the nomination. Nixon chose as his running mate the governor of Maryland, Spiro Agnew, whose fame rested on a harsh attack he had made on black leaders for failing to stop the inner-city riot in Baltimore following Martin Luther King's assassination.

As the campaign itself got under way, the big uncertainty was George Wallace. For a full year, Wallace and his staff had worked hard to get on the American Independent Party ticket on the ballot of all fifty states and had succeeded. The Wallace campaign started slowly, but after Bobby Kennedy's assassination and the Chicago convention, it picked up speed.

Wallace's support came primarily from voters who deeply resented what they saw as the breakdown of traditional values, the rise in crime and disorder, and the establishment's favoritism toward blacks. Many of the backlash voters were defectors from the Democrats, and the Humphrey campaign felt their loss keenly. The vice president also seemed likely to lose the McCarthyites, who linked him to LBJ. Among middle-of-the-road voters, the vice president's major problem was that he seemed a mere extension of Lyndon Johnson. Friends warned him that he must establish his independence or face certain defeat. But Humphrey was a deeply loyal man who could not bring himself to repudiate Johnson's policies. By late September, the Democratic campaign was faltering badly. A September 27 poll showed 48 percent of the voters supporting Nixon, with Humphrey at 28 percent and Wallace not too far behind the vice president, at 21 percent.

The Democratic campaign turned around in Salt Lake City on September 30, when the vice president gave a nationally televised speech that proposed more generous American conditions for negotiating a settlement in Vietnam. The shift, though small, was enough to give the campaign a badly needed lift. Suddenly contributions poured in, assuring the campaign more badly needed TV time. Meanwhile, the nation's influential union leaders began to speak sternly to their members. As governor of Alabama, Wallace had been bad for labor, they said, and good union men should not vote for him. And Wallace hurt himself. On October 3, he announced that Air Force general Curtis LeMay would be his running mate. LeMay was a military Neanderthal who wanted to bomb Vietnam "back to the stone age" and use nuclear weapons, if necessary, to win the war. Conservatives deplored the administration's decision to fight a limited war in Vietnam, but few voters cared to risk a nuclear holocaust over a marshy piece of ground in Southeast Asia.

As the campaign approached its final days, Wallace was sinking fast. Thousands of his supporters moved to Humphrey, who was soon closing the gap with Nixon. On October 26, after holding back petulantly for many crucial weeks, Lyndon Johnson finally decided that he was a Democrat after all. To help Humphrey before the election, he promised a bombing halt if Hanoi agreed to begin serious peace negotiations among the belligerents. He almost pulled it off. In the end, the stumbling block was the Saigon government, which, believing Nixon to be a tougher anti-Communist than Humphrey, refused to help the Democrats. They would not accept a separate Vietcong delegation to the Paris peace negotiations and would not join the talks. The negotiations collapsed.

Nixon, of course, won, but the race was close. Only half a million votes separated Humphrey from Nixon out of 73 million cast. Nixon took the Electoral College vote by 301 to 191. Wallace got almost 10 million popular votes and 46 from the Electoral College. The Democratic decade was over.

Robert Kennedy and the 1968 Presidential Campaign

Robert Kennedy occupies a special place in the life of the Sixties. Third son of the Joseph Kennedy clan, he was in some ways the most Irish. Joe Junior, the oldest, killed in combat in World War II, had had the smooth qualities of the ambitious executive. John, the president, was the debonair sophisticate, the family intellectual. Ted, the youngest, was the pampered rich boy who believed Daddy's money would buy anything. It was Bobby who retained the combativeness and the passion that we associate with Irish-American ethnicity.

RFK served his brother as attorney general and stayed on after Dallas under Lyndon Johnson for some additional months. As the nation's chief legal officer, he was considered a tough enforcer of the laws, at a time when the federal government was fighting massive resistance of the white South to federal civil rights rulings by Congress and the courts. He had also played a constructive role in Ex Comm, the small circle of advisers who had successfully maneuvered the nation through the dangerous Cuban Missile Crisis in 1962.

Robert Kennedy and Lyndon Johnson were not friends. Their antipathy went back at least to 1960, when RFK, as his brother's campaign manager, had opposed Johnson's choice as Jack Kennedy's vice-presidential running mate. He had stayed on in the cabinet after the assassination, but he became the rallying point of JFK loyalists who could not accept the legitimacy of Lyndon Johnson. In 1964, he left to run for the Senate from New York and won, though he was accused of being a "carpetbagger" who had no real connection with the state.

As a senator from New York, Bobby acquired a whole new set of advisers, young men more liberal than he who influenced his views on race, student dissent, and Vietnam. He developed a special rapport with the young and with blacks and Hispanics, and somehow, perhaps because of his scrappy Irish temper, he retained the support of the blue-collar whites who were defecting from the Democratic Party.

Bobby was the obvious choice of the "Dump Johnson" forces who wanted to challenge the president's bid for reelection in 1968. But at first he refused to consider it. He was reluctant to disrupt the Democratic Party, he said, and besides, replacing Johnson was a forlorn hope. Only after Eugene McCarthy's stunning upset of the president in the New Hampshire primary did he reconsider.

The selection here is Robert Kennedy's announcement of his candidacy on March 16 in the room of the old Senate Office Building, where he had first come to public attention as counsel of the McClellan Committee on organized crime and where, eight years before, his brother had thrown his own hat into the presidential ring. In it, he tries to deflect impressions that he is involved in a grudge fight against LBJ and that he is a spoil-sport for McCarthy. But both charges would stick—with good reason.

In the next three months, from Indiana on, Kennedy and McCarthy would battle it out on the primary trail. California was the last primary state, and there, on June 4, he narrowly defeated McCarthy. After a brief victory statement to his supporters, as he was leaving the Ambassador Hotel, he was shot and killed by a Palestinian immigrant who resented his pro-Israel views.

[*"Robert Kennedy Throws His Hat into the Ring,"* **Washington Post,** *March 17, 1968.*]

ROBERT KENNEDY THROWS HIS HAT INTO THE RING

I am announcing today my candidacy for the Presidency of the United States.

I do not run for the Presidency merely to oppose any man, but to propose new policies. I run because I am convinced that this country is on a perilous course and because I am obliged to do all I can. I run to seek new policies, policies to end the bloodshed in Vietnam and in our cities, policies to close the gaps between black and white, rich and poor, young and old, in this country and around the world. I run for the Presidency because I want the Democratic Party and the United States of America to stand for hope instead of despair, for the reconciliation of men instead of the growing risk of world war.

I run because it is now unmistakably clear that we can change these disastrous, divisive policies only by changing the men who are now making them. For the reality of recent events in Vietnam have been glossed over with illusions. . . . The crisis in gold,* the crisis in our cities, the crises on our farms and in our ghettos, all have been met by too little and too late.

No one who knows what I know about the extraordinary demands of the Presidency can be certain that any mortal can adequately fill that position. But my service on the National Security Council during the Cuban missile crisis, the Berlin crisis, and the negotiations on Laos and on the Nuclear Test Ban Treaty have taught me something about both the uses and the limitations of military power, about the value of negotiations with allies and enemies, about the opportunities and dangers which await our nation in the many corners of the globe to which I have traveled. As a member of the Cabinet and a member of the Senate, I have seen the inexcusable and ugly deprivation which causes children to starve in Mississippi, black citizens to riot in Watts, young Indians to commit suicide on their reservations because they lack all hope and feel they have no future, and proud, able-

---

*The reference here is the recent wave of gold hoarding, owing to an American balance of payments problem which had already developed—ed.

bodied families to wait out their lives in empty idleness in eastern Kentucky. I have traveled and listened to the young people of our nation and felt their anger about the war they are sent to fight and the world they are about to inherit. In private talks and in public, I have tried in vain to alter our course in Vietnam before it further saps our spirit and our manpower, further raises the risks of wider war, and further destroys the country and people it was meant to save.

I cannot stand aside from the contest that will decide our nation's future and our children's future. The remarkable New Hampshire campaign of Senator Eugene McCarthy has proven how deep are the present divisions within our party and country. Until that was publicly clear, my presence in the race would have been seen as a clash of personalities rather than issues. But now that the fight is one over policies which I have long been challenging, I must enter that race. The fight is just beginning and I believe that I can win.

I have previously communicated this decision to President Johnson, and late last night, my brother Senator Edward Kennedy traveled to Wisconsin to communicate my decision to Senator McCarthy. I made clear through my brother to Senator McCarthy that my candidacy would not be in opposition to his, but in harmony. My aim is to both support and expand his valiant campaign in the spirit of his November 30 statement.* Taking one month at a time, it is important that he achieve the largest possible majorities next month in the Wisconsin, Pennsylvania, and Massachusetts primaries.† I strongly support his effort in those states and urge all my friends to give him their help and their votes. Both of us will be encouraging like-minded Democrats in every state to select like-minded delegates to the National Convention, for both of us want above all else an open Democratic convention in Chicago, free to choose a new course for our party and country.

To make certain that this effort will still be effective in June, I am required now to permit the entry of my name into the California primary to be held in that month; and I do so in the belief, which I will strive to implement, that Senator McCarthy's forces and mine will be able to work together in one form or another. My desire is not to divide the strength of those forces seeking a change, but to increase it. . . .

Finally, my decision reflects no personal animosity or disrespect toward President Johnson. He served President Kennedy with the utmost loyalty and was extremely kind to me and members of my family in the difficult

---

*McCarthy's own statement of candidacy—ed.
†RFK was not on the ballot in those states and so could not compete there—ed.

months which followed the events of November 1963.* I have often commended his efforts in health, education, and many other areas, and I have deep sympathy for the burdens he carries today. But the issue is not personal; it is our profound differences over where we are heading and what we want to accomplish.

I do not lightly dismiss the dangers and difficulties of challenging an incumbent President; but these are not ordinary times, and this is not an ordinary election. At stake is not simply the leadership of our party or even our country—it is our right to moral leadership on this planet.

Eugene McCarthy and the "Children's Crusade"

Senator Eugene McCarthy of Minnesota was a Catholic theologian manqué. He received his undergraduate education in Catholic colleges and taught in several before running for Congress as a Democrat. Though he would find himself in the middle of the political storm during the Sixties, he never ceased to be in temperament the man of thought.

McCarthy represented a liberal state, but he was never a flaming liberal. In the Senate, he had not been an influential figure and seemed restless and dissatisfied with public life. When approached by Allard Lowenstein in late 1967 to challenge Johnson in the Democratic presidential primaries, he at first demurred but then, out of conscience, accepted.

Few believed that the McCarthy campaign was more than a personal expression of dismay at the evil war. No one had ever successfully displaced an incumbent president from the party ticket. But this time the skeptics were mistaken. Although the senator was an indifferent, even reluctant campaigner, his challenge to LBJ struck a resounding chord. To young men and women, especially, his cause seemed a way, finally, to do something practical and consequential to end the war. Hundreds of young idealists flocked to his campaign, many to follow it all the way to the Democratic convention in Chicago in late summer.

It was the March presidential primary in New Hampshire, the first of the series, that made McCarthy a viable candidate. The McCarthy forces had little money at first and were compelled to rely almost entirely on volunteers. This proved to be an advantage in the Granite State, where the enthusiastic young men and women were able to get past the flinty Yankee skepticism and talk to the voters about their candidate. As one New Hampshire Democrat noted: "These college kids are fabulous. . . . [They] knock at the door and come in politely, and actually want to talk to grown-ups, and people are delighted."

---

*That is, after the assassination of John Kennedy in Dallas—ed.

But the students had to make concessions. Few were flamboyant hippies, but many wore their hair long and dressed in the grungy way typical of the youth culture. Under the direction of Curtis Gans and Sam Brown, the campaign managers, they went "Clean for Gene," putting on skirts, jackets, ties, and slacks, and shaving off or cutting off excessive hair, if they expected to do active canvassing among New Hampshire's conservative voters.

In this selection below by Ben Stavis, we observe the Children's Crusade, as the New Hampshire McCarthy campaign was soon called, through the eyes of a young Columbia graduate student and his wife, who came to help in mid-February and in the end stayed all the way to the August national convention.

[**We Were the Campaign** *by Ben Stavis. Copyright © 1969 by Ben Stavis. Reprinted by permission of Beacon Press, Boston.*]

THE NEW HAMPSHIRE CHILDREN'S CRUSADE

When Roseann and I took a bus for Concord, New Hampshire, in early February 1968, we saw no other way to help end the war in Vietnam. With countless other Americans we had watched with horror and frustration as our country unleashed an ever larger war on the people of Vietnam, rendering modernization of backward countries impossible and preventing racial progress at home. There seemed no other way of stopping it. Newspaper advertisements, demonstrations, and protests were ineffective; even important senators were discovering [their] powerlessness. The supposed safeguard of democracy, the presidential election, seemed irrelevant. Throughout 1967 it seemed that the choice would be between Lyndon Johnson and Richard Nixon, leaving no choice to vote for peace....

Thus, when Senator Eugene McCarthy ... revealed interest in challenging the incumbent president for his party's nomination, I was encouraged.... I knew of Senator McCarthy because I had met him about six years earlier and liked him. He had visited Haverford College when I was a student there, participated in classes, and informally chatted about American foreign and domestic policy with students for several hours over coffee. He impressed me as a man of decency and integrity....

During December and January after McCarthy announced [his candidacy], while I stayed at Columbia University and studied for oral examinations for my doctorate ..., I followed with some concern the debate about McCarthy's candidacy.... McCarthy had not been a leader in the Senate against the war as [Wayne] Morse from Oregon and [Ernest] Gruening from Alaska had.... Even after the announcement of his candidacy, McCarthy's position remained weak....

Despite these misgivings, the logic of a presidential challenge remained. . . . Then, at the beginning of February, Roseann and I had a block of free time. . . . So on February 14, St. Valentine's Day, we took a bus to Boston and, next morning, another one to Concord, New Hampshire—almost four weeks before the New Hampshire primary. We walked into the headquarters about 10:30 A.M., suitcases in hand. Headquarters was an old electrical appliance store and, although it bore a sign MCCARTHY FOR PRESIDENT, it was not yet functioning.

We were quickly put to work. We shoveled rubbish from a side room, taped extension cords to the ceilings to support light bulbs, and carried pails of water to the basement to serve as fire extinguishers. A large wooden spool that had once held heavy wire was set on end to become a table for a borrowed coffee maker. Posters were put up to cover holes in the walls. Tables were placed over holes in the floors. We then began to stack cartons of literature and sort piles of posters. The campaign existed in the national press and on television, but it had barely begun in New Hampshire.

Roseann and I thought we might be able to coordinate some sort of office work, do some of the envelope stuffing—that sort of thing. We expected to stay for a week or two, on the assumption that the campaign would have many effective workers from the Senator's staff and from New Hampshire. An assignment the next afternoon forced me to reassess drastically. I accompanied two other students to Rochester, New Hampshire, about an hour's drive from Concord. We were to annotate voting lists with party affiliation, so as to avoid canvassing or sending mail to Republicans. The people of New Hampshire, seemingly not trusting any centralized bureaucracy, had no single location for party registration records. . . . At Rochester the records for one ward were at the police station; for the second ward, in the official's isolated farmhouse; for the third posted on the outside of a school. I volunteered to transpose party information from the latter list. For about two hours I stood outside in 15-degree weather shivering, carefully noting who was a Democrat and who was an Independent. . . .

While we were driving back to Concord, I began to understand that the McCarthy campaign was not the property of Senator McCarthy or the people of New Hampshire. If I was willing to stand in the cold, freezing wind and take down information, it was my campaign. . . . With this realization, we decided to stay, at least until the . . . election. Beyond that we made no plans. . . .

Original Staff

I should clarify what the word "staff" meant at that time in New Hampshire. A staff member was essentially anyone who worked during the week. He prepared materials to be used on weekends, then supervised the people who came on weekends. . . . The concept of staff involved no financial distinction. The full-time workers thought it likely that if the campaign got money, they would be fed; but that would come only when the wallets grew thin and the stomachs empty.

The original staff was composed almost entirely of graduate students. There were a few undergraduates, but generally their class schedules prevented them from spending great amounts of time with the campaign.

The office was headed by Sam Brown, a former National Student Association official, who knew a great number of students. He was registered at the Harvard Divinity School to keep his student standing. He kept his hair at perfect length: long enough so that he could pass as a student radical but not so long that he would be mistaken for a hippie. . . .

The counterpart to staff was volunteer. Of course everyone was a volunteer in the strict sense, but in New Hampshire volunteer meant part-time worker. Volunteers were the college students who came to work for the weekend. On weekends, the office quickly became cluttered with sleeping bags, portable typewriters, textbooks, and term papers in various stages of completion. The most important item of logistical support was a record player and hard-rock records. Each weekend meant a new set of records. After a week of the Beatles, Country Joe and the Fish came as a welcome change in the office environment. By the next weekend, everyone was overjoyed at having the Grateful Dead for a week.

At that time there were two major projects for volunteers. The first was to put out a mailing to all Democrats and Independents in New Hampshire. During the week, we philosophers, theologists, sinologists, economists, lawyers, and a few people with only bachelor's degrees all tore mailing labels, pasted them on envelopes, stuffed, sealed, stamped, and sorted by zip code. When masses of volunteers came for the weekend, we learned how to supervise. . . . All this work was geared to the throbbing rhythm of the hard-rock records. . . .

At the same time a small group of weekend volunteers experimented with another method of getting votes. We tried to canvass. Roseann and I went out with an experimental canvassing group to talk with the people of New Hampshire on the weekends of February 17 and 24. It was a chilling experience in many ways. First, it was cold and windy. The problem was partly overcome with long underwear, heavy clothing, and boots. Sunglasses helped reduce the intense glare from the snow. Second, people often had huge dogs near their houses, whose barks replace doorbells in alerting the household to the approach of a visitor. Only courage and careful checking of the length of tethers helped here. The reception by the voters was also chilly. There were numberless excuses for not talking with us. The people had guests, were eating, were getting ready for a funeral, or had sickness in the house. This kind of coldness could not be combatted with gloves; it needed quick response. One man would not let me in his house because he was hanging wallpaper and his house was a mess. He immediately agreed with me when I observed that the country was in a mess also. I didn't get into the house but did give him McCarthy literature and a smile. . . .

During the first attempts at canvassing the only adult interested in hearing about it was a stocky bald man who said he was a motivational analyst hired by the campaign. . . . He suggested ways of explaining to the voter how the war was related to tax increases and inflation. He urged us to try conversing with the voter instead of merely offering literature. . . .

Roseann started out as an assistant office manager. She helped Pat Reiley, a New York girl with flaming red hair. Pat had worked for a month at New York Coalition for a Democratic Alternative (as the New York McCarthy campaign was called). . . . Roseann, driven by her home economics training and her experience as a program director for a girls' camp, enlarged the job of assistant office manager. She kept the office well stocked with vitamins, enriched peanut butter, jelly, and bread. She solicited fruit from the sympathetic groceries and made everyone drink orange juice in the mornings. She kept a crude first-aid kit. . . .

Roseann's responsibilities included calling up mothers of the youngsters who came to the office and assuring them that their children were being helpful. . . .

The Staff Grows

After about a week and a half, our headquarters was tremendously strengthened by the arrival of several members of the Washington staff. We now had a campaign director in Curt Gans. Since he was thirty years old, he could rent cars. He could always be located by following some telephone wire or a trail of opened Pepsi bottles. . . . He was short and frail, with a crew cut . . . , and looked more like a mechanic than an organizer of a great political campaign. . . .

Although he had never run a large campaign, he had spent the previous several months traveling around the country organizing Concerned Democrats. Before that he had arranged peace rallies and sit-ins, so he had more organizing experience than anyone else in the Concord headquarters. . . .

The new staff was a major addition to the Concord headquarters. Our work now had direction, breadth, and money. We started getting more telephones, tables, cars, literature, and even money for eating. . . .

Gans wanted to project a campaign that was based on two elements: (1) local support and leadership, and (2) innocent students. There was something of a contradiction in both these images, for most of the students and staff were from out of state, and the innocence of the students could not be guaranteed. Thus Gans was often frightened that press stories would destroy the impression he was hoping to create. He even tried to keep his own existence a secret from the press. When the *Concord Monitor*, the local daily, carried a five-page story announcing that the McCarthy campaign had sent its key workers, Curt Gans, Sam Brown, and Harold Ickes to New Hampshire, Curt was infuriated and promised to fire whoever leaked the story to the press. The canvassers, the core of the campaign, might produce a bad press: they might get into fights or get caught smoking pot. A story revealing such behavior could puncture the entire image of the McCarthy Kids. Thus Gans carefully kept the press away from our canvassers frugging* at a Manchester party on a Saturday evening. He also insisted that only one thousand out-of-state students be allowed to canvass for the last weekend. This meant "turning off" about ten busloads. Gans carefully selected New York buses to be stopped, on the guess that heavy New York accents and a hard-sell semi-radical approach that might have been learned canvassing in New York would alienate the proud, independent, conservative New Hampshirites.

For the same reason, Gans tried to prevent people with beards from canvassing. Such men were assigned to help me, so they were out of sight in the basement, helping prepare maps and file cards for canvassing. The public image of the McCarthy campaign was "Clean for Gene" and marginal change in foreign policy (later it was radical change). But bearded students, SDS militants, officers of the New York's Twelfth Street Peace Action Committee, and unmarried couples were all helping prepare for canvassing. The few black volunteers were used fully and publicly in canvassing. . . .

When election day finally came, I slept through it, having worked all night until the polls opened getting maps and lists ready in Manchester. As the results came in that evening, I worked an adding machine and slide rule to tabulate those that were telephoned by field offices. We were hours behind the media. None of us had a confident prediction of the vote. Staff guesses of McCarthy's vote ranged from 8 percent to 60 percent. I had no

*The Frug was a popular dance of the day among college students—ed.

idea what we would get. Nor did anyone know what would be considered a good vote. We had to rely on the press after the vote was in to tell us whether it was respectable or not. If the press called 25 percent a strong showing for McCarthy, it would be that. Thus one reporter asked me what vote would satisfy me. I asked him how the press would interpret the vote. He said that 30 percent would be regarded as a very strong showing, so I figured that would be satisfactory to me, but publicly I said nothing. Gans insisted that no one either make a prediction or drop a hint as to what would be considered a good vote. He did not want the press to be able to say that we did not do as well as we expected to.

When the votes were tallied, I was somewhat surprised that a full 48 percent of the voters liked LBJ enough to write in his name. But since all the newscasters said that our 42 percent was a great victory for McCarthy, we were ecstatic. A heavy snowstorm had prevented our joining the main staff celebration in Manchester, but we watched it on television and celebrated with a pizza. On Wednesday someone attached a chair to the ceiling and labeled it "the overturned presidential seat." At a noon meeting Curt Gans told a joyous staff that we had changed the presidency and maybe the next president would be McCarthy. . . .

The Yippies Go to Chicago

Abbie Hoffman, Jerry Rubin, and Paul Krassner called the week-long demonstration they concocted for the Chicago Democratic convention a "Festival of Life." The three-some had long been agitators and gadflies, Krassner as publisher of the adversarial Realist, *Hoffman as a civil rights activist, and Rubin as a Berkeley antiwar leader. Sometime in the middle of the decade, they were all swept up in the counterculture wave and deposited on the coast of hippiedom. In 1967, Rubin and Hoffman orchestrated the Mobe's march on the Pentagon that opened with a zany Buddhist ceremony to levitate the building. By 1968, Hoffman was calling himself "a revolutionary artist."*

According to Hoffman's whimsical account, the three political cutups, coming down from an LSD trip on New Year's Day 1968, decided to create the Yippies,* a blend of counterculture and the New Left that would undermine the establishment through humor and ridicule. In their first escapade, the Yippies scattered money from the trading floor balcony of the New York Stock Exchange while the capitalists below awkwardly scrambled for the bills raining down. Then, in March, six thousand Yippies celebrated the spring equinox by invading New York's Grand Central Station and smashing the information booth clocks, the symbol of the nine-to-five commuter rat race.

---

*Supposedly an acronym for Youth International Party, but actually a blend of *yippie,* meaning "hooray," and *hippie.*

The big show would be Chicago, however. There the Democrats' "Festival of Death" would be turned into a "Festival of Life." Thousands of Yippies would descend on the Windy City during convention week and create a "perfect mess." The liberated young would divert themselves with "poetry readings, mass meditation, flycasting exhibitions, demagogic Yippie political arousal speeches, and rock music and song concerts." They would also disrupt the proceedings. Several hundred Yippie male studs would seduce the wives, daughters, and girlfriends of the Democratic delegates, and according to Krassner, to enhance the fun, the zanies would dump LSD into the city's water supply. Most of this was fantasy, but the Festival of Life was a clear attack on a sacred political ritual of the republic.

The promoters claimed they would draw thousands to Chicago. In fact, warned by Abe Peck of the Chicago Seed and by other underground press editors that Mayor Daley and the Chicago police would happily smash heads, only about two or three thousand Yippies came. But they were enough to trigger the chaos and street drama that the American public saw on their TV sets during the convention.

The government indicted Hoffman, Rubin, and six other antiwar leaders* for conspiring to incite a riot at the convention. After an unruly trial that continued the hijinks of the convention, all were convicted but acquitted on appeal.

This article, published six weeks before the convention, was Hoffman's call to action. It appeared in Krassner's The Realist *on July 7, 1968.*

[*Abbie Hoffman, "The Yippies Are Going to Chicago,"* **Realist,** *July 7, 1968.*]

THE YIPPIES ARE GOING TO CHICAGO

Last December a group of us in New York conceived the Yippie! idea. We had four main objectives:

1. The blending of pot and politics into a potlitical grass leaves movement—a cross-fertilization of the hippie and New Left philosophies.
2. A connecting link that would tie together as much of the underground as was willing into some gigantic national get-together.
3. The development of a model for an alternative society.
4. The need to make some statement, especially in revolutionary action-theater terms, about LBJ, the Democratic Party, electoral politics, and the state of the nation.

To accomplish these tasks required the construction of a vast myth, for through the notion of myth large numbers of people could get turned on

---

*The others were: Dave Dellinger, Tom Hayden, Rennie Davis, Lee Weiner, John Froines, and Bobby Seale. Seale's prosecution was later legally severed from the trial of the others.

and, in that process of getting turned on, begin to participate in Yippie! and start to focus on Chicago. *Precision was sacrificed for a greater degree of suggestion.* People took off in all directions in the most sensational manner possible:

"We will burn Chicago to the ground!"

"We will fuck on the beaches!"

"We demand the Politics of Ecstasy!"

"Acid for all!"

"Abandon the Creeping Meatball!"

And, all the time: "Yippie! Chicago—August 25–30."

Reporters would play their preconceived roles: "What is the difference between a hippie and a Yippie?" A hundred different answers would fly out, forcing the reporter to make up his own answers; to distort. And distortion became the life-blood of the Yippies.

Yippie! was in the eye of the beholder.

Perhaps Marshall McLuhan can help.

This is taken from an interview in the current Columbia University yearbook:

McLUHAN: "Myth is the mode of simultaneous awareness of a complex group of causes and effects. . . . We hear sounds from everywhere, without ever having to focus. . . . Where a visual space is an organized continuum of a uniform connected kind, the ear world is a world of simultaneous relationships. Electric circuitry confers a mythic dimension on our ordinary individual and group actions. Our technology forces us to live mythically, but we continue to think fragmentarily, and on single, separate planes."

INTERVIEWER: "What do you mean by myth?"

McLUHAN: "Myth means putting on the audience, putting on one's environment. The Beatles do this. They are a group of people who suddenly were able to put on their audience and the English language with musical effects—putting on a whole vesture, a whole time, a *Zeit.*"

INTERVIEWER: "So it doesn't matter that the Pentagon didn't actually levitate?"

McLUHAN: "Young people are looking for a formula for putting on the universe—*participation mystique.* They do not look for detached patterns—for ways of relating themselves to the world, à la nineteenth century."

So there you have it, or rather have it suggested, because myth can never have the precision of a well-oiled machine, which would allow it to be trapped and molded. It must have the action of participation and the magic of mystique. It must have a high element of risk, drama, excitement, and bullshit.

Let's return to history. Remember a guy named Lyndon Johnson? He was so predictable when Yippie! began. And then *pow!* He really fucked us. He did the one thing no one had counted on. He dropped out. "My God," we exclaimed. "Lyndon is out-flanking us on our hippie side."

Then Go-Clean-for-Gene and Hollywood-Bobby. Well, Gene wasn't much. One could secretly cheer for him the way you cheer for the Mets. It's easy, knowing he can never win. But Bobby, there was the real threat. A direct challenge to our theater-in-the-streets, a challenge to the charisma of Yippie!

Remember Bobby's Christmas card: psychedelic blank space with a big question mark—"Santa in '68?" Remember Bobby on television stuttering at certain questions, leaving room for the audience to jump in and help him agonize, to battle the cold interviewer who knew all the questions and never made a mistake.

Come on, Bobby said, *join the mystery battle against the television machine.* Participation mystique. Theater-in-the-streets. He played it to the hilt. And what was worse, Bobby had the money and power to build the stage. We had to steal ours. It was no contest.

Yippie stock went down quicker than the money we had dumped on the Stock Exchange floor. Every night we would turn on the TV set and there was the young knight with long hair, holding out his hand (a gesture he learned from the Pope): "Give me your hand—it is a long road ahead."

When young longhairs told you how they'd heard that Bobby turned on, you knew Yippie! was *really* in trouble.

We took to drinking and praying for LBJ to strike back, but he kept melting. Then Hubert came along exclaiming the "Politics of Joy" and Yippie! passed into a state of catatonia which resulted in near permanent brain damage.

Yippie! grew irrelevant.

National action seemed meaningless.

Everybody began the tough task of developing new battlegrounds. Columbia, the Lower East Side, Free City in San Francisco. Local action became the focus and by the end of May we had decided to disband Yippie! and cancel the Chicago festival.

It took two full weeks of debate to arrive at a method of dropping-out which would not further demoralize the troops. The statement was all ready when up stepped Sirhan Sirhan, and in ten seconds he made it a whole new ball game.

We postponed calling off Chicago and tried to make some sense out of what the hell had just happened. It was not easy to think clearly. Yippie!, still in a state of critical shock because of LBJ's pullout, hovered close to death somewhere between the 50/50 state of Andy Warhol and the 0/0 state of Bobby Kennedy.

The United States political system was proving more insane than Yippie!.

Reality and unreality had in six months switched sides.

It was *America* that was on a trip; we were just standing still.

How could we pull our pants down? America was already naked.

What could we disrupt? America was falling apart at the seams.

Yet Chicago seemed more relevant than ever. Hubert had a lock on the convention: it was more closed than ever. Even the squares who vote in primaries had expressed a mandate for change. Hubert canned the "Politics of Joy" and instituted the "Politics of Hope"—some switch—but none of the slogans mattered. We were back to power politics, the politics of big-city machines and back-room deals.

The Democrats had finally got their thing together by hook or crook and there it was for all to see—fat, ugly, and full of shit. The calls began pouring into our office. They wanted to know only one thing: "When do we leave for Chicago?"

What we need now, however, is the direct opposite approach from the one we began with. We must sacrifice suggestion for a greater degree of precision. We need a reality in the face of the American political myth. We have to kill Yippie! and still bring huge numbers to Chicago.

If you have any Yippie! buttons, posters, stickers, or sweatshirts, bring them to Chicago. We will end Yippie! in a huge orgasm of destruction atop a giant media altar. We will in Chicago begin the task of building Free America on the ashes of the old and from the inside out.

A Constitutional Convention is being planned. A convention of visionary mind-benders who will for five long days and nights address themselves to the task of formulating the goals and means of the New Society.

It will be a blend of technologists and poets, of artists and community organizers, of anyone who has a vision. We will try to develop a Community of Consciousness.

There will be a huge rock-folk festival for free. Contrary to rumor, no groups originally committed to Chicago have dropped out. In fact, additional ones have agreed to participate. In all about thirty groups and performers will be there.

Theater groups from all over the country are pledged to come. They are an integral part of the activities, and a large amount of funds raised from here on in will go for the transportation of street theater groups.

Workshops in a variety of subjects such as draft resistance, drugs, commune development, guerrilla theater and underground media will be set up. The workshops will be oriented around problem-solving while the Constitutional Convention works to developing the overall philosophical framework.

There will probably be a huge march across town to haunt the Democrats.

People coming to Chicago should begin preparations for five days of energy-exchange. Do not come prepared to sit and watch and be fed and cared for. It just won't happen that way. It is time to become a life-actor. The days of the audience died with the old America. If you don't have a thing to do, stay home, you'll only get in the way.

All of these plans are contingent on our getting a permit, and it is toward that goal that we have been working. A permit is a definite contradiction in philosophy since we do not recognize the authority of the old order, but tactically it is a necessity.

We are negotiating, with the Chicago city government, a six-day treaty. All of the Chicago newspapers as well as various pressure groups have urged the city of Chicago to grant the permit. They recognize full well the huge social problem they face if we are forced to use the streets of Chicago for our action.

They have tentatively offered us use of Soldiers' Field Stadium or Navy Pier (we would have to rename either, of course) for our convention. We have had several meetings, principally with David Stahl, Deputy Mayor of Chicago, and there remains but to iron out the terms of the treaty— suspension of curfew laws, regulations pertaining to sleeping on the beach, etc.—for us to have a bona fide permit in our hands.

The possibility of violence will be greatly reduced. There is no guarantee that it will be entirely eliminated.

This is the United States, 1968, remember. If you are afraid of violence you shouldn't have crossed the border.

This matter of a permit is a cat-and-mouse game. The Chicago authorities do not wish to grant it too early, knowing this would increase the number of people that descend on the city. They can ill afford to wait too late, for that will inhibit planning on our part and create more chaos.

It is not our wish to take on superior armed troops who outnumber us on unfamiliar enemy territory. It is not their wish to have a Democrat nominated amidst a major bloodbath. The treaty will work for both sides.

There is a further complicating factor: the possibility of the Convention being moved out of Chicago. Presently there are two major strikes taking place by bus drivers and telephone and electrical repairmen, in addition to a taxi strike scheduled to begin on the eve of the Convention.

If the Convention is moved out of Chicago, we will have to adjust our plans. The best we can say is, keep your powder dry and start preparing. A good idea is to begin raising money to outfit a used bus that you can buy for about $300 and use locally before and after Chicago.

Prepare a street theater skit or bring something to distribute, such as food, poems, or music. Get sleeping bags and other camping equipment. We will sleep on the beaches. If you have any free money, we can channel this into energy groups already committed. We are fantastically broke and in need of funds.

In Chicago contact *The Seed*, 837 N. LaSalle St.; in New York, the Youth International Party, 32 Union Sq. East. Chicago has rooming facilities for 25 organizers. Write us of your plans and watch the underground papers for the latest developments.

The point is, you can use Chicago as a means of pulling your local community together. It can serve to open up a dialogue between political radicals and those who might be considered hippies. The radical will say to the hippie: "Get together and fight, you are getting the shit kicked out of you." The hippie will say to the radical: "Your protest is so narrow, your rhetoric so boring, your ideological power plays so old-fashioned."

Each can help the other, and Chicago—like the Pentagon demonstration before it—might well offer the medium to put forth that message.

Violence in Chicago

In June 1968, that clamorous year of assassinations and riots, Lyndon Johnson created the National Commission on the Causes and Prevention of Violence headed by Milton Eisenhower, brother of the former president and respected ex-president of Johns Hopkins University. The commission would "examine this tragic phenomenon" of violence in the nation's life and recommend ways to lessen it.

The Democratic convention in Chicago had collapsed into a bedlam of thudding nightsticks, flying bottles, tear gas, Mace, and broken bones before the commission could finish its investigation. The commission quickly authorized a special panel to look into the Chicago disorders under the direction of Daniel Walker, a prominent corporation attorney and president of the Chicago Crime Commission.

The Walker report, issued on December 1, was over 230 pages long. Based on fourteen hundred eyewitness accounts, as well as films, photographs, and news stories, it did not deal gently with the Chicago police. Though subject to great provocation by antiwar demonstrators, they had failed to exercise the self-restraint and discipline that citizens had reason to expect. They had responded with "unrestrained and indiscriminate . . . violence . . . often inflicted upon persons who had broken no law, disobeyed no order, made no threat."

This excerpt from the Walker report describes the disorders on August 28, when the antiwar protesters, though denied a permit, tried to march on the convention amphitheater at the very time the delegates were choosing the Democratic presidential nominee. Having battled with protesters on the Chicago streets and in the parks for a week, the police were particularly hard on activists that day and, as the Walker report asserted, displayed a shocking lack of discipline. The account makes it clear why the media called the events of that afternoon and evening "a police riot."

[*From* **Rights in Conflict: The Walker Report to the National Commission on the Causes and Prevention of Violence** *(Washington, DC: U.S. Government Printing Office, 1968), pp. 246–61.*]

RIGHTS IN CONFLICT

Vice President Humphrey was now inside the Conrad Hilton hotel and the police commanders were afraid that the crowd might either attempt to storm the hotel or march south on Michigan Avenue, ultimately to the Amphitheater. The Secret Service had received an anonymous phone call that the Amphitheater was to be blown up. A line of police was established at 8th and Michigan at the south end of the hotel, and the squads of police stationed at the hotel doors began restricting access to those who could display room keys. . . .

At this time, says [a] police sergeant who . . . was now on duty at the Hilton, people were screaming foul language of every type at the police and shouting, "Who's your wife with now?" . . . "Where's your wife tonight?" Some were spitting on the officers and daring them to come and hit them. "The obscenities," says an attorney who was present, "were frequently returned in kind by the police. . . ."

The demonstrators . . . seemed bent on making their march to the Amphitheater. Obscenities and vulgar epithets were shouted at the police. There were also chants of "One, two, three, four; stop this damned war"; "Dump the Hump"; "Daley must go"; "Ho, Ho, Ho Chi Minh"; "The streets belong to the people"; and "Prague, Prague, Prague!"*

A policeman on Michigan later said that about this time a "female hippie" came up to him, pulled up her skirt and said, "You haven't had a piece in a long time."

A policeman standing in front of the Hilton remembers seeing a blond female who was dressed in a short red minidress make lewd, sexual

---

*The reference is to the recent invasion by Soviet troops of the Czech capital to put down a regime supporting the "Prague Spring," a political and cultural revolt against Soviet dominance since the 1948 Communist takeover. The chanters were implying a resemblance between the Chicago police and the brutal Red Army in Central Europe—ed.

motions in front of the police line. Whenever this happened, he says, the policemen moved back to prevent any incident. The crowd, however, egged her on, the patrolman says. He thought that "she and the crowd wanted an arrest to create a riot." Earlier in the same general area a male youth had stripped bare and walked around carrying his clothes on a stick.

An attorney who was present at the intersection, a member of the ACLU, later said that "perhaps ten people were on lampposts and shoulders of other people, waving at the cameras. . . . The noise was very loud. . . . I felt this was a violent crowd that came to fight and was looking for trouble."

The intersection at Balbo and Michigan was in total chaos at this point. The street was filled with people. Darkness had fallen, but the scene was lit by both police and television lights. As the mule train* left, part of the group tried to follow the wagons through the police line and were stopped. According to the deputy superintendent of police, there was much pushing back and forth between the policemen and the demonstrators. He said that this was where real physical contact began. . . .

The crowd was becoming increasingly ugly. The deputy superintendent states that demonstrators were pushing police lines back, spitting into officers' faces and pelting them with rocks, bottles, shoes, glass, and other objects.

While this was happening on Michigan Avenue, a separate police line had begun to move east toward the crowd from the block of Balbo that lies between Michigan and Wabash along the north side of the Hilton.

About 7:45 P.M., the police radio had crackled with a "10-1," an emergency code for "police officer needs help." A police captain was reporting imminent danger in front of the Hilton, and in response to his call, a reserve platoon had been ordered to the northwest corner of the hotel on Balbo. Shortly after that, all available vans in the vicinity were ordered to converge on the Hilton.

The reserve platoon, numbering some 40 policemen, had arrived by special . . . bus at Wabash and Balbo . . . under the command of a deputy chief of police. The men came from a skirmish with demonstrators at 14th and Wabash, several blocks southwest of the Hilton. . . .

As the bus unloaded, the unit formed up building-to-building across Balbo in four ranks of ten led by a deputy chief and a lieutenant.

---

*A feature of the Southern Christian Leadership Conference's Poor People's Campaign, the mule train was scheduled to take Ralph Abernathy to the amphitheater that evening to speak to the Democratic convention—ed.

At the same time, Sidney Peck* with his bullhorn was urging people to follow him west on Balbo in an effort to flee the Michigan intersection. "We saw the police approaching," Peck states. He says he called people back and urged the police "not to move against them." Over the loud-speaking equipment, Peck shouted, "Sit down and no violence will happen. Don't use any violence."

The deputy chief states, on the other hand, that he saw marchers coming toward his men. He felt that "a disorderly mob surging west on Balbo from Michigan, taking up the whole street and sidewalks, shouting and screaming slogans and insults [was] taking over the Blackstone and Hilton Hotel entrances with the intention of taking over these hotels."

The police moved east on Balbo toward Michigan Avenue at a fast walk. As they did so, the throng on Balbo backed east toward the intersection or crowded onto the sidewalk. By the time the officers reached the west edge of Michigan, they slowed to a determined walk. . . .

As a response to seeing the police phalanx . . . , says a law student who was standing near the front of the mob, the chant, "pigs . . . pigs . . . pigs" went up.

Policemen in the line of march claim that they suffered from more than verbal abuse. One officer states that in the vicinity of the Haymarket, a cocktail lounge in the Hilton's northeast corner with an entrance on Balbo, a bottle shattered about 18 inches behind him. He thought it was dropped from a hotel window. When the line reached Michigan, he said, he heard someone say, "Mother fucker, I'm going to kill you." He saw a man, about 33 years old, bearded and wearing a helmet, standing with a wine bottle in his hand, . . . ready to swing at me. I knocked the bottle out of his hand at that point, someone behind me hit me with some heavy object in the back and I fell on one knee. . . ."

The Balbo police unit commander asserts that he informed the sit-downs and surrounding demonstrators that if they did not leave, they would be arrested. He repeated the order and was met with a chant of "Hell no, we won't go." Quickly a police van swung into the intersection immediately behind the police line, the officers opened the door at the rear of the wagon. The deputy chief "ordered the arrest process to start."

"Immediately upon giving this order," the deputy chief later informed his superiors, "we were pelted with rocks, bottles, cans filled with unknown liquids and other debris, which forced the officers to defend themselves from

*Peck, an academic sociologist, was a leader of the Mobilization Against the War in Vietnam, or Mobe—ed.

injury. . . . My communications officer was slugged from behind by one of these persons, receiving injuries to his right eye and cheekbone." . . .

A patrolman who was in the skirmish line states that "the order was given to remain in position." But then, he says, one of his fellow officers "ran into the crowd, he was surrounded and I lost sight of him." At this point, the patrolman and other officers in the line "broke into the crowd," using their batons to "push away people who had gathered around" their fellow officer. . . .

The many films and videotapes of this time period present a picture which does not correspond completely with the police view described above. First, the films do not show a mob moving west on Balbo; they show the street as rather clean of the demonstrators and bystanders. . . . Second, they show the police walking east on Balbo, stopping in formation, awaiting the arrival of the van and starting to make arrests on order. A total of 25 seconds elapses between their coming to a halt and the first arrests. . . .

To many . . . witnesses, it seemed that the police swept down Balbo and charged, with clubs swinging, into the crowd without the slightest pause. What these witnesses may, in fact, have seen was a second sweep of the officers, moving east on Balbo after the first arrest. . . .

"There was just enough time for a few people to sit down before the cops charged," says the law student quoted earlier. "The guys who sat down got grabbed, and the cops really hit hard. I saw a pair of glasses busted by a billy club go flying through the air."

"The crowd tried to reverse gears," a reporter for a St. Louis paper says. "People began falling over each other. I was in the first rank between the police and the crowd and was caught in the first surge. I went down as I tried to retreat. I covered my head, tried to protect my glasses which had fallen partially off, and hoped that I would not be clubbed. I tried to dig into the humanity that had fallen with me. You could hear shouting and screaming. As soon as I could, I scrambled to my feet and tried to move away from the police. I saw a youth running by me also trying to flee. A policeman clubbed him as he passed, but he kept running."

"The cops were saying 'Move! I said, move, god dammit! Move, you bastards!'" A representative of the ACLU who was positioned among the demonstrators says the police were cussing a lot and were shouting "Kill, kill, kill, kill!" A reporter for the *Chicago Daily News* said after the melee that he too heard this cry. . . .

"People were trying to move but were clubbed as they did," the reporter for the St. Louis paper continued. "I fell to my knees, stumbling over somebody. . . ."

The crowd frantically eddied in a halfmoon shape in an effort to escape the officers coming in from the west. . . . At first, says [a] McGovern worker,* "the police just pushed the demonstrators with their nightsticks. The demonstrators [nearest the police] tried to move, but couldn't because of the press of the crowd. There was no place for them to go. . . ."

Thus, at 7:57 P.M., with two groups of club-wielding police converging simultaneously and independently, the battle was joined. The portions of the throng out of the immediate area of conflict largely stayed put and took up the chant, "The whole world is watching," but the intersection fragmented into a collage of violence.

Re-creating the precise chronology of the next few moments is impossible. But there is no question that a violent street battle ensued.

People ran for cover and were struck by police as they passed. Clubs were swung indiscriminately. . . .

"I saw squadrons of policemen coming from everywhere," a secretary . . . said. "The crowd around me suddenly began to run. Some of us, including myself, were pushed back onto the sidewalk and then all the way up against . . . the Blackstone Hotel along Michigan Avenue. I thought the crowd had panicked."

"Fearing that I would be crushed against the wall of the building . . . I somehow managed to work my way . . . to the edge of the street . . . and saw police everywhere."

"As I looked up I was hit for the first time on the head from behind by what must have been a billy club. I was then knocked down and while on my hands and knees, I was hit around the shoulders. I got up again, stumbling and was hit again. As I was falling, I heard words to the effect of 'move, move' and the horrible sound of cracking billy clubs. . . ."

"After my second fall, I remember being kicked in the back, and I looked up and noticed that many policemen around me had no badges on. The police kept hitting me on the head. . . ."

In balance, there is no doubt that police discipline broke [down] during the melee. The deputy superintendent of police states that—although this was the only time he saw discipline collapse—when he ordered his men to stand fast, some did not respond and began to sally through the crowd, clubbing people they came upon. . . .

While violence was exploding in the street, the crowd wedged behind the police sawhorses along the northeast edge of the Hilton was experiencing

*George McGovern, the Democratic senator from South Dakota, was a dove on Vietnam who had some delegate support against Humphrey—ed.

a terror all its own. Early in the evening, this group had consisted in large part of curious bystanders. But following the police surges into the demonstrators clogging the intersection, protesters had crowded the ranks behind the horses in their flight from the police.

From force of numbers, this sidewalk crowd of 150 to 200 persons was pushing down toward the Hilton's front entrance. Policemen whose orders were to keep the entrance clear were pushing with sawhorses. Other police and fleeing demonstrators were pushing from the north in the effort to clear the intersection. Thus, the crowd was wedged against the hotel. . . .

Films show that one policeman elbowed his way to where he could rescue a girl of about ten years of age from the viselike press of the crowd. He cradled her in his arms and carried her to a point of relative safety 20 feet away. The crowd itself "passed up" an elderly woman to a low ledge. But many who remained were subjected to what they and witnesses considered deliberate brutality by the police.

"I was crowded in with the group of screaming, frightened people," an onlooker states. "We jammed against each other, trying to press into the brick wall of the hotel. As we stood there breathing hard . . . a policeman calmly walked the length of the barricade with a can of chemical spray in his hand. Unbelievably, he was spraying at us." Photos reveal several policemen using Mace against the crowd. . . .

"Some of the police then turned and attacked the crowd," a Chicago reporter says. The student says she could see police clubbing persons pinned at the edge of the crowd and that there was "a great deal of screaming and pushing within the group." A reporter for a Cleveland paper said, "The police indiscriminately beat those on the periphery of the crowd. . . ."

As a result, a part of the crowd was trapped in front of the Conrad Hilton and pressed hard against a big plate glass window of the Haymarket Lounge. A reporter who was sitting inside said, "Frightened men and women banged . . . against the window. A captain of the fire department inside told us to get back from the window, that it might get knocked in. As I backed away a few feet I could see a smudge of blood on the glass outside."

With a sickening crack, the window shattered, and screaming men and women tumbled through, some badly cut by jagged glass. The police came after them.

"I was pushed through by the force of large numbers of people," one victim said. "I got a deep cut in my right leg, diagnosed later by Eugene McCarthy's doctor as a severed artery. . . . I fell to the floor of the bar. There were ten to twenty people who had come through. . . . I could not stand on the leg. I was bleeding profusely.

"A squad of policemen burst into the bar, clubbing all those who looked to them like demonstrators, at the same time screaming over and over, 'We've got to clear this area.' The police acted literally like mad dogs looking for objects to attack.

"A patrolman ran up to where I was sitting. I protested that I was injured and could not walk, attempting to show him my leg. He screamed that he would show me that I could walk. He grabbed me by the shoulder and literally hurled me through the door of the bar into the lobby. . . ."

In the heat of all this, probably few were aware of the Haymarket's advertising slogan: "A place where good guys take good girls to dine in the lusty, rollicking atmosphere of fabulous Old Chicago. . . ."

The Wallace Campaign

Few people outside of Alabama knew Governor George Wallace until the spring of 1963, when he denounced Martin Luther King's drive to desegregate the stores and businesses of Birmingham. Later that year, the governor defied the federal government when it sought integration of the University of Alabama. Wallace had already announced his racial stand in his inaugural address as governor: "Segregation now! Segregation tomorrow! Segregation forever!" By 1964, he had become the prime symbol of the irreconcilable racist South.

Wallace soon became spokesman of the backlash movement as a whole. Backlash voters considered blacks pampered by the government. Many undoubtedly were racists. But the backlash movement also swept up men and women with deep resentments against the other "excesses" of the decade—the antiwar movement, the student power movement, the counterculture, the liberalization of sexual attitudes and practices, the centralization of political power, the breakdown of law and order.

The backlash mood also expressed a populist resentment of elites—those who had imposed preferential racial programs on the nation; who defended the civil liberties of criminals; who wanted pupils bused from their own neighborhoods for the sake of racial balance; who called pornography free speech; who denounced their country's efforts to stop Communism in Vietnam—these were primarily members of the privileged classes, "limousine liberals" who were indifferent to the cost to common folk of their theories and programs while they themselves escaped the consequences. If backlash voters had been asked to specify the culprits by class, they would have listed college professors, intellectuals, rebellious students, media liberals, foundation officials, and federal bureaucrats.

Backlash voters were, not surprisingly, numerous in the South. But they were also common among blue-collar whites in the northern cities, especially among the children and grandchildren of eastern and southern Europeans.

Wallace drew on the backlash pool of social, political, and cultural resentment to advance his political career. In 1964, well before the Sixties turned ugly, he ran in several Democratic presidential primaries and did surprisingly well in a number of northern states. By 1968, he was ready to mount a serious effort to achieve national power.

The election laws of the United States are rigged against any third national party. But Wallace and his lieutenants managed to get his name on the ballots of all fifty states under the American Independent Party label. Financed by funds from Texas oil tycoon H. L. Hunt, from Kentucky Fried Chicken millionaire Colonel Sanders, and from the actor John Wayne, among others, he started his drive for the presidency with a bang. At the outset, he was almost neck-and-neck with Hubert Humphrey.

By the time Wallace arrived in New York in late October, his campaign had slipped as blue-collar workers, responding to labor leaders' attack on him as a union-buster and an enemy of the working man, returned to the Democratic fold. The speech excerpted here was delivered at Madison Square Garden on October 24, some two weeks before Election Day.

New York City was the heart of the enemy's country and, as the address reveals, Wallace was heckled aggressively. The speech was custom-tailored for the audience, however. Wallace scrupulously avoids mention of nuclear weapons to end the war in Vietnam. His running mate, General Curtis LeMay, had recently raised a storm by proclaiming that the world would not end "if we exploded a nuclear weapon." The governor was not going to repeat the proposal. Wallace also paraded on his stage that night every union official who dared to support him publicly. Most telling, he carefully avoided making a blatant racist appeal. Open racism did not sell as well in New York as it did in Alabama or Maryland.

Despite the guarded tone, however, enough of the backlash message came through to satisfy the angers felt by his constituents. Wallace did not carry New York, but he won 360,000 of the state's votes, about five percent of the total.

[Speeches of American Presidential Candidates, by Gregory Bush. Copyright © 1976, 1985. *Used and reprinted by permission of The Continuum Publishing Company.]*

GEORGE WALLACE CAMPAIGN SPEECH, 1968

Well, thank you very much ladies and gentlemen. Thank you very much for your gracious and kind reception here in Madison Square Garden. I'm sure *The New York Times* took note of the reception we've received here in the great city of New York. I'm very grateful to the people of this city and this state for the opportunity to be on the ballot November 5, and as you know we're on the ballot in all fifty states in the union. This is not a sectional movement. It's a national movement, and I am sure that those who are in attendance here tonight, especially of the press, know that our movement is a national movement and that we have an excellent chance to carry the great Empire State of New York. . . .

[At this point and at other points, as suggested by his responses, Wallace was interrupted by protesters.]

Well, I want to tell you something. After November 5, you anarchists are through in this country. I can tell you that. Yes, you'd better have your say now, because you are going to be through after November 5, I can assure you that. . . .

And, you came for trouble, you sure got it.

And we have R. H. Bob Low president of the MBC*— We—why don't you come down after I get through and I'll autograph your sandals for you, you know?

And Charlie Ryan, recording secretary of the Steam Fitters Local 818, New York City. We have been endorsed in Alabama by nearly every local in our state: textile workers, paper workers, steel workers, rubber workers, you name it. We've been endorsed by the working people of our state.

Regardless of what they might say, your national leaders, my wife[†] carried every labor box in 1966, when she ran for governor of Alabama in the primary and the general election. And I was also endorsed by labor when I was elected governor in 1962.

Now, if you fellows will . . . sit down, ladies and gentlemen, I can drown that crowd out. If you just sit down . . . all he needs is a good haircut. If he'll go to the barbershop, I think they can cure him. So all you newsmen look up this way now. Here's the main event. I've been wanting to fight the main event a long time in Madison Square Garden, so here we are. Listen, that's just a preliminary match up there. This is the main bout right here. So let me say as I said a moment ago, that we have had the support of the working people of our state. Alabama's a large industrial state, and you could not be elected governor without the support of people in organized labor.

Let me also say this is about race, since I'm here in the state of New York, and I'm always asked the question. I am very grateful for the fact that in 1966 my wife received more black votes in Alabama than did either of her opponents. We are proud to say that they support us now in this race for the presidency, and we would like to have the support of people of all races, colors, creeds, religions, and national origins in the state of New York.

---

*The Mobile Building and Construction Trades Council, a south Alabama trade union—ed.
†Lurleen Wallace, who ran as a stand-in for her husband because state law forbade him to serve another term—ed.

Our system is under attack: the property system, the free enterprise sys-tem, and local government. Anarchy prevails today in the streets of the large cities of our country, making it unsafe for you to even go to a political rally here in Madison Square Garden, and that is a sad commentary. Both national parties in the last number of years have kowtowed to every anar-chist that has roamed the streets. I want to say before I start on this any longer, that I'm not talking about race. The overwhelming majority of all races in this country are against this breakdown of law and order as much as those who are assembled here tonight. It's a few anarchists, a few activists, a few militants, a few revolutionaries, and a few Communists. But your day, of course, is going to be over soon. The American people are not going to stand by and see the security of our nation imperiled, and they are not going to stand by and see this nation destroyed, I can assure you that.

The liberals and the left-wingers in both national parties have brought us to the domestic mess we are in now. And also this foreign mess we are in. . . .

Now, what are some of the things we are going to do when we become president? We are going to turn back to you, the people of the states, the right to control your domestic institutions. Today you cannot even go to the school systems of the large cities of our country without fear. This is a sad day when in the greatest city in the world, there is fear . . . in every school building in the state of New York, and especially in the City of New York. Why has the leadership of both national parties kowtowed to the group of anarchists that makes it unsafe for your child and for your fam-ily? I don't understand it? But I can assure you of this—that there's not ten cents worth of difference with what the national parties say other than our party. Recently they say most of the same things we say. . . .

It's costing the taxpayers of New York and the other states in the union almost half a billion dollars to supervise the schools, hospitals, seniority and apprenticeship lists of labor unions, and businesses.* Every year on the federal level we have passed a law that would jail you without a trial by jury about the sale of your own property. Mr. Nixon and Mr. Humphrey, both three or four weeks ago, called for the passage of a bill on the federal level that would require you to sell or lease your own property to whomsoever they thought you ought to lease it to. . . . † When I become your president, I am going to ask that Congress repeal this so-called open occupancy law, and we're going to, within the law, turn back to the people of every state

*That is, for purposes of detecting race or gender discrimination, though the latter had not yet become a major issue—ed.

†The reference here is to the Open Housing law passed in April 1968, prohibiting discrimination in the sale or rental of a large proportion of the nation's houses and apartments—ed.

their public school system. Not one dime of your federal money is going to be used to bus anybody any place that you don't want them to be bused in New York or any other place.

Yes, the theoreticians and the pseudo-intellectuals have just about destroyed not only local government but the school systems of our country. That's all right. Let the police handle it. So let us talk about law and order. We don't have to talk about it much up here. You understand what I'm talking about in, of course, the City of New York, but let's talk about it.

Yes, the pseudo-intellectuals and the theoreticians and some professors and some newspaper editors and some judges and some preachers have looked down their nose long enough at the average man in the street: the pipe-fitter, the communications worker, the fireman, the policeman, the barber, the white-collar worker, and said we must write you a guideline about when you go to bed at night and when you get up in the morning. But there are more of us than there are of them because the average citizen of New York and of Alabama and of the other states of our union are tired of guidelines being written telling them when to go to bed at night and when to get up in the morning.

I'm talking about law and order. The Supreme Court of our country has handcuffed the police,* and tonight if you walk out of this building and are knocked in the head, the person who knocks you in the head is out of jail before you get in the hospital, and Monday morning, they'll try a policeman about it. I can say that I'm going to give the total support of the presidency to the policemen and the firemen in this country, and I'm going to say, you enforce the law and you make it safe on the streets, and the president of the United States will stand with you. . . .

You had better be grateful for the police and firemen of this country. . . . Yes, the Kerner Commission report, recently written by Republicans and Democrats, said that you are to blame for the breakdown of law and order, and that the police are to blame. Well, you know, of course, you aren't to blame. They said we have a sick society. Well, we don't have any sick society. We have a sick Supreme Court and some sick politicians in Washington— that's who's sick in our country. The Supreme Court of our country has ruled that you cannot even say a simple prayer in a public school,† but you can send obscene literature through the mail,‡ and recently they ruled that

---

*A reference to the *Miranda* and *Gideon* decisions, among others, on the rights of accused felons—ed.
†A reference to *Engel v. Vitale*—ed.
‡A reference, probably, to *A Book Named "John Cleland's Memoirs of a Woman of Pleasure" v. Attorney General of Massachusetts*. This decision liberalized the publication and sale of books formerly considered obscene—ed.

a Communist can work in a defense plant.* But when I become your president, we're going to take every Communist out of every defense plant in the United States, I can assure you.

The Kerner Commission report also recommended that the taxes of the American people be raised to pay folks not to destroy the country, and not to work. I never thought I would see the day when a Republican and Democratic report would call for taxes on the already overtaxed people of our country to pay people not to destroy. . . . Now the Kerner Commission report—who is it writes these reports, ladies and gentlemen? It's usually some pointed head from one of those tax-exempt foundations. When they recommend that taxes be raised on you and me, they don't have to pay taxes because they're tax-exempt. When I become the president, I'm going to ask the Congress to remove the tax exemption feature on those . . . foundations and let them pay taxes like the average citizen of New York pays also. . . .

We have a comprehensive platform that I hope you get copies of before the election, in which we have dealt with every problem that faces the American people. But let me tell you briefly about foreign policy. The Democrats and Republicans are always saying: "What do the folks at Madison Square Garden supporting the American Independent Party know about foreign policy?" I ask them: "What do you know about foreign policy? We've had four wars in the last fifty years. We've spent $122 billion of our money on foreign aid. We are bogged down in a no-win war in Southeast Asia, and anarchy in the streets. What do you know about foreign policy? You haven't been so successful in conducting American foreign policy in the last fifty years yourself. . . ."

We are in Vietnam whether you like it or not. I sincerely hope and pray that the conflict is soon over, but we should have learned one thing about our involvement in Southeast Asia—the same thing that Mr. Humphrey now says in his speeches: we should not march alone. I said last year in California that we should never have gone to Vietnam—by ourselves. We should have looked our allies in the face in Western Europe and our non-Communist Asian allies and said to them: it is as much your interest as it is ours, and you are going to go in with manpower, munitions, and money, and if you don't go and help us in Southeast Asia . . . we are not only going to cut off every dime of foreign aid you're getting, but we're going to ask you to pay back all you owe us from World War I right to this very day. . . .

*Refers to *Afroyim v. Rusk*, a Supreme Court decision invalidating a federal law excluding a Communist from working in a defense plant—ed.

I sincerely hope and pray that we have a successful negotiated peace. Well, I'll drown them out, come on. I sincerely hope and pray that we have an honorably negotiated peace to arise out of the Paris peace talks. . . . But if we fail diplomatically and politically in Southeast Asia, we're not going to stay there forever, we're not going to see hundreds of American servicemen killed every week for years and months to come. If we do not win diplomatically and politically in Paris . . . then in my judgment, we ought to end it militarily with conventional weapons and bring the servicemen home. If we cannot settle it diplomatically and politically, and could not win it militarily with conventional weapons, then I wonder why we're there in the first place? We're going to conclude this war either through honorable negotiations or conventional military power.

There's something else we ought to talk about and you see some of it here in the state of New York. We should stop the morale boost for the Communists in our own country. In every state in the union, this treasonable conduct on the part of a few, and their speeches, are printed in Hanoi, Peking, Moscow, and Havana. General Westmoreland* said it is prolonging the war, and it is causing New Yorkers and Alabamans to be killed in Southeast Asia. When you ask the Attorney General of our nation: "Why don't you do something about this treasonable conduct," do you know what he says? "We are too busy busing schoolchildren in New York and Los Angeles and we don't have the time." We also have some college students who raise money, food, and clothes for the Communists and fly the Viet Cong flag in the name of academic freedom, and free speech. We didn't allow that in World War II; we did not allow for anybody to call for Nazi victory, or Fascist victory.

There is such a thing as legitimate dissent. . . . But if you . . . say you long for Communist victory, every citizen in New York knows that one is dissent and the other is something else. I want to tell you that when I become your president, I'm going to have my Attorney General seek an indictment against any professor calling for Communist victory† and stick him in a good jail somewhere. When you drag a few of these college students who are raising money for the Communists and put them in a good jail, you'll stop that too, I can assure you. . . . We're going to destroy academic freedom in this country if we continue to abuse it. . . . Whether you agree with the war or not, we should agree that whatever we say or do

*William Westmoreland, the U.S. commander in Vietnam through 1968—ed.
†A reference to professor Eugene Genovese of Rutgers, who created a storm when he called for a Communist victory in Vietnam in the course of an antiwar rally in October 1965—ed.

should be in the national interests of getting the American servicemen home safely. . . .

That's all right. That's all right honey—that's right sweety-pie—oh, that's a he. I thought you were a she. . . .

Well, don't worry what the newspapers say about us. . . . Not a single thing have I said tonight that anybody can argue logically with, and that's the reason they call us extremists and want to say we're Fascists. . . . They want to say, well, they're evil folks. I want to tell these newspapers something. These large newspapers that think they know more than the average citizen on the street of New York haven't always been right. I remember the time *The New York Times* said that Mao Tse-tung was a good man, and he turned out to be a Communist. . . . They were mistaken about Castro.

They [the newspapers] are mistaken about our movement, and they are mistaken about the good people of New York State who are here tonight supporting our candidacy because the two national parties . . . have paid no attention to you. But they are paying attention to those who are making the most noise here at Madison Square Garden tonight and every other place in the country. . . .

Four years ago our movement received thirty-four percent of the vote in Wisconsin, thirty percent in Indiana, forty-four percent in Maryland. We have won nearly every radio and television poll in every state in the union, so we don't pay attention to the pollsters. . . .

You know, I like to tell this because . . . you've heard it before, but it's very good. Down in the state of Maryland that night four years ago in the presidential primary, I was leading up until about 9:30 with several hundred thousand votes in, and they called the mayor of Baltimore to the television and asked him what he thought about this man from Alabama running first in the presidential primary in our free state. . . . He said: "It's sad; it's sad. We'll never live this down. What has come over the people of the free state of Maryland?" Well, if he had gone out and asked a good cab driver of Baltimore, he could have told him. You vote for me, and you are going to be through with all that. Let me tell you now, you continue to support our movement until November 5, together we are going to change directions in this country, and we are going to return some sanity to the American government scene. I do appreciate you being here in Madison Square Garden tonight. Thank you very much, ladies and gentlemen.

Index

About the Author

Irwin Unger is a professor of history at New York University. He was awarded the Pulitzer prize in 1965 for *The Greenback Era* and has edited several standard history texts. He was a consultant and scriptwriter for the A&E series "Our Century" and was a historical consultant to the national art exhibit "Art and Politics in 1968," curated by Nina Castelli. He is the recipient of several Guggenheim fellowships and a Rockefeller Humanities fellowship.

Debi Unger is a journalist who has collaborated with Irwin Unger on *The Vulnerable Years, Twentieth-Century America* and *Turning Point: 1968*. She has also written "Portraits and Documents" for *These United States: The Questions of Our Past.*